Muhammad's
MONSTERS

A Comprehensive Guide to
RADICAL ISLAM
for Western Audiences

Muhammad's
MONSTERS

A Comprehensive Guide to
RADICAL ISLAM
for Western Audiences

David Bukay, editor

Balfour
Books

First printing: April 2004

ISBN: 0-89221-576-3
Library of Congress Number: 2003116052

Printed in the United States of America

Please visit our website for other great titles:
www.balfourbooks.net

For information regarding author interviews,
please contact the publicity department at (870) 438-5288.

Contents

FOREWORD

Islamic Fundamentalism and the Arab Political Culture 7
David Bukay

SECTION ONE:
ISLAM AS A WORLD THREAT

A New and More Dangerous Era 25
Anthony J. Dennis

Sacred Visions and Religious Terror: The Case of Islam 41
Charles Selengut

The Afghan Alumni and the Clash between Civilizations 59
Shaul Shay

How Islam Plays the Press 89
Joseph Farah

SECTION TWO:
ISLAM IN THE WORLD AND THE MINORITIES POLICY

The War of Islam Against Minorities in the Middle East 105
Mordechai Nisan

Genocide in Sudan 129
Patrick Sookhdeo

From Bosnia to Kosovo: The Re-Islamization of the Balkans 143
Raphael Israeli

Extremist Islamist Terror and Subversion in South Asia 167
K.P.S. Gill and Ajai Sahni

Muslim Immigration and the West 187
    David Pryce-Jones

Islamic Judeophobia: An Existential Threat 195
    Robert S. Wistrich

SECTION THREE:
ISLAM AND UNCONVENTIONAL WARFARE

Nuclear Programs of Arab and Islamic States: Capabilities,
    Strategies, and Implications 223
    Gerald M. Steinberg and Aharon Etengoff

The Chemical and Biological Threat of Islam 255
    Dany Shoham

Facing Insurgent Islam: A Grand Strategy for the West 281
    Yehezkel Dror

SUMMARY

What Is to Be Done? 317
    David Bukay

Glossary of Islamic Terms 324

About the Authors 331

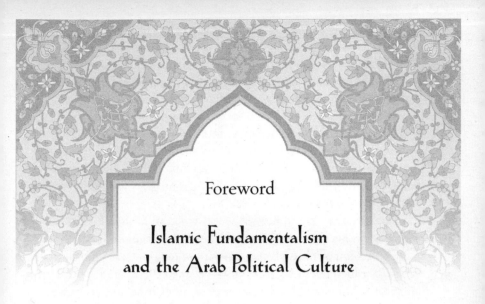

Foreword

Islamic Fundamentalism
and the Arab Political Culture

David Bukay

The 20th century was one of the most turbulent in human history, marked by total wars and severe ideological struggles. Two ideologies competed against the Western liberal-democratic system and were defeated unconditionally. The first, Nazism, was vanquished in a total war that exacted one of the greatest human and economic costs in history. The second, communism, was overcome after a political and ideological struggle that lasted three-quarters of a century. When it seemed that a "New World Order" had emerged and the period of total wars, and especially fanatic ideologies, had ended, the world became aware of the danger of fundamentalist Islam, whose borders, as Samuel Huntington has observed, are borders of blood.

Indeed, in several regards this is a more extreme danger, certainly a graver and more massive threat: there are many Islamic states in the world, there is a total Islamic population of over a billion human beings, and the reality is one of an extroverted and aggressive, totalistic religion with an ideology of perpetual expansion. It should also be stated clearly, even in the age of the "politically correct," that the problem is also one of Arabs, the "savage kinship" as scholars have called it, which is still immersed in many values of anarchic tribalism. We are not speaking of Islam as a religion, nor of the Arabs, per se. However, the combination of radical Arabs and fundamentalist Islam is deadly, and constitutes the greatest threat to the existence of modern society and culture. Their ideology is uncompromisingly murderous and nihilistic, and they are supported by millions of frustrated and destitute people who seek to convert the humiliating present back into the glorious past.

Islam constitutes a universal world view, an all-inclusive civilization that lays down positive and negative commandments for the believer. It is a comprehensive system of religion *(din)* and state *(dawlah)*, which does not distinguish between the kingdom of Allah and the kingdom of the ruler, and signifies total and exclusive submissiveness and devotion to the will of Allah. The Islamic ideal was the establishment of a political community *(ummah)*, and the goal was defined as achieving an Islamic order and political stability, while maintaining the unity of the community. Any rule is preferable to lack of rule, and any ruler can be accepted, because he is preferable to anarchy. Arab history, from the days of the prophet Muhammad to the present, is one of patrimonial leadership in military or monarchic authoritarian regimes. Yet, from the historical standpoint, political activity in the Arab world tended to encourage rebelliousness and political violence.[1] How can we explain this paradoxical phenomenon? The answer is fascinating: there is no need for legitimacy stemming from the people and its sovereign political will, since sovereignty comes from Allah, and the moment one rule is replaced by another, it becomes accepted and consented to. Everything is done according to the will of Allah, and the test is always the result. Whether an act has succeeded or failed, that is the will of Allah. This is the ideological-religious basis for violence in Islam. Today, this model endures even in the secular conception of rule, with sovereignty consisting of the leader's personality and the forcefulness of his rule.

The Islamic state is theocratic: Allah is the only source of faith, and the religious cult is the symbol of collective identity. Any criticism, any opposition, constitutes heresy. This orientation is linked to the legitimacy of the government. Islam completely rejects the

Western view that the state is the product of a "social contract." The state reflects and embodies the will of Allah. Sovereignty (*hakmi-yah*) stems from Allah alone and does not pertain to the will of the ruled. The Western doctrine of a right to oppose a bad government, and a duty to replace it, does not exist in Islam (Saddam Hussein's maintenance of power in Iraq, and Arafat's continuing to lead the Palestinians, are real-life examples). The question of the citizenship and of civil sovereignty is irrelevant. In this regard, it is clear what the army's role will be, and that the leadership will remain in power. From the standpoint of Islam, any attempt to alter the structure of legitimacy and sovereignty constitutes heresy and rebellion. The Arabic word for "state" is *dawlah*, which means dynasty, but connotes becoming or replacing (*Koran, Sura* 3, 134–140).

Most of the population is estranged from the government, and is not regarded as a factor to consider in conducting politics. The political culture is native (submissive) in the center and parochial in the periphery. There is no tradition of a civil society that constitutes the sovereign, and citizenship, as a critical phenomenon, is practically nonexistent. Political participation is on the level of supportiveness only, and mobility is low. Intellectual thought in Islam, like legitimacy and sovereignty, is also different from the Western concept, and this has important implications for basic principles and political behavior. The concept is atomistic rather than integrative, meaning that the principle of causality does not exist, since everything stems from the will of Allah. The result is the crystallization of a synthetic culture that manifests mental collectivism, with an overarching goal of preserving stability, and a fear of questioning the political order lest disintegration, anarchy, and disorientation result.

The values of Islam were profoundly influenced by the basic values of the Arabs in the *jahali* era. Allah is from the *jahali* period. He was regarded as a supreme god, and he had three daughter-gods: *al-Lat, al-Manat,* and *al-'uzza.* The cult of the stones was central in *jahali* Arab society, particularly the "black stone" in Ka'bah in Mecca. Another key example is the custom of the *hajj,* which was entirely incorporated into Islam. Apart from the customs that were replicated from the *jahali* era, it seems that only two of the five pillars of Islam (*arkan al-Islam*) — prayer (*salat*) and testimony (*shahadah*) — are originally Muslim.

David Bukay

The determinative affiliation is inward, involving the blood relations within the family or clan. This is manifested in the proverb, "I and my brothers against my cousin. I and my cousin against the neighbor, I and the neighbor against the foreigner." The duty to uphold the affiliative and clan-family framework against others exists without any connection to the question of right or wrong. The hostility and suspicion toward other tribes is deep and intense, and is well reflected in the relations between Arab states. There have never been relations of peace and fraternity between these countries, but rather a cold and alien détente. The summit conferences are a powerful filter for synchronizing the severe disagreements that exist. These summits are held when sharp disputes arise on the political agenda. To avert conflicts as well as the shame of failing to arrive at agreement, the Arab leaders decide to formulate a joint document in a festive conference that aims at covering up the shame and creating an atmosphere of solidarity. Even this goal is achieved only with great difficulty. To prevent failure, and the intensification of the collective Arab shame, the Arab foreign ministers meet before holding the summit to formulate a summary document. That document is then transmitted to the heads of state for approval. The leaders' level of participation manifests their agreement or opposition to the positions that have been reached. No less important, the defense and security agreements that are signed between Arab states are not worth the paper they are written on, and they are not regarded as applicable even by the signatories themselves.

From the state of affairs just presented, we may draw conclusions about the likelihood of reaching political arrangements with Arab states, let alone in the case of Arab land considered to be inhabited by infidels, such as the Crusaders and Israel. The attitude toward the foreigner shows fascinating paradoxes: on the one hand, courtesy, sympathy, and hospitality, yet on the other, an aloof suspicion. This indicates the social basis of the Arab-Islamic hatred, which is mingled both with fanaticism and feelings of inferiority toward the West. Peace is hardly a familiar phenomenon between the Arabs, and it is illusory to think they can reach peace with foreigners.

Muhammad succeeded in laying the political and intellectual foundation for the Islamic social system, but he failed to eradicate the tribal-clan structure. The tribes became part of Islam on the basis of the existing commonality of customs, and swore personal loyalty *(mubaya`ah)* to it because it was perceived as triumphant. This is a salient phenomenon among the Arabs, rooted in the spread of Islam, and it has major implications for the issue of Islamic fundamentalism: the victor is righteous, and the righteous always triumphs. The test for righteousness is the same as the test for success. These are facts dispensed by Allah; hence, Islam triumphs and succeeds because it is righteous.

In the tribal society, secular ideas held a central place and were expressed in the concept of "manhood" *(muruwwah)*. This refers to the traits of the perfect Bedouin man. The most important framework was that of maintaining the rules of tribal solidarity *(`asabiyah)*. The tribe was the primary social unit, the basis of personal and collective existence; hence the centrality of the collectivist rather than individualist approach. The crucial phenomenon in the society is that of honor. This is the supreme value, more important than life itself. *Sharaf* is a man's honor of the man. It is dynamic and can rise or fall in line with the man's activity and how he is perceived. `*ird* is the honor of the woman (and also refers to her pelvis, which is related to her modesty). `*ird*, unlike *sharaf*, is permanent and static. The woman was born and grew up with her honor, and her duty is to guard it closely. The moment `*ird* is lost, it cannot be restored, and the honor of the man is severely compromised.[2] Muslim tradition ascribes supreme importance to the man's honor and the woman's modesty. This is the basis for the status of women in Islamic society, and one of the primary concepts in Islam that fosters male-female inequality.[3]

The opposite pole of honor is shame. Researchers are not certain what is more important, the notion of honor or the fear of the shame that will be caused if honor is compromised. It is not honor, but shame that is the key issue. Public exposure is what harms a man's honor and humiliates him. The Arab is constantly engaged in avoiding whatever causes shame, in word and deed, while striving vigorously to promote his honor. Beyond shame and preventing its occurrence, there is vengeance, which is also to be displayed to all.[4] Arab culture reflects a collective ethos, and esteems tradition and honor. It is circumspect in regard to avoiding insult or causing shame; hence, it is better to lie so as to prevent conflict and not offend someone. Whereas the Jewish approach turns one cheek, on the basis of "We have sinned, we have transgressed, we have done wickedly," and the Christian approach turns the other cheek and discards responsibility, the Arab-Islamic approach is essentially aggressive: I have a problem? Then you are to blame. This constitutes open and emphatic defiance of everything that is perceived as wrong, unjust, and as inability to accomplish one's goals. There is no effort at compromise, certainly no tolerance and consent to the rights and rightness of the other. Nor is there any comprehension that relative concepts are involved. The phenomenon has been starkly evident in the Arab approach to the issue of Palestine. The conception is absolutely total. Justice and truth belong only to the Palestinians, in a manner absolute and without appeal, and the political discourse manifests this clearly.

Language is a cultural phenomenon of supreme importance. Prominent among the Arabs is the use of expressions, proverbs, metaphors, linguistic allegories, as well as exaggeration *(mubalaghah)* and glorification *(mufakharah)*. As a result, spoken Arabic is replete with exaggeration, verbal pathos, and the frequent use of high-flown phrases.

This approach contrasts completely with the language of understatement in Western culture. This linguistic contrast contributes to a major problem of communication between members of the two different cultural spheres. What happens in an encounter between Arab culture's language of overstatement and Western culture's language of understatement? This is one of the major causes of Israel's difficult position in world public opinion, which believes the Arab culture of exaggeration reflects an actual reality. The impact of the rich and beautiful Arabic language on Arab conduct is remarkable. There would not be such ardent feelings of veneration, such conscious and intensive use of the language, if these were not so powerfully propelled by the written or spoken word. The Arabic language is a mirror through which the Arabs examine the world. Even the language of the uneducated is very rich, and fosters exaggerations and excessive emphases. The Arabs are proud of their language and convinced that it is the greatest and most beautiful of the world's tongues.

The Arab personality abounds in contradictions. This is a deeply rooted duality: only a small part of the people is happy and content, yet they give strangers a warm and enthusiastic welcome. They are also intensely emotional, and easily prompted to extremes of hostility and resentment with no self-control. Under the influence of distress and fanaticism, they are capable of any act of cruel violence in an appalling magnitude. The shift can be dramatic and extreme. This is characteristic of tribalism: an admirable fatalism and passivity of self-control, along within an astonishing impulsivity and capacity for draconian, uncontrolled violence. All the mechanisms of hospitality, blessings, and affability are aimed at creating a defensive buffer, at mitigating the threatening interpersonal encounter.

Life in a hostile environment in the desert, with scarce resources, in social and political alienation, forged a society that acquiesces to the harsh reality out of political conformism, and accepts the rules of behavior that defined society's objectives in religious terms.

These are ingrained symptoms of behavioral polarity between:

a) unity and separateness,
b) honor and shame,
c) violent aggression and passive submission to rule,
d) fantasy that ascends to the heavens and the earthliness of the burning desert,
e) hatred of the imperialist West and admiration for its attributes,
f) the desire for anarchic desert freedom that reflects the turbulent and emotional personality,
g) and patience and endurance in the face of the harsh reality.

The tribal origins of the Arab Middle East were assimilated into a rural society. The urban society developed only in the 20th century, but retained the patterns of thought and activity of the rural-tribal frameworks. Indeed, in many respects Arab society manifests the desert anarchy, whether they wear fine tailored suits or gold *jalabas*. All this is reflected as well in the polar duality of Islam.

The phenomenon of the "return of Islam" has many names, according to the eye of the beholder: awakening; rebirth; return;

David Bukay

reassertion; resurgence; resurrection; fundamentalism; messianism; political Islam; Islamism; radical Islam; Islamic extremism; Islamic movement; Islamic fanatics. The Muslims refer to the phenomenon in positive terms: rootedness *(usuliyah)*; origins *(asliyun)*; Islamists *(Islamiyun)*; believers *(mu`minun)*; God-fearers *(mutadayinun)*. However, the notion of fundamentalism, which initially referred to the late 19th century Protestant movement in the United States, is the most useful, both because it is related to "rootedness" in Arabic *(usuliyah)* and because it is more understood and meaningful in the Western political discourse.

Only on September 11, 2001, after the terrorist strikes on the Twin Towers and the Pentagon, was the Islamic threat internalized in the West. It then began to penetrate the Western political consciousness that the Arab-Islamic political culture is aggressive and violent, can arouse popular forces that are enormous in scope, and embraces worldwide aspirations.

The Muslim weakness, compared to Western supremacy, left profound feelings of frustration and inferiority among the Muslims, a sense that their just, victorious religion had been humiliated by the infidel West. This reality is not only unfamiliar, but unacceptable, since it contradicts all the laws of Muslim logic. The reactions to the weaknesses of Islam were perceived and defined as religious. The problems were formulated in religious terms, and so were the solutions that were proposed for them: a return to the original Islamic tenets, with the goal of restoring in the present the achievements of the past, and applying the principles of the past to successful activity in the present.

The violent Islamic aggression does not stem only from frustration, the most prominent factor in social science theories of aggression. Islam is characterized by violent and aggressive principles and a radical ideology, whose source is in the Arab political culture. The combination between sweetness and amiability as preached by the Koran on the one hand, and the fanaticism of wild, destructive violence on the other, is amazing. The phenomenon of the suicide bombers, for example, is Islamic in nature: from Chechenya to Iran, Hizbullah, and the Palestinians. The society sanctifies the phenomenon of turning abject cowards who attack innocent, defenseless civilians, into heroes whose murderous deeds are approved by their families, not to mention the monetary rewards and adulation they receive. In the West, this phenomenon is neither perceived nor understood. It must be emphasized that it is not a matter of a few extremists. Yet the West has a hard time understanding why Islam does not work to eradicate the phenomenon.

The first fundamentalist movements in Islam developed on the periphery of the Arab world, amid the waning of the Ottoman Empire. Its devotees had an internal orientation, focusing on reforms or a revolution in Islamic society. The *Wahabiyah* movement in the Arabian Peninsula founded by Muhammad bin `Abd al-Wahab (1703–1792), was influenced by the radical, puritanical *hanbali* movement and the interpretations of Ibn-Taymiyah. The Sanusiyah movement founded by Muhammad bin `Ali al-Sanusi (1787–1859) in Cyrnaika (Libya) was a mystical and reformist movement, suited to the cultural values of North Africa. And the Madhiyah movement founded by Muhammad Ahmad bin `Abdallah al-Mahdi (1843–1885) flowered in Sudan as a puritanical movement similar to *Wahabiyah*. But the movement that led fundamentalist Islam into the 20th century was the reformist al-Salafiyah movement headed by Jamal al-Din al-Afghani (1838–1897), who preached pan-Islamic solidarity and resistance to Western penetration. The success of this movement was via its disciples, Muhammad `Abduh (1849–1905) and Rashid Muhammad Rida (1865–1935), who were active in Egypt. The triumphant stream was the radical activism of the Muslim Brotherhood led by Hasan al-Bana (1906–1949). This movement gained enormous success, and established influential branches in almost all the Arab states.

Geertz defines religion as a system of symbols that confers meaning on reality, formulates views and outlooks, supplies answers to all the issues, and creates an ethos for action.[5] It is commonly claimed that Islam is the political movement of the popular strata, and provides a solution to the social-economic-cultural difficulties of the Muslims. By contrast, we maintain that the Islamic awakening *(al-sahwah al-Islamiyah)* does not involve the return of Islam as a religion, since in fact it was always there, and never underwent a secularization process. What has occurred is that Islamic religion has become a significant factor in political discourse. Furthermore, there are many different Islamic movements that employ a variety of modes of attaining political ends and of gaining power via political and social mobilization of the masses. These are aggressive and violent movements that use modern technological tools to subvert Arab and Islamic states that are defined as secular.

The Islamic movements are not part of the regime, but their functional orientation is strongly political. Islam is, indeed, the most political of all the religions. In contrast to the Christian ideal of the kingdom of heaven, and the Jewish ideal of the messianic age, Islam sees the ideal as immediately applicable via the state so long as it functions according to the *shari`a*. In practice this means that Muslims strive for a blend of Arab nationalism and Islam in its fundamentalist formulation. The mixture of the two is tantamount to embark upon a revolution whose ultimate objective is the reinstatement of the Islamic caliphate embodied in the Ottomon Empire until the beginning of the 20th century.

The dominant notion in the West is that Muslims today are expressing disappointment and frustration over the failure of modernization. They are displaying a cultural rearguard battle against a modernity that dissolves their traditional value system. Our view differs. We contend that the current Muslim uprising is a political reaction that seeks to promote political objectives as an alternative to the existing regimes, and, no less significant, it seeks to counteract capitalist and communist ideology for which it regards itself as an alternative. The Islamic awakening is not a negation of modernity, but a reaction to its Western model. Western modernity is perceived as a direct threat to Islamic civilization, which is the most important collective framework of identity. Thus, the only possible resistance to the West's cultural onslaught is Islam in its fundamentalist form presented as a comprehensive system that provides all solutions (*al-Islam huwa al-Hall*) to the problems of society.

The Islamic solution is authentic and its roots run deep in the existing culture. Western penetration induced a severe reaction precisely among those who came into direct contact with the West, those in the middle class who experienced modernity and higher education. Modernity is perceived as the source of all sin, and permissiveness and materialism as a catastrophe. But the greatest sin of the West is to place the individual and the rule of reason at the center, as opposed to total submission and devotion to Allah.

The Islamic victory in Afghanistan and overthrow of the communist regime there in 1988 raised the issue anew, and served as proof that Islam could vanquish the infidels through the power of enthusiasm and religious faith. Indeed, Allah is with Islam, and Islam triumphs because he is just.

❧

Fundamentalist Islam has begun its march through Arab-Islamic society. Analysis of the causes of its rise focuses on a number of factors: a reaction to Western penetration, and a fierce animosity toward its presence and influence in the Arab political system. This mindset is prevalent among city dwellers, those who have had more direct contact with the West, and the educated middle class, who have experienced modernity and technology: first there was an economic conquest, then a military-territorial one. And when the Arab states succeeded in liberating themselves from Western colonialism, the Western cultural invasion began. The challenges of Western technology and the global village threatened the foundations of Islamic society. Second is the failure of the secular political alternative. The authoritarian regimes and patrimonial leadership repress and alienate the masses, who experience no political participation and exert no influence over how the government functions. The third factor is the collapse of the secular Arab ideologies, not only socialism and communism but also nationalism, Nasserism, and Arab unity, together with the Arab inability to solve the "question of Palestine." As a result of these processes, a severe dissonance developed between the world view of the Muslim Arab and the reality of his social-political environment. The cultural conflict of values acted as a strong catalyst for a return to the familiar world of Islamic values, which offered a lifeline in a stormy sea.

Alongside the ideas developed thus far, it remains important to focus on still another dimension of the current Muslim predicament, namely the crises of identity and legitimacy,[6] personal and collective. In Arab-Islamic society, no practical ideology developed that could provide a platform for nation building, a basis for socioeconomic development, enabling the formation of a civil society. The Islamic societies have mostly remained rural and traditional, hence suffused with a religious mentality. Most of the Arab states are in a pre-industrial stage, and some of them are in the feudal era, with

David Bukay

religion exerting wide influence over the population. The processes of vast and uncontrolled demographic growth had a destructive impact. The results are the subversion of the social and traditional frameworks, the widening of the socioeconomic disparities, and the frustration and anomie of an alienated society, in states that comprise non-political and non-civil societies.

The combination of a frustrated intellectual and religious minority, the force that exhorts and leads, and the indigent masses, the flock with its numerical magnitude, forms the basis for the rise and endurance of the Islamic movements, a raft in the storm that gave the population feelings of affiliation and self-worth.

In such circumstances, the conclusion of the Islamic movements was clear and unyielding: one must return to the sources, to pure and just Islam that offers solutions for all distress and need, especially for the cultural contradictions and identity crises of Arab society. Arab unity cannot be achieved, and a solution to the Palestine problem requires the overthrow of the secular Arab regimes. In place of the secular Arab state, what is offered is the pan-Islamic framework under the laws of the *shari`a*. Secularism is regarded as the gravest threat to traditional society. That is why secularism and Islam cannot join forces, a fact that only a few authors about Islam still fail to comprehend. Islam is a permanent opponent of secularism, and the Islamic awakening contradicts modernity.[7]

In the view of Lewis and Pipes, Islamic anti-Westernism stems from deep feelings of humiliation among those viewing themselves as the inheritors of the dominant civilization of the past, which was subjugated by those regarded as inferior. The more appealing Western civilization became, the greater the fundamentalist hostility and will to struggle against it.[8] It is worth, however, considering a different aspect of this attitude. The resentment and abhorrence are at Western culture, not necessarily at the West. It is not Western politics but rather the cultural ubiquity of the West, and the threat to Islamic society that shape the Islamic outlook and behavior. Under such circumstances, the Arabs put their ears to the ground to listen for ancient drumbeats calling them back to the Golden Age.

What are the main characteristics of Islamic fundamentalism? The Islamic movements represent different trends, varied plans of action, and different views of how to achieve objectives. They are complex, multi-dimensional movements that function mainly within national political systems, although they have links to regional (mutual influence and ties between movements and states) and international (sources of funding and activity) organizations. They play a major role in shaping the system of relations and conflicts in Arab politics at the level of government and of groups that oppose the government. They include groups acting within a messianic revolutionary regime, as in Iran; in a conservative and closed regime, as in Saudi Arabia; and in the coalition of a military regime, as in Sudan. At the same time, some of them function in violent opposition to the regime, as in Egypt, Algeria, Syria, and Tunisia; or in agreed partnership with the regime, as in Jordan (where there are also radical movements of the bin Laden type, which the state harshly represses).

The Islamic movements are deeply entrenched in most social and economic strata of Moslem society. Their leadership comes from the professional organizations of the educated, urban middle class (engineers, doctors, lawyers, teachers). The voice of the Islamic movements is the most clear-cut and assimilable. They are not only a political but a significant social force as well, arising from an educated and radical generation, with an academic background in the sciences, concentrated in the middle strata of the urban society. Moreover, they make intensive and sophisticated use of the media.

It is often claimed that the activism and militancy of the fundamentalist movements is essentially a defensive phenomenon, a way of fending off threatening Westernism, reflecting profound distress that issues in a blend of cultural and political protest, a perspective cultivated by a particular line of research in this field.[9] We maintain, however, that this approach provides only one possible view. A different perspective notes that the primary issue is not one of defensiveness and distress, but rather an attempt to cope with a hostile and dissonance-producing reality that involves relatively glaring contradictions to the notion of presumed Islamic superiority.

Islamic fundamentalism does not exhibit passivity but rather an iron determination to disseminate the values of religion, and provide Islamic answers to the maladies of modern society. This is not at all a defensive struggle. The Islamic movements do not display or express a sense of failure and self-protection, but rather an offensive push toward victory.

Despite their radical zealousness, the fundamentalist Islamic movements have displayed versatility and flexibility in their activity, and have undergone different stages that manifest an adaptive, pragmatic approach to changing circumstances. At first there emerged an all-embracing ideology, based on a just and righteous Islam rooted in the ancient teachings of the Prophet Muhammad. Since the mid-1960s the Islamic movements have shifted to the political sphere and made use of violence and terrorism, striving to overthrow secular Arab regimes. Since the mid-1980s they have made attempts to integrate into parliamentary systems by participating in elections and to seize power from within. Finally, in light of the political repression and manipulations of the regimes during elections, as well as the movements' gains through organized violence, two sub-groups have emerged within the fundamentalist movements: one decided to return to ancient Islamic origins and to social activity among the populace sanctioned by the regime; the other changed its strategy to join the training camps of Afghanistan, with the encouragement and aid of Saudi Arabia and the backing of the United States.

Belatedly, some Western nations have come to realize that fundamentalist Islam threatens not only the Arab and Islamic regimes, but its menace embraces the whole world. By now it is well known that the menace takes the form of terrorism and violence. Less well known is the fact that the enormous immigration of Arabs and Muslims into Western countries has serious implications for their political stability.

All the studies in this volume, with *two exceptions*, were written before bin Laden's terrorist attack on the United States on September 11, 2001. They include analyses of a wide variety of Islamic issues, and have critical implications for how this phenomenon is understood in the widest sense.

Endnotes
1 For a fascinating analysis of these movements, in terms of the "significance of heresy," the "revolutions in Islam," and "Islamic concepts of revolutions," see B. Lewis, *Islam in History: Ideas, Men and Events in the Middle-East* (London: Alcove Press, 1973).

2 R.T. Antoun, "On the Modesty of Women in Arab Muslim Villages: A Study in the Accommodation of Tradition," *American Anthropology*, 70/4 (August 1968): p. 671–697.

3 F. Mernissi, *Beyond the Veil: Male-Female Dynamics in Modern Moslem Society* (Bloomington, IN: Indiana University Press, 1987); L. Ahmed, *Women and Gender in Islam: Historical Roots of a Modern Debate* (Cairo, Egypt: American University in Cairo Press, 1993).

4 D.P. Ausubel, "Relationship Between Shame and Guilt in the Socializing Process," *Psychological Review*, 62/5 (September 1955).

5 C. Geertz, *The Interpretation of Cultures* (New York: Basic Books, 1973).

6 In other words, a crisis syndrome that is inherent to modernization processes, involving: identity, legitimacy, penetration, division, participation, and expectations. As we shall see, in Arab and Islamic politics the most important of these factors is identity. See L. Binder et al., *Crises and Sequences in Political Development* (Princeton, NJ: Princeton University Press, 1971).

7 H. Sharabi, "Modernity and Islamic Revival," *Contention*, 2/1 (1992): p. 127–138.

8 B. Lewis, "Roots of Muslim Rage," *Atlantic Monthly* (September 1990): p. 47–55; D. Pipes, "Fundamentalist Muslims between America and Russia," *Foreign Affairs*, 64/5 (Summer 1986).

9 E. Sivan, *Radical Islam* (New Haven, CT: Yale University Press, 1985); E. Sivan, *Religious Radicalism and Politics in the Middle-East* (Albany, NY: State University of New York Press, 1990).

Section One

ISLAM

AS A

WORLD

THREAT

A New and
More Dangerous Era

Anthony J. Dennis

I n the 1990s, fundamentalist Islam began to emerge as the only coherent ideology to pose a credible threat to the West. Islamic fundamentalism is clearly a global phenomenon. Its adherents can be found in an almost unbroken line from the Abu Sayyaf in the Philippines to the Armed Islamic Group in North Africa. This chapter will discuss the resurgence of Islamic fundamentalism in the post-Cold War era and will explain why this ideology represents a threat to the safety and security of the West in particular, and all non-Muslims generally, as demonstrated by the words and deeds of the fundamentalists themselves. Recent attempts by President Khatami of Iran to establish a more moderate and less confrontational brand of Islamic rule will also be addressed. This chapter will conclude with several recommendations for Western governments faced with the challenge of dealing with the Muslim fundamentalists in the international political arena today.

To understand the extent of the threat posed by Islamic fundamentalism to the non-Muslim world, it is important to understand the impact the end of the Cold War has had on the political landscape and to carefully consider the political agenda and salient characteristics of the transnational fundamentalist movement itself.

THE POST-COLD WAR WORLD: A MIXED LEGACY

The end of the Cold War left the world with a more mixed legacy than is generally admitted. While the defeat of communism and the peaceful annihilation of the Soviet empire represented a tremendous moral as well as political victory for the West, the collapse of the Soviet Union and its satellite empire also meant the extinction of a tremendous restraining influence on scores of ethnic and religious rivalries. One of the stabilizing facts of the Cold War competition was that both East and West kept their client states in check. While some rivalries were fueled during the Cold War, others clearly were suppressed by it. With communism's collapse, many nations forged in the crucible of communism died with it. The people of the former Soviet Union and of Yugoslavia, for example, have found that there is no longer anything that commonly defines and therefore unites them. As a result, nations have fragmented or have disappeared entirely with astonishing swiftness. Cut loose by the failed ideology of communism, many have fallen back on their long-suppressed religious identity as a principle of political organization and as a means of understanding themselves and their world. We should not be overly surprised to see new countries and even new empires arise from the ashes of the old.[1]

One can say that the end of the Cold War and the collapse of the Soviet Union have had at least three major effects. These watershed events created 1) an ideological vacuum, 2) a power vacuum, and 3) the largest weapons bazaar and black market in world history. Islamic fundamentalism as a political movement and as an ideology has benefited from each of these effects.

Ideological Vacuum

The collapse of the Soviet empire discredited communism as a viable ideology, especially in the eyes of developing nations. As a consequence, communism is no longer viewed as worthy of emulation. Yet, while communism was defeated, democratic ideals have not necessarily triumphed. Democracy, like communism before it, is essentially a non-indigenous ideology imported into Muslim territories only in the last one hundred years or so. By contrast, the notion of governance according to traditional Islamic principles is a familiar and appealing concept in these regions. Islam clearly has what one might call the "home field advantage."

The post-Cold War ideological vacuum has been filled by Islam as many leaders in the Muslim Middle East, North Africa, and Central Asia have fallen back on their "Muslim roots" for models of governance and as a way to remain politically relevant in the eyes of their largely Muslim populace. By the early 1990s, the language of socialism, with all its references to the liberation of the masses, the exploitation of capitalists, and the misdeeds of various imperialist powers, had become outdated. The language of fundamentalist Islam, with its disturbingly violent references to jihad, its moral and religious endorsement of terrorism against civilians, and its glorification of martyrdom, had taken its place.

Power Vacuum

The political universe, like the natural one, abhors a vacuum. At its height, the Cold War generally worked to suppress other political ideologies and movements as both the Americans and the Soviets (and their respective allies) committed tremendous resources to either democratic or communist parties and leaders in Asia, Africa, and the Middle East. Anyone not aligned with one or the other political camp was, at best, unfunded and ignored and, at worst, ruthlessly suppressed. Now that the superpowers have largely withdrawn from many of these areas, Islamic fundamentalism has had a chance to "break out" and evolve from being a relatively marginal political movement to a mainstream movement.

The increased popularity of Islamic rule in the post-Cold War era was eloquently demonstrated in Turkey, an economically advanced and westernized nation and a longtime member of NATO. In 1996, for the first time in modern Turkish history, the Islamic party's candidate for prime minister won in a stunning electoral upset, beating out candidates from the two mainstream parties, True Path and Motherland. The elevation of Necmettin Erbakan to the office of prime minister that year demonstrates that parties calling for a rejection of the West (including termination of military and diplomatic alliances with Western nations) and a return to traditional Islamic rule have substantial electoral clout, even in relatively wealthy and developed nations like Turkey. These parties are serious contenders for political power and should not be dismissed out of hand. Nor should their popularity be ascribed solely to poor economic conditions. Those who assert that Islamic parties are popular solely or principally because of poor economic conditions are able to make such declarations only by studiously ignoring the facts.

Elsewhere in the world, the absence of Soviet authority in places like Central Asia has given native leaders and local religious types in these areas a golden opportunity to politically organize. As predicted, we have seen parties calling for Islamic forms of government rise to some prominence throughout the former Soviet Central Asian Republics in the last ten years. The Islamic Renaissance Party, for example, was active in the immediate aftermath of the collapse of Soviet rule. In 1991, four of the former Soviet Asian Republics banned all activities of this party out of concern over its growing strength.[2] Where were the budding democratic parties at this time? They were, comparatively speaking, non-existent.

Black Market Weaponry

On the military front, the disintegration of the Soviet Empire and the concomitant loss of centralized control over its vast military arsenal have given the fundamentalist Muslims unprecedented access to weapons of mass destruction (WMD) capable of making relatively small terrorist groups or nations into world military powers literally overnight. In fact, there have been a number of detailed reports concerning the ease with which Soviet-made nuclear weaponry or other sophisticated military technology can be smuggled out of the country and purchased in the black market.[3] This is the world into which Usama bin Ladin and others have stepped, with ready cash in hand, and it is the reason why the fundamentalist movement represents such a grave threat to world peace in the present age.

DEFINITION AND OVERVIEW OF POLITICAL AGENDA

Before proceeding any further, let me state here as I have stated previously in other contexts that my remarks are limited to one politically active and politically radical segment of the vast Muslim world, and that I do not mean to suggest or imply that all 850 million to 1 billion of the world's Muslims are terrorists or necessarily supportive of terrorism of any kind. In fact, I consistently use the modifier "fundamentalist" in connection with the term "Muslim" in order to make evident that I am referring specifically to this radical segment.

The term "Islamic fundamentalist" is not a theological term but a politically descriptive one which describes persons or parties that have a very specific and defined domestic and foreign policy agenda. I tend to favor the foregoing term over the terms "Islamist" or "political Islam." "Islamist" is a colorless term that does not convey the return to the early days of the prophet's rule and the fundamentals of the early faith to which the modern day fundamentalists aspire. The term "political Islam" strikes me as similarly unedifying and even redundant since Islam is, by definition, a faith that has been intimately and inextricably involved in politics from the very beginning.

Domestic Policy

The Muslim fundamentalists seek on the domestic front the establishment of an Islamic theocracy or religious dictatorship (including, if necessary, the violent overthrow of the existing government), the adoption and strict application of the *sharia*, Islam's traditional legal code, and the eradication and expulsion of all non-Muslim influences on their society and way of life.

Foreign Policy

In terms of foreign policy, these groups adopt an implacably hostile and adversarial posture toward the West, with talk of military and terrorist strikes against it, the desirability of killing Western citizens, and the necessity (indeed the religious duty) of undertaking a jihad against America and other nations including Israel. As incredible and unrealistic as it sounds, the ultimate foreign policy objective of these groups is the conversion or extermination of all non-Muslim peoples including those living in Europe and North America. Sheik Omar Abdel-Rahman, the Egyptian cleric who was later convicted of involvement in the World Trade Center bombing in New York City, was quoted on the front page of the *Wall Street Journal* one month before that bombing as saying that his goal was to "show all Americans that they'll never be happy if they don't follow Islam."[4]

The Islamic Republic of Iran, in fact, has a clause in its constitution calling for spreading the Islamic revolution to other lands.[5]

Both Iran and Sudan have found that preaching jihad against America is a useful centerpiece around which to organize their foreign policy, and in Sudan's case — even their military and local militia.[6] Iranian government officials have been quite honest about their rhetorical and literal war against America. In 1991, Ali Akbar Mohtashemi openly admitted that "[i]t is necessary to target all U.S. objectives throughout the world" and stated that "Iranians are ready for sacrifice and Holy War."[7] Needless to say, normal diplomatic relations with such governments or groups in the face of these homicidal intentions are highly problematic at best.

Fundamentalist groups can be Shiites like the Islamic Republic of Iran or Sunnis like the regime in Sudan or the Taliban in Afghanistan. It should be noted that religious differences have not prevented Shia and Sunni groups or regimes, including Iran and Sudan, from working together against a common perceived enemy and do not present an insurmountable hurdle to transnational cooperation.[8]

PROGRAM OF CULTURAL DESTRUCTION

In addition to instituting strict Islamic rule inside their own countries, fundamentalists from several different areas of the Muslim world also have advocated a program of cultural destruction which ought to be roundly condemned by Muslim and non-Muslim alike. In Turkey the Islamic party, known formerly as the Refah (Welfare) Party and more recently as the Islamic Virtue Party, advocated banning ballet as a degenerate art form and the closing of women's shelters. The party has also advocated the destruction of those historical monuments and archeological sites within Turkey that do not glorify the nation's Muslim past. At one point, the fundamentalist mayor of Istanbul even called for the destruction of the magnificent and historic Byzantine-era walls around the city. It was only after the threat of an international outcry and expected pressure from Turkey's secular national government that this program of cultural destruction was at least temporarily abandoned. Nothing in the Koran would appear to authorize, let alone compel, this kind of cultural vandalism yet these disturbing initiatives appear to be part and parcel of the fundamentalists' domestic program.

Farther east in Afghanistan, the Taliban engaged in the most infamous act of cultural vandalism in recent times when, in March 2001, it ordered and swiftly carried out the destruction of thousands of irreplaceable ancient Buddhist statues that resided in the Kabul Museum and the dynamiting of the two largest stone-carved Buddhas in the world at Bamiyan.

SALIENT CHARACTERISTICS: HATRED OF THE WEST

Although I find the human rights abuses and the persecution of religious minorities (both of which lie outside the scope of this essay) extremely troubling from a moral as well as an international human rights law perspective, it is the fundamentalists' implacably hostile foreign policy and highly emotional rhetoric demonizing America and other Western nations which is of most concern to me because of the implications for future acts of terrorism against the West and because of the national security implications generally. We all know and have heard the slogans uttered by the highest levels of successive Iranian governments over the last 20-odd years which characterize America as "the Great Satan." This has been followed by chants of "Death to America!" in officially organized street demonstrations in Teheran. Sadly, this kind of rhetoric is common in fundamentalist circles and represents yet another barrier to productive communication between the Muslim and non-Muslim worlds.

A few more examples, out of many that could be recited, should suffice: In 1993, Sheik al-Tamimi, then the leader of Islamic jihad, was publicly quoted as saying, "I pray that Allah may tear apart America just as the Soviet Union was torn apart."[9] For his part, Sheik Abdel-Rahman made many tapes for his followers in which he called the USA a "den of evil and fornication."[10] Besides the bombings of the U.S. embassies in Tanzania and Kenya on August 7, 1998, which left 257 dead, Usama bin Ladin is perhaps best known in the West for his February 23, 1998, fatwa or religious decree calling for Muslims worldwide to kill Americans and their allies — civilians and military — wherever and whenever they can find them. "This is an individual duty for every Muslim" and "is in accordance with the words of Almighty God," stated bin Ladin as part of his decree.

Even the Palestinian Authority has gotten into the act. On July 22, 1997, the *Wall Street Journal* carried an excerpt of a July 11 sermon of Palestinian Authority Mufti Ikrama Sabri (an Arafat appointee, noted the *Journal*) at the Al Aqsa Mosque in Jerusalem. Sabri publicly prayed in part, "Oh Allah, destroy America, for she is ruled by Zionist Jews. . . . Allah will paint the White House black!"[11] At the time Arafat's appointee was publicly praying for the literal destruction of the United States and its historic symbol, the White House, American taxpayers, were providing Arafat's organization with millions of dollars in aid as part of the Clinton administration's efforts to buy peace in the Middle East.

REASONS FOR FUNDAMENTALIST FURY

There are several reasons for the Muslim fundamentalist world's hatred of the West. First of all, as a puritanical movement aspiring to return Islamic society to the early days of the faith, Islamic fundamentalism by definition is hostile to any outside influence that makes the achievement of that objective harder to attain. The world has become smaller with the advent of the Internet and the worldwide web, the globalization of trade, and the ease with which non-Western populations are able to access Western music, movies, theater, literature, television shows, and so forth. These developments are taken as a serious cultural threat by fundamentalist leaders who have called the Western cultural onslaught "Westoxification." Hence, we see vigorous efforts in many traditional Islamic countries to confiscate and destroy satellite dishes and radios as a way to prevent ordinary Muslim citizens from being exposed to Western culture and the free expression of ideas.

If the fundamentalists are living and governing according to God's law as they believe, then why, might they ask, is their civilization less advanced, their military less powerful, their people less healthy and less wealthy than the infidels living in the West? This is a source of great consternation and embarrassment to the fundamentalists. The fundamentalists view themselves as the heirs of the ancient Arabic empire founded by the prophet, and they are acutely conscious of their failure to live up to that grand inheritance.

They are also painfully aware of the fact that the material, scientific, political, military, and technological achievements of Western civilization dwarf the achievements of their own Islamic civilization in the modern age. Instead of blaming themselves, at some level they blame America and the West for reminding them of their own failings. The unqualified triumph of the West in defeating the Soviet Union in a virtually bloodless fight only adds to the pressure the fundamentalists feel either to define an alternative Islamic world order or be forced to fall in line with Western values and political and economic ideals.

Unlike the IRA or the Basque separatists, the Muslim fundamentalists aren't seeking merely the transfer of territory or the release of political prisoners. Nor is it America's long-standing record of friendly relations with Israel which alone make it a prime fundamentalist target. The stark and simple fact is, the fundamentalists hate Americans (and other Westerners) for who we are and, therefore, there is nothing we can do, no cognizable demands we could ever satisfy, short of stepping into a cultural gas chamber that would ever satisfy the essential demands of the Muslim fundamentalists.

THE KHATAMI PHENOMENON

President Mohammad Khatami of Iran deserves mention for the novelty of his ideas and the courageousness with which he has expressed them. He is that rare and endangered creature — a moderate politician in a fundamentalist Muslim state. Khatami is important because if the "Khatami revolution" sweeps away the unreconstructed aspects of the Iranian revolution leaving Iran with a less confrontational, more moderate and participatory form of Islamic-based government, then such an event will have removed one of the biggest stars in the fundamentalist constellation.

In his writings and public pronouncements, Mohammad Khatami has attempted to replace conflict between Islamic civilization and the Judeo-Christian West with dialogue.[12] Khatami uttered his now famous call for a "dialogue among civilizations" in an hour-long interview on the Cable News Network (CNN) which was broadcast worldwide on January 7, 1998. His statements stand in stark contrast both to the statements of the transnational fundamentalist movement and to the remarks of many of his colleagues in the Iranian government, including Iran's Supreme Leader Ayatollah Ali Khamenei who continues to adhere to a harsh, anti-American and anti-Western line. The appearance of individuals like Mohammad Khatami is a hopeful development because it provides an individual with whom it is potentially possible to have a peaceful and productive dialogue and because it breaks the monopoly the fundamentalists have held on much of the political speech emanating from the Islamic world of late. If Khatami survives and succeeds in his political quest, his presence will give powerful encouragement to other moderate, democratic forces working from within the Muslim world to combat the fundamentalists.

INSTITUTIONAL AND IDEOLOGICAL HURDLES TO REFORM

President Khatami faces both institutional and ideological hurdles to the realization of his vision of a more moderate, less confrontational Islam. He is like a man on a raft in the middle of a powerful and turbulent fundamentalist sea. On the political front, the power of the presidency in the Islamic Republic of Iran is overshadowed and circumscribed by the office of the supreme leader and the Council of Guardians. The president is not the most senior executive branch official in the Iranian government. As a result, President Khatami does not control Iran's foreign policy or its military and intelligence branches. He has also been powerless to prevent his own government's zealous prosecution and imprison- ment of many of his allies and supporters. Scores of Khatami's allies from the press, the universities, and from Iranian political circles have been sent off to prison for disagreeing publicly with the fun- damentalist line. Khatami's lack of executive authority in Iran has proven to be a great source of frustration for the president himself and for his supporters.

These institutional limitations constitute significant stumbling blocks on Iran's path to reform. They may also discourage other governments from initiating a dialogue or having relations with Iran out of concern that the cordial words of Khatami by no means reflect the actual attitudes and intentions of the Iranian government, which is controlled by hardliners under Supreme Leader Ayatollah Khamenei.

President Khatami's political vision, a vision which acknowledges and incorporates important aspects of Western political
thought, also faces significant ideological hurdles within the Muslim
world. These ideological hurdles represent additional friction points
between the Islamic and Western worlds. Islamic and Western conceptions of the state, the individual, and society are often totally at
odds. According to Western political thought, governmental power
arises from the governed. In contrast, in a theocracy such as exists
in Iran, governmental power is presumed to originate directly from
God. An Islamic ruler represents Allah's agent on earth. In such a
setting, liberal democratic institutions — including a robust multi-
party system, free and fair elections, and freedom of intellectual
expression including political expression — simply cannot work
since all political disagreements are ultimately religious disagreements, the penalties for which can be severe.

For a Shia cleric living in the theocracy that is Iran, Khatami
has made some daring and highly unconventional statements:

> The legitimacy of the government stems from the
> people's vote. And a powerful government, elected by the
> people, is representative, participatory, and accountable.
> The Islamic government is the servant of the people and
> not their master, and it is accountable to the nation under
> all circumstances.[13]

Khatami's views on government are plainly at odds with those
of his political opponents.

The profound gulf between Islamic and Western conceptions of
the state extends to the individual and society. To the fundamentalists, there is "no doctrine of human rights, the very notion of which
might seem an impiety. Only God has rights — human beings have
duties."[14] The whole Lockean concept of natural rights — or the
more modern concept of universal human rights — that predate
and are superior to the rights of any government to take them away,
finds no place in fundamentalist thought. In fact, the fundamentalists view the West's insistence on certain basic and universal human
rights as an arrogant attempt to place the rights and privileges of
human beings above God, and above God's agents on earth (i.e.,
the government run by the fundamentalists).

Anthony J. Dennis

Islamic rule as practiced in fundamentalist countries completely dominates both the individual and society. Islam, in its classic formulation, recognizes no separation between the religious and secular spheres. It represents a complete way of life for its followers regulating virtually every aspect of individual and group behavior. This leaves very little room to maneuver for reformers like Khatami.

Khatami's attempts to institute civil society and a fully functional democracy in the Islamic Republic of Iran encounter other troubles as well. Democracy and the whole concept of "human rights" are viewed by many as Western imports and as another legacy of colonialist rule. If the Muslim world which Khatami inhabits has any hope of reconciling democracy with religion, free speech with the authority of the religious establishment, and human rights (including especially women's rights) with the Koran, then ideally he and his supporters must find indigenous sources for such ideals in order to legitimize them in the eyes of the public and religious authorities alike. Otherwise, his program may be attacked and contemptuously dismissed by his fundamentalist opponents as "Western imports" whose adoption by the nation would represent a capitulation to the West and a betrayal of the Islamic revolution.

In summary, Khatami treads a difficult path both practically and intellectually. President Khatami and his supporters will have to work energetically to point out how aspects of their progressive political program in fact have their origins in the Koran and the Hadith (the Tradition).

We can wish Khatami well and do what we can, at arm's length and from across the waters, to encourage the growth and development of politically moderate voices within the Islamic world. Western governments cannot do much more than that since a close embrace of Khatami and his program may give his hard line opponents an opportunity to criticize him as a puppet of the West. In the meantime, we must still deal with the hostile intentions of the fundamentalist government of Iran and the deadly threats uttered by fundamentalist groups around the world against the United States and other Western countries.

POLICY RECOMMENDATIONS

Very briefly, several policy recommendations flow from the above state of affairs.

- **Condemn Words and Deeds, Not Religious Status:** We should condemn words and deeds, not religious status. No one should be condemned as a terrorist or supporter of terrorism merely because they happen to be followers of Islam. The West must avoid falling into the trap of condemning a particular religion. Rather, Western governments should condemn those individuals and groups who interpret Islam in such a way as to justify their violent actions.

- **Support Civil Society, Not Elections:** Western governments should not rigidly support calls for immediate elections in certain Islamic countries today which would only serve to betray democratic principles tomorrow. The West must not be beguiled by the fundamentalists in places like Algeria into betraying its allies by blindly joining calls for immediate elections. We should instead support and rally around the concept of "civil society" which consists of those governmental and nongovernmental institutions that are the prerequisite of a mature and fully functional democracy. I am referring here to the ground rules of a democratic system such as recognizing the rights of opposition parties; allowing political opposition and dissent to exist without the threat of torture, imprisonment, or death; allowing a free press, free speech, and the right to demonstrate peacefully; the right of minority religions to co-exist with Islam without persecution or harassment; the establishment of an independent judiciary; and so on. The institution of civil society ensures that a political culture will be in place that guarantees the orderly transition of power between elected governments and that future elections will in fact take place.

- **Deterrence is Dead:** We must recognize that the military doctrine of deterrence is dead. The cornerstone of America's and NATO's Cold War defense strategy — the deterrence doctrine — is not going to be sufficient in dealing with the transnational fundamentalist movement. How does one deter a fundamentalist soldier, terrorist group, or military detachment that believes the surest and swiftest way to heaven is to commit a terrorist act against a Western target and die in the course of that attack? You cannot "deter" that person or party in the conventional sense. You can only neutralize the threat.

Emphasis must be on thwarting such attacks, whether through the use of counter-terrorism measures or the deployment of missile defense systems to prevent a successful attack against America and its allies. The positive aspect of missile defense systems is that they are not offensive systems but defensive ones. They do not threaten particular adversaries or single out any one particular threat. They protect against all-comers, and there is very little danger that the Muslim fundamentalist countries or others will feel "threatened" or "discriminated against" as a result of the deployment of such defensive systems.

- **Money Does Not Always Talk:** Money does not solve all political or foreign policy problems. It would be condescending and naïve to assume that the fundamentalists would give up their dearly held, core beliefs in return for more economic aid. Such a clumsy attempt to "buy them off" would likely be met with derision and contempt even as it was being cynically accepted and exploited. Fundamentalists have had many chances over the years to take the easier and more peaceful path. The luscious fruits of global trade and world economic prosperity sit like a table filled with bounties before them. Nonetheless, the fundamentalists have refused to holster their weapons, remove their gas masks and sit down at the feast. Quite the contrary. They view Western economic prosperity and the promise of easy living as the temptations of the devil. Theirs is a different mental sensibility entirely.

CONCLUDING THOUGHTS

The Western democracies won the Cold War but they have not yet won the peace. While democracy and its economic corollary, capitalism, triumphed over communism in the 20th century, these ideals have not yet won a definitive victory over Islamic fundamentalism which many around the globe have seized upon as a rival ideology. A sizeable portion of the world's populace — stretching from Indonesia and the southern Philippines in the Pacific through Central Asia to the Middle East and Africa — has shown a willingness to embrace Islamic fundamentalism as a governing ideology. Given the fundamentalist movement's openly jihadist foreign policy toward the West, the world has now embarked upon a new and more dangerous period in human history.

Endnotes

1 Anthony J. Dennis, *The Rise of the Islamic Empire and the Threat to the West* (Bristol, IN: Wyndham Hall Press, 1996).
2 Ibid., p. 68.
3 "Russian Aide Says Gangsters Try to Steal Atom Material," *New York Times*, May 26, 1994, p. A5; "The Plutonium Racket," *Economist*, August 26, 1994, p. 39; Seymour M. Hirsch, "The Wild East," *Atlantic Monthly* (June 1994): p. 61.
4 "Egyptian Jihad Leader Preaches Holy War to Brooklyn Muslims," *Wall Street Journal*, January 6, 1993, p. A1, A5.
5 "Constitution of the Islamic Republic of Iran," *Middle East Journal* (1980): p. 185.
6 "Jihad," *Economist*, August 7–13, 1993, p. 42–43.
7 Reuters, October 28, 1991.
8 Dennis, *The Rise of the Islamic Empire and the Threat to the West*, p. 61, 76; James A. Phillips, "The Saddamization of Iran," *Policy Review*, Vol. 69 (Summer 1994): p. 7.
9 Reuters, March 11, 1993.
10 "A World Terrorist Link?" *Hartford Courant*, June 20, 1993, p. C1.
11 See "Notable and Quotable," *Wall Street Journal*, July 22, 1997, p. A14.
12 Mohammad Khatami, "Covenant with the Nation," first presidential inaugural speech, in *Islam, Liberty and Development* (Institute of Global Studies, Binghamton University, 1998), p. 150.
13 Ibid., p. 150.
14 Bernard Lewis, "Islam and Liberal Democracy," *Atlantic Monthly* (February 1993): p. 98.

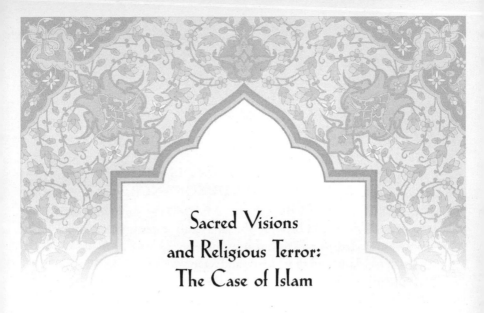

Sacred Visions
and Religious Terror:
The Case of Islam

Charles Selengut

Ll religions have, at their core, a sacred vision of the ideal
utopian community based upon their religious scriptures,
traditions, and laws. This is the case in Christianity with
its vision of a Christian society organized according to the gospels
and faithful to Jesus Christ as Lord and Savior, in Judaism with its
view of the ideal Jewish society based upon talmudic tradition and
observance of halacha, and in Islam whose history and theology
call for establishing societies and states under the sole authority
of Muslim religious leaders and governed by the Muslim *shari`a,*
religious law.

Islam, for complex historical reasons, has never religiously
accommodated to modernity and, with the exception of a small
cadre of liberal theologians and intellectuals,[1] its mainstream laity
and religious leadership have steadfastly maintained its classical
outlook and religious vision. Islam has refused to retreat to the
"private realm" of personal life and still asserts its rightful place in
the public sphere of government, the legal system, and civil society.[2]
Nonetheless, the forces of modernization and secularization are

worldwide and have affected Muslim as well as European societies and Islam has been confronted by its inability to carry out its religious vision as it finds Islamic religious, political, and social programs challenged by both Muslim states intent on modernization and an emerging global order antagonistic to its religious world view.

ISLAMIC DILEMMAS, RELIGIOUS DISAPPOINTMENT, AND COGNITIVE DISSONANCE

From the time of the prophet Muhammad onward, Islam has divided the world between the lands and states under Muslim control, referred to in Muslim jurisprudence as *Dar al-Islam*, the domain of Islam, and those lands and territories not under Muslim jurisdiction, called *Dar al-Harb*, the domain or abode of war. The faithful Muslim's duty is to engage in religious struggle, *jihad*, to transform non-Muslim lands, the *Dar al-Harb*, into *Dar al-Islam* lands, governed by Muslim law. The goal of *jihad* is not to force individual conversion, but the transformation, by forcible conquest if necessary, of non-Muslim areas into Muslim-controlled states, whereby they become part of the Islamic world, the *Dar al-Islam*. Islam, from its earliest periods, permitted monotheistic religions like Christianity and Judaism to maintain their religious institutional life but these communities, known as *dhimmi* communities, while permitting religious and economic rights, were consigned to an inferior status within Muslim society, and subject to special taxes and obligations. Unlike the *dhimmis*, who are tolerated minority communities, citizens of non-Muslim societies are seen as *harbi*, people living in a war zone, and therefore subject to conquest. For Islam, "there is a canonically obligatory perpetual state of war" between Islamic civilization and non-Muslim societies, which must be fought by faithful Muslims "until the whole world either accepts the message of Islam or submits to those who bring it."[3] The world, in the Muslim view, is divided between "Islam" and "war" and the devout Muslim believer must answer the call of *jihad* to advance Allah's message for all humankind. Theologically, Muslims should throw themselves into an unrelenting, unyielding, and unending *jihad* until their duty of world transformation is complete. Political reality, military considerations, and historical developments, however, makes this impossible even for the pious Muslim. *Jihad* is not fought in a divine battlefield but in the material world and a Muslim will find it necessary and permissible to delay or renounce the battlefield, for a time, in order to make alliances, obtain war materials, and assemble a capable force. A truce, however, is a temporary matter to be followed by a continuing *jihad*.

The precise contexts and meanings of *jihad* and *Dar al-Harb* have shifted in the course of Islamic history. In the earliest periods of Islamic history, when Islam was steadily advancing in the ancient and medieval world, it was assumed that all non-Muslim lands would be conquered and take their place in the greater *Dar al-Islam*. After the Spanish Reconquista and the expulsion of Islam from Europe, this classical view of total and constant *jihad* was modified somewhat to fit the gradual loss of Muslim hegemony. Despite these changes, the call to *jihad* remains central to Islamic doctrine and religious imagination. While the ultimate goal of *jihad* is the creation of a universal world community living according to the *shari`a*, the Muslim religious code based on the *Qur`an* and the various Islamic legal traditions, the immediate task of the faithful is to make certain that existing Muslim states remain loyal to Muslim teachings and practices.

Islam rejects the secular state and acknowledges no separation between a distinctly religious realm and a secular realm. The Islamic state is the community of believers, the *ummah,,* those faithful to Islam and living under Islamic law wherever they may be. National boundaries are irrelevant. Muslims may have state entities but the Muslim *ummah* transcends national or ethnic categories and includes all who are faithful to the Muslim vision. Allegiance then is not to any national state authority but to the *ummah* and to those Islamic religious leaders who will forge an Islamic entity which will be true, in every way, to the full gamut of Muslim law, custom, and government. Practically, this means the establishment and enforcement of *shari`a* law in all Muslim societies and in all international relations.

The Islamic civilization, envisioned, required, and desired by faithful Muslims, has not occurred. A recalcitrant reality involving the international community, modern economics, and international trade and, perhaps most painful of all, the passivity and, not infrequently, the antagonism of fellow Muslims have come together to deny the faithful their deepest religious goals.

Perhaps most painful and tragic for the Muslim faithful is the continued existence of an alien Jewish state of Israel. In the Islamic view, the State of Israel now illegitimately occupies, with the assent and backing of Western military power, Islamic lands. According to Islamic perceptions, hundreds of thousands of the Muslim inhabitants of Palestine were terrorized and forced to leave their ancestral home and the holy places of Islam, the Haram el Sharif in Jerusalem and the Ibrahimi Mosque in Hebron which are under Jewish control. Not to be discounted is the everyday consciousness and experience, by an indigenous and religiously autonomous Muslim community, of being a conquered people in what is considered a sacred center of Islam.

Disappointment is a stressful human experience, and religious disappointments in particular may be among the most painful of such states because the believers invest so much of themselves in a religious faith. The psychologist Leon Festinger has described the experience of religious disappointment as a state of "cognitive dissonance" — that is, a state where two elements of belief or "fact" turn out to be contradictory or inconsistent. Festinger argued that human beings seek consistency between their beliefs and goals and their experience of external reality, because of a human propensity for order and consistency. In a series of experimental studies, Festinger and his colleagues have demonstrated that the experience of cognitive dissonance leads to severe states of discomfort and to attempts, of all sorts, to reduce or eliminate the inconsistencies and discomfort.

> Dissonance produces discomfort and, correspondingly, there will arise pressures to reduce or eliminate the dissonance. Attempts to reduce dissonance represent the observable manifestations that dissonance exists. Such attempts may take any of three forms; the person may try to change one or more of the beliefs, opinions, or behaviors involved in the dissonance; to acquire new information or beliefs that will increase the existing consonance and thus cause the total dissonance to be reduced; or to forget

the importance of those cognitions that are in a dissonant relationship.[4]

The desire to reduce dissonance and disappointment is psychologically equivalent to the desire for food when hungry, or sleep when fatigued. Living with disappointment, being ridiculed for one's beliefs, and being unable to fulfill ones religious obligations are intensely difficult situations. As Peter Berger described it, the longer it continues "it becomes very difficult to take yourself seriously."[5] The Muslim faithful find themselves in such a psychological dilemma. Their essential religious theology and religious obligations — the call to *jihad*, the conquest of non-Muslim lands for Islam, the institutionalization of *shari`a,* and an essentially clerical leadership — are inherently in conflict with the nationalistic modernizing Muslim regimes and the democratic secular traditions of Europe and the United States. The challenge facing Islam is both religious and psychological and an appreciation of the Islamic dilemma must consider both.

ISLAMIC RESPONSES

There are three ways religious groups can attempt resolution to the experience of cognitive dissonance and chronic religious disappointment: surrender, reinterpretation, and revolutionary transformation. In the Muslim case, these correspond to what I will refer to as modernism, traditionalism, and militant Islam.

MODERNISM

Muslim modernism deals with the contradictions and dissonance engendered by Islamic faith by surrendering those elements of dogma and behavior which are in conflict with modern sensibilities and culture. In this fashion, the painful experience of dissonance is dealt with by rejecting implausible faith positions for the newer "truths" of modernity, science, and political reality. Perhaps the earliest modernist writing developed in 19th century British India where the Muslim community found itself living under severe colonial rule. After the British had suppressed the Muslim revolt of 1857, some Muslim intellectuals, wanting to accommodate the new political realities and because some were captivated by European superiority, began to abandon *jihad* and

conquest as an obligation for Muslims. One prominent accultur-
ated Muslim writer, Moulavi Cheragh Ali, who spoke for a whole
cadre of modernist Muslims, explained that all the verses in the
Qur`an relating to *jihad* were of historical importance only and
that Islam was opposed to *jihad* and had no call to wage wars of
conquest.[6] Ali's writings are of interest because he works so hard
to make a case for the similarity between European Christianity
and Islam.

For contemporary modernists, as well, the classical doctrines
of the division between *Dar al-Islam* and *Dar al-Harb* and the
obligation of aggressive *jihad* are rejected. Modernist scholars like
Mahmud Shalut and Abu Zahah argue that taking the full context
of the *Qur`anic* passages on *jihad* into account — "contextualized
interpretation" — demonstrates that Islam is opposed to violent
confrontation and is encouraged to make permanent peace with
non-Muslim communities. There is a full rejection of the classical
approach to Islamic treaties as temporary and limited in time as
exemplified by Muhammad's agreement with the Meccans at Hu-
daibiya.[7] Muslim modernists invoke the category of "silent *shari`a*"
to indicate that Muslims are left considerable leeway in decision
making because, in the modernist view, the *Qur`an* only prescribed
broad principles but has left details and specifics for the human
community to decide. For example, in their rejection of a religious
state, modernists argue, "there is nothing in the Islamic *shari`a* that
compels one to bind religion to state-setting, the *shari`a* does not
deal with any specific form of government." The modernists also
invoke the "silent *shari`a*" to show that Islam can be fully compat-
ible with western political democracy, pluralism, and equality. One
Muslim scholar has found Islam compatible with a Jewish state in
the Middle East.[8] The modernists are frequently pious and highly
acclaimed scholars of the *Qur`an* and its associated literature, but
their world view represents a surrender of classical Islam, as they
create a synthesis between modernity and Islam traditionalism.

TRADITIONALISM

Traditionalism is a complex phenomenon and presents elements
of surrender, resignation, and, despite all this, maintains crucial elements of the classical tradition. Traditionalists tend to ambivalence

both in language and action and, unlike modernists, refuse to out-rightly reject classical doctrine while de facto discouraging or even forbidding followers from strictly following those same scriptural admonitions. There is no cognitive or theological capitulation to political and cultural reality but there are elaborate reinterpretations of classical doctrine to make it compatible with current reality. Traditionalists engage in "cognitive and theological bargaining,"[9] willing to compromise on some issues so they can achieve the more important goals at some future point.

The Muslim Brotherhood organization in Egypt and Jordan and its affiliates all over the Muslim world, originally a sectarian revivalist movement and later, in the sixties and seventies, a radical revolutionary organization before it was transformed into a popular Islamic movement, illustrates the traditionalization response. These groups continue to affirm the complete legitimacy of *jihad* and ac-cept fully the obligation to create Islamic states which will govern in full conformity to religious law. But while they view the current leadership of Muslim nations as "infidels" and enemies of Islam, members of the Brotherhood serve in parliaments, in Jordan, Egypt, and elsewhere, and take their place as legitimate political parties. The Muslim Brotherhood justifies their participation by appeal to the *Qur`an*ic narrative of Joseph who, as a prophet doing divine bidding, took a most active role in the evil and idolatrous Pharaonic regime. Similarly, argue Muslim traditionalists, while we desire *jihad*, while we await a true Islamic state and world order, we can and are obligated to participate in governmental activity as did the prophets in the *Qur`an*ic narratives.[10]

Muslim Brotherhood members in the West Bank, Gaza, and Jordan, who, prior to the Intifada of the late nineties, refused to par-ticipate fully in organized violence against Israel and secular Muslim regimes, justified their inaction by appealing to Muhammad's *hijra*, migration to Medina, when he could not overcome the powerful opposition in Mecca and establish an Islamic state, only to return 13 years later and triumph over his opposition. Traditionalists argued that there is no violation of Muslim doctrine and no inconsistency or cognitive dissonance in their refusal to engage in a violent *jihad* at a time they saw as importune, because their course of action is fully compatible with the example of the prophet Muhammad. In the past, when challenged and even taunted by more activist groups for their refusal to engage in terrorist action against Israel, Brotherhood leaders proclaimed :

> Work for Palestine does not come in one form, that is bearing arms. It also includes awakening the youth to work for Palestine. Only the Muslims can undertake this duty, taking the youth out of their soft childhood to manhood, from nothingness to self realization, from fragmentation and diverse concerns to unity and cohesiveness. The Muslim Brotherhood does all these things and all such efforts are being made on the road to the liberation of Palestine which is part of the land of Islam.[11]

After a time, many of these traditionalist groups, like the Muslim Brotherhood in the West Bank, responding to pressure from more radical groups and to their growing sense of dissonance and infidelity to religious teachings, return to a more activist orientation. Traditionalism without engaging in violent confrontation is a difficult stance to maintain in the Islamic world.

MILITANT ISLAM: THE TRANSFORMATION OF REALITY

The transformation response seeks to change reality, to make it conform to religious expectations and dogma. Transformationists see modernists and traditionalists as faithless and weak-minded in their willingness to compromise their essential religious beliefs and goals. Militant Islam rejects Islamic modernism as theological surrender and apostasy. Traditionalism and its willingness to compromise aids and abets the enemies of Islam and deludes the Muslim faithful. Militant transformationists are pure believers, impatient with waiting and zealous to do battle for God. God spoke and his truth is literal. Any other response is blasphemous.

Muslim theology has not undergone liberalization, as has Christianity, nor has it been modified in a traditionalist mode as has Haredi Judaism with its rabbinical adjustments to new realities.[12] Islam has remained an essentially literalist Qur`anic tradition and deviations from the texts receive no legitimization or support from the religious virtuoso class of leading clerics. The militant response in its demand to engage in *jihad*, to make the literal texts come alive, to fulfill the precise demands of scripture is not sectarian or idiosyncratic as many Western secular observers imagine, but central to the inner life of Islam. The Islamic injunction to establish a universal Islamic society, to reclaim immediately Muslims lands and to establish *shari`a* as the state law is the Muslim obligation. Compromises, theological bargaining, and sophisticated reinterpretations do not ultimately address the failure of responsibility and the experience of dissonance for pious Muslims. The texts, the oral histories, and world view passed on within the closed Muslim world of Islamic schools, mosques, and universities worldwide do not permit abandonment of the classical traditions. One commentator put it this way:

> To a considerable extent, all Muslims are fundamentalists, that is they believe that the *Qur`an*, the holy scripture of Islam is God's final complete and perfected revelation for all mankind. The *Qur`an* is therefore the supreme guide for the human race, the direct words of God, covering all aspects of human life transmitted directly to his last prophet and messenger, Muhammad.
>
> Islam is God's plan for the world, every inch of it, not only just the Islamic regions. Islam is for everyone, whether one wants it or not. It is the duty of every Moslem to help expand the borders of Islam until every being on this planet acknowledges that "There is no God but Allah and Muhammad is his Messenger."[13]

Islam never rejected these beliefs and religious duties but they lay dormant in the Muslim world under the yoke of colonialism and later by the attractions of nationalism and economic modernization, whether in the form of socialism or capitalism.[14] Two 20th-century thinkers, the Indian Muslim Maulana Mawdudi and the Egyptian Sayid Qutb gave new life to the core Islamic goals, and in doing so ignited a transformation of Islam. Maulana Mawdudi argued that Islam is entirely incompatible with modernity and the modern state and that modernity in its rejection of God's laws for society and in its depraved moral order is actually identical to the *jahiliyah*, the barbarism and pagan immortality which Muhammad came to destroy and replace with the new moral and political order of Islam. Modernity is not a neutral matter, it is lethal to a genuine and faithful Islam and a Muslim cannot under any circumstance accommodate or compromise with *jahiliyah*. Qutb, who incorporated Madoodi's ideas in his own rejection of modernity, explained the following about *jahiliyah*:

> ... denotes rejection of the divinity of God and the adulation of mortals. In this sense, *jahiliyah* is not just a specific historical period (referring to the era preceding Islam) but a state of affairs. Such a state of human affairs existed in the past, exists today, and may in the future, taking the form of *jahiliyah*, that mirror image and sworn enemy of Islam. In any time and place human beings face that clear-cut choice: either to observe the Law of Allah in its entirety, or to apply laws laid down by man of one sort or another. In the latter case they are in a state of *jahiliyah*. Man is at the crossroads and that is the choice: Islam or *jahiliyah*.[15]

Qutb excoriated the modernists who sought to imitate Western societies or to define Islam in Western religious categories. Qutb went back to the texts and challenged the acquiescing Muslim clergy and politicians for failing to demand the full implementation of Islam in the political, social, and economic realm. Qutb's Islam is aggressive and all-encompassing, and he refused to dilute or compromise what he took to be authentic Islam.

Qutb worked for most of his life as an educational inspector for the Egyptian government and during the early part of his life felt that education and preaching could lead to the establishment of an Islamic state. The recalcitrance of the Egyptian state and his own religious development changed his position and led him to champion violent *jihad* as the correct path. His stay in the United States during 1949–52, studying educational administration, had a profound effect on him and highlighted for him the depravity and inferiority of the Christian West.

> During my years in America, some of my fellow Muslims would have recourse to apologetics as though they were defendants on trial. Contrariwise, I took an offensive

position, excoriating the Western *jahiliyah*, be it in its much-acclaimed religious beliefs or in its depraved and dissolute socioeconomic and moral conditions: this Christian idolatry of the Trinity and its notions of sin and redemption which make no sense at all; this Capitalism, predicated as it is on monopoly and interest-taking, money-grubbing, and exploitation; this individualism which lacks any sense of solidarity and social responsibility other than that laid down by law; that crass and vacuous materialistic perception of life, that animal freedom which is called permissiveness, that slave market dubbed "women's liberation."[16]

The Islamic response to this sordid, immoral, and God-denying situation, which Qutb now saw as invading Muslim countries, is a full uncompromising return to the fundamentals of Islam which for Qutb will only occur by means of a militant *jihad*. Moreover, the enemies of Islam are not only those who wage war against Muslims or deny Muslims their religious, political, or civil rights, but the entire world of *jahiliyah* whose very existence should not and cannot be tolerated by Islam. Islam has in this view a universal liberating and humanizing message for all humanity and it is inevitable that other religions and systems will not recognize the truth of the Islamic message. Consequently, these others powers must be "destroyed" and their leaders "annihilated." As Qutb explains, "Truth and falsehood cannot exist on earth. . . . The liberating struggle of *jihad* does not cease until all religions belong to God."[17]

Qutb went even further. Basing himself on the widely recognized medieval theologian Ibn Taymiyya, he argued that Muslim governments who are disloyal to Islamic law and do not rule according to *shari`a* are themselves to be classified as *jahiliyah* regimes and are rightfully to be violently overthrown. This was a revolution — which Qutb successfully carried out by his astute use of the legacy of the unimpeachable Ibn Taymiyya — certainly within Sunni Islam whose traditionalist leadership had for centuries been materially dependent and had accommodated the distinctly non-Muslim policies of the ruling elites. Historically, the fear of *fitna*, civil war, had been so great among the Sunni community that a great tolerance for religious compromise had been legitimated. Qubt's writings and revolutionary activity changed all that. *Jihad* and revolt were now back on the Islamic agenda. Qutb saw those willing to compromise as "spiritual and intellectual defeatists." He refused to tolerate dissonance between the Muslim texts and traditions and political and social reality and insisted on the transformation of reality in accordance with the Muslim vision.

Sayid Qutb was executed by the Egyptian government in 1956 for his Islamic revolutionary activity and is today a highly respected figure read by millions of Muslims all over the world, and he has inspired numerous revival and *jihad* organizations. Still, his writings on violence have elements of apology — he still seems caught in the traditionalist argument which defines *jihad* as a last if necessary resort — and his training as a teacher led him to believe that discussion and propaganda would bring some people to Islam. His revolutionary rhetoric, strong as it was, gave a place for *hijrah*, separation and migration from infidel regimes, and his writing on *jihad* lacked an immediate and programmatic quality.

The most sophisticated theological continuation of militant transformative Islam was taken by Abt al-Salam Faraj in his *Al-Faridah al-Gha'ibah, (The Absent Duty),*[18] a booklet which provided the theological justification for the assassination of Anwar Sadat. Faraj was executed by the Egyptian government in 1982 for his involvement in the assassination, but his work continues to be circulated widely, taken seriously by both establishment clerics and militants. He continues to be the major inspiration for Islamic "sacred terror"[19] worldwide, including followers in the United States, Europe, and India. He most recently has gained a readership in Muslim areas of the former Soviet Union whose religious leadership is increasingly adopting Qutb and Faraj as their religious inspiration.[20] Faraj's critical point is that *jihad*, violent and physical confrontation including death and destruction, is the "absent" and neglected duty of contemporary Islam. The *Qur`an* is clear: "Fight and slay the pagans wherever you see them, seize them, beleaguer them, and lie in ambush" (*Koran, Surah* 9:5).

Faraj dismisses any and all of the traditional restraints on *jihad*. Such arguments for limiting *jihad*, even those used by the most orthodox schools as excuses, are but examples of Muslim cowardice. *Hijrah* is ridiculed: "All this nonsense — about going out to the desert — results from denouncing and refusing to follow the right way to establish an Islamic state," writes Faraj.[21] It is the unwillingness to fight *jihad* that leads Muslim leaders to put their faith in preaching, propaganda, or scholasticism as ways to achieve the Islamic state. Muslims do not and will not achieve their divine mission without *jihad*. And the *Qur`an* puts it directly, "Fighting is prescribed for you and ye dislike it, but it is possible that ye dislike a thing which is good for you and you love a thing that is bad for you. But God knoweth and ye know not" (*Koran, Surah* 2:216). The high value the Muslim community puts on religious study and knowledge is similarly derided with Faraj's argument that the great ages of Muslim conquest and glory saw little scholarship but great *jihad*.

Faraj's expansion of *jihad* is most vividly seen in his encouragement of individual acts of religious violence and treachery (*fard ayn*)and his strong theological position that *jihad* needs no approval of Muslim religious authority and need not be limited by earlier ethical restraints against murder of children and certain other civilians. Moreover, the soldiers of *jihad* may use any and all methods, including deception and deceit, surprise attacks, trickery, and large-scale violence to achieve their religious goals. Throughout his writing, Faraj is clear that *jihad* means "confrontation and blood," and that no Muslim may legitimately avoid the call to *jihad*.

Faraj and his disciples laid the theological groundwork for a fundamentalist, aggressive, and increasingly violent Islam. In its emphasis on violence and murder and in its justification of individual and haphazard attacks, the new militants have religiously institutionalized *jihad* as every man's "sacred terror." The fact remains that the understanding of *jihad* and the nature of violence tolerated by Muslim authorities has been transformed after the publication of *Al-Faridah al-Gha`ibah*. This is not to say that Faraj's policy of violence is the actual Islam of most Muslims. Followers of such movements are not insignificant — likely in the hundreds of thousands worldwide — but the ultimate importance of these transformative militant thinkers is that they have created a sacred canopy under which purveyors of "sacred terror" can operate, collect money, and recruit new followers among the Muslim faithful. Qutb and Faraj were marginalized but their spiritual children are

Charles Selengut

among mainstream Muslims and it is these spiritual offspring who are setting the Islamic agenda.

This sometime quiet and sometime noisy transformation is occurring all over the Muslim world. The release from the traditional restraints on violence offered by Faraj and others has enabled Islamic activists all over the world to now legitimately proclaim individual *Fatwas*, religious verdicts, and threaten violence against anyone these activists define as "enemies of Islam."[22] The past obligation for consultation with recognized religious authorities served to limit violence and constrain *jihad*, but in this new decentralized and individuated understanding of *jihad*, there is increased likelihood for greater violent confrontation. The Palestinian Muslim Brotherhood, under the influence of the new theology, has now enlarged its active *jihad* activities and given its theological imprimatur to terrorist activity.[23] The Palestinian Authority and its supporters, once given to political and liberation movement rhetoric, has now appropriated the rhetoric of sacred terrorism associated with Islamic groups.[24] The current Palestinian Authority appointed *mufti* of Jerusalem and Palestine, Sheik Ikrima Sabri, explained that when mothers "willingly sacrifice their offspring for the sake of freedom, it is a great display of the power of belief. The mother is participating in the great reward of *jihad*. . . ."[25]

Western observers and diplomats are often shocked and scandalized by the growing legitimization of violence in the Islamic world. Muslims see things differently. Militant Islam and the new ideologies of "sacred terror," aimed at transforming political and social reality in accordance with Islamic injunctions, has released Muslims from the psychological stresses of religious inconsistency and cognitive dissonance. Islam is different and the transformative approach including violence and armed struggle emerges from classical texts and the lived history of Islam. We see here a spectacle of "realities in conflict." What, to outsiders, appears to be violence and terror is, from an Islamic perspective, an obligatory and ethical response to paganism, infidelity, or apostasy.

Westerners have their own ethnocentrism and frequently want to believe, against all evidence, that all religions are the same, that all religions condemn violence and promote tolerance and human brotherhood. Western secular humanists in their embrace of an ethic of moral relativism and secular nationalism have erroneously assumed that all peoples concur with this unique and unusual approach of modern Western civilization. Modernization and nationalism, along American and European lines, have not worked in the Islamic world.[26] While small economic and political elites have welcomed westernization and benefited from it, the bulk of the Muslim world has experienced, in the prescient words of Emanuel Sivan, only "doom and gloom" from an embrace of modernity. The mood now all over the Islamic world — from the Arabian Peninsula to Caucasus, in the Philippines, Indonesia, and among the émigrés to Western Europe and the United States — is for a search for Islamic authenticity. It is at this moment that militant transformative Islam has much to offer to Muslim seekers. It is a religion anchored in the sacred texts without apology. It is a bulwark against globalization and moral homelessness and it has a clear program to achieve the Muslim vision of "there is no God but Allah" throughout the world.

Endnotes

1 Charles Kutzman, editor, *Liberal Islam* (New York: Oxford University Press, 1998), p. 3–26.
2 Bruce Lawrence, *Defenders of God* (Columbia, SC: University of South Carolina Press, 1995), p. 189–226.
3 Bernard Lewis, *The Jews of Islam* (Princeton, NJ: Princeton University Press, 1984), p.21.
4 Leon Festinger et. al., *When Prophecy Fails* (Minneapolis, MN: University of Minnesota Press, 1956), p. 25.
5 Peter L. Berger, "Some Sociological Comments on Theological Education," *Perspective* (Summer 1968).
6 Quoted in Mustonsi Mir, "*Jihad* in Islam," in Hadia Dajani-Shakeel and Ronald A. Massier, editors, *The Jihad and Its Times* (Ann Arbor, MI: Center For Near Eastern and North African Studies, The University of Michigan, 1991), p. 119.
7 Ibid.
8 See "A Jewish Temple Under Al-Aqsa?" *Jewish Voice and Opinion*, Vol. 14, No. 2 (Oct. 2000): p. 10–12. Abdul Hadi Palazzi, a leader of the Italian-Muslim community, argues for the legitimacy of the State of Israel and moreover sees no religious requirement for the Jewish state to give up sovereignty over Muslim holy places like the Al-Aqsa mosque, providing that respect for the sanctity of Muslim sites is maintained.
9 This term is taken from Peter L. Berger, "Some Sociological Comments on Theological Education," *Perspective 9* (Summer 1968): p. 129–141.

Charles Selengut

10 Anas B. Malik, "Understanding The Political Behavior of Islamists: The Implications of Socialization, Modernization, and Rationalist Approaches," *Studies in Contemporary Islam*, Vol. I, No. 1 (Spring 1999): p. 19.

11 Ziad Abu-Amr, *Islamic Fundamentalism in the West Bank and Gaza: Muslim Brotherhood and Islamic Jihad* (Bloomington, IN: Indiana University Press, 1994), p. 31.

12 For the process of reinterpretation of Jewish eschatological expectations see Charles Selengut, "By Torah Alone: Yeshivah Fundamentalism in Jewish Society," M. Marty and S. Appleby, *Accounting for Fundamentalism* (Chicago, IL: University of Chicago Press, 1993).

13 A.S. Abraham and George Haddad, *The Warriors of God* (Bristol, IN: Wyndham Hall Press, 1989), p. 1.

14 Emmanuel Sivan, *Radical Islam: Medieval Theology and Modern Politics* (New Haven, CT: Yale University Press, 1985), chapter 3.

15 Ibid, p. 24, quoting Qutb.

16 Ibid., p. 68.

17 Quoted in Yvonne Y. Haddad, "Sayyid Qutb: Ideology of Islamic Revival," in John L. Esposito, *Voices of Resurgent Islam* (New York: Oxford University Press, 1983).

18 For a discussion and translation, see Johannes J.G. Jansen, *The Neglected Duty: The Creed of Sadat's Assassins and Islamic Resurgence in the Middle East* (New York: MacMillan, 1986).

19 I am using the term "sacred terror" to highlight the twin aspect of the phenomenon. The murder and mayhem caused by militant Islam is certainly terroristic, but the religious motivation and definition given to these activities renders them also as sacred activity, at least from the perpetrators' point of view. I later refer to this issue as one of "realities in conflict."

20 Muslim informants from Islamic areas of the former Soviet Union have reported that militant authors are read and discussed widely — there are no translations into native languages — and that the newly pious are particularly moved by these ideas.

21 See English translation of *Al-Faridah al-Gha'ibah* in Jensen, Jansen, *The Neglected Duty: The Creed of Sadat's Assassins and Islamic Resurgence in the Middle East,* p. 188. I have used "nonsense" instead of Jensen's "strange ideas."

22 "Killing for the Glory of God in a Land Far from Home," *New York Times*, January 16, 2001, p. 1 reports on the growing number of *jihad* activists and their international networks.

23 Abu-Amr, *Islamic Fundamentalism in the West Bank and Gaza: Muslim Brotherhood and Islamic Jihad.*

24 Jeffrey Goldberg, "Arafat's Gift," *New Yorker*, January 29, 2001, p. 52–67.

25 "An Interview with the Grand Mufti About the Pope's Visit," *Al-Ahram Al-Arabi* (Egypt), March 29, 2000. Translated by the Middle East Media and Research Institute <www.memri.org>.

26 Bill Musk, *Passionate Believing* (Turnbridge Wells: Monarch Publications, 1992), points out that in Muslim areas such as Yemen, Egypt, and Saudi

Arabia, statistics show that high levels of education are correlated with high levels of involvement in militant groups. The expectation that high levels of education would lead to lower levels of religiosity was proved wrong in Muslim countries. This has also been pointed out in Joyce M. Davis, *Between Jihad and Salaam* (New York: St. Martins Press, 1997).

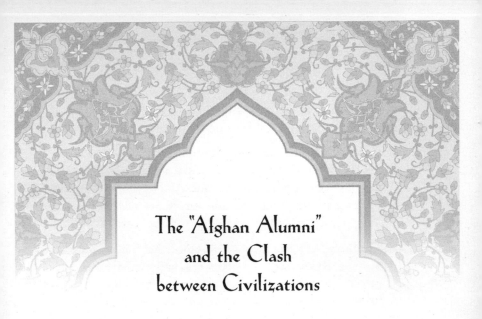

The "Afghan Alumni" and the Clash between Civilizations

Shaul Shay

I n recent years, some scholars have spoken of a clash of civilizations between Islam and modern secular (or Judeo-Christian)
democratic values and culture, or between Islamic civilization
and the West.[1] This trend gains surprising support from Osama
bin Laden, one of the most radical leaders of fundamentalistic
Islam.

Osama bin Laden set himself up as the leader of the "historical,
cultural, religious struggle between Islam and Jewish-Crusader pact"
which, he claimed, aimed at subjugating Islam and conquering the
Muslim holy places.[2]

In the summer of 1993, Professor Samuel P. Huntington, a
lecturer in international relations at Harvard University, published
an article entitled "The Clash of Civilizations?"[3] which caused a
stir within the international academic community. Three years
later, Professor Huntington published a book of the same name,[4]
in which he argues that the root of global conflict at the turn of
the century is neither ideological nor economic, but primarily
cultural.

Huntington divides the development of conflict in the modern world into four periods:[5]

1. **Conflicts between monarchs**: These conflicts were based on rival economic and territorial interests.

2. **Conflicts between nations**: Since the French revolution and the rise of nationalism, the principal actors in conflicts are no longer monarchs, but nations. As Huntington puts it: "The wars of kings are over, the wars of people had begun."[6] This stage lasted until the end of the First World War.

3. **Conflicts between ideologies**: Since the rise of communism in Russia, conflicts between nations have been replaced by conflicts between competing ideologies — first between communism, fascism, and democratic liberalism, and later between communism and democratic liberalism (the "Cold War" or "East against West").

4. **Conflicts between civilizations**: Since the end of the "Cold War," the clash between civilizations has become the primary cause of conflict.

Huntington argues that until the end of the "Cold War," Western culture dominated the modern world and shaped most of its significant conflicts, which he calls "Western civil wars."[7] At the end of the "Cold War" era, Huntington continues, Western culture lost its primacy, and the center of gravity in international politics shifted toward non-Western cultures. Conflicts between Western and non-Western cultures, and conflicts within the non-Western cultures themselves began to replace the "Western civil wars." From this point on, nations and states affiliated with non-Western civilizations ceased being the victims of Western colonialism, but became active, or even dominant, partners in the shaping of history.

During the "Cold War" period, nations were classified according to their political, economic, and technological advancement (developed and developing nations, First, Second, Third-World Nations, etc.). Huntington claims that this nomenclature is outdated and that today nations should be classified in terms of culture or civilization.

Civilization is defined by objective factors such as language, history, religion, customs, and institutions, and subjective factors such as the way people define themselves or their reference group. Therefore, civilizations may be defined as the broadest cultural entities with which people identify, or: "The highest cultural grouping of people and broadest level of cultural identity people have, short of that which distinguishes humans from others."[8]

Huntington goes on to list eight major civilizations in the modern world: Western, Slavic, Sino-Confucian, Japanese, Hindu, Latin American, Islamic, and African.[9] Of these, Huntington singles out Islamic civilization as the most militant, and emphasizes the inherent conflict between it and Western and other civilizations. He outlines the historical evolution of this conflict, starting with the Crusades, and continuing through the Ottoman Empire, Western colonialism, and the liberation wars of the Muslim states.

A glance at the map of international conflicts corroborates Huntington's premise: From West Africa to the Pacific Islands, Islam is engaged in violent conflicts with neighboring civilizations (known as "fault-line wars"). Huntington adduces the following conflicts in support of his theory.

- The Afghan War
- The Gulf War
- The conflict between Serbs and Albanians[10]
- The confrontation between Turkey and Greece
- Ethnic and religious confrontation in the former USSR[11]
- The war between Azerbaijan and Armenia

A more up-to-date list (up to 2000) lends further support to Huntington's contention.

- The civil war between Christians and Muslims in the Sudan
- The war between Christian Ethiopia and Muslim Eritrea
- The war in Kosovo between the Christian Serbs and Muslim Albanians

- The war in Chechnya and Daghestan, and insurrection against the pro-Russian regimes in Tajikistan and Uzbekistan

- The ongoing conflict with Iraq

- The war between India and Pakistan over Kashmir

- Subversion by Uighur Muslim nationalists in Western China

- The struggle between the Muslims and the Christian regime in the Philippines for control of Mindanao (Moro)

- The war between Indonesian Muslims and Christians in East Timor

- The Israeli-Arab conflict — a significant element in the conflict between Islamic and Western cultures, which has over the past decade adopted the guise of a Jewish-Muslim conflict

Although the political reality, as described above, reinforces Huntington's basic contention, a critique of some of his claims is in order. Our main criticism is that Huntington depicts all Muslim states as a single cultural bloc in conflict with Western and other civilizations. A more careful study of the regimes in Muslim states shows that the majority are secular regimes, or moderate and pragmatic Muslim regimes which, far from being in conflict with Western culture, have jumped onto the "modernization bandwagon" and adopted Western technologies, values, and ways of life. As well as modeling themselves on a Western lifestyle, many even rely on military, political, and economic aid from the West for their survival. Huntington has failed to differentiate between this dominant stream, and the fundamentalist Islamic stream, which, despite its militant anti-Western stance, still represents only a minority within the Muslim world.

John L. Esposito, criticized Huntington's concept: "Huntington's position emphasizes religious and cultural differences with confrontation. Areas of cooperation and the fact that most countries are primarily, although not solely, driven by national and regional interests are overlooked in his analysis."[12]

The two words "Islam" and "fundamentalism," which have become intimately linked in English usage in recent years, are "Western" terms and definitions dealing with a phenomenon taken from a different culture and environment.

Therefore, the nature of fundamentalist Islam and even the use of the term are hotly debated.[13]

The Muslim world today is torn by a deep internal conflict over the essence and purpose of Islamic society. The outcome of this internal conflict has dictated, and continues to dictate, the nature of the ties between Muslim civilization and Western and other civilizations.

The radical Islamic elements operate in all Muslim states at different levels of intensity. Their objective is threefold: to bring about the rule of Islamic law in Muslim countries, to establish new Islamic states, and to obtain independence for Muslim minorities in countries such as China, the Philippines, Serbia, and India, among others.

In other words, the radical Islamic struggle against foreign cultures may embrace one or several of the following four goals:

1. The overthrow of secular regimes in Muslim states and their replacement by Islamic theocratic regimes

2. Independence for Muslim minorities, and the establishment of independent Islamic states

3. The suppression of ethnic/cultural minorities seeking autonomy or independence in Muslim states

4. The neutralization of the influence of foreign — particularly Western — civilizations situated on the fault lines with Islamic culture.

The following three events have had a significant impact on the development of Islamic fundamentalism:

1. The Islamic revolution in Iran — This event turned Iran into a focus of radical *Shi`ite* Islam, exported the revolution to the Muslim world, and led to radical Islam's condemnation of the hegemony of the superpowers under the slogan: "Neither East nor West."

2. The victory of the Islamic *mujahideen* in Afghanistan — The defeat of the Soviet Union in battle was perceived by Islamic circles not only as a military victory, but also as a cultural one.[14] It created a broad cadre of seasoned, militant volunteers eager to disseminate fundamentalist Islamic ideas throughout the Muslim world.

3. The disintegration of the USSR — The collapse of communism left a political and ideological vacuum into which Islamic circles were only too eager to step.

The collapse of the Soviet Empire led to the creation of new states with Muslim populations, thereby furnishing a new arena of conflict for fundamentalist Islamic groups. Radical Islamic circles perceived the new geopolitical reality of the post-Cold War era, in which Islam spearheaded the ideological conflict with the West, as a mark of their success.

In Europe, meanwhile, for the first time in decades, the issue of Muslim identity arose among the populations of the Balkans (Bosnia, Kosovo, and Albania). For the first time, too, the religious and ethnic conflicts in this region presented radical Islam with an opportunity for gaining an ideological foothold in these areas.

In this chapter we shall be focusing on a recent phenomenon which clearly exemplifies Huntington's theory of the "clash of civilizations" — that of the "Afghan *mujahideen*" — the spearhead of radical Islam's struggle against heretical cultures. Despite their name, the "Afghan terrorists" are not affiliated with a specific movement or state, but see themselves as the representatives of Islam's relentless struggle against secular Muslim regimes and heretical cultures.

THE "AFGHAN ALUMNI"

Throughout the 1980s, Muslim volunteers from Muslim and Arab countries streamed into Afghanistan to help the Afghan *mujahideen* in their struggle against the pro-Soviet regime in Kabul and the Soviet occupying forces. Although no exact figures are available, it would seem that several thousand answered the call of the Afghan *jihad*, for religious, personal, or mercenary reasons.[15] During their stay in Afghanistan, the volunteers underwent military training and acquired extensive combat experience in guerrilla warfare.

The *mujahideen* and the Afghan volunteers were usually trained in camps in Pakistan, particularly in the city of Peshawar (near the Afghan border), which soon became the hub of *mujahideen* activity.[16] Instruction was given by Pakistanis, experts from Arab countries, and for a while also by Western — particularly official American — specialists.[17] The volunteers from Arab countries also trained in camps in the Sudan, Yemen, and Iran.

Although there are no records of the breakdown of volunteers by their affiliation to any of the Afghan rebel groups, many of the volunteers (some say as many as 3,500) would seem to have joined "Hizb Islam," Hekmatyar's extremist organization (where some of the volunteers continue to serve to this day, participating in its struggle against the current Islamic regime in Kabul).[18] After the collapse of the pro-Soviet regime in Kabul in May 1992, most of the volunteers — or "Afghan Alumni" — began returning home.

Despite the Pakistani government's declaration of January 1993[19] pledging to shut down the offices of the Afghan movements and expel illegal residents, in practice it has failed to keep its promise. To this day, many *mujahideen* continue to live in the camps of Peshawar and other places in Pakistan.

The ranks of the Afghan Alumni were swollen by the hundreds of Islamic terrorists who came to Afghanistan after the war to train in guerrilla and terrorist warfare, under the sponsorship of the various *mujahideen* factions. One of the outstanding leaders of these Afghan Alumni is Ahmad Shauqi al-Islambuli, the brother of President Sadat's assassin. Al-Islambuli and other radical leaders do not see themselves as terrorists, but rather as the proponents of a *jihad* designed to overthrow the "corrupt" regimes of Egypt, Algeria, Tunisia, and other Arab or Muslim countries.[20]

The Afghan Alumni's heroic participation in the *jihad*, their extensive combat experience, and their victory over the Soviet superpower, have today turned them into the vanguard of the Islamic fundamentalist and radical terrorist organizations.

Today, the Afghan Alumni operate in four capacities:

1. As leaders of the radical Islamic organizations in their countries of origin (Egypt, the Maghreb countries, Jordan, Saudi Arabia, etc.)

2. As founders of new terrorist organizations, such as Osama bin Laden's *al-Qa`idah* ("The Vanguard")

3. As the architects of "independent" terrorist cells which, while lacking a specific organizational affiliation, cooperate with other institutionalized terrorist organizations

4. As participants in the struggles of Islamic populations in places such as Bosnia, Kosovo, Chechnya, Tajikistan, and Kashmir[21]

Many of the countries which welcomed the volunteers' departure for Afghanistan, violently opposed their return, fearing that these battle-hardened, Muslim firebrands would join the ranks of the radical Islamic opposition in their countries of origin. Accordingly, the authorities of Egypt, Jordan, and most countries of the Maghreb tried to prevent the volunteers from returning, with varying degrees of success.

Sudan, and even Yemen, are today the Afghans' main sponsors, sheltering them before they infiltrate back into their countries of origin to join the ranks of the fundamentalist terrorist organizations there.[22] Iran, despite religious and ideological differences with the *Taliban* regime, shelters leaders of organizations affiliated with the Afghan Alumni. It supports several groups associated with the Afghan Alumni in Lebanon, Egypt, and Algiers and even sanctions the passage of activists and weapons through Iran to the *mujahideen* fighting in Chechnya.

Below is a breakdown of Afghan Alumni by country of origin.

ALGERIA

During the 1980s, many volunteers — an estimated several hundred to three thousand — left Algeria to fight alongside the Afghan *mujahideen*.[23] The Algerian *mujahideen* in Afghanistan (and Pakistan) were, and still are, divided between the supporters of the radical Islamic Salvation Front (FIS) and the supporters of Mahfoud Nahnah's more moderate Algerian "*Hamas*" movement. In the late 1980s, particularly after the *mujahideen*'s victory in Afghanistan, the battle-hardened volunteers, imbued with an Islamic revolutionary fervor, began returning home, where they joined radical Islamic organizations such as the "Armed Islamic Movement" (GIA) and the "*Al-Takfir-wal-Hijrah*" organization.[24]

Ali Belhaj, a leader of the Islamic Front, served as the spiritual father of most of the radical opposition organizations in Algeria. Some believe it was he who paved the way for the Afghan groups' absorption into the Islamic Front, with the aim of institutionalizing a focus of militant radical power as a counterweight to the political compromise advocated by some of the movement's leaders.[25]

The Afghans' first attack took place in November 1991 in the town of Gumhar on the Algerian-Tunisian border, when a group of fighters attacked a police station, causing many deaths and injuries.[26] From this point on, the struggle between the Algerian regime and the Islamic opposition intensified, with growing reports of involvement by the "Afghans" in terrorist operations throughout the country.

The terrorist activities of the Islamic organizations in Algeria, which began in 1991 with sporadic attacks against military and governmental personalities and institutions, have gradually escalated into a relentless civil war that has, so far, claimed at least 70,000 lives. In under a decade, the Islamic terrorists have succeeded in gaining control of many rural areas, and even some urban neighborhoods.

In 1994, the Islamic terrorists expanded their struggle by targeting foreign civilians and institutions in Algeria. Algeria currently has about 60,000 foreign workers, many of them working for the oil industry, which is the country's main source of revenue.[27]

From 1994 onwards, particularly in 1995–1996, the GIA began carrying out terrorist attacks abroad. All the attacks took place in France, or targeted French citizens abroad, to protest the French government's support of the Algerian regime. According to GIA spokesmen, the GIA's hostility toward France is a relic of the historical conflict between Algeria and France during the Algerian War of Independence in the early 1960s. Terrorist attacks by the GIA abroad included the hijacking of an Air France plane in December 1994, and two waves of attacks in France (July–Oct. 1995 and December 1996) in which some 20 people were killed, and dozens were injured.

The GIA, like other fundamentalist organizations in Arab countries, advocates the establishment of an Islamic regime ruled by Islamic law. Interestingly, although it sees the United States,

Israel, and Judaism as the enemies of Islam, none of its terrorist attacks have been specifically directed against American or Israeli targets. However, as part of its overall anti-French strategy, three of its attacks were directed against Jewish targets in France. The first (December 24, 1994) was an abortive car bomb attack against a Lyon synagogue, the second was a car bomb attack against a Jewish school in Villeurbanne near Lyon (September 1995), and the third was a letter bomb sent to the editor of a Jewish newspaper (December 1996).

The GIA terrorist attacks in France led to the exposure of an extensive GIA infrastructure in various European countries, particularly in France, Belgium, the UK, Germany, Italy, Sweden, and Spain. Logistic, financial, and operational ties were found to exist between the members of the small terrorist cells operating in these countries. The main objective of this European network was to smuggle funds and weapons to their comrades in Algeria.[28]

The European-wide crackdown against terrorists, sponsored by France, dealt a heavy blow to the infrastructure of the Algerian terrorist network, and effectively led to the cessation of terrorist attacks by GIA operatives abroad.

Unlike Palestinian and *Shi`ite* terrorist organizations, the GIA has so far refrained from carrying out "extortionist" terrorist operations in attempts to free dozens of its members languishing in various European jails. This may be due to the GIA's wish to focus on the struggle at home, and to avoid alienating European public opinion, which could harm its potential for exploiting Europe as a vital logistic base for its activities in Algeria.

Note that in 1998, as well, more GIA-affiliated terrorist cells were uncovered in Europe. The involvement of first- and second-generation immigrants from the Maghreb countries in attacks in France, and in Algerian terrorist cells in various countries in Europe, shows that the organization drew upon a large pool of potential volunteers from the poorer strata of the immigrant population who felt discriminated against and alienated in their countries of adoption. These populations served as a source of recruitment for new volunteers, some of whom were sent to Afghanistan for terrorist training in the early 1990s and others of whom volunteered to fight in Bosnia.

TUNISIA

Tunisian intelligence agents claim that in May 1992, Islamic extremists who had trained in Afghanistan tried to assassinate the president of Tunisia, Ben Ali, by attempting to down his plane with a portable missile. The attempt failed and the assassins were arrested. Today, the Tunisian security services are successful in containing extremist Islamic activity in Tunisia. Extremist Islamic organizations have been banned and most of their leaders have been arrested or have fled abroad, including Rashid Ghannushi, head of the "Al-Nahdha" ["Revival"] movement, who has been granted political asylum in London.

Nevertheless, the violent struggle between the Algerian regime and the Islamic opposition in neighboring Algeria, and the possible rise to power of an extremist Islamic movement there, will undoubtedly have far-reaching repercussions on developments in Tunisia.[29]

YEMEN

Yemen, today, is an important center of "Afghan" terrorist activity, due to the regime's "tolerant" attitude toward such activity. Yemen also serves as a meeting and transit point for Afghan Alumni throughout the world.

In December 1998, the Yemenite authorities arrested members of an extremist Islamic group who were planning to carry out attacks against British and American targets in Aden.[30] The group, headed by the London-based Muslim cleric Abu Hamza, who is identified with the radical "Supporters of *Shari`ah*" movement, included eight Britons and two Algerians. Members of the group reached Yemen using forged French passports, and were trained and equipped by a local fundamentalist Islamic organization called the "Islamic Army of Aden," led by Al-Mihdar, who was executed after his implication in the kidnapping of 16 European tourists.[31]

During Al-Mihdar's trial, it transpired that members of the "Islamic Army" kidnapped the European tourists in order to obtain the release of members who were arrested in December 1998.[32] The kidnapping saga was brought to an end by a rescue operation mounted by the Yemenite security forces, resulting in the death of the kidnappers and four hostages. A study of those involved in the two terrorist attacks in Yemen shows that some of them were trained in Afghanistan, and had ties with the Egyptian *jihad* organization supported by bin Laden.

EGYPT

In the 1980s, Egypt aligned itself with the Muslim and Western world by condemning the Soviet invasion of Afghanistan, and by providing aid to the *mujahideen* leading the struggle against the Kabul government and Soviet forces. In a show of solidarity, Egypt allowed volunteers to leave for Afghanistan to participate in the *mujahideen's* struggle. Most of the Egyptian volunteers who left for Afghanistan were members of the Muslim Brotherhood or of more radical organizations, such as the Egyptian "Muslim *jihad*."[33] At the time, the Egyptian authorities were relieved that the "revolutionary fervor" of the radical Islamic elements was being directed outside Egypt. This not only led to a decline in radical activity in Egypt but also strengthened Egypt's status within the Muslim community.

However, as we shall see, the issue of the "Afghan volunteers" became, in time, a "double-edged sword" for the Egyptian government. With the defeat of the Soviet forces and the collapse of the pro-Soviet administration in Kabul, the Egyptian volunteers began returning home, much to the dismay of the Egyptian authorities who, fearing an upsurge in radical terrorist activity in Egypt, did their best to prevent them.

Despite their efforts, some Afghan Alumni evidently found their way back into Egypt where they joined Islamic terrorist organizations. In 1992–1994, the "Afghans" were involved in a series of terrorist attacks in Egypt. Their trials, which came to be known as the "Trials of the Afghanistan Returnees," shed light on some of their activities as members of terrorist organizations working against the Egyptian regime. Below are some of the "achievements" of the Egyptian *mujahideen* in Afghanistan:

- The establishment of training camps in Afghanistan and in Peshawar in Pakistan[34]

- The dispatch of trained fighters back to Egypt, particularly via the Sudan[35]

- The preparation of false documents for these fighters[36]

- The cultivation of drugs and drug trafficking in order to finance the organizations' activities[37]

- Propaganda activity for terrorist organizations such as "*Tala`I` al-Fath*" ("Vanguards of the Conquest") and the Egyptian "*jihad*"[38]

- The planning and implementation of attacks in Egypt and other places (Afghan Alumni were among the perpetrators of the World Trade Center bombing in New York City)[39]

The Egyptian volunteers were involved in numerous terrorist activities in Egypt, among them violent activities in upper Egypt. In 1992–1993, extremist Islamic activists incriminated in these activities were arrested and tried in Egypt. During their interrogation, they admitted that they had trained in Afghanistan, and that they had planned terrorist attacks against the Egyptian security forces and Egyptian public figures,[40] such as the attempted assassination, in 1992–1993, of the Egyptian Information Minister, Sawfat al-Sharif, the Interior Minister,[41] and the Prime Minister, Atef Sidky. The assailants, who were caught, were found to be members of *Tala`I` al-Fath* — an organization that had been set up in Afghanistan.[42]

The Egyptian terrorist organizations chose tourism as their target, as the best way of harming the state's economy (tourism is the country's second most important source of revenue after the Suez Canal), and its image both at home and abroad. The spectacular terrorist attacks they mounted against tourists were designed to destabilize the regime on the one hand, and to attract new recruits, on the other.

Attacking tourists also served the ideological goal of destroying the representatives of the "heretical" Western culture that "contaminated" the Muslim world.

As a result of these attacks, the 1992–1993 tourist seasons in Egypt suffered serious losses amounting to several billion dollars. The most serious attack was that perpetrated by *Al-Gama`ah al-Islamiyyah* ["The Islamic Group"] against tourists in the Temple of Queen Hatshepsut in Luxor (November 1997), in which 58 tourists and 4 Egyptians were killed. The attack caused enormous damage to Egypt's recovering economy, in losses estimated at half a billion dollars.

The Coptic Christian minority, perceived by the fundamentalist organizations in Egypt as a cultural, ethnic, and religious foreign implant, and envied for its economic success, has also served as a target for terrorist attacks.

In November 1993, President Rabbani of Afghanistan visited Egypt and signed an extradition agreement and a security cooperation pact, whereby Egypt offered Afghanistan economic and security aid in return for Afghanistan's commitment to banning extremist Egyptian Islamic elements in Afghanistan and extraditing prominent activists such as Muhammad Shauqi al-Islambuli.[43] At the end of his visit, President Rabbani expressed his appreciation of Egypt's contribution to the victory of the Afghan *mujahideen*, condemned terrorism in all its forms, and declared that he would not allow Afghanistan to be used as a springboard for attacks against the regime in Egypt.[44]

Rabbani's wish to improve his country's standing with Egypt was not shared by his rival, Hekmatyar, who extended his patronage to the Egyptian fundamentalists in Afghanistan, and even offered Sheikh Omar Abdel Rahman political asylum (after Egypt requested his extradition from the United States for his involvement in the World Trade Center bombing). Since Rabbani's regime had no control over Hekmatyar's opposition movement,[45] Afghanistan failed to keep its promise to banish or extradite Egyptian fundamentalist terrorists residing in the country.[46] Consequently, Egypt announced that it could not honor the agreement.

The "heavy-handed" policy adopted by the security forces against the terrorist organizations in Egypt, and the expulsion of terrorists, limited their freedom of action, compelling them to resort to terrorist attacks abroad. Most of these attacks were in retaliation for the arrest, extradition, and assassination of their members abroad by Egyptian security forces, sometimes in cooperation with local security forces. These attacks included the attempted assassination of an Egyptian diplomat in Switzerland by the Egyptian *jihad* (November 1995), a suicide bomb attack against the police station in Rijeka, Croatia, by *Al-Gama`ah al-Islamiyyah*, (October 1995), and the bombing of the Egyptian embassy in Pakistan (November 1995). The most daring attack orchestrated by *Al-Gama`ah al-Islamiyyah* was the attempted assassination of Hosni Mubarak during his visit to Ethiopia (June 1995). (The terrorists chose this occasion on the assumption that security precaution there would be more lax than in Egypt.)

The Egyptian organizations, predominantly *Al-Gama`ah al-Islamiyyah*, were indirectly involved in international terror, through "Arab-Afghans" (Egyptian citizens who trained in the *Mujahideen* camps after the end of the war) who operated as individuals within autonomous Islamic terrorist cells abroad.

Note that the blind Egyptian cleric, Sheikh Omar Abdel Rahman, the supreme spiritual authority of *Al-Gama`ah al-Islamiyyah* and the Egyptian *jihad*, issued a *fatwa* (religious decree) sanctioning the activities of these terrorist cells.

In recent years, especially since 1998, the activities of the Egyptian organizations have been influenced by their ties with Osama bin Laden and his *al-Qa`idah* organization. *Al-Qa`idah* has recruited a substantial number of Egyptians. At least one of the drivers in the suicide bomb attacks in Nairobi and Dar-es-Salaam in August 1998, masterminded by *al-Qa`idah,* was an Egyptian citizen. The alliance between bin Laden and the Egyptian organizations is reflected in his close ties with leaders of these organizations, such as Ahmad Rifa`i Taha and Mustafa Hamza, heads of the political and military arms of *Al-Gama`ah al-Islamiyyah,* respectively, and especially Oman Ayman Zawahiri, head of one of the factions of the Egyptian *jihad*. Zawahiri has adopted bin Laden's new terrorist strategy of targeting American, rather than Egyptian objectives, on the grounds that the head-on confrontation with the Egyptian regime has caused the deaths of innocent people and has alienated Muslim public opinion in Egypt, while attacks against the American infidels were sure to elicit sympathy among the Muslims. That the Egyptian *jihad* adopted this strategy is evident in its planned attack on the U.S. consulate in Albania, (foiled in June 1998), and its involvement in the embassy attacks in East Africa in August 1998.

Al-Gama`ah al-Islamiyyah, the mainspring of the religious-military coalition envisaged by bin Laden, has for the past two years been divided in its policy regarding domestic and anti-U.S. terrorism. The unilateral declaration of a truce toward the Egyptian government by its imprisoned leaders (July 1997) caused a rift between the leadership in Egypt and the leadership abroad concerning the movement's policy and goals. The massacre of the tourists in Luxor (October 1997) intensified the polemic, in particular as a result of growing pressure by the Egyptian regime on members of the organization in Egypt and abroad. Omar Abdel Rahman's declaration from his prison in the United States, advocating peaceful means in pursuing the organization's objectives (October 1998), tilted the balance in favor of the "moderates."

Al-Gama`ah al-Islamiyyah has already officially declared a "cease-fire," and some members of the Egyptian *jihad*, after Ayman Zawahiri's resignation, have followed suit. This declaration has intensified the polemic within the Egyptian organization, and the question of whether the cease-fire will be observed remains to be seen.

THE JORDANIAN AFGHANS

In early 1994, a series of bombs exploded in several cinemas in Jordan.[47] Following arrests by the Jordanian security forces in 1995, a group belonging to the "*Bai`at al-Imam*" ["Homage to the Imam"] movement was discovered, headed by "Issam Muhammad al-Burqawi" (Abu Muhammad al-Muqadassi), a Palestinian originally from Jaffa, and a number of Afghan Alumni.[48] The organization, which disposed of weapons and explosives, aimed at overthrowing the regime in Jordan through a *jihad*, as part of an overall struggle to reform Islamic society. In the course of the investigation, it transpired that the terrorists had intended carrying out a range of terrorist attacks against people (public figures) or institutions (cinemas, hotels) they identified with corruption.

In December 1999, an Islamic terrorist organization, comprising Jordanian, Iraqi, Algerian, and Palestinian citizens bearing American documents, was uncovered in Jordan. The group was headed by Abu Hoshar who had already been arrested in Jordan (1993) for carrying out attacks there, but who had been granted a royal pardon. Abu Hoshar, who had trained in Afghanistan, returned to Jordan to set up the "Army of Muhammad," which was also partly composed of Afghan Alumni.[49]

On December 17, 1999, Halil Dik (an American of Palestinian origin), considered the architect of the abortive attacks in Jordan, was extradited to Jordan by Pakistan. The investigation of members of the organization showed that they intended carrying out attacks against Jewish and Israeli tourists in Amman's Radisson Hotel, against visitors to Moses' tomb on Mt. Nebo, against tourists passing through the Jordanian-Israeli border check post, and against pilgrims visiting the site of Jesus' baptism.[50]

ATTACKS BY AFGHAN ALUMNI AGAINST ISRAELI AND JEWISH TARGETS

The virulent rhetoric of *The Protocols of the Elders of Zion*, used by the Sunni Muslims against Judaism and Israel has not, so far, been translated into a consistent terror campaign against international Jewish and Israeli targets. Since the mid-1990s, however, Sunni Muslim organizations have been responsible for isolated attacks/ attempted attacks against Israeli and Jewish targets abroad. For example, on April 19, 1996, during the "Grapes of Wrath" operation in Lebanon, the Egyptian *Al-Gama`ah al-Islamiyyah* mounted an attack against tourists in the Europa hotel in Cairo, killing 17 Greek pilgrims. In its communiqué claiming responsibility for the attack, the organization stated that it had meant to target Israeli tourists who were known to frequent the Europa hotel.

As stated above (see section on Algeria), the Algerian GIA carried out three attacks against Jewish targets in France as part of its terror campaign in France. These attacks included two car bomb attacks, one near a synagogue in Lyon in 1994 (foiled) and one near a Jewish school in Villeurbanne. It was only because the school bell was late that a massacre of Jewish schoolchildren was averted. The third attack was a letter bomb sent to the editor of a Jewish newspaper in France (1996).

In 1995 and 1999, two organizations of Afghan Alumni which were planning attacks against Jewish and Israeli targets were discovered in Jordan (see section on Jordan above).

Particularly noteworthy is the growing involvement of Palestinian Afghan Alumni abroad in planning terrorist activities against Israeli targets. This has been particularly evident in recent terrorist activity in Jordan.

In February 2000, Sa`ad Hindawi, a Palestinian "Afghan veteran" hailing from Halhul, who lived in Lebanon for many years, was arrested in Israel, where he and his family had returned after the establishment of the Palestinian Authority. Hindawi, whose brother is the chief of police in Hebron, admitted that in 1998 he was trained in Durante — one of Osama bin Laden's camps in Afghanistan — in terrorist warfare and sabotage. Diagrams for assembling explosives were found in his possession.

Despite his denials, he was suspected of planning to carry out attacks against Israel, possibly in coordination with local Palestinians.[51]

Finally, it is worth noting that Sheikh Abdullah Azzam, a Jordanian of Palestinian origin, was the main ideologue of the Afghan Alumni and bin Laden's partner in setting up the "Services Office" (*Maktab al-Khidamat*) — the recruiting office for the thousands of Islamic volunteers who streamed into Afghanistan to take part in the battle against the Soviets. Although Abdullah Azzam was killed in a car bomb explosion in Afghanistan in 1989, his writings and philosophy continue to provide ideological fodder for the struggle against the "enemies of Islam."

A number of factors may explain the relatively small number of terrorist attacks by Sunni terrorist organizations against Israeli and Jewish targets abroad.

- These organizations see their main goal as the overthrow of the secular regimes in their own countries, and their replacement by Islamic regimes governed by the rule of Islamic law (*Shari`ah*).

- These organizations do not see attacks against Israeli or Jewish targets as means in themselves, but rather as part of an overall terrorist strategy against their non-Muslim rivals.

- These organizations tend to focus their terrorist activity against American objectives, in line with their view of the United States as Islam's main enemy.

Osama bin Laden, a proponent of this policy, has been sharply criticized for ignoring other "Islamic" problems, including the Palestinian problem. This criticism may have been one of the reasons behind the choice of Israeli and Jewish targets in the attacks perpetrated by the Egyptian *jihad*, *al-Qa`idah*, and the Islamic cells in Jordan, in 1995 and 1999.

AZERBAIJAN

Following the defeats suffered by the Azeri (Muslim) forces in their war with the Armenians (Christians) over control of the Nagorno-Karabakh region, Azerbaijan turned to Afghanistan in August 1993 for military aid. Afghanistan responded by sending 1,000 *mujahideen* warriors to help the Azeris. In October 1993, the Afghan *mujahideen* launched a surprise attack against the Armenian forces in the region of Zanglan (near the Iranian border), and even gained ground, before being repulsed by the Armenian forces. As far as we know, these *mujahideen* forces remained in Azerbaijan where they continue to help the Azeris in their struggle against the Armenians.[52]

CHECHNYA

The disintegration of the Soviet Union triggered a religious-national awakening in Chechnya, following which (September 6, 1991) the leaders of the separatist stream declared their secession from the USSR and the establishment of the Chechen Republic of Ichkeria.

President Yeltsin, refusing to condone this move, tried to bring about the downfall of the separatists by funneling aid to the opposition groups in Chechnya, and by direct military intervention. His failure created a situation of de facto independence for Chechnya, and led to growing tension between the countries. This tension reached a peak on December 11, 1994, when Russia invaded Chechnya. Since then, Russia and the Chechen separatists have been engaged in an armed confrontation which began as a regular war, but which has since evolved into guerrilla warfare and the use of terror by the Chechen forces.

Following the victory of the *mujahideen* in Afghanistan over Najibullah's pro-Soviet regime in 1992, the Afghan Alumni were free to help the Islamic struggle in various countries throughout the world, including Chechnya. Afghan *mujahideen* organizations, and since 1996 the *Taliban* regime, have been sending equipment, weapons, and warriors to help the Muslim separatists in Chechnya in their struggle against the Russians. Other Muslim organizations helping the Chechens are affiliated with the Saudi *Wahabi* movement, and even bin Laden's organization.

Moreover, the ranks of the Chechen fighters have been swollen by Afghan Alumni headed by Ibn-ul-Khattab, whose extensive combat and leadership skill, acquired in Afghanistan and Tajikistan, have proved of great service to the Chechens.

The "Afghan" volunteers' extensive experience in guerrilla warfare and terror and their familiarity with Russian tactics and vulnerabilities acquired in the wars against the Russians in Afghanistan and Tajikistan, have been of invaluable assistance to the Chechen warriors.[53]

BOSNIA

In 1993, about 200 Arab-Afghan *mujahideen* from Algeria, Sudan, and Saudi Arabia were found to be operating in central and northern Bosnia.

These *mujahideen,* as well as taking an active part in the war against the Serbian forces, ran educational activities designed to inculcate their fundamentalist world view on the Bosnian population. In an interview with a member of the *mujahideen*, he stated that his movement had two goals in Bosnia: to launch a *jihad* against the Serbs, and to educate Bosnian Muslims in the true way of Islam ("missionary" activity or *da`wah*).[54]

INDEPENDENT TERRORIST CELLS

One of the salient features of international terrorism in recent years has been the activity of autonomous, Islamic terrorist cells without any defined structural hierarchy, which operate through institutionalized terrorist organizations. The Afghan Alumni played a major role in the activity of these cells, through their training in Afghanistan and their ties with Islamic relief organizations, which supplied them with logistic and financial aid. These terrorist cells were responsible, among other things, for the World Trade Center bombing in New York City (February 1993) which left six dead and about a thousand wounded, plots to attack the UN building and the New York-New Jersey interstate tunnels (June 1993), the attack against the Philippine PAL jetliner (December 1994), and a planned offensive against American planes in Asia, scheduled for early 1995.

An investigation of these terrorist cells brought to light their ties with Islamic Non-Government Organizations (NGOs) such as the

"Muslim World League" (MWL), the "International Islamic Relief Organization" (IIRO), and Islamic cultural centers in Europe, such as the center in Milan. Members of these cells were also found to have close ties with Osama bin Laden.

AL-QA`IDAH [THE VANGUARD]

Another key organization in the activity of the Afghan Alumni, whose influence has been increasing in the international arena, is *al-Qa`idah*, an organization set up in 1988 by the Saudi millionaire Osama bin Laden.

Al-Qa`idah was set up by the "Services Office" (*Maktabal-Khidamat*), a Non-Governmental Islamic Relief Organization, to handle the recruitment, absorption, and placement of thousands of Islamic volunteers from 50 countries around the world in *mujahideen* camps in Pakistan and Afghanistan.

After the war, most of its activities were conducted from the Sudan and Afghanistan through a network of worldwide offices, including the United States (especially the "*Al-Kifah*" center in Brooklyn) and the Philippines.

Al-Qa`idah provided aid to other terrorist organizations, and worked for the radicalization of the Islamic movements operating in Chechnya, Bosnia, Tajikistan, Somalia, Kashmir, Yemen, and Kosovo. Its members were also involved in terrorist operations, such as the attacks against UN forces in Somalia in October 1993, in which 18 American servicemen were killed, and the attacks in Kenya and Tanzania in August 1998. There is also evidence pointing to a clear connection between *al-Qa`idah* and terrorist attacks that were planned and carried out by terrorist cells led by Ramzi Yousef in New York (1993) and in the Philippines (1994). *Al-Qa`idah* was likewise involved in the attack in Riyadh, in which six people, including five American servicemen, were killed (November 1995). The Saudis argued that bin Laden was not directly involved in the last two attacks, but that his militant anti-American rhetoric may have provided the inspiration for them.

THE ESCALATION OF THE CONFRONTATION BETWEEN BIN-LADEN AND THE UNITED STATES

In 1998, the issue of the Afghan Alumni became something of a cause *célèbre* after the spectacular attacks carried out by *al-Qa`idah* in East Africa. Bin-Laden, accused by the United States of masterminding these attacks, was portrayed by the Western and Arab media as epitomizing the threat of international fundamentalist terror. Bin-Laden lent credence to this claim by setting himself up as the leader of the "historical cultural-religious struggle between Islam and the Jewish-Crusader pact" which, he claimed, aimed at subjugating Islam and conquering the Muslim holy places.[55]

In interviews and statements, such as the June 1996 "Declaration of War"[56] and the February 1998 "*fatwah*," bin Laden paints a world view in which the entire world, especially the Middle East, is seen as the stage on which the deterministic battle for survival of the three major religions is being waged. In this struggle, a Jewish-Christian (or "Jewish-Crusader") alliance has evolved, personified by the United States and Israel (and World Jewry), which has conquered the holy Islamic places (Mecca, Medina, and Jerusalem), and aims to subdue Islam. According to bin Laden, this alliance is responsible for the systematic and deliberate slaughter of Muslims.

In order to win over the Muslim public, bin Laden sprinkles his rhetoric with historically loaded terms imbued with Islamic undertones, such as "crusaders" and *jihad*. He justifies the violence he preaches on the grounds that its purpose is to protect the Islamic holy places. By portraying the Muslim as victim, he minimizes his role as aggressor.

Bin-Laden believes that the use of violence and terror will show the community of believers that the enemies of Islam, even if seemingly invincible (like the United States and the Soviet Union), are in fact rendered vulnerable by their lack of faith. In this context, bin Laden relies heavily on the ethos of the victory of the Afghan *mujahideen* which, he holds, brought about the collapse of the Soviet Empire. He cites other examples of the weakness of the enemy (particularly the United States), such as the withdrawal of American troops from Somalia which, he claimed, was the result of the guerrilla activities he supported.

The attacks by the Saudi opposition forces in Riyadh (November 1995) and Dhahran (June 1996), which left 24 dead and dozens injured, were part of a two-pronged struggle: to "purge" the holy places (Mecca and Medina) of American control, and to bring about a moral-psychological victory for the Islamic warriors.

Bin-Laden had similar designs on the Israeli occupiers of the holy site of Al-Aqsa.[57]

During 1998, bin Laden had spun around him a web of Islamist organizations to counteract the Jewish-Crusader pact. On February 23, 1998, he convened the heads of a number of Islamic organizations in Afghanistan, and declared the establishment of the "Islamic Front for the Struggle against the Jews and the Crusaders" (hereafter the "Front"). The Front issued a *fatwah* signed by the leaders of five major Islamic organizations — Osama bin Laden, head of *al-Qa`idah*; Ayman al-Zawahiri, head of the Egyptian *jihad*; Ahmad Rifa`i Taha, leader of the Egyptian *Al-Gama`ah al-Islamiyyah*; Sheikh Miyar Hamza, secretary of the Pakistan Scholars Society (*Jama`at al-`Ulema*); and Fazlul Rahman, the emir of the Bangladesh *jihad* movement. Since bin Laden has no religious authority or military power to speak of, he needs the backing and support of these organizations. The clerics, particularly Sheikh Miyar Hamza, a high-ranking Islamic spiritual authority, lend a religious character to the decisions of the Islamic Front, while the heads of *Al-Gama`ah al-Islamiyyah* and the Egyptian *jihad* provide the military-terrorist infrastructure.

A *fatwah* issued by the Front called on Muslims throughout the world to consider it their personal duty to kill Americans and their allies, including civilians, in order to liberate the Holy Mosque in Mecca (read: Saudi Arabia) and the Al-Aqsa Mosque (read: Jerusalem and Palestine).[58]

In May 1998, in an interview with the ABC network, bin Laden declared before the American public the Front's intention to carry out global attacks against American citizens in retaliation for the American administration's "corrupt policy." Trilateral security cooperation between the United States, Egypt, and Albania foiled the attack planned by members of the Egyptian "*jihad*/Zawahiri faction" against the U.S. embassy in Tirana, and led to the extradition of its members to Egypt (July 1998). Following these events, the Front and the Egyptian *jihad* sent letters to the *Al-Hayat* newspaper[59] threatening to attack American targets. The next day (August 7), members of *al-Qa`idah* launched two sensational attacks against the U.S. embassies in Kenya and Tanzania, resulting in 291 dead and about 5,000 injured. Most of the victims were local people. Of the U.S. citizens who were the main target of the attack, "only" 12 were killed (Nairobi embassy employees).

The attacks in East Africa presented the United States with an opportunity for carrying out a limited military operation against the Afghan Alumni under the leadership of bin Laden and the Egyptian organizations. The evidence taken from those involved in the embassy attacks served to vindicate the U.S. bombing of *al-Qa`idah* bases in Afghanistan and the Sudan, and the violation of the sovereignty of the sponsor states involved. The American bombing (August 20, 1998) was directed against five *al-Qa`idah* camps in Afghanistan, and against a pharmaceuticals concern in Khartoum which, according to the United States, was financed by bin Laden, and manufactured chemical warfare components for him.

Alongside military and intelligence operations, the United States and Britain also explored the diplomatic avenue. The United States, for example, sent Ambassador Richardson to Afghanistan in an attempt to persuade the *Taliban* to hand over bin Laden or at the very least, to contain his anti-American activity and rhetoric. Britain for its part, was prepared to strike a deal with the *Taliban*, by authorizing the opening of a *Taliban* office in London, and clamping down on the Afghan opposition in London, in return for a restriction on bin Laden's activities.[60]

Meanwhile, the United States continued to cooperate with its Arab and European partners in rounding up members of *al-Qa`idah* and the Egyptian organizations, with some success. September 1998 saw the arrest of a number of key operatives in bin Laden's terrorist network, such as Wahdi al-Haj, a Lebanese Christian who converted to Islam. Al-Haj, who until 1994 had served as bin Laden's personal secretary in the Sudan, was instrumental in laying the groundwork for the August 1998 bombings in Kenya and Tanzania. He was arrested in Texas, where he had moved in 1997, probably with the intention of setting up a terrorist infrastructure in the United States.

On September 16, Mamduh Muhammad Mahmud Salim, one of bin Laden's senior aides, was arrested in Munich. Salim, who served as bin Laden's financial and logistics advisor, was responsible for procuring weapons (possibly even non-conventional weapons). Salim was extradited to the United States on December 24, 1998, where he is awaiting trial for participation in bin Laden's terrorist network.

Members of bin Laden's network have been arrested in London. Foremost of these is Khaled Fuaz, bin Laden's representative in London, a member of the Saudi opposition, and head of the "Advice and Reform" commission.

Egypt, too, during the second half of 1998, stepped up its counter-terrorist operations against Egyptian operatives abroad. In a joint American-brokered security operation, Egypt arranged for countries such as Albania, Azerbaijan, Bulgaria, South Africa, Ecuador, Saudi Arabia, Kuwait, and the UAE, to extradite members of the Egyptian *jihad* and bin Laden's terrorist network. This operation, later known as the "Albanian Returnees Affair," almost destroyed the Islamic umbrella organization.

Bin-Laden used the American bombing of Iraq (December 17–20, 1998) as a pretext once again to threaten American citizens for supporting the United States "massacre" of the Iraqi Muslim population. In a series of aggressive interviews with *Time, Newsweek*, and the BBC, he called on his Muslim brothers to renew their attacks against the enemies of Islam.[61]

Bin-Laden has proclaimed his intention to intensify efforts to obtain non-conventional weapons. He sees this as a religious duty, and accuses Muslims who obstruct such activity as sinning against Islam. Bin-Laden is deliberately vague about whether he possesses such weapons, and under what circumstances he would use them.[62]

Bin-Laden's attempts to acquire and manufacture non-conventional weapons had been closely monitored by the United States, even before he openly declared his intentions.

Indeed, the United States justified its attack on the pharmaceuticals plant in Khartoum on the grounds that the factory was manufacturing chemical weapon components for bin Laden. The extradition of Mamduh Salim (December 24, 1998), bin Laden's weapons procurer, from Germany to the United States, was also in connection with the acquisition of non-conventional weapons.

CONCLUSIONS

Islam has reemerged as an alternative to the perceived failure of secular ideologies. Islamic movements and organizations have become sources of legitimacy and mobilization, and Islamic movements span the religious and political spectrum from moderate to extremist. Islamic movements, both moderate and extremist, have proliferated and become agents of change. They establish modern political and social organizations and embrace advanced means to disseminate their message. Most of the movements function within civil society as social and political activists.

At the same time the extremists use violence to threaten the stability of many regimes.

The phenomenon of the Afghan Alumni has in recent years become an increasingly significant factor in the world of international terror and poses a real threat to the stability of Muslim regimes. It far transcends the narrow context of a terrorist organization or state-sponsored terrorism. Rather, it represents a militant religious-ideological current, which aims at bringing about a cultural revolution in an attempt to reinstate Islam's bygone glory. As such, the phenomenon of the "Afghans" clearly embodies the clash of civilizations that lies at the root of Huntington's premise.

The Afghan war gave rise to a number of exceptional processes in modern history, as described below:

- The creation of a kind of Islamic "*internationale*" through the recruitment of volunteers throughout the Muslim world to help the struggle of the Afghan *mujahideen*.

- The creation of a global network of radical Muslim terrorists through ties between these volunteers and radical Islamic movements throughout the Muslim world.

- The creation of a mystique of invincibility. The Islamic fighters' victory over the Soviet forces has won them international acclaim and has served as a source of inspiration to Islamists throughout the Muslim world.

- The creation of a broad-based cadre of highly motivated and experienced warriors, bent on exporting the Islamic revolution to the world at large.

Osama bin Laden is one of the outstanding "products" of the Afghan war, and his organization *al-Qa`idah* is one of the main expressions of the "Afghan" phenomenon. Bin-Laden views his struggle as part of the conflict between Islamic and other civilizations, particularly "the Jewish-Crusader Civilization," as he calls it.

As a cultural struggle, the worldwide Afghan struggle is being waged on three fronts: within Muslim countries (to reinstate the rule of *Shari`ah* law); in countries with Muslim minorities, situated on "fault lines" with other cultures (the Balkans, the Caucasus, Kashmir, etc.); and, internationally, in the struggle against Western, particularly U.S., civilization, which is perceived by the fundamentalists as the source of all evil, and the primary threat to Islam.

It looks as if the clash of civilizations as perceived by Huntington, at one extreme, and Osama bin Laden, at the other, is with us to stay, at least for the foreseeable future.

Endnotes

Some information in this chapter is taken from Shaul Shay and Yoram Schweitzer, *The "Afghan Alumni": Islamic Militants Against the Rest of the World*, The International Policy Institute for Counter Terrorism, The Interdisciplinary Center, Herzliya, Israel (September 2000).

1 John L. Esposito, "Political Islam and the West," *Joint Forces Quarterly* (Spring 2000).
2 David K. Schenker, "Bin-Laden and the Problem of State Supported Terrorism," *Policy Watch*, Washington Institute for Near East Policy, No. 346 (October 21, 1998).
3 Samuel Huntington, "The Clash of Civilizations?" *Foreign Affairs* (Summer 1993).
4 Samuel Huntington, *The Clash of Civilizations and the Remaking of World Order* (New York: Simon & Schuster, 1996).
5 Huntington, "The Clash of Civilizations?"
6 Ibid.
7 Ibid., Huntington is quoting William Lind.
8 Ibid.
9 Huntington includes both the Soviet Union and Communism in Western culture and ideology.
10 When the book was written, the tension between the Serbs and the Albanian Muslims in Kosovo had not yet erupted into war.
11 At the time of writing, war had not yet broken out between Chechnya and Russia.
12 John L. Esposito, "Political Islam and the West," *JFQ* (Spring 2000).
13 Martin Kramer, "Fundamentalist Islam at Large: The Drive for Power," *Middle East Quarterly* (June 1996).

14 Huntington later identifies Russia (after the disintegration of the USSR) with the Slavic culture, with which the Serbs are also identified.

15 According to an article in the weekly *Al-Usbu` al-`Arabi*, July 1992, their number was estimated at 12,000.

16 *Intelligence Newsletter*, France, July 9, 1992.

17 Conflict International (April 1994).

18 Hayyim Raviv, *Ba-Mahaneh* (August 1992).

19 *Al-Wasa*, London, February 15, 1993.

20 Ibid.

21 Yoram Schweitzer, "Middle-East Terrorism: The Afghan Alumni," in Shlomo Bron and Yiftah Shapir, editors, *Military Balance in the Middle East 1999–2000* (Cambridge, MA: Jaffee Center for Strategic Studies, MIT Press, 2000).

22 *Al-Sabah,* Tunisia, January 22, 1992.

23 Conflict International, April 1994.

24 *Al-Ahram,* Egypt, August 30, 1992.

25 Agence France Presse (AFP), February 11, 1992.

26 *Le Matin,* Algeria, December 4, 1991; Agence France Presse, Algiers, December 8, 1991.

27 Conflict International, April 1994.

28 *Conflict International,* July/August 1994.

29 Conflict International, April 1994.

30 AFP, October 17, 1999.

31 AFP, August 9, 1999.

32 *Al-Hayat*, May 5, 1999.

33 *Intelligence Newsletter,* France, July 9, 1992.

34 *Al-Wasat,* London, June 5, 1993.

35 *Ahir Sa`ah,* Cairo, June 10, 1993.

36 *Al-Ahram,* Cairo, June 10, 1993.

37 *Ruz al-Yusouf,* Cairo, July 19, 1993.

38 *Al-Ahram,* Egypt, December 4, 1993.

39 Jane's Intelligence Review Yearbook, 1993.

40 *Al-Sharq,* Qatar, July 27, 1992.

41 *Al-Gumhuriyya,* Cairo, August 20, 1993. Naziah Nitzhi Rashid, one of the assailants of the Egyptian interior minister, carried a forged identity card, bearing the Egyptian name Walim Naguib Saaifin. The card was forged in Afghanistan.

42 *Al-`Arabi,* Egypt, November 27, 1993.

43 *Al-Wafd,* Egypt, November 20, 1993.

44 *Al-Ahram,* Egypt, November 21, 1993.

45 Jane's Intelligence Review Yearbook, 1993.

46 *Al-Muharrir,* Paris, January 1994.

47 *Shihan,* Jordan, March 19, 1994.

48 N. Tal, *`Imut mi-Bayit, Hitmodedut Mitzrayim ve-Yarden `im ha-Islam ha-Kitzoni, (Domestic Conflict, How Egypt and Jordan Cope with Fundamentalist Islam)* (Tel Aviv University: Papyrus, 1999), p. 208.

49 *New York Times*, Internet, January 29, 2000.

50 AFP, quoting ABC news of January 21, 2000.

51 *Kol ha-`Ir*, March 26, 2000.

52 Conflict International, April 1994.

53 Internet, <http://www.Azzam.com>, November 20, 1999.

54 Jane's Intelligence Review Yearbook, 1993.

55 Magnus Ranstorp, "Interpreting the Broader Context and Meaning of bin Laden's Fatwah," *Studies in Conflict Terrorism* (October-December 1998) vol. 21.

56 Ely Karmon, "Terrorism á la bin Laden Is Not a Peace Process Problem," *Policy Watch*, Washington Institute for Near East Policy, No. 347, October 28, 1998.

57 Ibid.

58 "American Soldiers are Paper Tigers," Interview, *Middle East Quarterly*, Vol. V, No. 4, December 1998.

59 *Al-Hayat*, August 6, 1998.

60 *Al-Hayat*, February 12, 1999.

61 Yehudit Ronen, "The Khober Bomb," *Middle East Contemporary Survey (1996)*, p. 130–133.

62 Ibid., p. 582–586.

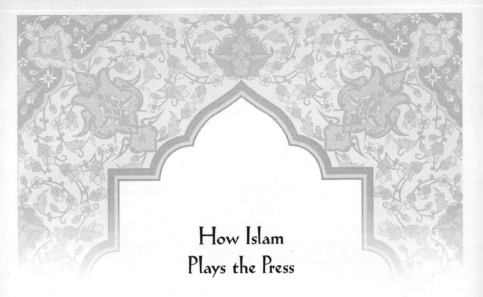

How Islam
Plays the Press

Joseph Farah

The world often views Islam as a seventh century anachronism. But the truth is, the Islamic world is playing and winning a sophisticated game of media manipulation in which powerful and wealthy police states and anti-democratic political movements are more often portrayed and perceived — at least in the context of the Arab-Jewish conflict — as victims rather than threatening oppressors. This chapter contrasts what Islamic leaders say about their intentions for the State of Israel in English while Western television cameras are rolling and what they say to their own constituents in Arabic.

HOW ISLAM PLAYS THE PRESS

Fiamma Nirenstein, who writes for the Italian daily *La Stampa* and the weekly *Panorama,* explains:

> The information coming out of Israel these days is heavily influenced by the political imagination of reporters and columnists and cameramen who have flocked to the scene from the four corners of the earth to cover this

latest installment of violence in the ongoing Middle East conflict.

They tend — they are expected — to place those clashes within an agreed-upon framework: the framework, roughly, of David (the Palestinians) versus Goliath (the Israelis). It is only when they fail to follow this paradigm that they, their editors, and their readers or viewers become confused.

Confused, that is, by the facts. "The culture of the press is almost entirely Left," Nirenstein, a veteran Middle East reporter, explains. "These are people who feel the weakness of democratic values; who enjoy the frisson of sidling up to a threatening civilization that coddles them even while holding in disdain the system they represent."

Nirenstein makes a profound point: "Even the most articulate and bold defenders of Israel seldom proclaim for newsmen that Israel has an absolute right to protect itself from violence directed at its citizens and soldiers." Yet, as she states so eloquently, "by contrast, Palestinian spokesmen like Hanan Ashrawi or Ziad abu Ziad or Saeb Erekat never miss an opportunity to begin their story from the top: 'This is our land, and ours alone, and the Jews who are occupying it are employing armed force against an unarmed people.' "

What's at the root of this media caricature? Nirenstein has two more cogent observations:

It is not just that we are talking about a profession, the world press, that is almost entirely uniform in its attitudes.

The truth is that Israel, as the Jewish state, is also the object of a contemporary form of anti-Semitism that is no less real for being masked or even unconscious. (Arab Holocaust-denial, more violent and vulgar than anything in the West, is rarely if ever touched on in the mainstream media.)

And there is something else as well: looking into the heart of the Arab regimes, preeminently including that of the Palestinians themselves, is simply too disturbing. For what one is liable to find there are disproportionate measures of religious and/or political fanaticism, bullying,

corruption, lies, manipulation, and a carefully nurtured cult
of victimhood that rationalizes every cruelty.[1]

Could the press possibly be this blind, this biased, this manipulated?

From 1903 through 1908, two young bicycle mechanics from
Ohio repeatedly claimed to have built a flying machine. They demonstrated it over and over again to hundreds of people, obtained
affidavits from prominent citizens who witnessed their efforts, and
even produced photographs of their invention at work.

Nevertheless, Orville and Wilbur Wright were dismissed as
frauds and hoaxers in the *Scientific American*, the *New York Herald*,
and by the U.S. Army and many American scientists.

But as Richard Milton points out in his entertaining book,
Alternative Science, the real shocker is that even local newspapers
in the Wrights' hometown of Dayton ignored the story in their
backyard for five years.

Despite the fact that witnesses repeatedly visited and wrote to
the *Dayton Daily News* and *Dayton Journal* over those years asking
about the young men in their flying machine, no reporters were
dispatched. No photographers were assigned.

Asked in 1940 about his refusal to publish anything about the
sensational accomplishments of the Wrights during those years,
Dayton Daily News city editor Dan Kumler said, "We just didn't
believe it. Of course, you remember that the Wrights at that time
were terribly secretive."

When the interviewer pointed out that the Wrights were flying
over an open field just outside of town for five years, Kumler grew
more candid: "I guess the truth is we were just plain dumb."

What excuses will the international press have when the truth
about their current heroes in the Middle East is no longer possible
to conceal?

It's getting there.

If you think you get an accurate idea of what Arab leaders
believe when you listen to Hanan Ashrawi interviewed on ABC's
"Nightline" or on CNN, think again.

Yasser Arafat and, indeed, other Arab leaders, have played a
skillful media manipulation game in the West, persuading most

Americans and most westerners that the Middle East crisis can be settled by rearranging a few borders — by Israel exchanging more "land for peace."

What you don't see on ABC or CNN — or even in the pages of the *New York Times* or *Washington Post* — are the harsh, racist, fighting words of Arab "journalists," politicians, activists, leaders, and even clerics recorded in the Arab-language media.

For instance, read the words of a leading cleric in Gaza in a sermon delivered October 13, 2000.

Dr. Ahmad Abu Halabiya, former acting rector of the Islamic University said:

> None of the Jews refrain from committing any possible evil. If the Labor party commits the evil and the crime, the Likud party stands by it; and if the Likud party commits the evil and the crime, the Labor party stands by it. . . . The Jews are Jews, whether Labor or Likud. . . . They do not have any moderates or any advocates of peace. They are all liars. They all want to distort truth, but we are in possession of the truth.
>
> O brother believers, the criminals, the terrorists — are the Jews, who have butchered our children, orphaned them, widowed our women and desecrated our holy places and sacred sites. They are the terrorists. They are the ones who must be butchered and killed, as Allah the Almighty said: "Fight them: Allah will torture them at your hands, and will humiliate them and will help you to overcome them, and will relieve the minds of the believers." . . .
>
> O brothers in belief, this is the case of the Jews and their habitual conduct, and what happened yesterday, and has been going on for two weeks, and before that for many years, and which will be repeated in future years unless we stand up like men and unless we have the known Muslim position, (the position) of those who wage *jihad* in the path of Allah, those who defend their rights and who sacrifice all that is dear to them. . . .

The hatred-drenched rhetoric is not directed only toward Israel. Here's more from Halabiya:

This is the truth, O brothers in belief. From here, Allah the almighty has called upon us not to ally with the Jews or the Christians, not to like them, not to become their partners, not to support them, and not to sign agreements with them. And he who does that, is one of them, as Allah said: "O you who believe, do not take the Jews and the Christians as allies, for they are allies of one another. Who from among you takes them as allies will indeed be one of them. . . ." The Jews are the allies of the Christians, and the Christians are the allies of the Jews, despite the enmity that exists between them. The enmity between the Jews and the Christians is deep, but all of them are in agreement against the monotheists — against those who say, "There is no God but Allah and Muhammad is his messenger," that is — they are against you, O Muslims.

Have no mercy on the Jews, no matter where they are, in any country. Fight them, wherever you are. Wherever you meet them, kill them. Wherever you are, kill those Jews and those Americans who are like them — and those who stand by them — they are all in one trench, against the Arabs and the Muslims — because they established Israel here, in the beating heart of the Arab world, in Palestine. They created it to be the outpost of their civilization — and the vanguard of their army, and to be the sword of the West and the crusaders, hanging over the necks of the monotheists, the Muslims in these lands. They wanted the Jews to be their spearhead. . . .[2]

Is there any compromising with people like this? Why is it that we in the West do not read such statements or hear them broadcast? It probably doesn't surprise us to know that such rhetoric is being spoken, published, and broadcast daily in the Arab world. But, how, in spite of such impolitic speech, does the Arab world continue successfully to portray itself as the victim in the conflict with Israel?

The Western world often views Islam as a seventh century anachronism. But the truth is the Islamic world is playing and winning a sophisticated game of media manipulation in which powerful and wealthy police states and freedom-squelching political movements are more often portrayed and perceived — at least in the context of the Arab-Jewish conflict — as victims rather than threatening oppressors. But what Islamic leaders say about their intentions for the State of Israel in English while Western television cameras are rolling and what they say to their own constituents in Arabic can be two diametrical opposites.

One of the most successful techniques currently being employed in the Arab world is an effort, through the international press, to revise basic Middle East history — even archeology — in ways so profane they suggest there is little hope of quenching the hatred in the hearts of Israel's foes.

In an interview with an Italian newspaper in March 2000, Sheik Ikrama Sabri, the Palestine Authority's top Muslim figure in Jerusalem, decreed that the Western Wall, the last remnant of the Jewish temple, has no religious significance to the Jews. "Let it be clear: the Wailing Wall is not a holy place of the Jews, it is an integral part of the mosque (grounds). We call it *al-Buraq*, the name of the horse with which Muhammad ascended to heaven from Jerusalem," he said.[3]

In fact, the Temple Mount area and the Western Wall are, according to Jewish scholars, the only truly holy sites of Judaism.

Yasser Arafat himself has made similar statements, claiming the city of Jerusalem has no real significance to Jews. In June 1998, he said on an Arabic television program, "Let me tell you something. The issue of Jerusalem is not just a Palestinian issue. It is a Palestinian, Arab, Islamic, and Christian issue."

Asked by the interviewer if one could also say it is a Jewish issue, he replied, "No. Allow me to be precise — they consider Hebron to be holier than Jerusalem."

Arafat is among those Arab leaders making the incredible suggestion that there was never a Jewish temple at the site. "Until now, all the excavations that have been carried out have failed to prove the location of the temple," he claims. "It is 30 years since they captured the city and they have not succeeded in giving even one proof as the location of the temple."[4] This was no casual remark by Arafat. In an earlier speech broadcast on Arabic radio, he said, "Let us begin from the holy Buraq wall. It is called the holy Buraq wall, not the Wailing Wall. We do not say this. After the holy Buraq revolution in 1929 . . . the Shaw International Committee said this is a holy wall for Muslims. This wall ends at the Via Dolorosa. These are our Christian and Muslim holy places."[5]

With such inflammatory rhetoric on the record, how do the Islamic forces maintain an edge in the battle for public relations in the Western media?

According to Judy Lash Balint, a veteran Middle East reporter who decided to report on the ideological axes her colleagues were grinding:

> For most of the American Colony Hotel-based Western correspondents, there are certain "given" assumptions that provide the backdrop for all their coverage. Topping the list is the notion that Palestinians are engaged in a noble struggle for independence and Israeli oppressors are using their might and muscle to stand in their way.

How do they arrive at these conclusions? "Journalists arrive at this view based both on experiences in their own native lands as standard-bearers for minority rights and other liberal causes, but also as a result of their reliance on local assistance here in Israel," she explains.

Since very few of the foreign correspondents in Israel are fluent in Hebrew or Arabic, they rely on a network of local sources as well as the service of "fixers" — locals who can "fix" situations for them. Currently, some 400 Palestinians Authority residents are in possession of Israel Government Press Office credentials.

Much of the current conflict is raging in Area A (under full Palestinian Authority control), so it is not surprising that the fixers are generally young U.S. educated Palestinians who know how to operate in PA territory and who introduce the journalists to their circle of acquaintances.

By contrast, explains Lash, correspondents generally get the Israeli point of view from official sources — currently bottlenecked with a one-man operation.

The bias in some of the major news bureaus in the Middle East is palpable, according to Lash. At the ABC-TV studio, for instance, the only map hanging in the office is dated March 2000 and displays the title, "Palestine."[6]

This anti-Israel press prism is hardly new, nor unique to the latest Arab uprising. Author Ze'ev Chafets made similar observations of the western press corps during coverage of the Lebanese war in the 1980s. He wrote:

> In conformity with the PLO-dependent security system, Western reporters ghettoized themselves and became, in effect, accomplices to their own isolation and supervision.
>
> They clustered around the Palestinian-run Commodore (Hotel) where they knew their movements, contacts, and outgoing communications would be monitored. Some of those with separate offices in the city found that they needed local Palestinian employees in order to establish contacts and guide them through the complexities of life in Beirut. These assistants were, in many cases, subject to the discipline of the PLO.
>
> Even reporters aware of the fact that their local employees might be a conduit to PLO intelligence were loathe to give them up; in many cases, such people were an invaluable buffer.[7]

What the Palestinian leadership cannot accomplish through its charm offensive and by providing friendly manpower to western reporters, they achieve through intimidation and coercion.

The Independent Committee to Protect Journalists, which monitors abuses against the press and promotes press freedom around the world, reports:

> In the nearly seven years since the Palestinian National Authority assumed control over parts of the West Bank and Gaza, Chairman Yasser Arafat and his multi-layered security apparatus have muzzled local press critics via arbitrary arrests, threats, physical abuse, and the closure of media outlets. Over the years, the Arafat regime has managed to frighten most Palestinian journalists into self-censorship.[8]

Is it reasonable to assume that foreign correspondents covering the same turf are not exercising similar self-censorship?

And because the Arab world is comprised only of totalitarian police states, unfriendly to Western news media, it ensures that international press attention remains focused on Israel. Those are the only images shown by television cameras — terrorist attacks, rioting, angry protests against "occupation."

All these factors combine to create a winning public relations agenda for the Arab world and its crusade against Israel.

Perhaps the final weapon in the arsenal of Arafat is what is often referred to as "the big lie."

In February 2001, a bus was the weapon of choice for Arab terrorists who crashed into a crowd of civilians, killing 8 and injuring 20. Technically, an Islamic terrorist organization known as *Hamas* claimed responsibility for the bus assault. Technically, Yasser Arafat and the Palestine Authority have plausible deniability.

But just read for yourself what Arafat actually said about the attack to see how he not only excuses it, he continues to condone this type of terrorism. "The combined attack on the Palestinian people by (Prime Minister Ehud) Barak and (Prime Minister-elect Ariel) Sharon has a direct effect on the mood of the people. The Israeli escalation is what brought about the attack," he said in Jordan.[9]

Arafat has mastered a propaganda technique known as "turnspeak." Turnspeak is achieved when you attack someone but claim, with some success, to be the victim of the attack. Over and over again, we see this happen in the Middle East on a daily basis.

In effect, a purveyor of turnspeak disseminates information that is the exact opposite of the truth — making it difficult for the real victims to respond in a way that is clearly understandable to the world.

Where was turnspeak first employed as a propaganda tool? In March 1939, some enterprising journalists recognized that Adolf Hitler was using "the big lie" in justifying Germany's invasion of Czechoslovakia.

Whose fault was it that Germany was forced to invade? It was the fault of the Czechs, of course. They were trying, Hitler claimed, to provoke a regional war by attempting to claim their land as their own.

"Thus the plight of the German minority in Czechoslovakia was merely a pretext . . . for cooking up a stew in a land he coveted, undermining it, confusing and misleading its friends and concealing his real purpose . . . to destroy the Czech state and grab its territories," wrote William L. Shirer about Hitler's gambit.[10]

How did much of Europe respond? They bought the big lie — hook, line, and sinker. They didn't want to risk an all-out war. So they rationalized that Hitler had some legitimate claims on Czechoslovakia.

Tell a big enough lie often enough and some people — often many people — will believe it. That is the lesson of turnspeak. And Arafat has learned it well.

It's not uncommon for the Arabs today — Arafat included — to refer to the Israelis as "Nazis" or fascists. Why do they do that? To provide cover for their own similarities and ties to the Nazis.

As author Joan Peters points out in her Middle East history, *From Time Immemorial*, Hitler's crimes against the Jews have frequently been justified in Arab writings and speeches. In 1940, Haj Muhammed Amin al-Husseini, the grand *mufti* of Jerusalem, requested the Axis powers to acknowledge the Arab right "to settle the question of Jewish elements in Palestine and other Arab countries in accordance with the national and racial interests of the Arabs and along the lines similar to those used to solve the Jewish question in Germany and Italy."[11]

Yasser Arafat's given name, as an Egyptian, was Abd al-Rahman abd al-Bauf Arafat al-Qud al-Husseini. That's right. He called the former *mufti* his "uncle."

Arafat will continue to say day is night and war is peace. We should expect it from him. That is the way the big lie works.

But how many more body bags do we need to see from terrorist incidents before the whole world recognizes Arafat for what he is — a bold liar whose ultimate goal remains, as always, the annihilation of the Jewish state?

Oh yes, Arafat will continue to maintain plausible deniability with regard to *Hamas* and *Hizbullah* and other terrorist operations. He will portray himself as a reasonable man, a man of peace. He will wax persuasively about his own victimhood. He'll tell you that the Israelis are the true obstacles to peace.

Understand what all that means when you hear it. That's just the way turnspeak works. He's practiced at the art of deception. He moves quickly in an effort to remain at least one step ahead of the truth. What he says is usually the exact opposite of reality — and he knows it.

Meanwhile, as Arafat and others execute a nearly flawless public relations offensive in the West — covering up their own warts while exposing both real and imagined horrors perpetrated by their Israeli foes — a cult of anti-Semitism unseen since the Holocaust sweeps through the Arab world.

And those perpetrating it are inventing allies — including America's founding fathers.

If you are to believe the vicious propaganda increasingly seeping into periodicals and speeches in the Arab world, Benjamin Franklin and George Washington hated Jews and warned against dealing with them.

For instance, Egypt's General Hassan Sweilem authored a two-part series in the weekly *October* titled "The Jewish Personality and the Israeli Action." Here's an excerpt:

> Historians, race-studies professors, and sociologists agree that humanity, throughout its long history, has never known a race such as the Jewish race in which so many bad qualities — base and loathsome — have been gathered.
>
> The Jews had a quality which distinguished them from others: whenever they gathered in a particular place and felt comfortable there, they turned the place into a den of evil, corruption, incitement to internal strife, and the spreading of wars," the official wrote. "The Jews took advantage of the lack of attention by the people and rulers to the plots and traps designed by the Jews.

Sweilem then retraces his version of "history" right up through the Holocaust, which he proclaims "a lie." "This is a huge lie which they managed to market around the world," Sweilem writes.

What is particularly noteworthy about the Sweilem slander is his use of false "quotations" about the Jews from America's founding fathers. Sweilem claims:

> The first American presidents warned against the danger of Jewish hegemony over American life. First and

foremost was President George Washington who warned in 1788: "It is troubling that the . . . nation has not purified its land from these pests. The Jews are the enemies of America's well-being and the corrupters of its prosperity." Further, Washington writes about the Jews: "They operate against us in a way much more effective than the enemy's armies. They endanger our liberty and our interests one hundred times more than the enemy. It is most troubling that the states have not begun long ago to follow them, because they are a plague (threatening) society."

Of course, anyone who has read the precious writings of George Washington can instantly recognize from the style alone, not just the substance, that this statement is a forgery through and through. But Sweilem continues to libel another of America's early statesmen. He wrote:

American President Benjamin Franklin said in his speech to the 1789 Constitutional Convention in Philadelphia: "A great danger threatens the United States — the Jewish danger. When the Jews settle down, we will discover that they are weakening the determination of the people, shaking up the ethics of trade and establishing a government. When they meet resistance, they will suffocate the nation economically."

Which history text did Sweilem use to find this quotation from Franklin, who, of course, never served as an American president? It turns out the forgery first appeared in 1935 in German in the Nazis' *Handbook on the Jewish Question*.[12]

There's a rising strain of anti-Semitism in the Arab world's popular press, its schools, and its official and unofficial rhetoric. As an Arab-American Christian, it repulses me — it offends me. Moreover, it makes me wonder how peace — true and lasting peace — can be achieved between Jews and adversaries with such enmity in their very hearts and souls.

America should recall what Washington actually wrote about the Jews, a people whose history he studied in the scriptures for clues about building a new civilization in the New World. In an August

1790 letter to Moses Seixas, the warden of the Hebrew Congregation of Newport, Rhode Island, the president wrote:

> It is now no more that toleration is spoken of, as if it was by the indulgence of one class of people that another enjoyed the exercise of their inherent rights. For happily the government of the United States, which gives to bigotry no sanction, to persecution no assistance, requires only that they who live under its protection should demean themselves as good citizens, in giving it on all occasions their effectual support.

Washington then concluded with a quotation from Micah 4:4: "May the children of the Stock of Abraham, who dwell in this land, continue to merit and enjoy the good will of the other inhabitants while everyone shall sit in safety under his own vine and fig tree, there shall be none to make him afraid."

Sadly, that, of course, is a Washington quote you're not likely to see reproduced anywhere in the Arab world today.

Endnotes

1   Fiamma Nirenstein, *Commentary* (January 2001), translated from Italian in *La Stampa.*

2   Special Dispatch No. 138-PA, Middle East Media and Research Institute, October 14, 2000, translated from Arabic by MEMRI.

3   *La Republica*, March 24, 2000 (MEMRI).

4   Al-Jezira television, June 28, 1998 (MEMRI).

5   Voice of Palestine, October 10, 1996 (MEMRI).

6   Judy Balint Lash, WorldNetDaily.com, March 6, 2001.

7   Ze'ev Chafets, *Double Vision* (New York: William Morrow, 1985).

8   Joel Campagna, *Bloodied and Beleaguered*, Committee to Protect Journalists, October 20, 2000.

9   WorldNetDaily.com, February 16, 2001.

10 William L. Shirer, *The Rise and Fall of the Third Reich* (New York: Simon & Schuster, 1960).

11 Joan Peters, *From Time Immemorial: The Origins of the Arab-Jewish Conflict over Palestine* (New York: Harper and Rowe, 1984).

12 Special Dispatch No. 166, December 16, 2000, MEMRI.

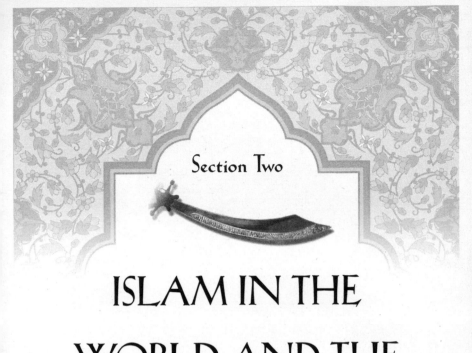

Section Two

ISLAM IN THE WORLD AND THE MINORITIES POLICY

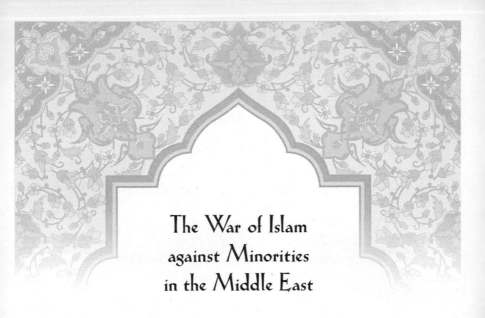

The War of Islam
against Minorities
in the Middle East

Mordechai Nisan

The rapid and triumphal Islamization of the Middle East beginning in the seventh century, west to North Africa, north to the Caucasus, and east to China, is one of the most profound, permanent, and awesome conquests in history. This military and religious campaign welded a collective consciousness and constituted a political strategy whose primary concepts included: Muslim holy war *(jihad)*, the Islamic territorial abode *(dar al-Islam)*, and martyrdom *(shuhada)* on the one hand, juxtaposed to infidels *(kuffar)*, tolerated non-Muslim scriptuaries *(ahl al-dhimma)*, and the non-Islamic territorial abode of warfare *(dar al-harb)*. The mission of Islam was spearheaded by the "sword of Muhammad" in order to impose Allah's last revelation over all mankind and throughout the world. Among the various methods employed, in particular in the Middle East terrain but not only, were deportation, colonization, conversion, repression, and at times massacre of native populations.[1]

The transformation of the broad Mideastern environment was a process of many centuries that culminated in the defacing and refashioning of many lands and peoples. Byzantine Asia Minor, Armenian Anatolia, and much of Kurdistan, became Muslim Turkey. The Sudan as the land of Kush, Nubia, and Black Africa assumed an Islamic and Arab face. Lebanon's Pheonician and Christian heritage has been swamped by Islam and Arabism. Mesopotamia, Assyria, and part of Kurdistan were in the grip of Arab-Muslim Iraq. The pre-Islamic Berber/Imazighen/Kabyle character of North Africa struggles in the face of integralist and violent Islam. And Israel, reverberating with the Hebrew-Jewish legacy in the Holy Land, confronts the Islamic contention that Palestine is a sacred *waqf* domain belonging to the Muslims alone.

While the debate continues regarding the actual historical treatment meted out by Muslims to non-Muslims, Jews and Christians in particular,[2] the spirit of *our* times in the late 20th and early 21st century is dominated overwhelmingly by Islamic fundamentalism linked to a comprehensive Muslim assault for glory and power. The names of Ayatollah Khoumeni (Iran), Osama bin Laden (Afghanistan), Sheikh Hasan Nasrallah (Lebanon), and Hasan Turabi (Sudan), are some from among the heroic revolutionaries in the Muslim pantheon of iconic figures. Resonating into the boroughs of London, the arrondissements of Paris, and the neighborhoods of Jersey City, Detroit, and Chicago, Islamic movements and messages carve out their territory of influence in the quest for ultimate domination within the public domain of discourse and politics.

This is so in the remaining bastions of the (so-called) Christian West and with every greater immediacy and fury within and a bit beyond the Middle East. In May 1998, Libyan leader Mu`ammar Qadhdafi declared that Jews and Christians hate Muslims and insult Muhammad, the prophet of Islam. In the light of this charge, and that by Saddam Hussein of Iraq that Israel defiles Muslim and Christian sanctuaries, the Islamic world is expected to take the road of *jihad* in order to achieve peace and justice in the world.[3] The *mujahid* bin Laden, evoking the slogan of the "Great Islamic Republic" throughout the Middle East, repeated the militant refrain in Peshawar in September 2000, calling for war against Jews in Palestine and Christian Americans in Saudi Arabia.[4] A year later, the September 11, 2001, Islamic terror attacks in the United States brought home the seriousness and immediacy of bin Laden's intentions. His *al-Qa`idah* movement had struck ruthlessly at the political and economic centers of American power.

Meanwhile, attacks in the Far East against Christians and churches in Indonesia, and in Nigeria and the Ivory Coast in Africa, in the year 2000 signaled the scope of the Islamic offensive. The Pakistani "Army of the Righteous" stated the need for *jihad* against non-Muslims, especially Jews and Hindus, while the march of Allah's soldiers continued in Bosnia and Kossovo, Chechnya and Kashmir, Palestine and Lebanon.

Of special importance in this regard is the Christian character of Lebanon and the Jewish ethos of Israel as primary targets of Islam's war against the traditional infidel communities. In 1980, at an Islamic Summit Conference in the Pakistani city of Lahore, the goal was set to have the Middle East totally Islamic with the elimination of the Christians of the Orient and the Jews of Israel. This imperialistic if not genocidal intention appears high on the Muslim agenda until today, considering the pace and direction of events in both occupied Lebanon and *intifada*-infested Israel.

In an interesting development, the Tibetan Dali Lama condemned both Christians and Muslims in January 2001 for their practice of actively seeking converts. The non-aggressive religions of Hinduism and Buddhism apparently fear for their future. But it is evidently clear that the truly aggressive religion in this era is not Christianity, but rather putative and militant Islam with its explicit agenda of expansion worldwide.

Islam in its formative historical stage surfaced as a conquering and colonizing religious movement that arrogated public space and political power for itself alone. This serves as a model for reproduction in any future era thereafter, subject to the exigencies of power opportunities that are available to the Muslims. There are no fixed frontiers to delimit the scope of the future expansive drive, nor are there any moral or juridical restrictions in pursuing the war. Rather, the exaltation of battle by whatever means is designed to vindicate Islam's global primacy. The horrors of victory, perhaps for the victors and the vanquished alike, are tangential to the satisfaction of exacting tribute and earning respect from the cringing adversaries of Islam. In this scenario, the minorities in the Middle East are fated, as capitalists for Marx, to disappear in the dustbin of history.

1. *Dhimmis*:

(a) Jews

Islam in its koranic and traditional self-consciousness consid-ered the monotheistic religious communities of Jews and Christians worthy of no more than a "protected and tolerated" status under Muslim rule. However, with the modern political founding of a Jewish State of Israel and a predominantly Christian state of Leba-non, the normative hierarchy of power was overturned when the inferior, subjugated *dhimmi* minorities arrogated the right to govern themselves, and even to dominate Muslims as less-than-equal citizens in both Israel and Lebanon. An uncompromising Muslim response was deemed necessary, and certainly legitimate, to re-establish the primacy of Islam in these two Mideastern countries.

Both Pan-Arab nationalism and local Palestinian nationalism had rejected the Zionist claim to Jewish statehood in 1948 and de-veloped a variety of political and military approaches to undermine and unravel Israel's existence. Islam, though active in the pre-1948 struggle, emerged more recently as an alternative and yet comple-mentary Palestinian framework of belief and dedication, mobiliza-tion and warfare, against the rebellious *al-yahud* of irremediable and obstreperous character. Though a majority in their land and state, the Jews of Israel would be reduced to their minority status in order to re-confirm Muslim primacy.

There were different ways by which the integrity of Jewish iden-tity and the security of Jewish life were disparaged and denied in the past. Jews in Arab lands were considered at times no more than "Arab Jews" in a sweeping assimilative embrace. Living within the parameters of Islamic civilization seemed emblematic of Jews being virtual "Muslim Jews." But the stridency of the modern Palestinian Muslim movements, with their doctrinal rejection of Israel and their violent mode of armed struggle, sharpened the active war of Islam against the Jewish people.

Modern Zionism, as the national liberation movement of the Jewish people, is defamed in the Muslim world as a colonial aggres-sion and invasion that must be repelled by the defensive *jihad* of Islam.[5] According to the Palestinian Islamic Resistance Movement (*Hamas*) in Article 13 of its covenant, any concession of the land of Palestine is a concession of the religion of Islam. This linkage of politics and religion is a central theme in classical Islam culled for active application. When the liberation of Palestine is achieved through *jihad*, the rule of Allah will descend and shape the moral and religious life of the Muslims, as the alien Jews will be defeated. Sheikh Ahmad Yasin of *Hamas* had stated in 1989 that "the solution [to the conflict] is a Palestinian Islamic state on all of Palestine where Arabs, Jews, and Christians will live under Islamic rule."[6] This recalls the model of the *dhimma* (the apocryphal/historical Muslim pact with infidels) that dogmatically denies equality, dignity, or independence to non-Muslim minorities.

The outburst of *Intifada al-Aqsa* in September 2000 revealed the surging energy of Palestinian Muslims to confront Israel in a spirit of sacrifice and devotion, with hundreds dead and many more hundreds wounded in the first few months thereafter. Jerusalem, as the third holiest city in Islam, was the political target in this new phase of warfare. The *Aqsa* mosque situated on the Jewish Temple Mount (*Har Ha-bayit*), known by the Muslims as *Haram al-Sharif*, evoked a koranic image and the legend of Muhammad's nocturnal visit to the Holy City. Sheikh Ikrima Sabri, Arafat-appointed *mufti* of Jerusalem and Palestine, called for "sacrifice until Allah's victory" and considered the Jews as cowards. To liberate *al-Aqsa* at the cost of child martyrs is an honor to the parents of the *shuhud*.[7]

The Islamic ethos of warfare throughout Judea, Samaria, and Gaza, and even within pre-1967 Israeli borders as well, merged from within with the national Palestinian ethos of "armed struggle" (PLO Covenant, Art. 9). It also converged from without with the religious furor emanating from the Islamic Republic of Iran and its promotion of terrorism globally, the virulent Islamic hostility in Egypt to Israel, and *Hizbullah*'s *Shi`ite* victory against the Israeli army in south Lebanon, from which the IDF withdrew in late May 2000. In December of that year at a "Jerusalem Day" celebration in solidarity with the Palestinian *intifada*, *Hizbullah*'s Secretary-General Hasan Nasrallah referred to Israel as "a cancer that needs to be removed at its roots."[8] The intense conviction of religious truth that fills Muslim hearts and minds bolsters the Islamic and Palestinian ambition of politicide against Jewish Israel. The Jews who survived as a pseudo-tolerated minority have no right to assert themselves as a sovereign majority people.

For its part, Yasser Arafat's Palestinian Authority established in the context of the Oslo Accord from 1993 continues its animosity and rejection of Israel in the traditional Islamic idiom. The school texts used in the educational system in Palestinian-controlled areas, as in the towns of Ramallah, Kalkilya, and Hebron, portray Jews as "the enemies of the prophets and the believers," morally stained by "fanaticism" and "treachery," and committed to "racial discrimination." The Western Wall is not a Jewish site, but part of the *Haram* precinct, and the land of Palestine belongs to the Muslims and their brother Christians [sic.].[9] The formal and written PLO commitment to peace with Israel was not followed by the promotion of a message of accommodation, respect, and co-existence. Israel, demonized as the predator and pariah from the past, remained castigated as the Palestinians' enemy even after the peace process was launched in Washington. War against the Jews characterized, as before, the new era of peace.

(b) Christians

The "religious and ethnic cleansing" by Islam of what once was the Christian Orient, or largely the Byzantine Orthodox Middle East, is but a euphemism for cultural and human genocide and the willful decimation of primordial native peoples. Once the majority population, Christians in the beginning of the 21st century constitute just three percent of the region's inhabitants, numbering approximately 15 million, facing more than 350 million Muslims in Turkey, Iran, and all the Arab countries. The religious and historical cradle of Christianity has long become the Muslim-Arab heartland, and even symbolic Bethlehem and Nazareth, which long retained Christian majorities, have succumbed to Muslim majority domination.

The basic trend among Eastern Christians in the 20th-century was immigration to the West. This population movement was stimulated by endemic physical insecurity, indiscriminate plunder, religious persecution, and political discrimination directed against virtually all the Christian communities across the region. In fact, the same forces of exclusion and oppression operate in the beginning of our 21st century as well.

- The Armenian genocide of 1915–16 by the Turks, which led to the death of a million and a half people, merits primary mention due to the scope of this horrific crime against humanity. The ancient Armenian people had become a small and vulnerable minority in its homeland. The historical nexus of circumstances and incompatibilities gave birth to a policy of deportation with instances of fanatical Muslim mobs crying *"Allahu Akbar"* (God is great), as they burned and butchered the defenseless Christians in the cities of Ayntab and Birecik.[10] Turkish nationalism and Islamic passion turned on the Armenians with a satanic ferociousness.

- The massacre at Simel in Iraq of some 600 Assyrian Christians — though Assyrian sources claim close to 3,000 were murdered in the immediate vicinity — in early August 1933 marked the denouement in the history of an ancient Eastern community. Claiming independence in the area of the Lower Zab and Nineveh area but promised only minority guarantees after World War I, the Assyrians were abandoned by the British to the new Iraqi regime, *Sunni* by religion and Arab by national consciousness.

Meanwhile, in the area of Tur Abdin in southeastern Turkey in the 1990s, Muslim fundamentalists under the name *Hizbullah* spread their net of terror, seized Christian villages, forced women to wear the veil, and murdered priests. Abouna Symeon, a monk, related that the Muslims say, "We should go back to Europe where Christians come from . . . as if our ancestors weren't here for centuries before the first Muslim settled here."[11] More recently, an Assyrian *Suryani* priest, Yusuf Akbulut, in Diyarbekir, was put on trial for calling on Turkey to recognize the Ottoman murder of the Armenians during World War I, and charging also that the Turks had used the Kurds to kill Christians.

Hiding the truth of the past has served in conjunction with destroying any future hope for the ancient Christian communities of the Fertile Crescent, across Armenia, Assyria, and Kurdistan, in the mountains of Hakkiari and Urmia, in the valley of Sapna and the village of Amadiya. Assyrian refugees in London prefer to refer to their lost homeland as "Mesopotamia," recalling the Assyrian Kingdom from 612 B.C.E., rather than call it Iraq with its Arab-Muslim significance under the ruthless Baathist regime of Saddam Hussein.[12]

Under the mournful circumstances, the dream of a national revival and return can filter but in the recesses of Assyrian imagination while divorced from the political realities of the contemporary Middle East.

The Maronites of Lebanon, with a profound historical religious and national presence in the mountain stronghold of Bsharre and Zghorta, Jubail and Kesrouan, have been confronted by the resurgence of militant Islam in recent decades. Faced with Palestinian terrorists and Syrian occupiers, Lebanon's Christians also struggled with Iranian-supported *Shi`ite* movements that, in particular *Hizbullah*, seek to establish an Islamic Republic. Sheikh Fadallah and other religious authorities consider the Khoumeini revolution in Iran a precedent, certainly an inspiration, for their spiritual and political aspirations in the "land of the cedars."

The outbreak of Lebanese-Palestinian warfare in April 1975 began, appropriately enough in this Islamic *zeitgeist*, with a PLO shooting at a church ceremony in the East Beirut Christian neighborhood of Ayn Rummanah, killing four Maronites. Palestinian massacres of Christians followed in 1976 in Damour, exhibiting gang-rapes and mutilated bodies, and in Ayshiyyah, exhibiting burnt bodies in the church. The fighting and slaughter continued, and hundreds of thousands of Christians fled the country. Beginning in the 1980s, *Hizbullah* conducted warfare against native Christians and the Israeli military presence in south Lebanon. When Sheikh Nasrallah's own son was killed in battle in 1997, he expressed his paternal sadness but added that according to Islam, true life begins in Paradise with the martyr's death.[13] Meanwhile, in the northern city of Tripoli, where the Islamic Unity movement (*Tawhid*) is active, the 90 percent *Sunni* majority harassed the Christian shopkeepers and pasted pictures of Muslim leaders on public walls.

Lebanon, constituted after World War I as a primarily Christian state, symbolized the strengths and hopes of Christians throughout the region. But the downfall of Lebanon in recent decades is a sobering indication of the advance of Islamic power and Arab influence. Noteworthy in its irony, in addition, is the fact that both small Israel and Lebanon, as the two Western-oriented democratic countries in the region, and representing the Judaic and Christian civilizations in the ancient Orient, have been victimized by the forces of a ferocious brand of Islam. A popular Arab-Muslim refrain regarding the mournful fate of the Jews and the Christians threatens "first the Saturday people and then the Sunday people" targeted by Islam stalking its prey.

Egypt is the home of the largest single Eastern Christian community, overwhelmingly, of the Orthodox Copt church, that is estimated at over five million within a total population of approximately 70 million people. The spirit of Arab nationalism and Islamic revivalism have contributed manifestly to shaping the public domain as culturally inhospitable, discriminating in employment and political office-holding, restrictive in religious privileges and practice, and threatening the physical security of Christians.

Egypt has a deep Islamic identity, not only an overwhelming Muslim majority population, in a period of intense popular religious consciousness. The Muslim Brotherhood represents the sweep of Egypt's national Islamic identity, and other militant and violent groups actively engage in escalating the tone in Islamic discourse. The constitutional amendment which in 1980 recognized that "the Islamic shari`ah [law] is the principal source of legislation," and the assassination of President Sadat as a "heretic" by the *jihad* organization, were each in their own way acts that demonstrated Islam grabbing the political high ground in Egyptian society. The Christians, by implication, felt the increasingly suffocating and intimidating atmosphere.

The Copts of Egypt have requested that the state authorities grant them human and minority rights. But Copts have for many years been excluded from high political, administrative, and military posts. They have called for media broadcasting whose message would recognize their legitimate place in Egyptian life; but instead, public figures call for imposing the traditional *jizya* poll-tax on Christians, while Sheikh Omar Abd-el Rahman, of the 1993 Twin Towers bombing notoriety, reportedly issued *fatawat* to kill the Christians of Egypt.

The language of political oppression and linguistic doublespeak employed in Egypt, and then internationally, identifies Muslim assaults against Christians as mere "sectarian tension" (*fitna ta`ifiyya*) in a way intended to hide the identity of the aggressor and the victim.[14]

The starkest instance of recent years was the pogrom against the Copts in Kosheh and neighboring communities in Upper Egypt in late December 1999–early January 2000. What began as an argument between a Christian fabric merchant and a Muslim customer ended with the killing of 22 Copts. Chillingly reminiscent from other times and peoples was a rumor instigating the violence to the effect that Christians had poisoned the wells. In March it was reported that the Kosheh killers had been acquitted in court.[15] Traditional Islamic legalism frowns upon convicting a Muslim who injured or even murdered a *dhimmi*.

The condition of the Copts is deteriorating in all domains of Egyptian society. Other examples include attacks against churches, as at Kaser Rashwan in El-Fayoum province in August 2000, imposition of Friday and not Sunday as the day off from school as in the Christian village of El-Biadieah in March that year, forced conversions of Christians to Islam, and political intimidation of Christian figures like the patriarch of the Coptic Catholic Church to publicly support the Mubarak regime.

The Sudan in Black Africa, and its southern zone in particular, is the focus of another case in the war of Islam against Christianity in these troubled times. Since 1955, a civil war between the Arab-Muslim north and the African-Christian/animist south has left two million dead and hundreds of thousands of refugees in neighboring countries. In addition, more than three million Sudanese, overwhelmingly in the south, were at risk in the year 2000 from famine and drought. It was the proclamation of Islamic law in 1983 by General Numeiri, and the doctrinaire role of the National Islamic Front led by Hasan Turabi thereafter, that signaled the intensification of the life-and-death struggle for freedom and identity for the southerners. Headed by American-educated John Garang from the large Dinka tribe, the Sudan People's Liberation Movement and its military SPLA wing, then renewed the guerrilla war against the Khartoum regime, in the hands of Gen. Omar

Hassan Al-Bashir since seizing power in 1989. The long war is largely forgotten by the world.

A complex web of cultural, religious, and economic issues sheds light on the longevity and horror of the suffering and struggle. The historical 19th-century slave trade in southern Sudan, conducted by unrepentant Arab traders/missionaries,[16] continues in the throes of present-day warfare with the government's purpose to break the popular back of the southern rebellion and convert the captives to Islam. Abducted boys, uprooted from their native environment, are brought north to Khartoum and forced to become Muslims, while some are sent back to the south for missionary or military purposes.[17] The war in the south down to Equatorial province and Juba, the local capital, is unrelenting, with the Sudanese Army and its Muslim militias unwilling to tolerate an end other than the complete domination of the southerners, if not their physical — certainly cultural and religious — annihilation. We note that prior to the British withdrawal from Sudan in 1955–56 the south officially spoke English (not Arabic), had Sunday and not Friday as the day of rest, and freedom for Christianity was the dominant motif of the educational and religious milieu. But the independence of Sudan in 1956 signified the enslavement of the south.

The discovery of oil in the southern area of Bentiu complicated and exacerbated the north-south conflict, for it girded the military loins of Khartoum to preserve control over the region. Yet the SPLA, joined with Nubian and other opposition forces within the National Democratic Alliance, pursues the struggle in the area of Kassala in the east in an attempt to cut off Khartoum from its hinterland and then force a political settlement acceptable to southern aspirations and interests. Meanwhile, the program of Islamization and Arabization remains at the core of the Sudan government's strategy, a policy of ethnic cleansing as Arab tribesmen push African inhabitants farther south, especially away from the oil site of Bentiu. International oil interests and large numbers of Chinese security personnel stationed in support of the Khartoum regime bode ill for the southern struggle.

The vision of a new Sudan, as proposed by John Garang, is an idyllic image of a pluralistic country that recognizes autonomy for the south, freedom of religion for non-Muslims, and national unity for the country as a whole.[18] But when land falls under *dar al-Islam* and is sanctified for Muslim rule, it is inconceivable that it would be voluntarily relinquished in a magnanimous act for conflict-resolution. Moreover, it is an Islamic imperative to expand into lands not yet populated by Muslims and transform them through mosque construction, religious conversion, and *dhimmi* subjugation. This is indeed the historical script and political prescription concerning the events transpiring in the Sudan during many decades of continued warfare.

2. Heterodox/Heretical Non-Muslims:

(a)*Alawites/Nusairis*

According to legend, a *Shi`ite* from southern Iraq called Ibn-Nusair fashioned a radical interpretation of Islam's origins and dogmas in the tenth century in a way that launched a new sect. His doctrine concerning the deification of `Ali, Muhammad's cousin and son-in-law in Mecca, on the one hand, and the existence of a trinity of celestial powers on the other, stood in absolute contradiction to orthodox Islamic belief.[19] There arose, therefore, a new community of faith with highly syncretic features of Christian and pagan and perhaps Persian vintage, worshiping nature, promoting mixed dancing with unveiled women, as a schismatic *Shi`ite* sect set free from its presumably initial Islamic moorings. There were never mosques in the Nusairi mountain enclave in northwestern Syria, no sign of prayer, and no pilgrimage to Mecca.

This minority had apparently turned into an apostate community from Islam, and that act of heresy was met by hostility and rejection by the religious and political authorities in the Muslim East. A *fatwah* by Ibn-Taimiyya in the 14th-century considered the *Nusairis* an aberration and forbade to bury them in Muslim cemeteries or to eat meat from their slaughtered animals. In his view, the Nusairis were more infidel than Jews and Christians.[20] Efforts by the Mamluks and the Ottomans to have them accept Islam failed.

In the 20th century, the *Nusairis*, now commonly known as *Alawites*, sought recognition for their separate identity within their own regional autonomous zone in Syria; and yet alternatively, depending on the political situation, they wanted acceptance from the surrounding Muslim world. In 1936, the *mufti* of Jerusalem acknowledged *Alawites* as Muslims and later in the early 1970s, under far different political circumstances, *Imam* Musa Sadr in Lebanon declared that the sect is part of the *Shi`a* branch of Islam. This religious maneuver remained, we may assume, farcical in the eyes of the large Muslim *Sunni* population in Syria where Hafiz al-Asad, a son of the *Alawites* from the mountain village of Qardaha, ruled with an iron fist. The Muslims considered Asad's Baathist regime an atheistic anathema in the hands of a heretical minority dictatorship that represented only 12 percent of the Syrian population.

Events in Syria, like the massacre of 20,000 people in the stir of Muslim Brotherhood rebelliousness in Hama in 1982, illustrated the incongruity of *Alawi* rule over a society suffused with Islamic faith and Arab nationalist fervor. The fact that Asad, prior to his death in June 2000, was successful in transferring power to his son Beshar does not assure the long-term ability of the *Alawite* sect to impose its domination over the Muslims of Syria. The day of reckoning may come when Islam, as in its imperial past, recovers Damascus and the country from its apostate rulers from the mountain.

(b) *Druzes*

The appearance of the *Druze* sect in early 11th-century Egypt was a manifestation of a *Shi`ite-Fatimid/Isma`ili* faith and regime that elevated the caliphal figure of Al-Hakim bi-Amr Allah to divine status. This fundamental distortion of orthodox *Sunni* Islam led to the persecution (*mihna*) of the new community, which then set its sights on acquiring a safe haven in the southern mountainous area of Lebanon, in Jabal `Amil and Wadi al-Taym. The new *Druze* religion departed from Islam, though at times the adherents pretended to be regular Muslims (*taqiyah*), but actually divorced themselves from Koran and *shari`ah* law. Religion had given birth to this new community, leaving the *Druze*s hardly more than allegorical Muslims, with monotheistic faith but without the doctrinal and behavioral paraphernalia of Islam.[21] The *Bani Ma`aruf*, as they call themselves, consider their particular monotheism within an existing monotheistic Middle East to be a special brand, as a philosophical and syncretic quality fills the *Druze* spiritual universe with a fragrance of depth, eclecticism, and unadulterated purity.

The history of the *Druzes* is one of an introverted, secret sect surrounded, and sometimes endangered, by the *Sunni* Muslim majority in Lebanon, Syria, and beyond. Their religious leaders (*Uqqal*) preserved the collective integrity of this small minority group and, with lay military chieftains, always fought attempts, as in the effort by the Ottoman Turks at the turn of the 20th century, to impose Islam upon the *Druze*s in the southern Syrian Hawran region. At a minimum, the *Druze*s were put under Muslim religious authorities even though they claimed that they are independent of the *shari`ah*.

After Israel's establishment, the *Druze* minority in the Carmel and Galilee areas was allowed to administer their own communal courts, no longer subordinated to Islamic law. This development was a result of the Jewish-*Druze* relationship which had begun in the 1930s, and reflected traditional *Druze* anxiety with *Sunni* Muslims, in this case the Palestinian Arabs. The *Druze* ended up agreeing to full conscription into the Israeli army. In the background of this fascinating military brotherhood between two small Mideastern peoples is the symbiosis in the biblical tale of Moses and Jethro his father-in-law, whom the *Druze* claim as their spiritual ancestor.

(c) *Alevis*

This highly mysterious group, which may number as much as ten or more million people in Turkey, seems to be an offshoot of *Shi`ism* but with an extreme emphasis on the divinity of "Ali." Devoid of basic Islamic practices, like fasting in the month of Ramadan or mosque attendance, the *Alevis* reject *shari`ah* law and assume the proprietorship of an esoteric religious tradition, which may have absorbed Christian and pagan ideas. They also do not intermarry with *Sunnis* in Turkey.

When Muslim fundamentalism surfaced powerfully in Turkish society and politics, the *Alevis* cautiously maintained a low public profile. At the end of the 1990s, however, and though generally considered of non-Turkish ethnic identity, they adopted a more visible presence in Turkish cities and towns, erecting houses of worship known as *cemevi,* as in Ankara the capital.[22] They may consider that the constitutional character of Turkey as a secular republic will always buttress them while containing the challenge of Islam as a rival political doctrine. This will then allow the wayward *Alevis* the opportunity to feel free to declare their religious identity without inviting any menacing Islamic response.

3. Non-Arab Muslims:

(a) Kurds

The imperial rule of Islam dominated Kurdistan and its millennial-old native Kurds in the days of the Abbasid caliphate, the Ottoman sultanate, and the Safavid dynasty, and so, too, under their successor states — Iraq, Turkey, and Iran — in later and contemporary periods of Middle Eastern history. In the heights of their rugged mountain hearth the Kurds, subjugated by the Arab conquest, accepted *Sunni* Islam but in a way that their core collective identity remained rooted in their particular cultural, ecological, and ethnic way of life. Religious and national identity are often fused, as for Eastern Orthodoxy and Russian identity, or Catholicism and Irish nationality. In the Middle East, Arab nationalism has a *Sunni* Islamic hue, as if to be an Arab is to be a Muslim, or to be an Iranian is to be a *Shi`ite*.[23] What then of Muslim Kurds?

The consequences of this linkage between nationality and religion are for certain minorities, like Muslim Kurds, harsh and fatal. Such a minority is, at one and the same time, denied any independent or honorable national significance while subordinated to the overarching religious community of which it is a member but that is dominated by another people. In the words of Firat, a Kurd, in a private communication from January 2001:

> Islam is actually the main reason that the Kurds cannot unite [because they are nominal Muslims with other non-Kurd Muslims under the common faith of Islam], and one of the main reasons that Kurds do not have a country of their own [as they are subjected, as in Iraq and Syria, to the pan-Arab political framework].

Kurds were traditionally not considered mainstream, observant, and loyal Muslims by dominant Muslims like the Arabs. First, we have the exceptional case of the Yezidis in the valley of Lalish north of Mosul, with their pre-Islamic faith or apostasy from Islam, worshiping the peacock angel Melek Tawus, who as recently as the 1990s feared the construction of a mosque in Dohuk, northern Iraq, as a sign of impending religious persecution.[24] Secondly, saint worship and holy shrines were more predominant than *shari`ah* conformity and mosque attendance for the Ahl-e Haqq Kurdish adherents, as in Kermanshah in western Iran. Thirdly, *Sufi* mystical orders, like the *Qadiri* and *Naqshbandi*, muted formal Islamic commitment in favor of spiritual and moral exercises. Fourthly, popular Kurdish culture, it seems, only tangentially conformed to Islamic norms and probably more often diverged from them, as eccentrically engaging in mixed bathing.[25]

In the 20th century, the Kurds demanded and fought in vain in their pursuit of statehood as an expression of the surge of ethno-nationalism in their ranks. Conducting minority insurgency with great tenacity over many decades in Turkey, Iran, and Iraq produced, however, no political gain. With a fundamental denial of the very existence of the coherent ethnic-linguistic community of over ten million Kurds in the country, Turkey practiced a harsh policy of cultural repression and physical deportation. The indictment and imprisonment of sociologist Ismail Besikci became the *cause célèbre* in the struggle for Kurdish recognition in the 1980s. In Iraq, three million Kurds fought a guerrilla war under the charge of Mustafa Barzani, but the campaign collapsed in 1975. The variety of Kurdish parties/militias — KDP, PUK, PKK — continued armed struggle across the Kurdistan homeland, but division within and brutal repression without left the Kurds subjugated to the repressive states under which they live. In 1988, Saddam Hussein's forces unleashed the Anfal campaign to destroy his non-Arab Kurdish compatriots. The gassing of 5,000 villagers in Halabja became the symbol of Iraq's "final solution" policy against the Kurds. In 1992, in the aftermath of the Gulf War and the liberation of Kuwait from Iraq's clutches, the Kurds were able to establish a regional administration, but not more than that, with its capital in Arbil.

(b) *Amazighen* — Berbers/*Kabyle*

The struggle of the native *Imazighen* (especially Berbers in Morocco and *Kabyles* in Algeria) against the Arab-Muslim invasion of North Africa from the seventh and eighth centuries continued without interruption into the period of the contemporary state-system.

Based on an ancient oral language (*tamazight*) rooted in the historical geography of Kabylia, the Rif, and Atlas mountains in particular, preserving an indigenous culture of ethnic fidelity and customary law, this minority of 15 million people persists, sometimes rebels, but lacks independence and statehood. These Berber communities adopted *Sunni* Islam early on, but their commitment to the faith was traditionally considered weaker than love of their Berber hearth and their tenacity in maintaining Berber identity at all costs. They apparently lent money at interest, despite the Islamic prohibition, and considered saints rather than learned *ulema* the venue for sanctity and blessing.[26]

The Algerian war for independence from French colonialism (1954–62) found Kabylians, like Belkacem Krim, Ramdane Abane, and Hocine Ait-Ahmed, in the forefront of the armed FLN struggle. They dedicated their energies for a free Algeria that would accommodate the Berber minority, its language and culture, as a respectable component of the country's national profile. Instead, Algeria with a certain *jacobin* centralized apparatus was soon defined as an "Arab-Muslim" entity that conjured up an old-new cultural-linguistic colonialism. Furthermore, the connection between language and sanctity regarding the dominant role of Arabic as *the* state language marginalized the Berber tongue as a parochial folk fossil. It was virtually impossible to speak Berber in the Algerian public domain, though approximately eight to nine million speak it in their homes.

It was this repressive situation that led Mouloud Mammeri in the 1970s to initiate his struggle for legitimizing the Berber language and poetry as expressions of a revived culture. So, too, the courageous efforts of Lounes Matoub, who never felt Arabic to be his own language, to speak and sing in his native though stigmatized Berber dialect as an act of resistance. But Matoub, aged 42, was murdered in June 1998, perhaps by state security forces, perhaps by Islamic terrorists, with the civil war in Algeria raging since 1992, and targeting any and everyone.[27] Known for his anti-Islamist sentiments and proud Kabyle identity, Matoub once recalled how it was intimidating to utter a word in the Berber language on a bus in Algiers. He made an effort *not* to learn Arabic, and at his funeral the mourners chanted, "We are not Arabs!"

The Berber minority has been defiant in the face of violence and repression, demanding "democracy and culture" in a pluralistic ethnic Algeria. The people of Kabylia demonstrated in late April 2001 to commemorate the "Berber Spring" from 1980 in a proud act of ethnic self-affirmation. But in confrontations with the Algerian security forces, 30 unarmed youth were killed. The Berbers faced both Islamic and state terror with terrible human losses.

In Morocco, where the Berbers traditionally enjoyed liberty in the rural Bled es-Siba areas, the war against French rule in the 1950s arose within a context of national and Islamic unity of the entire population. Yet independence meant the Arabization of Morocco in rejection of the French and Berber languages — even though the Berber proportion of the total population is estimated as high as 40 percent. The Alawite monarchy served as a unifying Arab-Islamic institution, and assumes this political pretension for the new king Muhammad VI, since his ascension to the throne in 1999. Inasmuch as the dynasty claims descent from Muhammad the prophet of Islam, and the king identifies himself in the classical caliphal role as "commander of the faithful" (*Amir al-Mu`minin*), he is a unifying point of reference for all Muslims, Arabs, and Berbers alike.

The implication of these aspects in contemporary Moroccan society and politics is the diminution of the Berbers' status and their language in national life. Amazigh families in the south of Morocco have been displaced with Arabs, and *Amazigh* place-names have been purged and replaced with Arab ones. Only Arabic is an official language and it is even prohibited for *Imazighen* to record traditional names in birth registers. It is reported that many younger Berbers are not able to speak any one of their three *Tamazight* dialects which yet constitute one language, and that moreover the language is a handicap in the economic realm for which spoken Arabic is required.[28]

4. Power and Rights:

The treatment of minorities in Middle Eastern Muslim countries is part of a comprehensive strategy of exclusion, homogenization, and repression in the public and political arenas. Traditionally autocratic authoritarian regimes, from Algeria to Iran, engage in policies that deny or restrict human rights for all persons and peoples.

The regime rather than an active citizenry stands at the center of politics. It is often, though not always, the case that Islamic law or Muslim norms serve as a legitimizing pillar in the imposition of a single code of behavior that buttresses the regime.

In Saudi Arabia, where Islamic punishments (*hudud*) are applied, seven Nigerians charged with bank robbery in May 2000 were summarily beheaded.[29] In Sudan, whose penal code is inspired by *shari`ah* law, 19 men had limbs amputated for the same crime of bank robbery in late January 2001.[30] In the same period, the Palestinian Authority under Yasser Arafat executed two Palestinians (one in front of a large cheering crowd in Nablus) who were accused of collaboration with Israeli secret services. Beyond the aspect of judicial arbitrariness in the procedures preceding the sentencing, it is suspected that such punishments are the result of inner clan rivalries among the Palestinians and not necessarily the product of a commitment to Palestinian national solidarity.

In the domain of thought and culture, free-thinkers and public critics have been victims of government repression that reflects Islamic concerns. In the year 2000, Egyptian authorities arrested well-known human rights activist and scholar Saad al-Din al-Ibrahim on charges of fomenting divisions and tensions in the country due to his promotion of civil and minority, that is, Coptic, rights. He was later sentenced to a prison term. Author Salaheddin Mohsen, also of Egypt, was also sentenced to three years in prison in January 2001 because his writings were deemed offensive to Islam. These examples illustrate that Islam represents intellectual and political rectitude even though the government, headed by President Husni Mubarak, itself represses Islamic movements who use violence to achieve their objectives. Official Egypt, like monarchical Jordan, accommodates Islam, while at the same time containing its anti-regime animus.

While Islam is a powerful force of repression within Arab countries, it is also a catalyst for expansion and a virtual assault on the West beyond the Middle East. The decay of Christianity as a political cultural entity, along with its porous democratic ethos, exposes Western countries to Islamic penetration in Europe and North America.[31] September 11 as a seminal rupture in the consciousness of the United States looms large in this regard. This is of a piece with the vulnerability and weakness of Christian communities in the Muslim world. In the 19th century and even earlier, Russia, France, and Britain took an active interest in the safety and welfare of Oriental Christians; in the 20th century, national self-determination and decolonization served to liberate the Arabs and Muslims, but block the road for Christian minority freedom. The independence of Iraq and Egypt, among other countries, placed Arabs above non-Arabs, and Muslims above non-Muslims.

The halcyon days of European concern for Christians and even military intervention on their behalf, as with the French military expedition to Lebanon in 1861, vanished from the arena of practical politics. When the United States intervened in the Persian Gulf in 1990–1991 on behalf of Kuwait and Saudi Arabia, it demonstrated its global and regional strategic priorities; and when it accommodated Syrian occupation of Beirut and almost all of Lebanon in the same years, it obtusely abandoned Christians (and others) to a foreign and oppressive regime. Nonetheless, it is worth mentioning the initiative of the American Congress in the 1990s to express concern for enfeebled Christians in the Middle East, and for Lebanon in particular, in declaratory and legislative decisions.

International organizations, particularly the United Nations and its agencies, have lacked the requisite determination and resources to assure the rights of minorities in the Middle East. The Universal Declaration of Human Rights from 1948 made no reference to "minority rights," while the right to "self-determination" itself is judged inferior to the right of a state to maintain its national and territorial integrity. The rights of indigenous peoples have been recognized, but no country is agreeable to the notion that such peoples should enjoy the option of secession against the right of the state to assert its complete sovereign prerogatives over its entire territory. The Covenant on Civil and Political Rights, in Article 27, does acknowledge the right of minorities "to enjoy their own culture, to profess and practice their own religion, or to use their own language."[32] Yet a centralized political regime, anxious about the majority-minority rift within the country, will not agree to grant extensive rights to a dissident group which might thereafter threaten the survival of the country. Nor are some states even willing to recognize the minority's separate existence: Turkey traditionally called the Kurds "mountain

Turks," while Egypt mockingly considers Copts a natural part of the Egyptian people and therefore unworthy of special rights or considerations.

The goal of freedom and dignity for all old Middle Eastern peoples is a noble vision. The most reasonable solution, however, may be one in which the state refrains from interference in the life of the minority so long as it recognizes the right of the state to its sovereign existence.[33] In the religious and political milieu of the Muslim and Arab Middle East, more than this — and even this — seems hardly feasible in the days ahead.

Endnotes

1 On the status of non-Muslims in the eyes of Islam, see Yohanan Friedmann, "Classification of Unbelievers in *Sunni* Muslim Law and Tradition," *Jerusalem Studies in Arabic and Islam*, Vol. 22 (Jerusalem: Magnes Press, The Hebrew University 1998), p. 163–195. For a general historical overview, see Bat Ye'or, *The Decline of Eastern Christianity under Islam: From Jihad to Dhimmitude* (London: Associated University Presses, 1996).

2 A recent contribution to this historical debate appears in M.A. Muhibbu-Din, "Ahl al-Kitab and Religious Minorities in the Islamic State: Historical Context and Contemporary Challenges," *Journal of Muslim Minority Affairs*, Vol. 20, No. 1 (2000): p. 111–127.

3 The Associated Press, May 1, 1998, quoted in *Middle East Quarterly*, Vol. VII, No. 4 (December 2000): p. 85; and *Jerusalem Post*, December 25, 2000.

4 *Pakistan Observer*, September 2, 2000; and a report from *The Copts: Christians of Egypt*, Vol. 17, Nos. 1 & 2 (January 1990): p. 3.

5 Sheikh Abdallah Azzam, born in Palestine in 1941 and assassinated in Pakistan in 1989, wrote a compelling *fatwah* (Islamic legal decision) on the subject called "Defense of the Muslim Lands," (translated from the original Arabic) distributed on Internet site <http://www.hoct.com/islam/defence.htm>.

6 Ronni Shaked and Aviva Shabi, *Hamas: From Faith in Allah to the Path of Terror* [Hebrew] (Jerusalem: Keter, 1994), p. 112.

7 *Al-Ahram al-Arabi*, October 28, 2000, quoted by Middle East Media Research Institute (MEMRI), Dispatch no. 151, November 8, 2000.

8 *Daily Star*, Beirut, December 22, 2000, quoted in the *Monthly Digest*, published by The Jerusalem Institute For Western Defence, Vol. 13, No. 1 (January 2001): p. 7.

9 Research on Palestinian textbooks is conducted by The Center for Monitoring the Impact of Peace, and most of the above quotations are drawn from the Center's Newsletter, issue 4, available on their Internet site <http://www.edume.org>.

10 See the authoritative study by Vahakn N. Dadrian, *The History of the Armenian Genocide* (Oxford: Berghahn, 1995), p. 147–151.

11 A. William Dalrymple, *From the Holy Mountain: A Journey in the Shadow of Byzantium* (London: Flamingo, 1998), p. 97.

12 Madawi Al-Rasheed, "The Myth of Return: Iraqi Arab and Assyrian Refugees in London," *Journal of Refugee Studies,* Vol. 7, Nos. 2/3 (1994): p. 199–219.

13 Nasrallah interviews in *Al-Safir*, Beirut, September 16, 1997, and *Der Spiegel*, October 20, 1997.

14 *Aequalitas*, Vol. 4, No. 1 (March-April 1999): p. 6, published by the Canadian-Egyptian Organization for Human Rights, Chomedey-Laval, Quebec. Note also from the CEOHR, "A Communication on Violations of the Rights of the Copts in Egypt presented to the Center for Human Rights-United Nations Office at Geneva," April 9, 1996.

15 Information from <http://www.copts.com> and *Cairo Times*, January 13–19, 2000, p. 6–8.

16 Alice Moore-Harell, "Slave Trade in the Sudan in the Nineteenth Century and its Suppression in the Years 1877–80," *Middle Eastern Studies*, Vol. 34, No. 2 (April 1998): p. 113–128.

17 Author's interview in January 2001 with an anonymous rebel referred to as Philip who fought in the bush with the Sudan People's Liberation Army.

18 John Garang, *The Vision of the New Sudan: Questions of Unity and Identity*, edited by Elwathig Kameir (Cairo: Consortium for Policy Analysis and Development Strategies, 1997).

19 Meir Bar-Asher and Aryeh Kofsky, "The Nusayri Doctrine of `Ali's Divinity and the Nusayri Trinity According to an Unpublished Treatise from the 7th/13th Centuries," *Der Islam*, vol. 72, no. 2 (1995): p. 258–292.

20 Rene Dussaud, *Histoire Et Religion Des Nosairis* (Paris: Librairie Emile Bouillon, 1900), esp. p. 29–30.

21 Silvestre De Sacy, *Exposé de la Religion Des Druzes* (Amsterdam: Adolf M. Hakkert, 1964, orig. 1838).

22 Krisztina Kehl-Bodrogi, "The New Garments of Alevism," *ISIM Newsletter* (5/00): p. 23.

23 Henry Munson, "Islamism and Nationalism," *ISIM Newsletter* (5/00): p. 10.

24 Christine Allison, "Oral History in Kurdistan: The Case of the Badinani Yezidis," *The Journal of Kurdish Studies*, Vol. II, 1996–1997, p. 37–48. See also John S. Guest, *Survival Among the Kurds: A History of the Yezidis* (London: Kegan Paul, 1993).

25 C.J. Edmonds, *Kurds, Turks, and Arabs: Politics, Travel, and Research in North Eastern Iraq 1919-1925* (London: Oxford University Press, 1957), p. 204–205.

26 *The Encyclopaedia of Islam*, Vol. II (London: Luzac, 1927), p. 596–602.

27 On Lounes Matoub and his murder, see the Internet site of the World Algerian Action Coalition <http://www.waac.org> and the report in the *Washington Times*, June 29, 1998. In the Kabylian city of Tizi-Ouzou, Berber rioters destroyed public property in an outburst of collective anger.

28 Yamina El Kirat, "Some Causes of the Beni Iznassen Berber Language Loss," *Langues et Stigmatisation Sociale Au Maghreb – Peuples Mediteraneans*, Vol. 79 (Avril-Juin 1997): p. 35–53.

29 *Guardian* (Nigeria), May 20, 2000, reported in the *Monthly Digest of News from the Moslem World* issued by The Jerusalem Institute for Western Defence, vol. 12, no. 6 (June 2000): p. 11.

30 The Sudan Victims of Torture Group (SVTG) of London reported this information on February 2, 2001, that was distributed by Internet site <http://www.msanews@msanews.mynet.net>.

31 I examined this subject in my book *Identity and Civilization: Essays on Judaism, Christianity, and Islam* (Lanham, MD: University Press of America, 1999), esp. p. 144–153.

32 Patrick Thornberry, "The UN Declaration on the Rights of Persons Belonging to National or Ethnic, Religious and Linguistic Minorities: Background, Analysis, Observations, and an Update," in Alan Philips and Allan Rosas, editors, *Universal Minority Rights* (Finland: Abo Akademi University Institute for Human Rights, 1995), p. 20.

33 For a thoughtful discussion, see Anthony D. Smith, "Ethnic Nationalism and the Plight of Minorities," *Journal of Refugees Studies*, vol. 7, no. 2/3 (1994): p. 186–198; also my article "The Minority Plight," *Middle East Quarterly*, vol. III, no. 3 (September 1996): p. 25–34.

Genocide
in the Sudan

Patrick Sookhdeo

P rolonged civil war and systematic persecution of the Christian and Animist minorities in Muslim-majority Sudan have been largely ignored by the global community, and all the while the hostilities continue. The term genocide is used frequently in reference to Rwanda or Bosnia. It is estimated that over 2 million non-Muslims have been killed in the Sudan and at least 4½ million displaced,[1] but the world hesitates to call this genocide. The term genocide is defined in Article 2 of the Genocide Convention adopted by the UN in 1948:

> Genocide means any of the following acts committed with the intent to destroy, in whole or in part, a national, ethnical, racial, or religious group, as such: 1. Killing members of the group; 2. Causing serious bodily or mental harm to members of the group; 3. Deliberately inflicting on the group conditions of life calculated to bring about its physical destruction in whole or in part; 4. Imposing measures intended to prevent births within the group; 5. Forcibly transferring children of the group to another group.

Using this definition as a reference, this chapter will discuss the context of the Sudanese genocide phenomenon and why the international community has so far allowed it to continue.

CONFLICT

The population of the Sudan is made up of 140 ethnic groups of whom around 36 percent is Arab. Of the 117 languages spoken, Arabic is the official language of the north and English is the official language of the south. Approximately 70 percent of the population are Muslim, 20 percent Christian, and 10 percent Animist.[2] Yet the Sudan was declared an Islamic Republic in 1983, the official religion is Islam, and the culture promoted by the regime is an Arab-Islamic one. The conflict in the Sudan is usually described as a war between the mainly Muslim north and mainly non-Muslim south, but this is complicated by the issue of the Nuba region. This region is in central Sudan, covering 30,000 square miles in South Kordofan. It is a very fertile region and is home to around 50 ethnic groups. It also has a unique African cultural tradition that is retained in the face of the Islamization/Arabization of the surrounding areas. Despite the fact that many people in this region are Muslims, they have also become victims of the regime's Arabization policy which seeks to usurp all manifestations of African society. Finally, the development of the oil industry in the Sudan has had a negative impact on the minority groups in several ways to be discussed later in this chapter.

The Sudan has never been a truly unified entity. Since 1820, the dominance of northern Muslim regions has shaped the character of the country. The invasion by Egypt under Muhammad Ali Pasha in 1820 served to institutionalize slavery in the Sudan with the north exerting power over the south. Slavery had already been internalized in society in northern Sudan but the Turko-Egyptian rule post-1820 introduced orthodox Islam and Arabic culture as a further divisive tool. According to classical Islamic law, three of the founders of the four main schools, Hanbal, Malik and Shafi, say that when the laws of unbelief become visible in a region, this makes it *dar al-Harb* (place of war). Therefore, unless *Shari`ah* is applied in the south, it will remain a place of war according to Muslim doctrine.

By the time the British became involved in the administration of the Sudan in 1900, the north and south were basically two different countries which were administered differently. The British made no attempt to alter this situation and instead they upheld the status quo. When power was handed over to the Sudanese, a conference was held in Juba in 1953, attended by delegates from both regions in order to discuss the administration of the north and south. After some days of discussion, the south voted for separate administration, possibly in a federal state. However, after the conference the northern delegates were able to persuade the southerners that the poorer south would not develop unless it was fully integrated with the north in one country. The conference was reassembled and the decision was taken that the north and south should remain together as one nation, even though the British administration foresaw the problems that could arise if the north were allowed to dominate the south, particularly if the Arabs would relocate to the south to take over senior government positions.

Elections were held in 1953 and a number of excellent southern candidates were elected to Parliament. These people were pressured to follow the government line when it came to the ratification of a constitution. As a result, the idea of safeguards for the south in the constitution was scrapped and the entire country was brought under a single government. In this way, the north was able to use political and administrative unification to increase its position of dominance and manipulate the situation to ensure its authority. From this strong legal position, the new regime was able to begin the imposition of northern Islamic/Arab culture on the peoples of the south. It seems plausible that a federation, or at least some form of safeguards for the south, could have prevented the spiral into civil war which continues to this day and has caused the Sudan's institutionalized practice of genocide.

GENOCIDE

Once the intentions of the north became clear, conflict between the north and south broke out even during the period of transfer of power. The first civil war lasted from 1955–1972. Military power was not the only tool used by the north to succeed in this conflict. Other weapons have also been used throughout the Sudan's modern history in an attempt to wipe out particular peoples and their customs. In 1972, the Nimeiri regime instructed government departments in the Nuba Mountains not to provide services to people who raised pigs or were "unable to dress properly [i.e., in an Islamic way]." The local *Baggara* (Arab) communities killed tens of thousands of pigs in an attack on a valuable food source and on Nuba cultural pride. In Islam, the pig is considered an unclean animal and Muslims are prohibited from eating its meat, so this was a specific attack on the non-Muslims of the region and on Muslims who follow Islam nominally along with their African traditions.[3]

Because of the way that politics and society in the Sudan have polarized into north/south, Arab/African, and Muslim/non-Muslim, the government has never been able to maintain a regime of peace and tolerance. The political and military balance of power thus far favors the north. That state of affairs cannot be reversed without a complete and sincere commitment to secular democratic government. There is even a lack of power sharing or agreement between the northern political parties because politics in the Sudan are based on ideology. Therefore, "political rivalry between the northern political parties make it unlikely that the *Umma* and DUP will risk disentangling themselves from their religious sectarian roots in favor of genuine secularism."[4] As noted above, according to Islamic ideology, the Sudan must be part of the *dar al-Islam* under the rule of Islamic law. The civil war against the south and Arabization/Islamization policies justify this end in the eyes of the leaders in Khartoum.

The current regime came to power in a military coup in 1989 after the civil war began in 1983 following the implementation of Islamic law. The regime remains a military one dominated by the National Islamic Front (NIF) who regard the civil war as *jihad*. Now led by Omar al Bashir, the ideological power behind the NIF until 1999 was Hassan al Turabi. According to his philosophy, Islam is essential to create a Sudanese identity and a cohesive society. He also believes it is necessary to challenge the West. This is the reasoning behind the NIF's continuation of the forced Arabization/Islamization of the Sudan and the elimination of those who constitute an obstacle to this goal. The regime also aims to rival Saudi Arabia as the home of Islam. Saudi Arabia is seen by many Muslims as corrupt because of its relations with the USA. The main grievance of Osama bin Laden and the *al-Qa`idah* network is the presence of

U.S. troops on Saudi soil. They perceive this as an attack on the Islamic faith because it defiles holy Islamic territory.

Furthermore, the notion of Islamic lands in the *dar al-Islam* concept is underlined by a *hadith* (a saying or tradition of Muhammad) believed to have been uttered by Muhammad on his deathbed in 632 A.D. It states: "Umar heard the Messenger of Allah (peace be upon him) say: I will expel the Jews and Christians from the Arabian Peninsula and will not leave any but Muslims."[5] A similar *hadith* reads, "One of things that the Messenger of Allah (may Allah bless him and grant him peace) said during his last days, 'May Allah fight the Jews and the Christians. Two religions shall not coexist in the land of the Arabs.' "[6] These *hadith* were the justification for the territorial expansion of Islam under the rule of Caliph Umar in the seventh century. In a similar way, the regime claims that its actions to Islamize the state are religiously justified and hence legitimate.

The scorched earth policy is another of the regime's tactics to remove the human obstacles to the Islamization/Arabization of the Sudan. This is the deliberate destruction of land and resources in order to create man-made famine. Crops, cattle, and property are burned or looted, and the people who once lived off this land are forced to move to government controlled "peace camps" or face starvation. These "peace camps" are referred to as concentration camps. Here the Islamic indoctrination process is carried out on vulnerable displaced people. Often the people targeted under this policy are those who live in areas where oil companies are operating in order to clear the area for further oil exploration and extraction. Oil has become a further complicating factor giving the regime incentive and financial resources to increase their campaign against the people of the southern and Nuba regions. Amnesty International has called this "the human price of oil" in the Sudan and has documented the cleansing of ethnic groups such as the Dinka and the Nuer from their land in order to secure the territory for oil fields.

On November 8, 2001, a class action complaint against Talisman Energy, Inc. was filed in New York on behalf of Rev. John Sudan Gaduel and the Presbyterian Church of Sudan and three individual plaintiffs. The complaint alleged that Talisman knowingly participated with the government of the Sudan in ethnic cleansing in order to create an empty area for Talisman's oil exploration and extraction. The complaint claimed that Talisman provides financial and logistical support for the regime knowing that they are engaged in *jihad* against non-Muslim civilians. Profits from oil enable the government to continue its genocidal campaign, while Western involvement in the area means that human rights violations are often overlooked by Western nations.

Approximately 4½ million people in the Sudan have been internally displaced without compensation or support. While some of these people went to the north on their own accord to escape the devastation of the south, others were forced to leave because of the total devastation resulting from the ongoing war. The fate of those who stay includes the threat of homelessness, murder, starvation, arrest, and torture. There is no medicine to treat the children, many of whom carry some form of disease. The people who migrated established shantytowns ringing Khartoum, but here again they came under attack. In December 1991 and January 1992, government forces bulldozed the makeshift homes of the shanty towns. The inhabitants were then rounded up and taken out to the desert. At these sites in the desert there were no facilities, no food, no water and no housing materials. They were surrounded by desert and security guards, who allow only Islamic aid agencies to enter these camps.

The bombing of civilians is a further danger to the Sudanese minority groups. At times these people undergo almost daily bombing raids. According to data compiled by humanitarian aid workers in the Sudan, bombings of civilian targets is occurring more frequently than was realized. During 2000, at least 113 bombing raids were recorded.[7] The research was based on information from the UN's Operation Lifeline Sudan, other international relief groups and an analysis of aid programs operated by local church groups in southern Sudan. The targets are not always military but are often civilian targets, such as schools, churches, refugee camps, and hospitals. On February 8, 2000, forces loyal to the regime in Khartoum attacked a Catholic school in the Nuba Mountains, killing 14 children and wounding 17. A teacher was also killed. According to a February 11 Reuters report, Dirdiery Ahmed, an official in the Sudanese embassy in Nairobi told Reuters that "The bombs landed where they were supposed to land."[8] The number of schools targeted by the regime show that this is one of their tactics. By destroying the education infrastructure, the hope, skills, and strength of the next generation of their enemy are undermined.

As well as the obvious obstacle that churches pose to the Islamization process, they also serve as a place of strength and unity for the Christian communities in time of conflict and devastation. Therefore, churches and Christian leaders have become targets for attack. Churches are burned down and pastors arrested. On December 29, 2000, a government plane bombed Fraser Cathedral in Lui, Equatoria Province. The building was destroyed. In another incident that took place in April 2001, All Saints Cathedral in Khartoum City came under attack after rioting broke out. Open-air Easter meetings scheduled for Khartoum's Green Square were called off, and while a meeting was being held in the Cathedral to discuss the decision, government troops stormed the building firing tear gas. Seats and cathedral properties were destroyed. There were many arrests and over 50 people were flogged. Yet despite such incidents as these, there is evidence to show that the church has undergone phenomenal growth in the Sudan, even though Christian communities and lands have been and continue to be decimated by a regime intent on destroying them.

The bombing campaign of the Sudanese regime also targets humanitarian sites. Since 1997, international aid organizations have been forbidden from operating in many of the poorest and most devastated regions of the Sudan. Only Muslim aid organizations are allowed to operate in these areas and there are reports that they have withheld food and other services from non-Muslims who refuse to convert to Islam. The UN's World Food Program itself has been threatened and must inform the regime when and where it is to make food drops in those areas where it is allowed to operate. In one incident on October 9, 2001, Sudanese government aircraft arrived 15 minutes before a scheduled food drop in Bahr el Ghazal and bombed the assembled crowd, causing the UN to stop their operations in that area.[9] In November 2000, the UNHCR (United Nations High Commissioner for Refugees) staff at Kassala had to be evacuated after coming under artillery fire. The offices were raided, equipment was seized, and staff was detained. On the May 9, 2001, a Red Cross airplane was fired on in Juba, in southern Sudan. The co-pilot was killed and the Red Cross was forced to discontinue its flights.[10] On November 11, 2001, government of Sudan forces used artillery to attack relief planes from the UN's World Food Program which were arriving in Nuba for a food drop operation. These examples clearly illustrate how the most vulnerable people in the Sudan are being attacked in numerous ways and international efforts to prevent this are being obstructed and then conveniently ignored by the UN itself. In this manner, the regime is able to destroy the infrastructure and lay waste to vast swathes of territory.

SLAVERY

Another facet to the genocidal practice taking place in the Sudan is the use of the slave trade. According to the United Nations Special Rapporteur on the Sudan and the U.S. State Department, the government of Sudan is the only one in the world today engaging in chattel slavery. Slavery has a long history in the Sudan, with the people of the north as the slave masters and the people of the south as the slaves. Today it is a weapon of war and part of the Islamization policy of the regime. Women and children from the south are abducted and forced into slavery. Many are forced to convert to Islam and there are reports of sexual abuse.[11] From the time of former President Mehdi in 1986, Arab militias have been taking women and children as booty with government knowledge, while looting cattle and burning property. Soldiers are encouraged and rewarded for fathering children by non-Muslim women because a child of a Muslim father is considered to be Muslim according to Islamic law. This policy effectively encourages the kidnap and rape of non-Muslim women. In October 2001, Christian Solidarity International liberated 4,041 Sudanese slaves in defiance of the regime. Interviews revealed that 90 percent had been physically abused, over 80 percent had been forced to convert to Islam, and 75 percent of female slaves over 12 had been gang-raped.[12]

Yet the Sudan is party to the 1926 Slavery Convention (as amended in 1953). Article 1 (1) of that convention defines slavery as "the status or condition of a person over whom any or all of the powers attaching to the right of ownership are exercised." Article 1 (2) defines the slave trade as "all acts involved in the capture, acquisition or disposal of a person with intent to reduce him to slavery." In fact, the prohibition of slavery is one of the fundamental principles of international law. Article 4 of the Universal Declaration on Human Rights provides that "No one shall be held in slavery or servitude; slavery and the slave trade shall be prohibited in all their forms." Slavery is prohibited in Article 8 of the International Covenant on Civil and Political Rights (ICCPR) and this Article is considered to be non-derogatory. Therefore, its violation can never be justified. Article 5 of the African Charter, promulgated in 1963, also prohibits the practice:

> Every individual shall have the right to the respect of the dignity inherent in a human being and to the recognition of his legal status. All forms of exploitation and degradation of man, particularly slavery, slave trade, torture, cruel, inhuman or degrading punishment and treatment shall be prohibited.

The capture and indoctrination of children is a particularly widespread phenomenon in the Sudan. Not only are children captured as part of the military conflict, but also children on the streets are picked up and placed into closed camps. These children are given Arabic names and undergo forced instruction in Islam.

It is clear that the right to religious freedom is denied in violation of international law. For example, Article 14 of the Convention on the Rights of the Child (CRC) stipulates, "States parties shall respect the right of the child to freedom of thought, conscience and religion." Every child should also have the right to an identity as stipulated in Article 8 (1) of the CRC, which protects the child's right to "preserve his or her identity, including nationality, name and family relations as recognized by law without unlawful interference." Clearly, the regime has little regard for the rule of law when it would prevent the full implementation of its Islamization program. Parliament was dissolved in 1999 and since then a state of emergency has persisted, which affords even more power to President Bashir and further reduces his accountability to the Sudanese people and domestic and international actors.

The Political Act that came into force in 1999 was supposed to relax the ban on opposition parties. However, the reality remains unchanged and opposition groups are either banned or are denied political freedom. The judiciary is not independent and the Supreme Court has upheld the right to extract confession under torture and the use of crucifixion as a form of execution. The National Security Act, as amended in December 2000, allows the security forces to detain people for up to 123 days before a legal challenge can be made. Effectively, this means that detainees can be held for an indefinite period of time by the regime without any charge being made against them. In the 57th UN Commission for Human Rights report of March 2001, there were concerns raised about the independence of the legal system, which is considered to be one of the most important ingredients for holding the government to account and for the rule of law to operate. Clearly, internal legal remedies are inadequate to solve or even control the human rights violations in the Sudan and genocide is the result.

ISLAMIC LAW

Islamic law was introduced in 1983 and was the catalyst beginning the current phase of the civil war. The substitution of secular with Islamic law in many areas illustrates how the north has been able to politically dominate the administration of the Sudan. The dominance of the north prevails because of the underlying imbalance of power between the north and its culture over the south. Although Islamic law is not applied in the ten southern states where Christians are a majority, this could change in the future. Islamic law does apply however to non-Muslims living in the majority-Muslim areas of the north. Islamic punishments include amputation and stoning. Yet this violates the government of Sudan's international obligations with regard to Article 5 of the Universal Declaration of Human Rights and Article 7 of the International Covenant of Civil and Political Rights. Both prohibit the use of torture or cruel, inhumane treatment. Dress codes have been introduced which require women to wear Islamic dress. Many of those caught who do not comply with this are beaten. The Constitution of 1999 provides for freedom of religion. In practice, this is of little value since there is scant regard for the rule of law and the judiciary has little independence from the executive, especially under the current state of emergency. The

Constitution also states that the *Shari`ah* and custom are the sources of legislation. This allows the government to Islamize the legal system "legitimately."

The implementation of Islamic law has also had an impact on the status of non-Muslims and their non-Islamic faiths. In Islam, Christians and Jews are referred to as "people of the book," because they have revealed books, which are recognized by Islam. Unlike followers of pagan religions, "people of the book" are permitted to live in Islamic territories, the *dar al-Islam*, but their status is of a second-class citizen called *dhimmi*. They may retain their faith and are not obliged to convert to Islam, but must pay a tribute tax called *jizyah*, and are bound by a list of strict conditions, including regulations on the clothes they wear, their homes, and conduct. Their worship should not be obvious to the larger Muslim community, so singing should not be audible, nor is the wearing of religious symbols such as the cross permitted. In conduct, the non-Muslim should be always subservient to the Muslim. The *Qur`an* states:

> Fight those who believe not in God nor the last day, nor hold that forbidden which hath been forbidden by God and his Apostle, nor acknowledge the religion of truth (even if they are) people of the book, until they pay the *jizyah* with willing submission and feel themselves subdued.[13]

These regulations were first set out in Umar's Edict in 634 A.D. after the defeat of Damascus by the Muslim army. In addition, the building of churches or synagogues required permission from the ruler. In the Sudan, it has been approximately 30 years since permission was last given for a church to be built. Many of these regulations are to enforce the belief that Muslims are superior people, as is written in the *Qur`an*. Chapter 3, Verse 110 states:

> Ye [the Muslims] are the best of Peoples, evolved for mankind, enjoining what is right, forbidding what is wrong, and believing in God. If only the People of the Book had faith, it were best for them: among them are some who have faith, but most of them are perverted transgressors.

Clearly the NIF ruling regime is based on a religious model that lends justification for their campaign to subject all of the Sudan and the Sudanese peoples to an Islamic form of government.

PROSPECTS

The U.S. House of Representatives adopted Resolution 75 on June 15, 1999, which finds that "the National Islamic Front government is deliberately and systematically committing genocide in southern Sudan and the Nuba Mountains among others."[14] Yet sanctions against the Sudan were dropped recently. There is an increasing awareness of the tragedy in the Sudan, and since 1998 a growing number of groups have been trying to highlight the five main genocidal actions of the Sudan regime.

These five actions are:

1. The government ban on humanitarian aid flights resulting in mass starvation

2. The indiscriminate aerial bombing of civilian and humanitarian targets

3. Slavery and the slave trade

4. Forcible Islamization, through the implementation of the *Shari`ah*, indoctrination of children in schools and camps and the use of food aid as an incentive to convert

5. The deliberate creation of starvation and displacement through the scorched earth policy and the clearing of territory for oil extraction

There are some international attempts to secure peace in the Sudan. Former U.S. Senator John Danforth's visit in November 2001 resulted in the agreement to four principles that must be fulfilled in order to discuss arrangements for peace talks. These four principles are:

1. Allowing humanitarian access to SPLA-held (Sudan People's Liberation Army) areas of the Nuba Mountains and the establishment of a cease-fire in the region

2. Respecting a cease-fire for vaccination programs to proceed

3. A cessation of aerial bombardment against civilian targets

4. Action to stop enslavement, in the form of a commission to investigate cases and release people held in captivity

Expectations that these conditions will be fulfilled are not high and the United States has threatened to disengage from the peace process. In fact, there was fighting in December 2001 in violation of the cease-fire agreed to by the government of the Sudan in order to allow food aid to be delivered in the Nuba Mountains.

The Sudanese government has no real incentive to end the war at present since it is obtaining support through oil revenues. Recently there have been increasing signs that Kenya is willing to support the north in return for oil. Any alliance between Kenya and the north of the Sudan would further isolate south Sudan. On top of this, the current political climate since September 11, 2001, has resulted in efforts to appease Islamic leaders in order to maintain an international coalition. Without an increase in awareness of the conflict in the Sudan and the suffering of the non-Arab, non-Muslim minorities, the political, economic, and military imbalance in favor of northern Sudan is unlikely to be rectified. Religious and ethnic groups in the Sudan are in very real danger of being undermined and destroyed by an aggressive campaign of bombing, abduction, slavery, displacement, starvation, and indoctrination.

The government has also fostered fighting among southern rebel groups. By dividing and therefore weakening the opposition, the regime can maintain the conflict. However, on January 7, 2002, two key southern groups, the SPLA/SPLM (Sudan People's Liberation Movement) and the SPDF (Sudan People's Democratic Front), announced a merger to solidify their struggle for self-determination. A stronger opposition could encourage a more adaptable stance from the government in regard to the minorities, their identity and religions. The people of the south continue to campaign for a solution based on the IGAD (Inter-Governmental Authority on Development) agreement signed by the Sudanese government in 1997. According to this agreement, a solution to the conflict should be based on autonomy for the south. Talks in January 2002 in Switzerland have produced a cease-fire agreement for Nuba, but its actual impact will only become clear with time. A just and lasting peace remains unlikely at the present time since this agreement applies only to Nuba and as the regime still continues the deliberate targeting of humanitarian, religious, and educational sites, showing that this is clearly more than merely a military conflict. According to the definition of Article 2 of the UN Genocide Convention, this conflict is nothing less than genocide in the Sudan.

Endnotes

1 U.S. Commission on International Religious Freedom, 2001 Annual Report on International Religious Freedom; Sudan.
2 Peter Hammond, *Faith Under Fire in Sudan* (South Africa: Frontline Fellowship, 1996), p.123.
3 Peter Verney et al., *Sudan: Conflict and Minorities* (United Kingdom: Minority Rights Group International, 1995), p. 34.
4 Ibid., p.40.
5 Umar ibn al-Khattab *sahih muslim*.
6 Al-Muwatta of Imam Malik, Umar ibn Abdul Aziz.
7 <www.afrol.com/News/sud015_113_bombattacks.htm>.
8 United States Commission on International Religious Freedom, <www.uscirf.gov/hearings/15feb00/gassisPT.php3>.
9 <www.freedomhouse.org/religion/sudan/chronology%20since%209-11.htm>.
10 <www.afrol.com/News2001/sud009_icrc_plane.htm>.
11 U.S. Department of State Country Report on Human Rights Practices, 2000.
12 <www.freedomhouse.org/religion/sudan/chronology%20since%209-11.htm>.
13 Yusuf Ali, translation of the *Qur`an*, Chapter 9, Verse 29.
14 <www.freedomhouse.org/religion/sudan/index.htm>.

From Bosnia to Kosovo: The Re-Islamization of the Balkans

Raphael Israeli

THE PROBLEM

On February 12, 1997, on the occasion of the `Id al-Fitr Festival, the Uighur rebels in Chinese Central Asia published, on their internet site, an appeal to all Muslims to heed the unfolding events in Bosnia. "What kind of festival is this," they asked, "when 250,000 Muslims are being murdered, tortured, and raped in Bosnia?" They sent their heartfelt thanks to the "Iranian people who are sending help in spite of the West's embargo," and accused the West of "stopping the Muslims when they were about to win, while at the same time aiding the Serbian Fascists." Evidently, the Uighurs in China's northwest had their own axe to grind when they used the universal festival which linked all Muslims together to draw attention to their own plight in Xinjiang, where their own land was being "robbed" by the "fascists" of China. However, as they thanked the Iranians for their assistance to the Bosnians, they might also have been referring to the backing that Islamic countries in the

Middle East were providing the Uighurs and other Islamic groups in China,[1] something that was recognized by and caused alarm in the midst of the China leadership.[2]

In April 1998, the State Department published its annual report on global terrorism. Among other things, it referred to the unidentified terrorists who acted against the international presence in Bosnia, and especially to the Mujahidin who had served in the Bosnian army during the civil war, but were now engaged in warrant killings. According to that report, the Bosnian government began arresting some of those loose terrorists, and by November 1997, it had incarcerated 20 of them, who were identified as Arabs or Bosnian Muslims.[3] In 1998 there were reports that Iranian intelligence agents were mounting extensive operations and even infiltrated the American program to train the Bosnian army. According to those reports, more than 200 Iranian agents were identified as "having insinuated themselves into Bosnian Muslim political and social circles . . . to gather information and to thwart western interests in Bosnia." Those agents, it was believed, could be helpful in planning terrorist attacks against NATO forces or targets.[4] Taken together, these reports do identify the "unidentified terrorists" mentioned above. Moreover, these reports link together into an Islamic International centered around Iran indicating that most of the major terrorist activities are carried out by Islamists: from the Israeli Embassy in Buenos Aires (1992); the international gathering of Islamic terrorist organizations in Teheran (1997); the *Hizbullah* stepped-up activities against Israel in the late 1990s; the arrest in Israel of Stefan Smirak, a would-be "suicide-bomber" for *Hizbullah* (November 1997); the attacks against American interests in the Gulf, East Africa, and on American soil (throughout the 1990s),[5] to say nothing of the Muslim separatists in China, and the Islamic resurgence in Bosnia and Kosovo.

People today speak of the clashes between Serbs and Muslims in Bosnia, and Serbs and Albanians in Kosovo, in terms of ethno-national conflicts, with the more numerous Serbs figuring as the oppressors and their rivals as the underdogs and the oppressed. *Prima facie,* the very usage of the terms Serbs (and Croats for that matter) against Muslims, equates the latter (essentially members of a faith and civilization) to the former who clearly belong to religio-ethnic groups. This points to the fact that not only did Yugoslavian statism and universalistic communism fail to obliterate ethnic and kinship identities (real or imagined), but that communal interest overrides the state umbrella, economic interest, or even sheer common sense. But this also raises the question of whether Islam, a universal religion predominant in more than 50 countries around the world, is, or can be, perceived as a nationalism that is particularistic by definition.

THE HISTORICAL UNDERPINNINGS

After the Arab conquests had exhausted the immense primeval energies released by Islam since its inception in the 7th century and up until the 9th century, the Turks of Central Asia who arrived on the scene in the 11th century gave a new impetus to Islamic expansion, this time into the heart of Europe.

The Ottoman state, which reached Vienna at the pinnacle of its existence, was multi-ethnic and multi-religious, and under its Muslim-majority dominance, Christians, Jews, and others lived side by side for many centuries. However, this co-existence was not born out of a modern concept of tolerance of the other on the basis of acceptance of differences and equality to all, but on a sense of superiority, which tolerated the others in spite of their inferiority. Thus, even though Turks, or Muslims, may have constituted the minority population in some areas of the Empire, they reigned supreme by virtue of their Muslim master status, while the various Christian groups (and Jews for that matter) were relegated to the status of "protected people" (the *dhimmi*).[6] Christians and others who had integrated into the Ottoman system by embracing Islam, speaking Turkish, and going into the Imperial service, soon became part and parcel of the Ottoman culture, even when they kept their attachment to their ethnic origin and to their mother tongue. The case in point were the Bosnians, many of whom felt privileged to go into the *devsirme* system by enrolling their boys in the prestigious janissary corps, and in the course of time were Islamized though they preserved their Slavic roots and language.[7]

The Balkans were conquered by the Ottomans from the middle of the 15th century on. Serbia fell in 1459, and four years later Bosnia, with Herzegovina succumbing to the conquerors in 1483. Caught between the economic interest of milking the taxpaying *dhimmis*, which necessitated maintaining the conquered population in place instead of expelling or converting it by force, and the military and security needs which required that the Muslim population be numerous enough to ensure the loyalty to the Empire, the Ottomans tended to implement the latter choice in the Balkans. They adopted a policy of deporting the native populations and settling their own people, or other conquered people, in their stead, thus ensuring that no local minority should envisage any insurgency among a Muslim population. In Bosnia, the process of Islamization was reinforced by the turncoats who flocked to Islam and became the worst oppressors of their former coreligionists; so much so that the Bosnians were notorious for their role in the Ottoman administration, military, and especially the janissaries.[8]

As late as 1875, long after the introduction of the *tanzimat* reforms which were supposed to redress the situation of the non-Muslims throughout the Empire, the British ambassador in Istanbul reported that the Ottoman authorities in Bosnia recognized the impossibility of administering justice in equality between the Muslims and the Christians, inasmuch as the ruling Muslim courts accepted no written or oral evidence from Christians. One 1876 report from Bosna-Serai (Sarajevo) by the British Consul in town, tells the whole story:

> About a month ago, an Austrian subject named Jean Udilak, was attacked and robbed between Sarajevo and Visoka by nine Bashi-Bazouks. The act was witnessed by a respectable Mussulman of this time named Nouri Aga Varinika, and he was called as a witness when the affair was brought before the Sarajevo Tribunal. His testimony was in favor of the Austrian, and the next day he was sent for by the vice-president and one of the members of the Court and threatened with imprisonment for daring to testify against his coreligionists.[9]

As Hans Majer tells us above, Muslims and Christians (and Jews for that matter) could keep to themselves in their own communities, with their lifestyles, rituals, and festivals running without hindrance, except in case of intermarriage. For here, the only allowed combination was Muslim men taking in Christian (or Jewish) wives, which consecrated their joint offspring as full-right Muslims. The result was that while non-Muslim culture merged into the predominant Islam, there was also an outside input into the Muslim culture with material culture (food, dress, habits, language, etc.) growing to become common to all. All this was acceptable to the Ottoman authorities, who were reluctant to interfere, but as soon as the *dhimmis* became wealthy and were conspicuous in their dress and demeanor, it was considered a provocation to the Muslim population and dealt with accordingly. Christians who wanted to improve their lot in Bosnia and Albania could always do so through conversion to Islam or seek the protection of their Muslim family members.[10]

Toward the end of the Ottoman rule, as economic problems arose and the state was no longer able to enforce law and order in the face of the nationalist awakening in the various provinces of the Empire, local rule grew more despotic in an attempt to hold on to the territories that were slipping out of the Porte's grip. The notions of equality coming from liberal Europe, which made the maintenance of legal and religious inequities untenable, conjugated into national terms, and spelled out independence from the Ottoman yoke since the idea of a ruling Empire held together by Islam was no longer operative. It was ironically the Ottoman attempts at modernity, opening up the system, addressing individuals instead of traditional communities, which brought its downfall and opened the new vistas of nationalism and independence in the Balkans as elsewhere, a situation not unlike Eastern Europe after the Gorbachev perestroika in the late 1980s and early 1990s. But in view of the Greek and Bulgarian plans for a Balkan Federation under their aegis, to take over from the Ottomans,[11] and the tax repression imposed by the Bosnian Muslims, the Serbs rose up in arms (1875), and many of them ran into hiding, leaving behind children, the old, and women, something reminiscent of the horrors of the Bosnian War and then the Kosovo War more than one century later. Preydor and Banja Luka were the most harmed by the insurgents when Serb churches and homes were burned.[12]

After the Berlin Congress and the occupation of Bosnia by the Austro-Hungarian Empire, the Serbs allied with the Muslims against the occupiers, who were supported by the Catholics in the province. The Hungarian governor of the province tried valiantly but unsuccessfully to create a new Bosnian identity merging together its three principal communities.[13] But the annexation of Bosnia by the occupiers in 1908 created a new alliance: the Serbs, who wished their merger with Serbia, were pitted against the Croat-Muslim coalition who would rather reconcile to their occupation than allow the Serbs to implement their dream. As a result, repression of the Serbs in Bosnia, coupled with the expulsion of Serbs from Kosovo, brought the bitterness of the occupied Serbs against their oppressors to a record level. Sukrija Kurtovic, a Bosnian Muslim, sought the differentiation between ethno-nationality and religion, and pleaded for the unity of the Bosnians with the Serbs in one single national group by reason of their common Serbian roots, arguing that Islam was a common religion of the Bosnians and the Turks, but that in itself did not make them share any national common ground.[14] The idea of Yugoslavism, a larger entity where all the ethnic and religious groups could find their common identity, came to the fore after the Balkan wars and precipitated World War I following the Sarajevo murder of the heir to the Austro-Hungarian throne in 1914. That war reinforced the Croat-Muslim alliance in Bosnia, which swore to expel the Serbs from Bosnia altogether and acted upon its vow by perpetrating large-scale massacres of the Serbs, and demonstrated the vanity of an all-Yugoslavian identity.[15]

A Yugoslavian state was created in 1918 nevertheless, which once again attempted to fuse its components in the ethnic and linguistic domains and leave, as befits a modern European state, the question of religion to the realm of each individual. However, while the Serbs and the Croats of Bosnia could look up to Belgrade and Zagreb respectively, the Muslims were left to vacillate between their Muslim, Ottoman, local, and Slavic roots. At first they allied with the stronger Serbs and turned their eyes on Belgrade where they ensured for themselves some privileges, but wary of the competition between the Croats who championed their nationalism and the Serbs who regarded themselves as the guardians of Yugoslavian unity, they focused more and more on their local and religious identity in the form of a Muslim party (JMO), while the Serbs and the Croats continued to claim that the Muslims of Bosnia were of their respective origins.[16]

During World War II, the renewed Croat-Muslim alliance had tragic consequences, inasmuch as under the shelter of its collaboration with the fascists and the Nazis, it brought about the murder, forced conversion, or expulsion of a million Serbs. After 1945, Yugoslavia was reconstituted, this time on its Soviet model, with its various components recognized on ethnic or linguistic grounds, and since 1971 on religious grounds for the Muslims of Bosnia. Since then, what was ethnic and religious sentiment for the Bosnians turned into a national identity, in spite of the paradox under which communism offered them nationalism based on faith.[17] This immediately reinforced their coalition with the Croats in order to scuttle Serbian hegemony in the federated communist Yugoslavian state, especially in view of the demographic presence of Serbs in all the federal republics, particularly in Bosnia and Croatia. So, once again, instead of using the idea of Yugoslavia to merge the populations of Bosnia-Herzegovina, the idea of faith (Islam and then Orthodox and Catholic Christianity) became a vehicle for reinforcing the hatreds and suspicions, which only waited for the end of the Tito rule and the Communist regime to burst out in violence and war. After the disintegration of Yugoslavia in the early 1990s, the Croats and Serbs of Bosnia expressed their wish to join their respective national republics, while the Muslims naturally regarded such a dismantling of what they viewed as their national state as detrimental to their national existence. None of the rival national groups possessed a demographic majority to claim legitimacy to rule all the rest, and the road was wide open to war.

THE IDEOLOGICAL UNDERPINNINGS

In 1970, well before the collapse of the Yugoslavian order imposed by Tito and the outburst of communal nationalism which instigated the process of its disintegration, a political manifesto was written by an unknown Muslim in Bosnia, Alija Izetbegovic (born in 1925), but not immediately released to the public. It was, however, duplicated and made available to individual Muslims who circulated it among their coreligionists apparently to serve as a guide for a Muslim order to replace the godless Communist system in Bosnia. That pamphlet is known as the *Islamska Deklaracija* (the Islamic Declaration). In 1983, after Tito's death but while the Communist state was held together, a trial took place in Sarajevo where the author and some like-minded individuals were prosecuted for subverting the constitutional order and for acting from the standpoint of Islamic fundamentalism and Muslim nationalism. Significantly, after the fall of Communist power, the accused were publicly rehabilitated, and the Declaration was then officially published in Sarajevo (1990). Izetbegovic, at the head of his Democratic Action Party (SDA) won the majority of the Muslim votes in the first free elections in Bosnia-Herzegovina (November 1990), but his pamphlet was obscured and not heard of again. Judging from the wide appeal of his later book, *Islam Between East and West*, which was published in English in the USA (1984), in Turkish in Istanbul (1987), and in Serbian in Belgrade (1988), and from the developments in the Bosnian war in the mid-1990s, one might be well advised to take a look at it.

The declaration, which in many respects sounds and looks like the platforms of Muslim fundamentalists elsewhere (e.g., the Hamas Charter),[18] assumes that its appeal will be heeded by Muslims around the world, not only by its immediate constituency. It accuses the West of wishing to "keep Muslim nations spiritually weak and materially and politically dependent," and calls upon the believers to cast aside inertia and passivity in order to embark on the road of action.[19] And like Muslim radicals such as Sayyid Qutb of Egypt, who urged his followers to reject the world of ignorance around them and transform it according to the model of the prophet of Islam, the Declaration of Izetbegovic also calls upon the millions to join the efforts of Muslim individuals who fought against the *Jahiliyah* (the state of ignorance and godlessness which had preceded the advent of the prophet),[20] and dedicates the text to the memory of "our brothers who have laid their lives for Islam,"[21] namely the *shuhada'* (martyrs) of all times and places who had fallen in the cause of Islam.

The manifesto, again like other Muslim radicals, not only addresses itself to the restoration of Islam in private life, in the family, and society, but also expressly shuns local nationalism of any sort and substitutes for it the creation of a universal Islamic polity (the traditional *umma)* "from Morocco to Indonesia."[22] The author awakens his people to the reality where "a few thousand true Islamic fighters forced England to withdraw from the Suez Canal in the early

1950s, while the nationalist armies of the Arabs were losing their battles against Israel," and where "Turkey, an Islamic country, ruled the world," yet when it tried to emulate Europe it dropped to the level of a Third World country. In other words, it is not nationalism that makes the force of Muslim nations, but their abidance by Islam in its universal version. Therefore, it does not befit Muslims to fight or die for any other cause but Islam, and it behooves Muslims to die with the name and glory of Allah in their hearts, or totally desert the battlefield.[23] Translated into the Bosnian scene, Muslims ought not take part in, or stand for, any form of government which is not Islamic and any cause which is not connected to Islam. To the Bosnians, whom Izetbegovic addressed, there were only two options left: either to subscribe to Muslim revival and its political requirements, or be doomed to stagnation and oblivion.[24]

As against the perceived failure of Turkey and other Muslim countries due to "the weakening of the influence of Islam in the practical life of the people," the author posits that "all successes, both political and moral, are the reflection of our acceptance of Islam and its application in life."[25] Therefore, while all defeats, from Uhud at the time of the prophet to the Sinai War between Israel and Egypt, were due to "apostasy from Islam," any "rise of the Islamic peoples, every period of dignity, started with the affirmation of the *Qur`an*." The author complains that in the real world the *Qur`an* is being recited instead of practiced, mosques are "monumental but empty," the form took over from substance, as the Holy Book turned "into a mere sound without intelligible sense and content."[26] This reality was caused, laments the author in line with other Muslim fundamentalists, by the Western-inspired school system in all Muslim countries.[27]

Secularism and nationalism, the products of that foreign educational trend, took over the minds and hearts of the new generation of Muslims. The masses, who do not submit to these fleeting concepts which are foreign to Islam, chose indifference. But if they are rightly guided they can rise to action provided they are spurred by "an idea that corresponds to their profound feelings, and that can only be the Islamic idea," instilled by a new intelligentsia that "thinks and feels Islam" and would ultimately "fly the flag of the Islamic order and together with the Muslim masses initiate action for its realization."[28] This new Islamic order should unite "religion and law, upbringing and force, ideals and interests, the spiritual community and the state, free will and coercion," for "Islamic society without Islamic rule is incomplete and impotent; Islamic rule without Islamic society is either utopia or violence."[29] This, in effect, means, in the vein of other Muslim fundamentalist platforms, that the Muslim state ought to enforce ("coerce") the Islamic order, short of which violence would erupt by necessity. For, according to this scheme, and contrary to the European concept of a liberal society where the individual is prized, a Muslim "does not exist as an individual entity," and he must create his Islamic milieu in order to survive, by way of changing the world around him if he does not want to be changed by others.[30]

This would mean, in the Bosnian context, that only a religiously based society, on the model of religious associations (*jemaat*) is viable, and no provision is made for non-Muslims or for a multi-religious or multi-cultural society in its midst. (See the question of minorities below.)

The question of life in such a Muslim community is left unclear. On the one hand, the manifesto assures the "equality of all men"[31] and discards divisions and groupings according to race or class. But, if man's value is determined according to one's "integrity, and spiritual and ethical value,"[32] and these noble qualities are grounded in Islamic creed and value system, then only if one is a good Muslim can he be considered worthy. This is all the more so when the concept of the *ummet*, the universal congregation of all Muslims is taken as the "supra-nationality of the Muslim community," and Islam and Pan-Islamism define its boundaries: "Islam determines its internal and Pan-Islamism its external relations," because, "Islam is its ideology and Pan-Islamism its politics."[33] By Islam, the author means certain limitations on private property in order to ensure a fair distribution of wealth based on *Qur`an*ic precepts. The restoration of *Zekat* (paying of alms, one of the Five Pillars of the Faith) to the status of a public obligation as of old, and the enforcement of the *Qur`an*ic prohibition of collecting interest, are seen as the instruments to achieve social justice.[34]

Izetbegovic, in intending to establish the "Republican principle," namely that power should not be inherited, defeats his purpose by positing at the same time the *Qur`an*ic "recognition of the absolute authority of Allah, which means the absolute non-recognition of any other omnipotent authority," for "any submission to a creature which implies unsubmission to the Creator is not permissible."[35] This, of course, would have a direct ramification on the entire question of sovereignty, democracy, authority, and power. In this scheme, the idea of the inviolability of the individual is totally rejected, as it is made clear that in statements of equality of all men notwithstanding, and "irrespective of man's merits" he must submit to the Islamic order where there is a "synthesis of absolute authority (in terms of the program) and of absolute democracy (relative to the individual)."[36] It takes a lot of intellectual acrobatics to extricate the meaning of this "absolute democracy" that is strapped to the "absolute authority" of the divine *Qur`an*ic message under which the believer is expected to operate. For, while the author subscribes to the idea that all men, including the prophet, are fallible, and worshiping them is a "kind of idolatry," he assigns "all glory and praise to Allah alone, because Allah alone can judge the merits of men."[37] This, of course, would render any process of election between men impossible, and anyone who reaches a position of authority can only gain legitimacy if he submits to the "absolute authority" of the *Qur`an*ic teachings.

Part of this brand of democracy is insinuated to us when the author suggests that in his envisaged Islamic order the mass media "should be controlled by people of unquestionable Islamic moral intellectual authority. Perverts and degenerates should not be allowed to lay their hands on these media . . . and use them to transmit the senselessness and emptiness of their own lives to others. What can we expect if people receive one message from the mosque and a totally opposite one from the TV relay?"[38] The author does not spell out the criteria to judge the "emptiness and senselessness" of journalists under his regime, nor does he explain how he, or anyone else, can judge any person when all judgment is left to Allah. But he dares, under the heading of "Freedom of Conscience,"[39] to suggest all those limitations on the media, which would certainly make them anything but free, the protestations of the author notwithstanding.[40]

While the statement that "there can be no Islamic order without independence and freedom" may still sound plausible, in view of the Islamic regimes of Iran and Saudi Arabia, it is vice versa, namely that "there can be no independence and freedom without Islam"[41] which seems a bit presumptuous by any stretch of the imagination. For that would mean that the freest and most democratic nations of the world are in fact deprived of freedom and independence as long as they do not see the light of Islam. Unless, of course, he means that the idea applies only to Muslim peoples. In that case, the author argues, only if the Muslims assert Islamic thought in everyday life can they achieve spiritual and political liberation. Moreover, he claims that the legitimacy of the ruler in any Islamic nation will always depend on the extent of the ruler's commitment to Islam, short of which he turns for support to foreigners who maintain him in power.[42] Conversely, if he acts according to Islamic requirements, he thereby achieves the true democracy by consensus which is inherent in Islam and which alone makes violence redundant.[43] But the road to this utopian state of affairs is not obtained in "peace and tranquility, but in unrest and challenge."[44] That means that like other Muslim fundamentalist movements which promise their constituencies sweat and blood, and they earn credibility and appeal in so doing, the Islamic Declaration under discussion treads the same road to contrast with the empty promises of rulers in the Islamic world who make sweeping pledges of peace and prosperity but are unable to deliver.

Now comes the problematic issue of the relations between the Muslim host culture and minority guest cultures under the Islamic order. The manifesto provides religious freedom and "protection" to the minorities, "provided they are loyal," something that smacks of the traditional Muslim attitude to the *dhimmi* (protected people) under its aegis. The interesting aspect of all this is that when the situation is reversed, namely Muslim minorities dwelling in non-Muslim lands, their loyalty is made conditional on their religious freedom, not the other way around. Moreover, even under such conditions, the Muslims are committed to carry out all their obligations to the host community "with the exception of those that are detrimental to the Muslims."[45] The question remains unanswered as to who is to determine what is detrimental to Islam, and when and where. Assuming that the status of Muslim minorities would depend on "the strength and reputation of the Islamic world community," it would mean two things:

1. There was a possibility, in Izetbegovic's thinking, that the Muslims of Bosnia would remain a minority. Indeed, their rate is about 40 percent of the total population (and growing, due to higher birth-rate), and if the Catholic Croats and Orthodox Serbs of Bosnia should gang up against them (something quite unlikely), this manifesto still provides them with a chance for survival.

2. In either case, the Bosnian Muslims are counting on the intervention of the world Muslim community, something that was to be corroborated during the Bosnia and then the Kosovo wars.

Again, like the Hamas and other branches of the Muslim brotherhood, this manifesto proclaims the primacy of education and preaching, in order to conquer the hearts of the people before power, a prerequisite of the Islamic order, is conquered. "We must be preachers first and then soldiers,"[46] is the motto of the manifesto. Force to take over power will be applied "as soon as Islam is morally and numerically strong enough, not only to overthrow the non-Islamic rule, but to develop the new Islamic rule," because "to act prematurely is equally dangerous as to be late in taking the required action."[47] The author is confident that this can be done, because "history is not only a story of constant changes, but also of the continual realization of the impossible and the unexpected."[48] The model for the new Islamic order, which the manifesto puts on the pedestal, is Pakistan, the Muslim state that, in spite of its many deficiencies, remains the "great hope" of Izetbegovic.[49]

Under the heading "Christianity and Judaism," the manifesto determines the future relationships of the envisaged new Islamic order with those two faiths, which the author considers "the two foremost religions" and the "major systems and doctrines outside the sphere of Islam."[50] Nonetheless, the author distinguishes between Jesus and the Church. The former, he says, in line with *Qur'an*ic teachings, is part of divine revelation while the latter, as embodied in the Inquisition, is abhorrent to his heart. At the same time, however, as is the normative Islamic wont, he accuses Christianity of "distorting certain aspects" of the divine message while accusing the Church of intolerance.[51] Similarly, he differentiates between

Jews and their national movement — Zionism — idealizing the times when they lived under Islam, but he totally rejects their plea for independence and nationhood.[52] So, as long as the Jews are submissive and stateless in their *dhimmi* status within the Islamic state he envisages, all is well, but to dare to declare independence and stand up to the Islamic world — that is unforgivable. He claims that Jerusalem is not only a Palestinian city but first of all a Muslim one, and therefore he warns the Jews, who "have created themselves" the conflict with the Arab regimes (not the Arab or the Muslim people), that a prolonged war will be waged against them by Muslims until they release "every inch of captured land." He threatens that "any trade-offs or compromises which might call into question these elementary rights of our brothers in Palestine will be treason which can destroy even the very system of moral values underpinning our world."[53]

In sum, this passionate message of Izetbegovic, based on the *Qur`an* and the revival of Islam, addresses the universal congregation of all Muslims, and strives to establish an Islamic world order based on *Qur`an*ic precepts. The idea of nationalism, any nationalism, is totally rejected in favor of the Islamic republic, which alone can respond to the challenges of the modern world and restore to Islam its glory and preponderance. Like the platform of the Hamas and other fundamentalists, the text of *Qur`an* rather than the commentaries of the Muslim establishment, provides the rationale for the cultural, social, and political revolution that the author proposes to undertake. Indeed, the profuse citations from the Holy Book that we find interspersed throughout the text of the Declaration bear witness to *Qur`an*ic hegemony in the thought and plans of the author. Moreover, by positing the listed principles as deriving from the Holy Scripture, namely the eternal and immutable Word of Allah, the document creates the impression of a divinely guided program, which is not given to debate or consideration.

While in Serbia in 1998 and 1999, when I met academics, politicians from the opposition, and journalists who did not hold much sympathy for their government, but were at the same time concerned about the revival of Islam in the Balkans, I was given more details about Izetbegovic and his Islamic activities. It is said that immediately after World War II, in the spring of 1946, as a member of the "Young Muslims," he, together with Omer Behmen (later vice president to SDA Party), and Dr. Shachirbay (father of Muhamed Shachirbay, the Bosnian ambassador to the UN), started an illegal magazine — the *Mujahid*, in which the following song was published:

> The earth throbs, the mountains quake,
> Our war cry resounds through the land.
> Heads held high, men old and young,
> In a holy *jihad* our salvation lies.
> **Chorus:** The time has come, onward brethren.
> Onward brethren, onward heroes,
> To the Jihad, to the Jihad let us go.
> Proudly the green banner flies,
> Close ranks beneath it in steel-like file.
> Let the brotherhood of Islam bind us,
> Let us scorn death and go to the battle.
> **Chorus:** The time has come, onward brethren. . . .
> With our war-cry "Allah Akbar,"
> Rot the old and corrupt world.
> For the joy and salvation of mankind,
> Boldly, heroes, let us go into battle!
> **Chorus:** The time has come, onward brethren. . . .

These themes are strikingly similar to those propagated in cassettes by the Hamas organization[54] to glorify the death for the cause of Islam in the course of jihad. They also strikingly form the same thinking which produced the Islamic Declaration analyzed above.

THE CONCEPT OF GREATER ALBANIA

During the turmoil which swept the Balkans on the eve of the Berlin Congress (1878), the Albanians, as an ethnic group, came up with the concept of including within their fledgling national entity all the Albanians of the Balkans, beyond the geographic boundaries of Albania itself. Being Muslims, the Albanians, like the Islamized Bosnians, enjoyed a privileged status in the Ottoman Empire. In 1878, the Albanian League was established in Prizren, which presented the Greater Albania plan. While the Albanians constituted the majority in the core areas of Albania proper, their proportion in Kosovo did not exceed 44 percent.[55] Like in the case of Bosnia where ethnicity was religion-bound, there could not exist an Orthodox Croat, nor a Catholic Serb, nor a Bosnian who was not Muslim.[56] So in Albania, Islamized Serbs, Greeks, and Bulgarians became *ipso facto* Albanians. In 1912, an attempt was made under Austro-Hungarian auspices to implement the idea, followed by another such attempt under the Italian fascists in 1941. The third attempt, initiated at the end of the 1990s as a result of the collapse of the Soviet Union and Yugoslavia, translated into tearing Kosovo, by now predominantly Albanian-Muslim, from Serbian sovereignty, following up on the Bosnian experience which had subtracted that province from Serbian-Yugoslavian hegemony.

The precedent of Bosnia, which had allowed in 1971, ironically under the Communist rule, the recognition of Bosnia's nationalism as Muslim, would now propel the ethnic Albanians to revive their Islamic heritage and claim their Muslim identity which *ipso facto* would justify their separation from the Serbs. At first, the awakening of the Albanians was undertaken along the ethno-national track. Prior to 1971, the break between Maoist Albania and Yugoslavia had occasioned the Albanian revolt in Kosovo (1968), but after the normalization of their relationships in 1971 the Albanians turned to cultural propaganda by peaceful, if subversive, means. Interestingly enough, like the Palestinians who are competing with Israel over their ancestral land by conveniently claiming that they are the descendants of the ancient Cana'anites who had preceded the Israelites on the land, the Albanians now advanced the claim that they inherited the ancient heritage of the Illyrians who were the original inhabitants of Kosovo.[57] This resulted in the Albanian rebellion of 1981, in which they demanded the status of a republic (no longer an autonomous region within Serbia, like Voivodina in the north), still within the six-republic Yugoslavian Federation. After the fall of communism in Albania, the new regime recognized in 1991 the self-declared Republic of Kosovo, and its head, Ibrahim Rugova, opened an office in Tirana.[58]

The disintegration of Yugoslavia by necessity revived the old dreams of a Greater Albania, which now eyed not only Kosovo, but also parts of Macedonia, Greece, Serbia, and Montenegro, where an Albanian population had settled over the years. The rising of

Muslim consciousness in the Balkans, after the Bosnian precedent, and the spreading of the Izetbegovic doctrine, now acts as a catalyst to draw together, under the combined banners of Greater Albania and Islam, all the Albanian populations of that region. In 1992, Albania joined the Conference of Islamic Countries, and it has been working to attract support of other Islamic countries to the Greater Albania plan, actually presenting itself as "the shield of Islam" in the Balkans.[59] It has been noted that while the Albanian demographic explosion in Kosovo, which has allowed them to predominate and demand secession, has not taken place in Albania itself,[60] perhaps an indication, as in Palestine and Bosnia, that the "battle of the womb" heralded by nationalists and Muslim fundamentalists, is not merely a natural growth but may be also politically motivated.

CONCLUSIONS

While in Serbian national terms the loss of Kosovo to the Albanians is equivalent in their eyes to Israel losing Jerusalem,[61] in international terms, the importance of this issue lay in the emerging pattern of the re-Islamization of the Balkans. True, the immediate concern of the Serbs is to what extent can a minority which achieves a local majority within their sovereign territory, demand the right of secession, especially when that demand is backed up by irredentist claims of a neighboring country. If that should be the case, then entire areas of the United States populated by Mexican-Americans, or parts of Israel where the local Arab population has achieved the majority, or the Kurdish populations of Turkey, Iraq, Iran, and Syria, or Arab enclaves in France, could raise the question of their autonomy and ask for their right to secede. For that matter, the Croats and Serbs of Bosnia could also revert to their initial demand at the outset of the Bosnian crisis to merge with their respective national entities. The larger concern, however, is to what extent the settling patterns of the Albanians can disrupt the physical continuity between the major Christian powers of the Balkans: Greece, Macedonia, Serbia, Bulgaria, and Romania; or, more importantly, whether a new continuity of Islamic settlement, from Bosnia through Kosovo and now southern Serbia, can link up with the Muslims of Bulgaria to achieve a geographical continuum with Muslim Turkey. In view of the Islamic Declaration analyzed above, which does not accept the present state of affairs in the Balkans and Turkey, and makes provision for an Islamic revolution to redress the situation to its liking, the Bosnia and Kosovo events seem only to be an ominous precursor of things to come.

These concerns have been raised due to the perverse link that has been established in real politics between Muslim fundamentalist powers like Saudi Arabia and Iran who seek to further the penetration of Islam into the Balkans, against Western interests, and the inexplicable rush of that same West to facilitate that penetration which is already turning against it. From the Muslim point of view, things are easy and goals are clear: to ensure the continuity of a Muslim presence from Turkey into Europe, namely to revitalize a modern version of the Ottoman Empire. True, the present successive governments of Ankara are committed to secularism of the Kemalist brand under the guardianship of the military. But as the Erbakan experience has shown (1996–1998), when democracy is allowed to operate, then the Algerian scenario may have the upper hand and an Islamist government may be elected to power that may also opt for the strengthening of the Islamic factor in Europe. Muslim fundamentalists across the world, from the Uighurs of Chinese Turkestan to the Arabs of the Middle East; from the Mujahidin of Afghanistan to the disciples of Izetbegovic in the Balkans, do not hide their designs to act for the realization of this new world order.

A summon by the Saudi scholar Ahmed ibn-Nafi` of Mecca, which was circulated to all centers of the Pan-Islamic Salvation Committee at the outset of the conflict in Bosnia, states in no uncertain terms:

> Let it be known, brothers, that life in this ephemeral world differs immensely from the life lived in keeping with the principles of *jihad*. . . . Fortunate is he whom Allah enlightens in this life . . . by waging a *jihad* for Him. Following Allah's instructions, the Pan-Islamic Salvation Committee has devised a holy plan to clean the world of unbelievers. We entrust you to see to the imminent establishment of the Caliphate in the Balkans, because the Balkans are the path to the conquest of Europe.[62]

This appeal was by no means an isolated case. In the same month of August 1992, a poster was plastered on walls in Sarajevo, signed by the spiritual head of the Iranian Revolution, Imam Khamenei, which accused the Western nations of not preventing the genocide against the Muslims of Bosnia, due to their innate hostility to Islam, and urged them to clear the way for Iranian Mujahidin and other young Muslims to wage the war and "drive the Serbs from this Islamic country."[63] In Zagreb, which at the time was the ally of the Muslims against the Serbs, a local journal echoed that call:

> The Muslim nation in Iran began its revolution with "Allahu Akbar!" and succeeded. On the territory of Yugo-slavia, the Serbs could not tolerate a Muslim [Izetbegovic] as the president of Bosnia-Herzegovina. Their only rival is Islam and they fear it. The time is approaching when Islam will be victorious.[64]

While the traces of Iranian and other Muslim volunteers' *jihad* in Bosnia were rife, Western reactions seemed more and more obtuse. Except for the theory that the United States had to please Saudi Arabia as it had done during the Gulf War when it desisted from occupying Baghdad, other explanations range from sheer misunderstanding of the dangers that Islamic fundamentalism poses to the West to cold-blooded commercial gains in the short run which obscure the long-term strategic considerations. If that quandary raised many eyebrows in the West during the Bosnia War, where the United States and European powers supported Bosnia at the detriment of the Serbs, so much more so for the intransigent, costly, and destructive military intervention of NATO in Kosovo. As it is known, war does not determine who is right, it only determines who is left. It is time to draw the balance of who is left and what is left from that war.

The "good guys" of NATO had set out, under the cover of a barrage of propaganda, to address the humanitarian problem of "ethnic cleansing," forgetting the "ethnic cleansing" that the Serbs had suffered over centuries in Bosnia and Kosovo. While accusing the Serbs of inflicting collective punishment on the entire Kosovar-Albanian population for the sins of the Kosovo Liberation Army, they have themselves destroyed the lives and livelihoods of millions of innocent Serbs, depriving them of bridges, potable water, supplies, municipal services, broadcasting stations, and what not. And all that while relentlessly repeating in their harrowing press briefings that they held no grudge against the Serbian people, only against their leader. The real questions for the horrors of that war were never raised by NATO, and certainly never answered: What has caused the mass uprooting of people from Kosovo, including Serbs? Was it only Serbian abuses against the Albanian population, or perhaps also the fear of people who were caught in the crossfire? Why were only the elderly, women, and children the ones who ran away to safety in refugee camps? Was it only because the Serbs callously imprisoned or exterminated able-bodied men, or perhaps because they were recruited into rebellious KLA troops who aided NATO's designs? Was Serbia encouraging or preventing ethnic cleansing? One day we were told that the refugees were pushed across the borders of Kosovo, another time we were told that they ran away by themselves, and yet another time we were assured that the Kosovars were prevented by the bad Serbs from crossing in order to serve as human shields. Who could take these inconsistencies seriously?

The havoc that was wreaked on Kosovo, far from settling the issue, on the contrary, aggravated it: the Serb population was almost totally forced out of the province, and those who stayed could only do so under the protection of the NATO or UN forces. Two months after they had "established order" there, a *New York Times* editorial had this to say about it:

> Kosovo remains lawless and violent. There are no local police, or judges. . . . NATO is doing an uneven and un-satisfactory job of preserving order. . . . Local thugs, rogue fighters of the Kosovo Liberation Army, and Albanian gangs slipping [from Albania] across the unpatrolled borders, have taken advantage of the law enforcement vacuum to terrorize the Serbian and Gypsy minorities and drive them from their homes. . . . The same violent elements also prey on Kosovar Albanians subjecting people to extortion, and potential political rivals and suspected collaborators with the previous Serbian authorities, to intimidation and murder. . . .

NATO must rethink its overly indulgent attitude toward the KLA, which has been permitted to postpone the deadline for surrendering heavy weapons and expects to see its former fighters included in the new local police forces.[65]

One year later, in July 2000, chaos seemed to be still prevailing, and the parties determined that the Kosovars want independence from Serbia, and the Serbs want to prevent it lest the Greater Albania plan comes to be implemented with the related instability in Macedonia and other areas inhabited by Albanians.[66] The UN troops are supposed to impose a "substantial autonomy" for the Kosovars under Serbian sovereignty, but that does not seem to be in the making, but Albanians who live in Serbia Proper may want to draw UN troops across the border. Reports from the spot identify a "Kosovo-wide problem of attacks on [Serb and other] minorities, harassment, intimidation, and persecution" and the "vicious Albania-based mafia that is spreading crime."[67] The irony in all this is that while the problem of Bosnia remains unsettled, with the Serb and Croat entities there entertaining their hopes to join their motherlands, and the Kosovo issue festering as an open wound, NATO finds itself backing, or at least seeming indifferent to the Islamic takeover in the heart of Europe.

Robert Cohen-Tanugi, in his series of articles which has drawn world attention,[68] proposes the thesis that the USA is basically interested in promoting Islamic radical states to create the "Green Belt," loyal to it, around Russia and China, and its subsidiary, the "Green Diagonal" designed to link Central Europe with Turkey, in order to restore the power and hegemony of this pivot of American strategy to its Ottoman times. That is the reason, he claims, for American determination to advance the cause of Islamic revival in Bosnia and Kosovo and, conversely, to eliminate nationalist Serbia which stands as the major obstacle on that road. However, rising fundamentalist Islam, which is inimical to the United States in particular and Western culture in general, will not necessarily play the American game and may turn against its benefactors sooner and with more vengeance that either the United States or its European allies suspect.

Endnotes

1 See Lillian Craig-Harris, *China Considers the Middle East* (London: Tauris, 1993), p. 275.

2 Xinhua News Agency, February 20, 1990.

3 *Patterns of Global Terrorism*, The U.S. Department of State, April 1998.

4 Policy Watch No. 296, p. 3, 1998, The Washington Institute, citing reports by the *New York Times* and the *Washington Times*.

5 Ibid.

6 For the details of the *dhimmi* status within the Empire, see Hans Majer, "The Functioning of a Multi-Ethnic and Multi-Religious State: The Ottoman Empire," in Slavenko Terzic, editor, *Islam, the Balkans and the Great Powers (XIV-XX Centuries)*, Vol. 14 (Belgrade: The Serbian Academy of Science, 1997), p. 61 ff.

7 Ibid., p. 63.

8 Bat Ye'or, *The Decline of Eastern Christianity under Islam: From Jihad to Dhimmitude* (London: Associated University Presses, 1996), p. 132.

9 Ibid., p. 176–177. For documents about the inequities in Bosnia against the Christian population, see also p. 421–427.

10 Terzic, *Islam, the Balkans and the Great Powers,* p. 67–68.

11 Vrban Todorov, "The Federalist Idea as a Means for Preserving the Integrity of the Ottoman Empire," in Terzic, *Islam, the Balkans and the Great Powers,* p. 293–296.

12 Jean-Paul Bled, "La Question de Bosnie-Hercegovine dans La Revue Des Deux Mondes," in Terzic, *Islam, the Balkans and the Great Powers,* p. 330, citing *Revue ded Deux Mondes,* Paris, Vol II, No 1 (1876): p. 237–254.

13 Dusan Batakovuc, "La Bosnie-Herzegovine: le System des Alliances," in Terzic, *Islam, the Balkans and the Great Powers,* p. 335–343.

14 Ibid., p. 343–344.

15 Ibid., p. 346.

16 Ibid.

17 A. Popovic, "La Politique Titists envers les Religions et ses Consequences," in M. Bodzemir, *Islam, et Laicite: Approches Globales et Regionales*, (Paris: Harmattan, 1996), p. 98–102.

18 Raphael Israeli, "The Charter of Allah: the Platform of the Hamas," in Y. Alexander, editor, *The Annual of Terrorism, 1988-89* (Nijhoff, the Netherlands, 1990), p. 99–134.

19 Alija Izetbegovic, *Islamska Deklaracija* (the Islamic Declaration), introduction, p. 1–2.

20 Ibid., p. 2.

21 Ibid.

22 Ibid., p. 3.

23 Ibid., p. 4.

24 Ibid.

25 Ibid., p. 12.

26 Ibid., p. 14–15.

27 Ibid., p. 16–17.
28 Ibid., p. 19.
29 Ibid., p. 20.
30 Ibid.
31 Ibid., p. 26.
32 Ibid., p. 27.
33 Ibid., p. 27–28.
34 Ibid., p. 29–30.
35 Ibid., p. 30.
36 Ibid., p. 31.
37 Ibid.
38 Ibid., p. 33.
39 Ibid.
40 Ibid., p. 34.
41 Ibid., p. 35.
42 Ibid.
43 Ibid., p. 35–36.
44 Ibid., p. 37.
45 Ibid., p. 40.
46 Ibid., p. 45.
47 Ibid., p. 45–46.
48 Ibid., p. 46.
49 Ibid., p. 48.
50 Ibid., p. 55–57.
51 Ibid., p. 55–56.
52 Ibid., p. 56–57.
53 Ibid., p. 57.
54 See, for example, R. Israeli, "Islamikaze and Their Significance," in *Terrorism and Political Violence,* vol. 9, no. 3, (Autumn 1997): p. 112–113.
55 Jovan Canak, editor, *Greater Albania: Concepts and Possible Consequences* (Belgrade: The Institute of Geo-Political Studies, 1998), p. 8–11.
56 Jens Reuter, "From Religious Community to Nation: The Ethnogenesis of the Bosnian Muslims," in Terzic, *Islam, the Balkans and the Great Powers,* p. 617–623.
57 Canak, *Greater Albania: Concepts and Possible Consequences,* p. 42–43.
58 Ibid.
59 Ibid., p. 47–48.
60 Ibid., p. 49.
61 Duro Fuletic, "Consequences of a Possible Creation of 'Greater Albania,' " *Review of International Affairs,* vol. L, no. 1085–6 (October–November 1999): p. 23.
62 The handwritten Arabic text of the epistle of August 17, 1992, appears in Hadzivukovic et al., *Chronicle of Announced Death,* p. 52.
63 The text of the summons, with Khamenei's picture, appears in Serbo-Croat, ibid., p. 54.

64 Vecernui List, Zagreb, August 9, 1992.

65 *New York Times,* editorial, August 6, 1999.

66 See report by Therese Raphael, *Wall Street Journal,* July 7, 2000.

67 See Flora Lewis, "The Kosovo Mission of the UN Is Left to Fail," *Herald Tribune,* March 10, 2000, p. 8.

68 Robert Cohen-Tanugi, in *Diaspora/Le Lien,* no. 112 of July 30, 1999; no. 117 of October 22, 1999; and no. 120 of December 3, 1999.

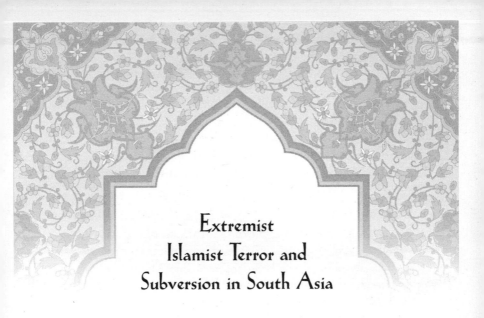

Extremist
Islamist Terror and
Subversion in South Asia

K.P.S. Gill and Ajai Sahni

In the Indian State of Jammu and Kashmir (J&K), 3,288 persons were killed in the year 2000, making this by far the bloodiest year since the beginning of the campaign of terror that seeks secession of the Muslim majority state from the Indian Union. Within India, Kashmir is perceived as a theater of a proxy war launched by Pakistan to secure the territories it has failed to seize through open warfare on three occasions in the past.[1] After the nuclear tests at Pokhran and Chagai in 1998, Western analysts saw it as a potential flashpoint for a nuclear confrontation between India and Pakistan, and these fears were heightened during the "undeclared war" in the Kargil sector of J&K in 1999, when the Pakistani leadership issued veiled threats of an exercise of the "nuclear option."[2] Increasingly, however, the international focus has been shifting to the burgeoning danger of extremist Islamic terrorism located in Pakistan and directed against India.

The tragic toll of life in Kashmir is certainly the most visible manifestation of the threat of extremist Islamist terrorism in the South Asian region at this juncture, but is far from an adequate index of its magnitude. The danger is equally great, and perhaps more urgent within Pakistan itself, as it becomes increasingly uncertain whether its leadership is "master or victim"[3] of the militant fundamentalism it fueled for its campaign against the Russian presence in Afghanistan through the 1980s, and continues to stoke in pursuit of its strategic ambitions in Kashmir. Ahmed Rashid notes the devastating potential of Pakistan's flirtations with "fundamentalist" mass mobilization:

> In the late 1990s the repercussions were much more pervasive, undermining all the institutions of the state . . . law and order broke down as Islamic militants enacted their own laws and a new breed of anti-Shia Islamic radicals, who were given sanctuary by the *Taliban*, killed hundreds of Pakistani Shias between 1996 and 1999. This sectarian bloodshed is now fueling a much wider rift between Pakistan's *Sunni* majority and *Shi`a* minority and undermining relations between Pakistan and Iran. At the same time, over 80,000 Pakistani Islamic militants have trained and fought with the *Taliban* since 1994. They form a hard core of Islamic activists, ever ready to carry out a similar *Taliban*-style Islamic revolution in Pakistan.[4]

Out of this unstable vortex, the "warriors of (extremist) Islam," the *mujahideen*, reach out into the fratricidal confrontations of the Balkans; into the new and volatile realities of Central Asia, and beyond, into the peripheries of China; from Pakistan, through Kashmir, into every theater of existing or emerging conflict across the Indian sub-continent; and far into southeast Asia — wherever "Muslim grievances" and "oppression" can be discovered or invented, and wherever there is violence to be exploited to further their encompassing vision of an all-conquering Islam.

Terror is at the heart of this vision, conceived by the ideologues of extremist Islam, not merely as a transient tactic, but as the essential objective of their "war to advance God's purpose on earth." Terror struck into the hearts of the enemies is not only a means; it is an end in itself. Once a condition of terror has been planted in the opponent's heart, hardly anything is left to be achieved. It is the point where the means and the end meet and merge. Terror is not a means of imposing decision upon the enemy [*sic*]; it is *the decision we wish to impose upon him.*[5]

Consequently, it is not surprising that the idea of a "geographical shift of the locus of terror from the Middle East to South Asia"[6] is being increasingly and vigorously propounded, identifying Afghanistan, Pakistan, and Kashmir as the new loci and primary sources of extremist Islamic militancy. There are, however, some difficulties with this notion. The first and more obvious is the fact that there is no evidence of any sudden or abrupt "shift," or a radical discontinuity in the situation at or around the time this thesis was propounded. Afghanistan's spiral into chaos has been an inexorable fact for over a decade, as has Pakistan's complicity and steady decline. Even a cursory glance at fatalities in Kashmir would confirm, moreover, that terrorism has been at comparable levels in this theater for over a decade.[7]

More significantly, however, it is dangerous to focus inordinately on the transient geographical location or concentrations of terrorist incidents, activities, and movements, to the exclusion of their ideological and material sources, their state sponsors, or their intended targets and proclaimed goals. The error here is the belief that the threat of Islamic terrorism is contained within the regions of its most visible manifestation. Extremist Islam must be recognized for its essential character as an ideology, and terrorism as a method that it accepts and justifies. A method will be adopted wherever it is perceived to have acceptable probabilities of success. An ideology extends wherever it has believers. These are the actual limits or foci of extremist Islamic terrorism.

A closer analysis would indicate that it is more accurate to speak of the *spread or expansion of the sphere of terrorism,* rather than any dramatic "shift." Indeed, as terrorists and their state sponsors secure even limited successes in one region, their methods are adopted in others, threatening an ever-widening spectrum of nations and cultures. It is now increasingly clear that no nation in the world is entirely free of the threat from extremist Islamist terrorism — and this includes not only the affluent, or "decadent," as the Islamist would have it, West, but also Muslim majority "Islamic" nations that do not conform to the extremist Islamist's notion of his faith and its practices. The extremist Islamist vision is not limited to its current sphere of militancy, or to the economic and political jockeying for control of Central Asia that some "Great Game" theorists believe, but to God's "universal empire." "The world is divided into opposing forces,"[8] Altaf Gauhar insists, adding that, "there is no common ground between secularism and Islam." Allah Buksh Brohi is even more explicit:

> Many Western scholars have pointed their accusing fingers at some of the . . . verses in the *Qur`an* in order to contend that the world of Islam is in a state of perpetual struggle against the non-Muslims. As to them, it is sufficient answer to make, if one were to point out, that the defiance of God's authority by one who is His slave exposes that slave to the risk of being held guilty of treason and such a one, in the perspective of Islamic law, is indeed to be treated as a sort of that cancerous growth on that organism of humanity, which has been created "Kanafsin Wahidatin" that is, like one, single, indivisible self. It thus becomes necessary to remove the cancerous mal-formation even if it be by surgical means (if it would not respond to other treatment), in order to save the rest of Humanity. . . . The idea of Ummah of Muhammad, the prophet of Islam, is incapable of being realized within the framework of territorial states, much less made an enduring basis of *viewing* the world as having been polarized between the *world of Islam* and *the world of war.* Islam, in my understanding, does not subscribe to the concept of the territorial state.[9]

The "surgical" removal of the "cancerous malformation" that is the non-Islamic world, is what the Islamist terrorists believe they are engaged in.

ISLAM IN SOUTH ASIA

South Asia comprises the largest concentration of Muslims in the world, with over 395 million people professing Islam as their

faith. Indeed, India has the second largest population of Muslims
— after Indonesia — for any country: nearly 142 million.

Countries	Population	Muslims Absolute Number	Muslims % of Population
Bangladesh	129,194,224	114,078,499	88.3%
Bhutan	2,005,222	100,261	5%
India	1,014,003,817	141,960,534	14%
Nepal	24,702,119	741,064	3%
Pakistan	141,553,775	137,307,162	97%
Sri Lanka	19,238,575	1,346,700	7%
Total	1,330,697,732	395,534,220	29.72%

Total and Muslim populations of South Asian countries[10]

As a region, South Asia has a long history, both of communal
confrontation and violence, on the one hand, and of co-existence
within an eclectic culture that has accepted differences, on the other.
This dualism is ingrained in the unique and diverse set of practices
and beliefs that comprise Indian Islam. There is, consequently, a clear
note of caution that must be sounded here. There has been a long
and widely acknowledged process of the demonization of Islam over
the years — indeed, perhaps over the centuries. John Esposito rightly
warns against "the temptation to view Islam through the prism of
religious extremism and terrorism," and identifies the "demonization of a great religious tradition due to the perverted actions of a
minority of dissident and distorted voices" as "the real threat."[11]

The total strength of extremist Islamic terrorists in India would
number a few thousand in a population of 142 million. The number
of those who sympathize with their cause would certainly be many
times greater, and those who are ambivalent in their responses
could be a significant proportion of the total population. The fact,
however, remains that even the sum of all these would only be a
very small fraction of those who seek to live in peace, within the

culture of coexistence that has become the essence of the Indian *Weltanschauung*.

This is not the case with India alone. Even in Pakistan, the country marked by the most rabid and widespread extremism in this region, the constituency of militant Islam is small in proportion to the total population, and this has repeatedly been borne out in the occasional elections that have been held in that country between its extended periods of military rule. Despite decades of military patronage, a continuous flow of governmental and international funding, and a political discourse dominated by Islam, the electoral performance of religious "fundamentalist" political parties, the *Jamaat-e-Islami* (JEI), the *Jamaat-e-Ulema-e-Islam* (JUI) and the *Jamaat-e-Ulema Pakistan* (JUP), has been dismal. In 1988, they won 11 seats out of 207 in the National Assembly, claiming a mere 6.6 percent of the vote. In 1990, they slipped down to 10 seats, with 5.4 percent of the vote. In 1993, the Pakistan Islamic Front (PIF), headed by the JEI, bagged 3 seats, and electoral support for all religious parties was a bleak 3 percent. *The JEI and the JUP boycotted the 1997 elections, and two seats were returned in the National Assembly to the JUI (Fazlur Rahman faction) that participated.*

This said, it must also be emphasized in the strongest terms possible that moderate Islam is, today, under deep, penetrating, and sustained attack in every concentration of Muslim populations throughout south Asia, and there is a "hardening" of beliefs that may lend itself to the extremist *jihad* in an uncertain future. The demonization of Islam is loudly protested, both by neutral scholars and by the apologists for extremist Islam. But there is a neglect of an even more vicious process of the demonization of all other faiths and nations among the people of Islam — and this goes beyond the "Great Satan," America, or the "Brahminical conspiracy" of "Hindustan," or the visceral anti-Semitism of the Arabs, to embrace all *Kafirs* or non-Muslims, and also all Muslims who do not conform to the perverse vision of extremist Islam. There is a profound ideology of hatred that is being fervently propagated through the institutions of Islam, particularly the *madrassas* or religious schools and seminaries that are proliferating rapidly across South Asia, and it is winning many ardent converts. As stated before, these are still a minority among south Asia's Muslims; but this is a vocal, armed, well supported, extremely violent and growing minority. The majority, by contrast, has tended to passivity and conciliation, and there is little present evidence of the courage of conviction or the will for any moderate Islamic resistance to the rampage of extremist Islam.

THE WEB OF TERROR: EROSION AND ENCIRCLEMENT

The primary focus and target of the armies of *mujahideen*, and their suicidal hard core, the *fidayeen*, who pour out of the *madrassas* and Pakistani terrorist training camps, at present, is the Indian State of Jammu and Kashmir (J&K). The leadership of the terrorist movement in J&K passed out of the hands of local militants, and to groups created by and based in Pakistan as far back as in 1993, when the most powerful terrorist group indigenous to the state, the Jammu & Kashmir Liberation Front (JKLF) led by Yasin Malik, chose to give up arms and seek a "political solution" to its grievances. The JKLF still demands Kashmiri "independence," and is strongly opposed to any amalgamation with Pakistan. The Pakistan-based groups, quite naturally, are far more amenable to a merger with that country.

Terrorist groupings enjoyed substantial mass support, particularly in the Kashmir Valley,[12] as long as the movement for secession remained indigenous. Progressively, however, a process of disillusionment with the activities of Pakistan-sponsored militants has combined with exhaustion to diminish this base, and terrorism is now sustained purely on inputs — ideologies, material, and increasing numbers of men — from across the border. Currently, the most active terrorist groups in the state maintain headquarters in Pakistan, and include the *Hizb-ul-Mujahideen* (HuM),[13] linked to the JEI in Pakistan; *Lashkar-e-Toiba* (LeT), the armed wing of the *Markaz-ad-Da`awa-wal-Irshad*; the *Harkat-ul-Jehad-e-Islami* (HuJI) and the *Harkat-ul-Mujahideen* (formerly the *Harkat-ul-Ansar*), linked to the JUI, the Pakistan *Tablighi Jamaat* and to the *Hizb-e-Islami* of Afghanistan; *al Badr*; and the recently formed *Jaish-e-Muhammad* (JeM). There are another score of minor and dormant groupings, also located in Pakistan. The umbrella *Muttahida Jihad* Council coordinates the activities of 13 of the most prominent terrorist factions (14 till the HuM was expelled for declaring a brief unilateral cease-fire in July 2000).[14]

The years 1997, 1998, and the first half of 1999 had seen a gradual decline in violence and fatalities in J&K, but there was a radical escalation after the Kargil War of May–July 1999. The trends underwent a further deterioration after two cease-fires. The first was announced unilaterally by the Hizb-ul-Mujahiddeen in July 2000, and the second, again unilaterally, by the Indian Prime Minister, A.B. Vajpayee, in November 2000. Also, the possibility of an emerging peace process threatened the entrenched interests and ideological ambitions of the extremist Islamist groups in Pakistan, and of their official sponsors there. A total of 26,226 persons have died in this conflict between 1988 and 2000. These include 10,285 civilians, 12,375 terrorists, and 2,566 security force (SF) personnel. Among the civilian fatalities, 8,712 (nearly 85 percent) have been Muslims.[15]

Significantly, the proportion of foreign mercenaries and *mujahideen* involved in the military activities in the state has been steadily rising, from a mere 6 percent in 1992 to an estimated 55 percent today.[16] A majority of these are drawn from Pakistan and Pakistan-occupied Kashmir (PoK). Also, some "Afghan Alumni"[17] and terrorists from Afghanistan and at least 11 other countries have been identified in Kashmir. The number of foreign terrorists killed in J&K has risen steadily since 1991, when their activities were first noticed in the state, and particularly after 1993, when the main indigenous militant group, the JKLF, came overground.

The conflict in Kashmir has been substantially documented in the context of Pakistan's strategy and "overriding interest . . . to achieve internal security by provoking instability among its neighbors."[18] There is, however, comparatively little understanding of the extremist or pan-Islamic agenda in the rest of South Asia, and of its integral links to the strategies and tactics that prepared the ground for terrorism in Kashmir.

As with much of South Asia, the culture and religious practices of the Muslims of Kashmir had little in common with the rigid and distorted version of *Wahabi* Islam emanating from Saudi Arabia that dominates contemporary extremist Islamists. Kashmiri Islam was steeped in the mysticism and values of the devotional *Sufi* order, and the Kashmir Valley was viewed as a unique and inspirational example of secular values at the time of partition and independence, and in the decades that followed. The emergence of terrorism in the state was preceded by decades of religious mobilization and reorientation centered primarily in the mosques in the valley. When terror broke out in the late 1980s, it was the mosques and the *madrassas* that provided the motivation, the moral sanction, and the initial impetus, not only to the violence, but to the near complete ethnic cleansing of the valley of its Kashmiri *Pandit* minority.[19] It is interesting that, among the priority targets of the terrorists was the network of secular schools, most of which were shut down under threats, especially in rural areas, progressively forcing the children into the only surviving "educational" institution, the *madrassa* or "schools of hate" that created new "supply lines" for *jihad*.

There is, today, a sustained effort to replicate these processes of religious mobilization and an extremist Islamist reorientation throughout South Asia, albeit with mixed results. In India there have been several political factors and events contributing to higher levels of communal polarization. Nevertheless, general communal conflict as expressed in the incidence of communal riots has declined. Political parties are yet to abandon the electoral strategy of exploiting religious sentiments and insecurities, but the mass base and credibility of those who seek to do so has suffered steady erosion. Nevertheless, the intent and strategy of Pakistan's covert agencies and extremist religious groupings is increasingly apparent in a wide range of activities intended to provoke communal confrontations, engineer terrorist incidents, and recruit soldiers for a pan-Islamic *jihad* in pockets of Muslim populations across India. This is compounded by a process of "encirclement" and massive demographic shifts that deepen the danger, particularly along India's eastern borders.

During a three-day annual congregation of the members of the *Markaz-ad-Da`awa-wal-Irshad* at Muridke near Lahore on February 6, 2000, the *Amir* (head) of the *Markaz*, Hafiz Mohammad Saeed, declared that Kashmir was a "gateway to capture India" and that it was the aim of the *Markaz* and its military wing, the *Lashkar-e-Toiba*, to engineer India's disintegration. Saeed added that his organization's campaign in Hyderabad (Andhra Pradesh) and Junagadh (Gujarat) were among the highest priorities. Abdul Rahman Makki, the LET's ideologue, expanded on this theme, proclaiming that the group had opened a new unit in Hyderabad to liberate the Indian city from "un-Islamic Indian rule."[20] These declarations are, at once, an expression of the pan-Islamic ambitions shared by all extremist Islamist groups operating in the region, and a reiteration of Pakistan's larger strategy of destabilizing India beyond the scope of the supposed "core issue" of Kashmir.

Within this larger design was a series of 13 bomb blasts in various churches in Andhra Pradesh, Karnataka, and Goa between May and July 2000,[21] executed by an obscure Islamic sect created in 1924, the *Deendar Anjuman*. The *Anjuman* is headed by Zia-ul-Hassan, the son of its founder, who is based in Peshawar, Pakistan, where the sect goes by the name *Anjuman Hizbullah*. Hassan is also said to have floated a militant organization, the *Jamat-e-Hizb-ul-Mujahideen* in Pakistan, in order to "capture India and spread Islam." Intelligence sources indicate that Hassan is bankrolled by the ISI, and the Indian Union Home Minister stated in Parliament that investigation had established the fact that linkages existed between the *Deendar Anjuman* and Pakistan's covert intelligence agency.[22] Investigations have exposed a network of the *Anjuman*'s subversive activities extending across several small towns and urban centers, including Nuzvid, Atmakur, Kurukunda, Palem, Vijayawada, Khammam, and Nandyal in Andhra Pradesh; and Batakurki, Ramdurg, and Hubli in Karnataka.

On February 14, 1998, a series of 19 explosions left over 50 dead and more than 200 injured in the Coimbatore district of Tamil Nadu.[23] Investigations and subsequent arrests exposed the involvement of a wide network of extremist Islamist organization across South India, including the Indian Muslim, Mohammadi Mujahideen, the Tanzim, Islahul Muslimeen, the *Jihad* Committee in Tamil Nadu and the Islamic Sevak Sangh, subsequently banned and revived as the People's Democratic Party (PDP), headed by Abdul Nasser Madani.

By far the most dramatic serial blasts engineered by the ISI took place in Bombay on March 12, 1993. They revealed a unique pattern of operation that has gradually consolidated itself over the years, namely, the use of organized criminal networks to execute terrorist strikes. Nearly 1,800 kilograms of RDX and a large number of detonators and small arms had been smuggled through the west coast of India prior to these blasts that killed over 300 persons and targeted critical commercial infrastructure, including the country's largest stock exchange at Dalal Street. The explosions were executed by the notorious D-Company headed by Dawood Ibrahim. Ibrahim now lives in Karachi, and runs India's largest criminal empire through aides located outside India, and primarily in the Middle East.[24]

India's northeast is another interesting area of emerging Islamist militancy. In that area it has appeared along with major demographic shifts that hold significant dangers for the future. Illegal migration on a large scale across the border from Bangladesh is the most potent single factor in the destabilization of this region. In November 1998, the governor of Assam, Lt. Gen. (Ret.) S.K. Sinha, submitted a report to the Indian president in which this infiltration was estimated to encompass at least six million people. Most of this increase was concentrated in a few areas, thereby exerting a dramatic impact on local demography and, hence, on politics. According to the report, four districts of Assam — Dhubri, Goalpara, Barpeta, and Hailakandi — had been transformed into Muslim majority districts by 1991 as a result of this mass infiltration. Another two districts — Nagaon and Karimganj — have had a Muslim majority since 1998 and yet another district, Morigaon, is fast approaching this position.[25] This demographic destabilization, combined with widespread violence and political instability in the region, has created a unique recruiting ground for the Islamists, and there has been a veritable efflorescence of Muslim terrorist groups operating along India's borders with Bangladesh in the northeast. In Assam alone, there are over 15 terrorist groups operating under an Islamic banner,[26] and the ISI's role in funding and arming these groups has now been fairly well documented.[27]

Serial bombings and overt terrorist movements, however, cannot be a measure of the penetration that has been achieved by the extremist Islamists and their state sponsors. Large-scale acts of terror represent the culmination of years of preparation that are reflected in motivation, mobilization, and organizational development. Evidence of these processes is mounting throughout India, and is reflected in the number of fundamentalist and of subversive groups that exist, and the geographical spread of their activities. The most prominent of these include the *Jamaat-e-Islami Hind* (JEI Hind), the All India *Milli* Council (AIMC), All India *Jihad* Committee (AIJC), the People's Democratic Party (PDP, formerly the Islamic *Sewak Sangh*), All India Muslim Federation (AIMF), Muslim United Front (MUF), *Tamil Nadu Muslim Munnetra Kazhagam* (TNMMK), National Development Front (*Kerala*), *Tabligh Jamaat*, Students Islamic Movement of India (SIMI), Students Islamic Organizations (SIO), *Al Umma*, *Al Jihad*, and the Muslim *Sena Sanghathan*, *Ikhwan-ul-Muslameen*, *Islami Inqalabi Mahaz*, *Tanzim Isla-ul-Muslameen*, and the Minorities United Front, among others.

Each of these organizations runs one or more non-governmental organization (NGO), many of which have offices abroad. Very substantial funds are received, and a range of interactions, including frequent "*Tablighi* conferences" with foreign delegations, are organized. The flow of funds is primarily through what is known as *hawala* (illegal) channels, and while Pakistan largely defines the patterns of use and the beneficiaries, the preponderance of such transfers originate in Saudi Arabia, Kuwait, United Arab Emirates, Qatar, and Oman. Thus, very substantial transfers of foreign funds generated under the pretext of providing relief to the Coimbatore riot victims are believed to have been used for the Coimbatore blasts.

The range, volume, and persistence of such subversive activity throughout the country is a measure of Pakistan's tenacity and the intensity of the extremist Islamist vision more than it is of the impact these activities have had thus far on the larger Muslim community in India. The tragic loss of life, the wasted human and developmental resources, and the atmosphere of fear and suspicion that sporadic incidents of terrorism generate notwithstanding, India has the flexibility, the resilience, and the political space to absorb a significantly higher level of subversive and extremist Islamist activities than it has experienced thus far. Nevertheless, the sheer lethal quality of weaponry and explosives, the possibility of escalation to a new generation of chemical and biological weapons, and the inherent uncertainty of the politics of a complex society characterized by immense religious and cultural diversity, make the existing risks and levels of activity unacceptable.

These risks are even greater and less acceptable in countries where such space is wanting, where political instability is at higher levels, and where the roots of democracy are yet to take firm hold of the soil. Islamist subversion is more of a threat to the peace and stability of the regime in neighboring Bangladesh, where religious extremism has emerged as a major threat to the prevailing political order and to internal security. There are grave and immediate dangers to peace and stability in Bangladesh: the revival of the activities of the Jamaat-e-Islami, the return to Bangladesh and its politics of Pakistan-backed elements who collaborated closely with the genocidal campaign of 1971 in what was then East Pakistan,[28] the rising rhetoric of Islamic *Hukumat* (rule), and the deepening linkages between militant Bangladeshi groups and the extremist Islamists in Pakistan, Afghanistan, and West Asia. Here again, the pattern of funding, subversion, and mobilization through the mosque and the *madrassa* is clearly in evidence.

Prior to independence, there were 1,467 *madrassas* in Bangladesh. Their number has currently risen to over 6,500, with more than 90,000 teachers and about 1.8 million students. A large number of these institutions have been established as a result of massive foreign aid, primarily from Gulf countries, and largely unmediated by official channels. Bangladesh's *madrassas* are the chief recruiting ground for Islamic militant groups, including several that are linked to Pakistan and also to Osama bin Laden's *al-Qaʿidah*. The latter category includes the *Harkat-ul-Jehad-e-Islami*, which was established by Shawkat Osman, alias Sheikh Farid in 1992 with bin Laden's backing, and which has an estimated strength of about 15,000. The *Harkat* maintains six camps in the hilly areas of Chittagong, where the cadres are given arms training. Several hundred recruits have also been trained in Afghanistan. The cadres, recruited mainly from among students of various *madrassas*, style themselves as the "Bangladeshi *Taliban*." Reports suggest that religious fanatics supported by foreign aid are actively conspiring to establish "Islamic *hukumat*" by waging war and killing progressive intellectuals, as well as various minority groups and "heretical" sects, such as the *Ahmadiyas*.[29]

In addition to the JEI, the prominent fundamentalist Islamist political parties in Bangladesh include the Muslim League, *Tabligh*

Jamaat, Jamaat-e-Tulba, and *Jamaat-ul-Muderessin.* One significant pro-Iranian group, the Islamic *Shasantantra Andolan* (Movement for Islamic Constitution), is also active. The subversive activities of the ISI and foreign extremist Islamist agencies in Bangladesh increased radically after Sheikh Hasina's broadly secular *Awami* League came to power in June 1996, and this has contributed to an upsurge in militant and fundamentalist political activity. Superimposed over a history of military coups, politics dominated by the rhetoric of Islam, and increasing international linkages, including networks with insurgent groups operating in India's northeast, extremist Islamic militancy constitutes the most serious existing internal security threat in Bangladesh.

The security agencies of the infant democracy of Nepal are also being challenged by rising extremist Islamist activity, despite the fact that Muslims constitute a bare three percent of the population. At the present time, these activities are aimed primarily against India, but they are linked with organized criminal operations. Moreover, the destabilization of pockets of Muslim concentrations in the Terai region bordering India are a cause of increasing concern for Kathmandu. A succession of recent reports has documented increased activities of the ISI and by the Pakistan embassy in Kathmandu. Again, these activities involve strong organized criminal networks and prominent political leaders who target India and reinforce the Islamist agenda within Nepal.[30] The Muslim pockets of the Terai, especially Bardiya, Banke, Rupendehi, and the Parsa-Morang belt have seen increasing *"Tablighi"* activities, and the construction of mosques and *madrassas* with financial flows from Pakistan, often coming directly from the embassy in Kathmandu, from Saudi Arabia and from a range of pan-Islamic organizations. Over the past two decades, more than 275 mosques and *madrassas* have been built in the four districts of Rupandehi, Banke, Kapilvastu, and Bardiya alone. There are some 15 major *Tablighi*/fundamentalist organizations in Nepal, and at least five of these are well within the ambit of Pakistan's influence and control. These include the *Jamaat-e-Millat-e-Islamia*; the Nepal Islamic *Yuba Sangh*; the Nepal Muslim League; the Nepal Muslim *Ekta Sangh*; and the Democratic Muslim Welfare Association. Nepal is, consequently, emerging as an important "staging post" for Pakistan's strategy of erosion and encirclement against India, and is increasingly the preferred route for terrorist movements to various areas of low-intensity conflict in J&K and the northeast.

In Sri Lanka, the Muslim community and emerging fundamentalist forces have generally aligned themselves with the interests of the government. The island nation's Muslim population is mainly Tamil, but has been driven out of the ethnically cleansed northern areas controlled by the Liberation Tigers of *Tamil Eelam* (LTTE), and is now concentrated along the eastern coast, the northwest coast, Kandy, and suburban Colombo. Islamic fundamentalist mobilization in Sri Lanka began after a succession of attacks on the Muslims by the LTTE in the early 1990s, after which the government decided to arm the Muslim youth for self defense. The conflict between Hindu and Muslim *Tamils* resulted in the polarization of mindsets on the issue of religious identity. There are, today, nearly a dozen Muslim fundamentalist organizations in Sri Lanka which are funded by foreign countries, primarily Saudi Arabia, with at least two political parties drawing significant support from Iran.

THE EXTREMIST ISLAMIST *INTERNATIONALE*

The threat of extremist Islamist terror in south Asia must be estimated, not just in terms of visible violence and subversion, but the unique and lethal mix of a virulent and vigorously propagated ideology; international and state support and sponsorship; the movement of experienced cadres across theatres that span the entire world; and the access to and destructive potential of contemporary weapons and information technologies. Pakistan's experience and the Afghan war have given rise to "a kind of Islamic *"internationale"* through the recruitment of volunteers throughout the Muslim world" and "a global network of radical Muslim terrorists."[31] Among these are the experienced and ideologically motivated Arab Afghans, with their roots in west Asia.[32] South Asia is, moreover, awash with small arms and lethal explosives.[33] The recovery of gas masks from bunkers held by Pakistani forces and irregulars during the Kargil War,[34] and recent reports regarding Osama bin Laden's intent to use chemical weapons,[35] suggest that extremist Islamic forces and their state sponsors are, at least, evaluating the possibility and impact of the use of weapons of mass destruction (WMD) in their low-intensity wars in various countries.

It is not necessary to belabor the obvious point that there are "many Islams," and that the adherents of the murderous mix of religion and terror are only a small fraction of Muslims in the world. There is, however, a difficulty that needs to be confronted, namely, the separation of legitimate religious, educational, and charitable activity by Islamic religious institutions, including the *madrassas*, from overt or covert support to terrorism and a militant Islamist agenda. This difficulty is enormously compounded by the ideological continuity among those who currently propagate the dogmas of Islamist extremism from the fringes of Europe through Asia and Africa, as well as by the continuity of sources of finance and support through every theatre of Islamist terrorism and "fundamentalist" subversion in the world.

Endnotes

1 1947–48, 1965, and 1971.
2 On May 31, 1999, for instance, the Pakistani foreign secretary, Shamshad Ahmad warned, "We will not hesitate to use any weapon in our arsenal to defend our territorial integrity." Given the overt nuclearization of Pakistan in May 1998, this threat had obvious connotations. "Any Weapon Will Be Used, Threatens Pak," *Hindu*, June 1, 1999, citing an interview in *News/Jang* newspapers.
3 Also see "Master or Victim: Pakistan's Afghan War," in Ahmed Rashid, *Taliban: Islam, Oil and the New Great Game in Central Asia* (London & New York: I.B. Tauris Publishers, 2001), p. 183–195. Jessica Stern refers to this as a typical "principal-agent" problem, observing that the interests of the state (principal) and those of the militant groups (the agent) are not fully aligned. See "Pakistan's Jihad Culture," *Foreign Affairs,* November–December 2000, at <http://www.foreignaffairs.org/issues/0011/stern.html>.
4 Ibid., p. 194.
5 Brig. S.K. Malik, *The Quranic Concept of War* (New Delhi: Himalayan Books, 1986), p. 59.
6 Ambassador Michael A. Sheehan, Coordinator for Counter-terrorism, U.S. Department of State, Statement for the Record Before the House International Relations Committee, July 12, 2000, <http://www.usinfo.state.gov/topical/pol/terror/00071702.htm>. Ambassador Sheehan was echoing Secretary of State Madeline Albright's earlier statement (of May 1, 2000) that there had been an "eastward shift in terrorism's center of gravity" toward south Asia.

7 Total Fatalities: 1990 – 1177; 1991 – 1393; 1992 – 1909; 1993 – 2567; 1994 – 2899; 1995 – 2795; 1996 – 2903; 1997 – 2372; 1998 – 2261; 1999 – 2538; 2000 – 3288. Source: <www.satp.org>.

8 Altaf Gauhar, *The Challenge of Islam* (London: Islamic Council of Europe, 1978), p. 309.

9 Allah Buksh K. Brohi, Preface, in Malik, *The Quranic Concept of War*, p. xix–xx

10 Estimated figures in the *CIA World Factbook 2000*, <http://www.odci.gov/cia/publications/factbook/indexgeo.html#t>.

11 John L. Esposito, *The Islamic Threat: Myth or Reality* (New York & Oxford: Oxford University Press, 1999).

12 The state of J&K comprises a total area of 152,298 square kilometers, with a population of 6,815,000. It is divided into three regions: the Muslim majority Kashmir region (HQ Srinagar), with an area of 15,898 square kilometers and a population of 3,977,000; the Hindu majority Jammu region (HQ Jammu), with an area of 26,293 square kilometers and a population of 2,538,000; and the Buddhist majority Ladakh region (HQ Leh), with a population of 300,000, <www.jammukashmir.nic.in>.

13 The Hizb has recently reduced its operation, first after its own unilateral cease-fire of July 2000, and subsequently after the Indian prime minister's declaration of cease-fire. The Hizb is the largest terrorist group in J&K, and is dominated by "local" cadres. The other groups are primarily drawn from Pakistani and other foreign elements.

14 Data about, and analysis of, Kashmir are primarily based on research and documentation at the Institute for Conflict Management and the South Asia Terrorism Portal, <www.satp.org>.

15 Up to December 31, 2000. The data are based on the South Asia Terrorism Portal's compilations from official and media sources in India, <www.satp.org>.

16 The proportion of foreigners among the *active* militants would be higher, as much as 75 percent, since the Hizb reduced its operations.

17 Shaul Shay and Yoram Schweitzer, "The 'Afghan Alumni' Terrorism: Islamic Militants Against the Rest of the World," *ICT Papers*, The International Policy Institute for Counter-Terrorism, Herzilya, September 2000, Volume 6.

18 Mark Husband, *Warriors of the Prophet: The Struggle for Islam* (Colorado & Oxford: Westview Press, 1999), p. 9. Also see Manoj Joshi, *The Lost Rebellion: Kashmir in the Nineties* (New Delhi: Penguin Books, 1999); Tavleen Singh, *Kashmir: A Tragedy of Errors* (New Delhi: Penguin Books, 1996).

19 Over 400,000 Kashmiri Pandits, out of an original population in the Kashmir Valley of 425,000 prior to 1989, continue to be displaced. Official records indicate that some 216,820 of them live as migrants in makeshift camps in Jammu, another 143,000 in Delhi, and thousands of others are now dispersed across the country. Many of those registered at the camps have also been dispersed according to the exigencies of employment and opportunities for education, trade, or business. There has been little effort

to facilitate their return to the valley in recent years. Earlier attempts were neutralized by brutal campaigns of selective murder, including the killing of 7 Pandits at Sangrama in Budgam district in March 1997, 3 at Gul in Udhampur district in June 1997, 26 in the massacre at Wandhama in Srinagar district in January 1998, and 26 at Prankote in Udhampur district in April 1998. The possibility of reversing the terrorists' ethnic cleansing of the valley remains remote, and there are now reports of a hidden migration from some of the border areas in the Jammu region where the Hindus are a minority, <www.satp.org>.

20 Praveen Swami, "The 'Liberation' of Hyderabad," *Frontline*, vol. 17, issue 10, May 13–26, 2000, <www.frontline.com/fl/1710/17100390.htm>.

21 "Church Blast Cases Busted; 15 Arrested," <indiainfo.com>, July 17, 2000, <http://news.indiainfo.com/2000/07/17/blast.html>.

22 "Centre May Consider Ban on ISI-Backed Deendar Anjuman," New Delhi, *Indian Express*, August 4, 2000.

23 "30 Killed as Serial Blasts Rock Coimbatore," <http://www.indiaserver. com/thehindu/1998/02/15/front.htm#Story1>; "Panic Following Blasts," <http://www.indiaserver.com/thehindu/1998/02/15/thb02.htm#Story2>; "Union Home Ministry Reviews Situation," <http://www.indiaserver.com/ thehindu/1998/02/16/thb01.htm#Story5>; "Six Extremists Die in Coimbatore Blasts, Toll 44," <http://www.indiaserver.com/thehindu/1998/02/16/ thb02.htm#Story1>; "Arrests Throughout the State," <http://www.indiaserver. com/thehindu/1998/02/16/thb02.htm#Story2>.

24 See Ghulam Hasnain, "At Home in Exile," *Outlook*, New Delhi, November 20, 2000, also available at <www.outlookindia.com>, p. 30–38.

25 "Report on Illegal Migration into Assam Submitted to the President of India by the Governor of Assam, November 8, 1998," <http://www.satp. org/India/Documents/Assam_Illegal Migration into Assam.htm>.

26 <http://www.satp.org/India/Assam/Terrorist Outfits/Terrorist Groups_Assam.htm>.

27 "ISI Activities in Assam: Statement Laid on the Table of the House of Assam Legislative Assembly Under Item No. 12, Dated April 6, 2000, by Shri Prafulla Kumar Mahanta, Chief Minister, Assam," <http://www.satp.org/ India/Documents/Assam_ISI Activities in Assam.htm>.

28 In July 2000, for instance, the Bangladesh president, Sheikh Hasina, spoke out strongly against the *Jamaat-e-Islami* and its leader, Prof. Gholam Azam, after the murder of seven student leaders by the student wing of the JEI, the *Islami Chattra Shibir. Haroon Habib,* "Hasina Declares War on Jamaat," New Delhi, *Hindu,* July 25, 2000.

29 "Bangladesh Assessment 2000," South Asia Terrorism Portal, <http://www. satp.org/Bangladesh/Assessment Bangladesh.htm>.

30 "ISI in Nepal: Guest of Dishonour," <http://www.india-today.com/ today/20000117/nation4.html>; "Nepal was one of the most important hubs for the ISI as far back as 1990," <http://india-today.com/ ntoday/extra/isi_rep/interview1.html>; "Terrorism: The Kathmandu

Nexus," <http://www.india-today.com/itoday/20000612/nation2. html>.

31 Schweitzer and Shay, "The 'Afghan Alumni' Terrorism: Islamic Militants Against the Rest of the World," *ICT Papers,* p. 19.

32 Rashid, Taliban: Islam, Oil and the New Great Game in Central Asia, p. 128–140.

33 According to estimates, some 3.5 million small arms are currently available for various conflicts in this region. Thousands of kilos of sophisticated explosives, mainly RDX and PETN, are routinely recovered each year from terrorist and criminal groups, and thousands of kilos of these explosives are actually used in the unnumbered incidents that take place across south Asia. Recoveries by state forces now include ballistic missiles.

34 Brahma Chellaney, "Sign and Violate," *Hindustan Times,* New Delhi, September 8, 1999.

35 "Bin Laden Seeking Chemical, N-Arms: CIA," *Times of India,* New Delhi, February 3, 2000.

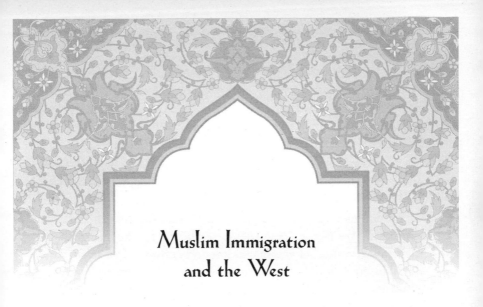

Muslim Immigration and the West

David Pryce-Jones

The arrival of Muslims in the West in any sizable numbers is a very recent and rapid development. The mosque in Woking, not far from London, is the only one in Britain which has celebrated its centenary. In the early 1950s, the Muslim population of Britain was 23,000. Between 1961 and the present, this rose from 82,000 to over one million.

Sweden went from having virtually no Muslims in 1950 to 200,000 today. Starting from almost nil in the 1960s, in Belgium and the Netherlands there are today respectively 260,000 and 450,000, with about 500 mosques altogether. The Muslim presence in Germany began in 1961 and Turks numbering some 1.9 million now form over three-quarters of the Muslims there.

France had incorporated Algeria into the legal definition of the French nation, and Algerians began to settle in France in the early part of the century. Today there are over four million Muslims living there from all the Maghreb countries (Morocco, Algeria, and Tunesia).

In the last 30 years an estimated five million Muslims have immigrated to the United States, half a million to Australia, about the same number to Argentina, and so on in many countries of the world.

This topic cannot be understood without reference to circumstance and historicity. Down the course of history, movements of population of any scale have provided constant impetus to violence and warfare, often in ethnic and religious clashes impervious to diplomacy and resolution. Is it different now? In the *dar al-Harb* where unbelievers lived, a Muslim was traditionally considered unable to fulfill the obligations of his faith, and so in the event of emigration faced a challenging choice between separatism and assimilation. Are Western countries experiencing for the first time in their midst minorities whose religion and culture are so separatist that they are cannot be assimilated? Or in the contrary event of assimilation, what will be the role of Islam? Does "Muslim" remain an appropriate definition, or has it become secondary to Frenchman, Swede, German, and so on? These questions are novel and it is in the media that the answers to them will be tested, and public opinion shaped as a result.

The political conjuncture of the world after 1945 set in flow this particular movement of population. The ending of Western colonialism and the independence of countries, hitherto colonies, were among the complex factors conditioning events. Muslim immigrants carried to the West diversities from home; they were *Sunni* and *Shi`a*, with factionalisms, regional cultural and social habits, community and clan loyalties all their own. Structures from the old days of empire came to be reproduced in one Western metropolis and another. The majority of British Muslims are from the Indian sub-continent, and they are adherents of the *Jama`at at-Tabligh*, a non-political movement of latter-day *Sufis*, founded in India in the 1920s by Muhamad Ilyas. Libyans tend to move to Italy, Surinamese to the Netherlands, Maghrebi Arabs to France, and so on.

To give an example of what happens in practice, the city of Leicester in 1991 had a population of 270,493, of whom 14 percent were Hindu, 4.3 percent Muslim and 3.8 percent Sikh. The Leicester Muslims were mostly Gujurati-speaking *Deobandis*, who are *Jama`at at-Tabligh* associates. The 50 separate Muslim organizations in just this one city include the *Dawoodi Bohra Jamaat*, the *Ahmadiyya* Muslim Association, the *Ismaili Jamaat*, the *Rawal* Community

Association, the *Gujurati* Muslim Association, the *Surati Muslim Khalifa* Society, the King Faisal Jam-e Mosque, the Islamic Center, and much else to delight sociologists. Altogether in Britain there are about one thousand Muslim organizations. In France, there are as many as three thousand separate Muslim organizations.

Transplanted as they have been from countries of origin, these organizations obviously have the aim of defending a particular religious and ethnic identity, rather narrowly defined. Most are religious or cultural in aim. The *imam* and the mosque are central to the many communities. Patronage and power are at stake locally, and inevitably the appointment of the *imam* attracts the attention of the authorities in the country where the *imam* and community originated. A particularly public example was the protracted struggle over control of the Paris mosque and associated religious trusts in France. In the end, the appointment of an *imam* approved by the Algerian government emphasized Algier's overall control of Islam in France. In comparable power struggles, *imams* in several British mosques have been deposed. *Imams* in Germany and Belgium have been murdered.

The media provide the forum in which such developments are assessed. Community politics are rough stuff, it is accepted, and what Muslims do among themselves is largely their own business. But undoubtedly the sudden and swift process of immigration and community-building by Muslims — so visible in architecture, clothing, food, social habits — contains the potential for arousing racism and xenophobia in the host countries of the West. Now and again the popular press makes an outrage of some unwonted incident, for instance an Iranian diplomat who for the feast of *Eid al-Kabir* slit a sheep's throat in a London suburban street, or another Iranian who insisted on marrying a 12-year-old girl in defiance of national law but, he claimed, in accordance with *Shari`ah*. He was deported. The underlying issue is: Are these people coming as others have come before them, to assimilate to national ways including democracy, or is this a reverse colonialism, and the host countries will be expected to adapt to their ways, indeed eventually to become *dar al-Islam*?

In general terms, the answer is already clear. Evidently attracted by democracy and capitalism, immigrants are not just integrating, but actually assimilating. At the grass roots, emotional attachments may not change, but direct ties to the homeland are diminishing. Second, and now third, generation immigrants are already likely not to know the language spoken by elder members of the families. French youths of Maghrebi descent often cannot speak or read Arabic. In spite of special television and radio programs in Bengali, Urdu, or Gujurati, the same is true of youths in Britain whose families came from the Indian sub-continent.

Muslims in the West now have their own media in which to air the culture-clashes erupting from new values and expectations. Here is a typical letter from a young woman published in December 1996 in *Trends*, which describes itself as "Britain's Biggest Selling Muslim Magazine."

> I had an arranged marriage when I was very young. I always used to get top grades at school, but then my future husband and his family made it clear that they did not want me to do my exams, but rather get married. So against my will I was married and now have two children. My husband is at times sensible and good but he will not let me study. I have tried to discuss this with him but he has a hundred and one excuses ready. He makes me cry but still he won't change his mind. I am very unhappy and feel that I have sacrificed so much and given up my youth.

Many, perhaps most, Westerners are secularized to the extent of knowing little or nothing about any religion at all. Insofar as Islam as a religion enters their horizon, they are likely to feel warmer toward it than toward Christianity. Islam continues to call for traditional values, and in particular for family solidarity and community, which is otherwise weakening and which many thoughtful people regret. The Prince of Wales is one who regularly appeals for Islam along these lines. A bishop informs the world that he has spent Lent reading the *Qur`an*. Not long ago Muslim vigilantes cleared prostitutes and drug dealers from the streets of a Birmingham suburb where Muslims lived, and British public opinion approved that they had redressed a failure of the law and policing. Brigitte Bardot complaining that the *muezzin* drowns out church bells is exceptional enough to make headlines.

The sort of people who are anxious to find fault with their own kind and their own society sometimes claim that the media present unfavorable stereotypes of Muslims. An example is a paper put out by the Runnymede Trust under the title of *Islamophobia*, a rather strained Arabic and Greek compound. But it offered virtually no evidence of anything serious. With exceptions of no great importance in one or two countries, immigrants have the same rights and duties as everyone else.

This reasonably positive picture has two shadows, one cast from the Western side, the other from the Muslim. Nobody seems to have had the wisdom to foresee that the drive to build common European institutions, and in all probability some ultimate federation, would provoke backlash nationalistic reactions damaging to foreigners and minorities, Muslim immigrants perhaps first and foremost. The historic nation-state brought about the drafting of constitutions, the rule of law, enfranchisement, and civic rights. Under the pressure of uniting Europe, the nation-state is being drained of these past achievements, and this is weakening democratic essentials, accountability of the authorities, the rule of law, and that trust in the state which the citizen must have if he is to obey its demands.

Feeling themselves improperly represented, unable to obtain a hearing, people in Europe are turning to new nationalist — and to some extent, tribalist — parties: the National Front in France, the Austrian Freedom Party, the Flemish Bloc, the Basque ETA, and dozens of groupings in Germany and Sweden and elsewhere, some of them clandestine and inclined to terrorism. Seeking to protect national and even tribal identities in what is now a recurrent pattern across Europe, these parties and their members encourage xenophobia and racism, which are rising to ever-higher levels of violence culminating in arson and murder.

One extreme, as usual, feeds another. Unable to integrate to an abstract, non-sovereign concept like Europe, Muslims increasingly find themselves relegated to the same uncomfortable neither-quite-in-nor-quite-out position that they were in the old Soviet Union, and so fall back on Islam for their primary identity. If really they are to be a tribe, then they may as well be the *umma*, or community of the faithful. The opening is thus created for Islamism.

David Pryce-Jones

Islamism preaches separatism as the overall solution — with the long-term objective of converting any and all countries in the *dar al-harb* to Islam. Called by its proper name, this is a reverse colonialism.

Iran and Arab countries have exploited Islamism to project power and foreign policy aims. What might look like a community organization for immigrants in a number of cases turns out to be sponsored and paid for to serve one or another absolutist ruler. An estimated 47 of the British Muslim organizations are thought to be fronts for *Hamas*. Bradford boasts of the Saddam Hussein Mosque, in effect a propaganda outlet designed to further that ruler's interests in the city where the Rushdie controversy started.

Some of this is covert. Either Iran or Saudi Arabia, or sometimes disconcertingly both in their religious and ethnic cold war, sponsor groups like *Hizbullah*, *Hamas*, *Hibz ut-Tahrir*, the *Al-Kifah* Society in America. Likewise, they sponsor individuals in the style of Dr. Kalim Saddiqi, paid for by Iran to advocate the establishment of a separate Muslim parliament in Britain. Mysteriously financed, the Syrian-born Sheikh Omar Bakri appears on television to praise the *Taliban* or terrorists in Yemen, and to warn Westerners that soon they will be stoned to death for their sins.

And some of the activity is overt. The Arab press of Beirut was destroyed in the Lebanese civil war. London now has more than 50 newspapers published in Arabic, and many more magazines and journals. Controlled, for the most part directly owned, by members of the al-Saud royal family, these publications promote Saudi interests primarily, but sometimes serve as a forum for debate otherwise not available. During the 1991 Gulf War, the columnist Khalid Kishtainy could write about Saddam Hussein in a style which would have been his death-sentence at home. A former Libyan Prime Minister is able to publish an article in *Sharq al-Awsat,* arguing that any peace terms that the Arabs can obtain with Israel is better than more dispute and war.

Falastin al-Muslima, the main *Hamas* paper, is published in a glossy format in a London suburb. The Bahraini and Libyan oppositions, the Tunisian Islamist movement *Al-Nahda*, the Algerian front *Islamique de Salvation*, are among many others publishing abroad in this manner. Western countries today seethe with an underworld of

Arab and Iranian paid agents, hit squads, dissidents, and adventurers who are responding not to local conditions but transplanted domestic considerations. Who exactly is manipulating whom is never very obvious, and truthful and accurate reporting is hard to come by. What the Westerner observes is the exploitation of one issue after another — Bosnia, Palestine, Afghanistan, Chechnya — or the abuse of the open society through the attempted assassination of the pope or the bombing of the World Trade Center in New York, manufactured causes like the Rushdie affair or the wearing of headscarves by Muslim girls in French schools.

Banned in the Middle East, *Hizb ut-Tahrir* claims the right of free speech in Britain in order to dedicate itself to a *Khilafah*, or unified Islamic state, in Europe. Its meetings provoke violence. In its publication, *Al-Khilafah*, in December 1996, an editorial declared, "All over the world the twin evils of freedom and democracy have reaped havoc with people's lives." The founder of a group of his own, *Al-Muhajiroun*, Sheikh Omar Bakri writes in one of his numerous pamphlets, "Democracy is a concept the West has conjured to destroy the Islamic state." Elsewhere he elaborates, "The idea of a democratic society is deceptive, dangerous, and unworkable. The party considers it is *haram* (forbidden) to establish or participate in parties which call for capitalism, socialism, secularism, nationalism, or any other religion other than Islam. We are surrounded by a sea of *Kafir* (unbelief): *Kafir* thoughts, practices, and *Kafir* systems of life. Homosexuals, adulterers, fornicators, will be killed, and Jews too."

Such threats are in open defiance of British law, which forbids expressions of hate. A leaflet distributed lately at the Saudi-financed Central Mosque in Regent's Park typifies many hundreds of such incitements to ordinary Muslims. "Do something to prove that on your shoulders there stands a head, not a piece of cheese. Throw a stone, trigger a bomb, plant a mine, hijack a plane, do not ask how."

Democracy sometimes appears paralyzed by those who take advantage of its freedoms in order to abuse them for undemocratic ends. Islamists make out that all Muslims are in their mold, or must be compelled to be. Their leaders raise suspicions and us-or-them hatreds, which do untold harm to ordinary people who ask for nothing more than to be integrated as democratic citizens who happen also to be Muslim. Whether Western or Muslim, the media provide perhaps the only immediately available means to rescue such people from such leaders.

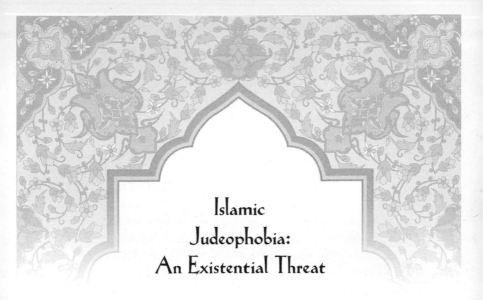

Islamic Judeophobia: An Existential Threat

Robert S. Wistrich

I

On November 18, 1947, Hitler's closest confidante, Albert Speer, wrote down the following recollection in his Spandau prison diary which today sounds so eerily prophetic:

> I recall how [Hitler] would have films shown in the Reich Chancellory about London burning, about the sea of fire over Warsaw, about exploding convoys, and the kind of ravenous joy that would then seize him every time. But I never saw him so beside himself as when, in a delirium, he pictured New York going down in flames. He described how the skyscrapers would be transformed into gigantic burning torches, how they would collapse in confusion, how the bursting city's reflection would stand against the dark sky.[1]

In September 2001, this frenzied Wagnerian imagery became fact. The Islamic terrorist perpetrators of the September massacres, like the Nazis and fascists of 60 years ago, speak a language of unquenchable hatred not only for America and the West but also for Israel and the Jewish people as such.[2] These Muslim radicals have consciously chosen a cult of death, turning the motif of sacrifice and martyrdom into something urgent, elemental, pseudo-religious, and even mystical.[3] Their Bible may be the *Qur`an* and not *Mein Kampf*, but the mental structures and world view behind their actions do have striking analogies with German National Socialism.[4] The Muslim fundamentalists — like the Nazis before and during the *Shoah* — rant against the "anonymous powers" of globalization and the plutocratic West (symbolized by the World Trade Center and the city of New York) as fiercely as they battered the citadels of Soviet Communism in Afghanistan more than a decade ago. Like their totalitarian predecessors, they (falsely) claim to speak for frustrated, underprivileged, and impoverished masses betrayed by more traditional Arab and Muslim ruling elites and ruthlessly exploited by international capitalism. To the radical Muslims, "Jewish" New York as much as the Zionist state of Israel, is the incarnation of satanic evil, just as Wall Street embodied the general headquarters of corporate wickedness and cosmopolitan Jewry to the Nazis and other pre-war Fascist true believers.[5] Anti-Semitic conspiracy theories lie at the very heart of the Muslim fundamentalist and Arab nationalist world view today — linking together plutocratic finance, international freemasonry, secularism, Zionism, and communism as dark occult forces led by the giant octopus of international Jewry — whose alleged aim is to destroy Islam and to subvert the cultural identity of Muslim believers.[6]

This mythical structure of thought is in many ways virtually identical with Nazi anti-Semitism despite the fact that it has undergone a process of "Islamicization" and the quotation of verses from the *Qur`an* to justify monstrous terrorist acts. Fundamentalist Islam has the same totalitarian, pseudo-messianic aspiration to world hegemony as German Nazism or Soviet communism. It also articulates a latent and sometimes explicitly genocidal rhetoric in its assault on "Jewish-Crusader" civilization that conjures up alarming echoes of the past.[7] For militant Islamic groups like *al-Qa`idah*, the *Taliban*, *Hamas*, *Hizbullah*, Islamic *jihad* and many others, anti-Semitic, anti-Zionism serves as an intrinsic part of their nihilist-totalitarian mindset. The *jihad*ist terrorists are committed to violence, bent on total confrontation with the infidels on the either/or politics of victory or death, and embrace an outlook rooted in a Manichean polarization between the forces of light and darkness. The bin Ladens of this world are driven not only by fanatical extremism, by their loathing of "Christian crusaders," heretics, dissenters, Jews, women, and their rejection of America and Western modernity *per se* — they hate civilization in a way that is radically nihilist.

It is highly characteristic that the September 11 terrorist attacks against the United States were greeted with such rapture in many parts of the Muslim world, including in the Palestinian Authority. For example, the *mufti* of Jerusalem, preaching his Friday sermon at the *Al-Aqsa* Mosque, openly called for the destruction of Israel, Britain, and the United States: "Oh Allah, destroy America, for she is ruled by Zionist Jews. . . . Allah will paint the White House black!"[8]

Other Muslim clerics like Sheikh Ibrahim Mahdi focused their efforts more on praising "suicide bombers" in Israel. In words aired repeatedly by PA Television, he enthusiastically encouraged the cynical sacrifice of children as being acts of so-called "martyrdom" against Israel:

> All weapons must be aimed at the Jews, at the enemies of Allah, the cursed nation in the *Qur`an*, whom the *Qur`an* describes as monkeys and pigs. . . . We will blow them up in Hadera, we will blow them up in Tel Aviv and in Netanya. . . . We bless all those who educate their children to *jihad* and to martyrdom.[9]

The current wave of Muslim suicide bombings, Israelophobia, and terrorism appear to enjoy massive resonance among most Palestinians and a large number of Arabs and Muslims. Islamic anti-Semitism has also spread with electrifying speed among Muslim and Arab immigrants in the Western democracies. Many of these immigrants already carry with them the anti-Semitic baggage of their mother countries and cultures, exacerbated by intensive media coverage of the escalating Middle East conflict. In September and October 2000 this resulted in an alarming increase in Muslim/Arab anti-Semitic assaults on Diaspora Jewish communities (especially in

Robert S. Wistrich

Europe) — including the burning of synagogues, arson, desecrations, physical attacks, letter bombs, and vitriolic verbal incitement of the most intimidating kind.[10] Such attacks have assumed near-epidemic proportions in countries like France which have a large Muslim population (about six million mainly Maghrebin immigrants) and a substantial, though much smaller community of around 600,000 Jews.[11] The dangerous combination of radical anti-Zionism (ominously sliding into anti-Jewishness in the liberal and leftist French media) fused with the Islamist Judeophobia of the Muslim immigrants, has seriously alarmed French Jewry.[12] So, too, in Great Britain a similar pattern of Muslim anti-Semitism is emerging that has made Anglo-Jews (already alarmed at the Israel-bashing of the BBC and the liberal British media) increasingly anxious.[13]

The anti-Semitic fallout from the terror attacks and the ensuing anthrax scare has been a revealing index for the depths of Muslim Arab hatred for America, Israel, and the Jews. Initially, the reactions were those of celebration and joy expressed with particular vehemence by fundamentalist circles, for the humbling of [American] "arrogance, tyranny, and boastfulness."[14] The Egyptian-based journal of the Muslim Brotherhood rapturously greeted Osama bin Laden as "a hero in the full sense of the word" and prayed that his followers would eventually "eradicate America and its 'infinite justice.' " Another Egyptian weekly rejoiced that "America is on the way to collapse, like all the empires of oppression throughout history."[15] As *Al Ahram Al Arab* expressed on October 4, 2001, America was finally tasting the poison of its own ruthless oppression, and with the collapse of "the city of globalization" [New York] so, too, it was boldly predicted that "the theory of globalization will be buried."[16] The Pan-Arab opposition weekly *Al Usbú* made it very clear that it could have no sympathy for America in its grief and one columnist even confessed that watching the inferno in New York "[those moments of] exquisite, incandescent hell" were "the most precious moments of my life."[17] A Nasserist weekly expressed undisguised satisfaction at the fact that "the Americans are finally tasting the bitterness of death."[18] Even columnists on the Egyptian Liberal Party daily *Al-Ahrar* felt that uninhibited delight was a national and religious obligation since "the U.S. position in the Arab-Zionist conflict causes Arabs to rejoice over every disaster visited upon the American government."[19]

For the Muslim Brotherhood, the terror strike was nothing less than "divine retribution," not least because the Americans "preferred the apes [i.e., the Jews] to human beings, treating human beings from outside the U.S. cheaply, supporting homosexuals and usury."[20] Islamic radicals, Pan-Arabists, and Nasserists all felt a common elation at the sudden collapse of the "mythological symbols of arrogant American imperialist power" and the blow which they believed had been struck on behalf of embattled Muslims in Palestine, Iraq, Kashmir, and other trouble spots on the planet.

But no less swiftly, across Muslim and Arab society, the blame for the terrorist and anthrax attacks was firmly placed on the Zionists, the Israeli government, and the Mossad. The Syrian Ambassador to Teheran was quoted as saying on good authority that "the Israelis have been involved in these incidents and no Jewish employee was present in the World Trade Organization building on the day."[21] According to the Syrian government newspaper *Al Thawra*, Israeli Premier Ariel Sharon thereby sought to divert attention from his aggressive plans toward the Palestinians.[22] He had supposedly created this golden opportunity in order to cause maximum damage and provoke a deep schism in Arab-American relations.[23] In the Jordanian newspaper *Al-Dustour* on September 13, 2001, an article appeared (by no means exceptional) which argued that the Twin Towers massacre was in fact "the act of the great Jewish Zionist mastermind that controls the world's economy, media, and politics. . ." and the diabolical plot was rapidly leading the world to a global disaster.[24]

In the same issue, a Lebanese-Jordanian Holocaust denier warned Arabs against the "Jewish-Zionist hands behind the terrible event"; another Jordanian columnist emphasized the prevailing Arab wisdom "that Israel is the one . . . to benefit greatly from the bloody, loathsome terror operation."[25] The Egyptian Sheikh Mohammad Al-Gamei'a, former *imam* of the Islamic Culture Center and Mosque of New York, also had little doubt that the Jews were behind the September terrorist attacks. "The Jewish element is as Allah described. . . . We know they have always broken agreements, unjustly murdered the prophets, and betrayed the faith."[26] The

theory that Mossad, Israel's intelligence service, was behind the
Twin Tower bombings was especially popular in Muslim Pakistan.
Major General Hamid Gul, former head of Pakistan's own intel-
ligence service, was adamant:

> I tell you, it was a coup [attempt], and I can't say for
> sure who was behind it, but it's the Israelis who are creating
> so much misery in the world. The Israelis don't want to see
> any power in Washington unless it's subservient to their
> interests and President Bush has not been subservient.[27]

In support of the Zionist conspiracy theory, the Lahore-based
Jihad Times and other media in Pakistan endlessly recycled the
legend that around 4,000 Israelis and Jews working in the World
Trade Center had received a secret directive from the Mossad not
to report for duty on September 11. The attacks had allegedly been
ordered by the "Elders of Zion" in reaction to the anti-Israel bash-
ing that had been handed out at the Third UN Conference against
Racism in Durban.[28]

The notion that contemporary Jewry exercises a "media dictatorship" deliberately seeking to poison relations between Islam and
the West has indeed become widespread in many Muslim circles.
Even more popular is the idea that Jews manipulate the Western
mass media as a whole, especially in the United States.[29] The *Iran
Daily* claimed, for example, that since September 11 the West had
been swamped by the propaganda of "Zionist circles [who] have
been almost uncontrollably emitting their profound contempt of
Islam. . . ."[30]

The Palestinian Journalists Association also insisted that the
western media were completely under the thumb of international
finance and Zionist Jews.[31] The Palestine Ministry of Information
website went even further and declared that there was an absolute Jewish monopoly of the U.S. news media. A small minority
had "the power to mold our minds to suit their own Talmudic
interests...[they had] a decisive influence on our [American] political
system and virtual control of the minds and souls of our children,
whose attitudes and ideas are shaped more by Jewish television
and Jewish films than by their parents, their schools, or any other
influence."[32]

The anti-Israel and anti-Semitic conspiracy theories that have been escalating in the Arab and Muslim world since September 11 are not in themselves new. But they do reveal a highly inflammable cocktail of anti-Westernism, ideological fanaticism, raw hate, and irrationality that underlies a significant strand of contemporary Muslim thinking. The attitude to the Jews, in particular, with its vehement language and emphasis on "radical solutions" is disturbingly reminiscent of the 1930s and 1940s. The anti-Semitic stereotypes are as frequent in those countries such as Jordan or Egypt that have peace treaties with Israel as they are in Syria, the Palestinian Authority, Saudi Arabia, or other Gulf states. Examples abound and could be multiplied *ad nauseam*: In *Tishreen*, a government-owned Syrian daily, the editor-in-chief, Mohamed Kheir al-Wadi, writing in January 2000, took it for granted that "Zionism created the Holocaust myth to blackmail and terrorize the world's intellectuals and politicians."[33]

A month later, an editorial in another government-controlled Syrian newspaper, *Al-Thawra*, written by Muhammed Ali Bouzha, stated with the same self-evident tone: "Israel has revealed itself as an entity steeped in racism, hate, and state-sponsored terrorism, which has surpassed even the Nazis in its criminal acts of murder, destruction and devastation and in its disdain for humanity."[34]

Sometimes, too, Holocaust denial and the "Zionism-is- Nazism" myth are fused, as in the response of state-owned Syrian radio in late February 2000 to the then Israeli Foreign Minister David Levy's stern warning to Lebanon from the rostrum of the Knesset to rein in the *Hizbullah*. Syrian radio promptly accused Israel of "playing the role of the Nazi executioners, who according to the Zionists, burned the Jews in Auschwitz." On February 28, 2000, the state-run Lebanese television echoed this Syrian propaganda by running an ad showing images of casualties from IDF attacks on Lebanon juxtaposed with Nazi concentration camps, followed by the words: "Same hatred. Same racism. Same criminality. Same history."[35]

In the Gulf states, too, Levy's statement was taken as proof that "Zionism was the descendant of Nazism."[36] Despite his efforts to attain peace, Israeli Prime Minister Ehud Barak — like his less conciliatory predecessors such as Begin, Shamir, Netanyahu, or Ariel Sharon today — also found himself regularly portrayed in

Nazi uniform with a *swastika* armband, as Israeli warplanes bombed Lebanon. Predictably, the caption in *Al-Watan* read: "In Lebanon Israel Is Behaving Like the Nazis."[37]

Nor is it any great surprise to discover that Israelophobia and anti-Semitism have been equally present in the Egyptian media at the turn of the millennium — in spite of the 1979 Peace Treaty with the Jewish state. Comparisons of Israel with the Nazis, denial of the Holocaust, and medieval blood libels regularly appear in the government-backed press (including in the largest dailies, *Al-Ahram* and *Al-Goumhurriya,* and the popular magazine, *October*) as they do in the leftist, Nasserist, and fundamentalist opposition newspapers. Worse still, the cartoons consistently deform Jews. They are almost always dirty, hook-nosed, money-grabbing, vindictive, scheming, and cruel.[38] The extremely hostile visual and verbal stereotyping in a country still considered the hub of the Arab world — one, moreover, whose newspapers, magazines, and books help to shape public opinion throughout the region — is both dangerous and alarming.

II

The examples of anti-Semitic falsehoods are not only innumerable, but consistently outrageous. Israel is repeatedly alleged by Egyptian (and Jordanian) news sources to be distributing drug-laced chewing gum and candy, intended to make women sexually corrupt and to kill children. *Al-Ahram*, the leading government-sponsored daily in Egypt, expostulates in great detail in a special series how Jews use the blood of Gentiles to make *matzah* for Passover. An Egyptian intellectual, writing in *Al-Akhbar*, less than a year ago, explains that the Talmud (described as the Jews' second holiest book), "determines that the '*matzahs*' of Atonement Day [sic] must be kneaded 'with blood' from non-Jews. The preference is for the blood of youths after raping them."[39]

This was a favorite motif of the late King Feisal of Saudi Arabia, who not only insisted that Jews carried out the ritual murder of children, but argued that this proved "the extent of their [the Jews'] hatred and malice toward non-Jewish peoples."[40]

On the eve of the new millennium, the Arab writers' weekly organ in Damascus brought the blood libel up to date with the following literary gem:

The [Passover] Matzah of Israel is soaked with the blood of the Iraqis, descendants of the Babylonians, the Lebanese, the descendants of the Sidonese, and the Palestinians, the descendants of the Canaanites. This Matzah is kneaded by American weaponry and the missiles of hatred pointed at both Muslim and Christian Arabs. . . .[41]

On the first day of the third Christian millennium, the Syrian weekly escalated its Israelophobe attacks to the "notorious Camp David Accords" and the "dirty Satanic methods used [by the Zionist Entity] . . . to destroy the fabric of Egyptian society." These "Zionist" methods included spreading AIDS among Arab youngsters by sending "pretty HIV positive Jewish prostitutes to Egypt and dispensing chewing gum to arouse sexual lust."[42] This absurd calumny — widely diffused among Egyptians and Palestinians — was no doubt grist to the mill for Syrian opponents of any "normalization" with Israel.

The West eventually received an all-too-rare public glimpse of the brutal anti-Jewish bigotry so commonplace in the Arab world, when the young Syrian president, Bashar Al-Assad, welcomed His Holiness Pope John Paul II on a historic visit to Damascus in early May 2001. The Syrian host did his best to fuse together in a single sentence the core message of European Christian and Islamic Judeophobia. It was a memorable feat of insipid and mindless vilification: "They [Israelis and Jews] try to kill all the principles of divine faiths with the same mentality of betraying Jesus Christ and torturing Him, and in the same way they tried to commit treachery against the prophet Muhammad."[43]

The anti-Jewish poison that rose so naturally to Assad's lips has today become a staple feature of the Palestinian Authority's educational program. In Palestinian textbooks, reference to Jews is minimal except for negative generalizations that attribute to them character traits of trickery, greed, and barbarity. Schoolbooks invariably insinuate that Jews never keep agreements as Muslims do.[44] The Jewish connection to the Holy Land is generally denied or else it is confined to antiquity and virtually ignored after the Roman period. There is no reference to Jewish holy places or to any special connection of the Jews or of Judaism to the city of Jerusalem.[45] Hebrew is not considered to be one of the languages of the land

and Zionism is mentioned solely in the context of alien intrusion, invasion, or infiltration. The state of Israel is not recognized at all and its territory is referred to only by terms such as the "interior" or the "1948 lands." By definition, the Jewish state is presented as a colonialist usurper and occupier.[46] Brutal, inhuman, and greedy, it is held exclusively responsible for obliterating Palestinian national identity, destroying the Palestinian economy, expropriating Palestinian lands, water and villages.[47]

The maps in Palestinian textbooks, without exception, disregard Israel's existence and that of its 5.5 million inhabitants. The Palestine that stretches from the Jordan River to the Mediterranean Sea is designated as purely and exclusively Arab.[48]

Nor have Palestinian clerics, intellectuals, and writers hesitated in recent years to dismiss or distort the historical reality of the Holocaust even as they accuse Zionism of being the heir of Nazism. An article by Hiri Manzour in the official Palestinian newspaper on April 13, 2001, brazenly asserted that "the figure of six million Jews cremated in the Nazi Auschwitz camps is a lie," while pretending that this hoax was promoted by Jews as part of their international "marketing operation."[49] The "big lie" technique, first perfected by the Nazis, is however by no means confined to Holocaust-related issues. Palestinian officials do not shrink, for instance, from the most outlandish and libelous allegations about Israeli "crimes against humanity."

At the UN Commission on Human Rights in Geneva on March 17, 1997, Nabil Ramlawi stunned delegates by declaring that "Israeli authorities . . . infected by injection 300 Palestinian children with the HIV virus during the years of the *intifada*." The commander of the Palestinian General Security Service in Gaza mendaciously attacked Israel for encouraging "Russian Jewish girls with AIDS to spread the disease among Palestinian youth."[50] The PA Minister of Supplies, Abdel Hamid al-Quds, even told the Israeli newspaper *Yediot Aharonot* that "Israel is distributing food containing material that causes cancer and hormones that harm male virility and spoiled food products . . . in order to poison and harm the Palestinian population."[51]

In the same perverse vein, Suha Arafat, wife of the PA president, at a press conference in the presence of Hillary Clinton (then-first lady), falsely accused Israel of poisoning Palestinian air and water. Yasser Arafat himself, at the 2001 world economic forum in Davos, Switzerland, shocked his distinguished audience by insisting in front of Israeli Foreign Minister Peres that Israel was using depleted uranium and nerve gas against Palestinian civilians. Film clips from official PA television were fabricated to show the alleged victims racked by convulsions and vomiting. In other cases, there were scenes of rape and murder supposedly carried out by Israeli soldiers, "re-enacted" specially for the cameras.[52]

The antagonism not only lies far deeper and goes well beyond the issue of "settlements." Indeed, it extends to the entire Jewish national project, to Israel's very existence in the Middle East and to the rejection of what Saddam Hussein repeatedly called the "criminal Zionist entity." We need to recognize that a culture of hatred has arisen which has become *an end in itself*, rather than a form of politics by other means.

III

In the current Arab dispensation, Israel is not merely another face of European racism or Nazism but actually "a double Nazism."[53] To quote that renowned political thinker, President Bashar Assad of Syria, Israel is "more racist than the Nazis." Fiamma Nirenstein has ably summed this kind of defamation as follows:

> Israel has been transformed into little more than a diabolical abstraction, not a country at all but a malignant force embodying every possible negative attribute — aggressor, usurper, sinner, occupier, corrupter, infidel, murderer, barbarian. . . . The uncomplicated sentiment produced by these caricatures is neatly captured by the latest hit song in Cairo, Damascus, and East Jerusalem. Its title: "I Hate Israel."[54]

This frightening image of the Jewish state as the incarnation of malignant evil naturally encourages the idea that all the Jews of Israel should be wiped out. Not only that, but on a soil fertilized by demonology, the cult of martyrdom more readily flourishes and loses its last moral inhibitions. The Muslim fundamentalist clergy plays a particularly deleterious role in the current cycle of incitement.

Robert S. Wistrich

In June 2001, the PA television broadcast Sheikh Ibrahim Mahdi's sermon blessing, "whoever has put a belt of explosives on his body or on his sons and plunged into the midst of the Jews."[55] There are unfortunately thousands of such sermons preaching violence against Jews. Equally horrifying is the enthusiasm with which so many Arab and Palestinian columnists greet the suicide bombers who destroy innocent Israeli lives. The terrorists enjoy overwhelming moral support in opinion polls from among the Palestinians. However, the *jihad* against Israel is seen by Islamists in particular not only as a military-political battle for the inalienable "sacred Muslim soil" (*Waqf*) of Palestine, but also as a struggle to defeat America and the occult power of the Jews.

For the best-known leader of *Hizbullah* in Lebanon, Ayatollah Fadlallah, the state of Israel is simply a military arm of the wider Jewish conspiracy, the nucleus for spreading their economic and cultural domination. According to Fadlallah, there is a "world Jewish movement working to deprive Islam of its positions of actual power." The Jews wish to control the economic potential and resources of the Islamic world, to weaken it spiritually over the question of Jerusalem and geographically over Palestine.[56] For Fadlallah, this is a battle for culture itself even more than for Palestinian land or for Jerusalem. It is an apocalyptic, Manichean vision of conflict. As Martin Kramer has put it, this is "a view of Muslim and Jew locked in a total confrontation which will continue until one side completely subjugates the other."[57]

Any peace agreement with Israel would, in the eyes of the Islamists, fatally subject the Muslim world to complete Jewish domination. According to *Hamas* spokesman Ibrahim Ghawshah, if there were ever a compromise between Arabs and Israelis, then "Israel will dominate the region like Japan dominates southeast Asia, and the Arabs will all become employees of the Jews."[58]

The specter of "Jewish domination" which underpins much of contemporary Islamic anti-Semitism is part of its comprehensive vision of a worldwide Jewish conspiracy. This is a world view that has steadily gathered force since the crushing Arab defeat at the hands of Israel in 1967. That humiliating loss was not just a blow to Arab pride, machismo, and national ambition but a reflection for many Muslims of the crisis of Islam, of a lethargic, backward society and culture defeated by a powerful, modern, technologically advanced, and highly motivated Zionist enemy. The secularist pan-Arab nationalism and Arab socialism that had previously held sway were in part discredited. In their place came the new trend toward seeing Islam as being engaged in a fateful battle for civilization.[59] In a curious echo of neo-Marxist rhetoric, the "Zionist invaders" were perceived by radical Muslims as "white settler colonizers" threatening the cultural identity of Islam itself.

Shortly after the disaster of June 1967, more conservative fundamentalists exacerbated and sharpened the traditional image of Zionism and the Jews into something so utterly vile and perverse that it could only merit total eradication.[60] Virtually all the Arab theologians assembled in Cairo in 1968 stigmatized Jews as "enemies of God" and "enemies of humanity"; as a criminal riff-raff rather than as a people. Their state was the illegitimate culmination of allegedly *immutable* and *permanently depraved* characteristics. As their Holy Books amply demonstrated, "evil, wickedness, breach of vows, and money worship" were "inherent qualities" in the Jews which had become horrifyingly visible in their conquest of Palestine.[61] In line with this conservative pattern of thought, President Sadat of Egypt on April 25, 1972, referred to the Jews as "a nation of liars and traitors, contrivers of plots, a people born for deeds of treachery," who would soon be "condemned to humiliation and misery," as prophesied in the *Qur`an*.[62] The head of the Academy of Islamic Research, Dr. Abdul Halim Mahmoud, was even more explicit in an influential book published a year after the Yom Kippur War: "Allah commands the Muslims to fight the friends of Satan wherever they are found. Among the friends of Satan — indeed, among the foremost friends of Satan in our present age — are the Jews."[63]

IV

Arab and Muslim anti-Semites have in recent decades annexed the symbols and expressions of European anti-Semitism, even as they "Islamicized" its language. A particularly significant example in which Arab anti-Semitism has proven itself to be virtually identical with neo-Nazi, racist, and "anti-Zionist" forms of Western Judeophobia, is Holocaust denial. Indeed, in recent years this has become one of the central planks of Arab and Muslim anti-Semitism.[64] One finds a growing readiness among Muslims to believe that the Jews consciously *invented* the "Auschwitz lie," the "hoax" of their own extermination, as part of a truly diabolical plan to achieve world domination. In this super-Macchiavellian scenario, the satanic archetype of the conspiratorial Jew — author and beneficiary of the greatest "myth" of the 20th century — achieves a gruesome and novel apotheosis.

One of the attractions of Holocaust denial to Arabs clearly lies in its radical challenge to the moral foundations of the Israeli state. This debunking critique is what motivated Mahmoud Abbas (better known today as Abu Mazen), who later emerged as the chief PLO architect of the Oslo peace accords. He wrote in 1983 a Holocaust denial book entitled *The Other Side: The Secret Relationship between Nazism and the Zionist Movement*. In it, Abu Mazen suggested, for example, that the number of Jewish victims of the *Shoah* was "even fewer than one million."[65] In the 1980s, a former Moroccan army officer, Ahmed Rami, also began to develop a much more fully fledged and violently anti-Semitic Holocaust denial campaign from Stockholm, Sweden, where he founded "Radio Islam." Under the cover of "anti-Zionism" and ostensibly defending the Palestinian cause, Rami called for "a new Hitler" who would rally the West and Islam against the cancer of "Jewish power," and free it from the mendacious yoke of "Talmudism" and the Holocaust industry.[66]

In Iran, too, beginning in the early 1980s, an embryonic form of Holocaust denial already existed alongside Stürmer-like caricatures of the "Talmudic Jew," the obsessive promotion of *The Protocols of the Elders of Zion* and repeated calls to eradicate the Zionist cancer from the planet.[67] Holocaust denial was a logical final step for militant Khomeini-style radicalism which totally demonizes Zionism, seeing in it a uniquely malevolent and insidious 20th century reincarnation of the "subversive and cunning spirit of Judaism."[68]

Against this historic background, it is no surprise to find the present-day leader of Iran, Ayatollah Ali Khameini, claiming:

> There is evidence which shows that Zionists had close relations with German Nazis and exaggerated statistics on Jewish killings. There is even evidence on hand that a large number of non-Jewish hooligans and thugs of Eastern

Europe were forced to emigrate to Palestine as Jews . . . to install in the heart of the Islamic world an anti-Islamic state under the guise of supporting the victims of racism.[69]

The *mufti* of Jerusalem, Sheikh Ikrima Subri, not to be outdone, told the *New York Times* in March 2000: ". . . we believe the number of six million is exaggerated. The Jews are using this issue, in many ways, also to blackmail the Germans financially. . . . The Holocaust is protecting Israel."[70]

Other Palestinians have also become explicitly defamatory in recent years about the Holocaust. Hassan al-Agha, professor at the Islamic University in Gaza City, declared on a PA cultural affairs television program in 1997:

> . . . the Jews view it [the Holocaust] as a profitable activity so they inflate the number of victims all the time. In another ten years, I do not know what number they will reach. . . . As you know, when it comes to economics and investments, the Jews have been very experienced even since the days of *The Merchant of Venice*.[71]

A sinister example of this popular genre can be found in a recent article by the editor of *Tishreen* (Syria's leading daily). Two years ago, he accused the Zionists of cynically inflating the Holocaust "to astronomic proportions" in order "to deceive international public opinion, win its empathy and blackmail. . . ." Israel and the Jewish organizations, he wrote, encourage "their distorted version of history" in order to squeeze ever more funds from Germany and other European states in restitution payments. But they also use the Holocaust "as a sword hanging over the necks of all who oppose Zionism."[72] According to the Syrian view, the Zionist effort to paralyze human memory, logic, and discussion was bound to fail: "Israel, that presents itself as the heir of Holocaust victims, has committed and still commits much more terrible crimes than those committed by the Nazis. The Nazis did not expel a whole nation nor bury people and prisoners alive, as the Zionists did."[73]

The European "revisionist" most frequently mentioned as a source for Arab Holocaust deniers was the French left-wing intellectual (and convert to Islam) Roger Garaudy. Indeed, the trial and conviction of Garaudy in France in 1998 for "*négationisme*," would make him a hero in much of the Middle East.[74] Among his admirers was the former president of Iran, Ali Akbar Hashemi Rafsanjani, who in a sermon on Teheran Radio, declared himself fully convinced that "Hitler had only killed 20,000 Jews and not six million," adding that "Garaudy's crime derives from the doubt he cast on Zionist propaganda."[75]

The Garaudy Affair, stemming from the French author's 1995 book *The Founding Myths of Modern Israel* (which argues that Jews deliberately fabricated the Holocaust for financial and political gain) is so revealing in several ways. First, there is the vitality of the Holocaust-denial anti-Semitism right across the Muslim and Arab worlds. The Arabic translations of Garaudy's work also became bestsellers in many Middle Eastern countries, though only in France itself was he charged with inciting racial hatred.[76] Many Arab professionals eagerly offered their services to help Garaudy. The binding ideological cement behind this outpouring of solidarity was a *Protocols*-style anti-Semitism which regards it almost as a self-evident truth that the Holocaust was indeed a Zionist invention. Hence, the very favorable reaction to Garaudy's theses by so many Arab newspapers and magazines or by clerics like Sheikh Muhammad Al-Tantawi, well-known politicians like Rafiq Hariri, or intellectuals such as Muhammad Hassanin Haikal.[77]

It is no less revealing that Palestinian intellectuals, clerics, and legislators have themselves shown great reluctance to incorporate any aspect of the *Shoah* into their teaching curricula, fearing that it might strengthen Zionist claims to Palestine.[78] Hatem Abd Al-Qader, a *Hamas* leader, explained in a recent internal Palestinian debate that such instruction would represent "a great danger for the formation of a Palestinian consciousness"; it would directly threaten Palestinian political dreams and religious aspirations, such as the promise by Allah that the whole of Palestine was a sacred possession to the Arabs.

According to the Palestinian intellectual Abdallah Horani, Israel and the Zionists should hardly be offered Palestinian assistance to propagate their "lies" and their "false history" of the *Shoah*. In his view, the very raising of this issue was part of an American-Israeli plot to efface Palestinian national memory in favor of the globalizing "culture of peace" and to prepare the ground for an ideological-cultural penetration of Palestine by the West.[79] The head of the Palestinian Islamic *jihad* in Gaza, Sheikh Nafez Azzam, was more brief and categorical: "To wish to teach the *Shoah* in Palestinian schools contradicts the order of the universe."[80]

V

A central feature of Arab and Muslim anti-Semitism continues to be the categoric refusal to accept Israel's right to exist and its moral legitimacy. This fundamental premise has been aggravated by an education relentlessly directed toward hatred of Israel and the Jews. In this propaganda, Israel is the scapegoat for the continuous Arab inability to achieve political unity, economic development, or other national goals. Frustration at the failure to successfully modernize has led to the displacement of rage on to Jews and the Jewish state as "agents of Western imperialism, globalization, and an invasive modernist culture in the region."

There is an implicit as well as an explicit anti-Semitism that underlies this exclusivist nationalist rhetoric and it is sharpened by what has become a completely dehumanized portrait of Israelis. They are branded as murderers, criminals, riff-raff, the scum of the earth. Israelis are simply a collection of rootless, nomadic Jews who illegally stole a land that was not their own, in order to create a "Nazified" state based on dreams of world domination as laid out in *The Protocols*. For many Muslims today, this "artificial" and evil state which exploits the "imperialistic" Judaic religion and its concept of a "chosen people" in order to seize ever more Arab land is pictured like a spreading cancer that must be surgically removed if Islam is to survive.[81]

Arab and Muslim anti-Semitism have always had a sharp political edge which derives from the intensity of the Arab-Israeli conflict. But the Palestinian territorial dimension should not blind us to the fact that anti-Semitism also has an autonomous dynamic of its own.[82] There is a distinctive, underlying structure to Arab-Muslim anti-Semitic ideology (some of it Christian in origin) beyond immediate political circumstances, government propaganda, the territorial conflict with Israel, or the instrumental use of imported anti-Jewish stereotypes and symbols.[83] It cannot be wholly divorced from the rise of modern Arab nationalism which constructed an ideology of "Arabism" (*al-`uruba*) inimical to the Jewish and foreign presence in the Middle East. This organic nationalism facilitated a stereotypical way of thinking about all "outsiders" (including Jews) as "aliens" and enemies. Already in Nasser's Egypt during the 1950s and in the *Ba`ath*ist movements of Syria and Iraq, it was apparent that a Western and even a "Nazified" anti-Semitism could be easily grafted on to the pan-Arab vision of a single, powerful, homogeneous Arabic-speaking nation. The historic resentment against Western colonialism and imperialism as well as the bitterness provoked by successive defeats at the hands of Israeli Jews, greatly intensified this frame of thought. Conspiracy theories postulating that "international Zionism" (conceptually merged into "world Jewry") is locked in eternal enmity toward the Arab nation became as widespread among Arab nationalists as they are in fundamentalist circles.[84]

It is no secret that secular pan-Arab nationalists, already before 1967, regarded Israel's existence and consolidation as a "cultural-challenge." What was driven home with such shocking clarity by the Six Day War was the fact that the previously powerless and defenseless Jewish *dhimmis* had not only successfully risen up and created an independent Jewish state (as in 1948) but were now able to decisively crush several Arab armies on the battlefield. One can perhaps best explain the peculiar emotional rage behind Arab-Muslim anti-Semitism as an attempt to deflect the unresolved traumas which this unexpected Israeli military and technological prowess inflicted on the Arab psyche.

The Six Day War greatly intensified the demonology of Zionism and the Jews, especially among Muslim fundamentalists. There was a deep sense of humiliation over the loss of Islamic territory in 1967 and the capture of the holy city of Jerusalem by the Israelis. Not by accident, fundamentalists now posed the conflict much more sharply in terms of a struggle between Islam and the Jews — a battle of culture, civilization, and religion.[85] The Jewish victory became for them a symptom of Islam's malaise and degradation — of its inability to recover the religious sources of its past glory and overcome the challenges posed by a "decadent" if powerful Western modernity. A radical rejection of all things "Western" and the belief that only Islam is the solution (*Islam huwa al-hal*) fused with a new vision of the Jewish danger — of Israel as total enemy and existential threat.

Another conspicuous feature of contemporary Arab-Islamic anti-Semitism is the fixed, almost static quality of its underlying stereotypes. Jews are constantly denigrated as irremediably evil, corrupt, immoral, intriguing, deceitful, and greedy creatures, or else they are vilified as racist, colonialist, and fascist "vampires" sucking Arab blood. Twenty years ago, a prominent Egyptian scholar wrote about the Jews and the Israel-Arab conflict in exactly the same anti-Semitic language that is so commonplace today: ". . . for Jews are Jews; they have not changed over thousands of years: they embody treachery, meanness, deceit, and contempt for human values. They would devour the flesh of a living person and drink his blood for the sake of robbing his property."[86]

It was in response to such defamation that the historian Bernard Lewis — a leading authority on Middle Eastern history — chillingly observed in 1986:

> The volume of anti-Semitic books and articles published, the size and number of editions and impressions, the eminence and authority of those who write, publish, and sponsor them, their place in school and college curricula, their role in the mass media, would all seem to suggest that classical anti-Semitism is an essential part of Arab intellectual life at the present time — almost as much as happened in Nazi Germany, and considerably more than in late 19th and early 20th century France.[87]

Lewis believed, however, that this Arab hatred lacked the visceral and intensely intimate quality of central and east European anti-Semitism. He claimed that in Arab lands it was "still largely political and ideological, intellectual and literary," lacking any deep personal animosity or popular resonance.[88] Despite its vehemence and ubiquity, Middle Eastern Judeophobia at that time was seen largely as a function of the Arab-Israeli conflict, cynically exploited for propaganda reasons by Arab rulers and intellectual elites: it was "something that comes from above, from the leadership, rather than from below, from the society — a political and polemical weapon, to be discarded if and when it is no longer required."[89]

This assumption, in my view, was overly optimistic and intellectually questionable even at the time that it was made. In recent years, this has become ever more apparent as the anti-Semitic virus has taken root in the body politic of Islam to a shocking degree. More than ten years ago I wrote that "an anti-Jewish Arab ideology has crystallized and acquired its own momentum over the course of the past few decades, one that has distorted and blackened the image of the Jew in ways that were historically unprecedented for the Islamic world.[90]

In the year 2004, it is no less clear that while very little has changed in the basic repertoire of Islamic Judeophobia, it has unfortunately become more widespread, intense, radicalized and militantly religious in character. The horrifying murder of the *Wall Street Journal* correspondent Daniel Pearl in Pakistan, cruelly exemplified the existential threat that this violently anti-Jewish ideology represents. His last words before he was decapitated by his fanatical Muslim captors were, "I am a Jew." He was butchered not simply because he was an American and an investigative journalist but for the simple fact of his birth. To be born a Jew has become, for many Islamic fascists, as it was for Hitler and the Nazis, an *a priori* reason to be executed.[91]

Endnotes

1 Quoted in Albert Speer, *Spandau: The Secret Diaries* (New York: Macmillan, 1976), p. 80.
2 For a vivid account of the steady drumbeat of a malignant anti-Americanism in the Arab world, see Fouad Ajami, "The Sentry's Solitude," *Foreign Affairs*, vol. 80, no. 6 (November/December 2001): p. 2–16.
3 *Memri Dispatch*, no. 226, June 8, 2001, quotes the highest ranking Palestinian Authority cleric, the Jerusalem *mufti*, Sheikh Ikrem Sabri as follows:
"Our enemies [i.e., Israel] think that they scare our people. We tell them: in as much as you love life — the Muslim loves death and martyrdom. There is a great difference between he who loves the hereafter and he who loves this world. The Muslim loves death and [strives for] martyrdom."
4 In this context, Hitler's consistent popularity in the Arab world is significant. See Robert S. Wistrich, *Antisemitism. The Longest Hatred* (New York: Pantheon, 1991), p. 247. For a characteristic recent example, see the columnist Ahmad Ragab's "Thanks to Hitler" (on behalf of the Palestinians) in the government-sponsored Egyptian newspaper *Al-Akhbar*. Quoted in *Memri Dispatch*, no. 208, April 20, 2001.

5 See Robert S. Wistrich, *Hitler's Apocalypse* (New York: St. Martin's Press, 1986), p. 154–193; and Bernard Lewis, *Semites and Anti-Semites* (New York/London: Norton, 1986), p. 140–163. Lewis emphasizes that it was the Arab leadership that initiated approaches to Nazi Germany between 1933 and 1945.

6 One can find such conspiracy theories in the work of Sayyid Qutb, the great Egyptian Muslim fundamentalist writer, executed by Nasser in 1966, who saw the struggle with the Jews as a cosmic and fateful war for Islam. See Ronald L. Nettler, *Past Trials and Present Tribulations. A Muslim Fundamentalist's View of the Jews* (Oxford/New York: Pergamon Press, 1987), p. 44–57.

7 See *Yediot Aharonot*, December 28, 2001, p. 10–13, 28–29 for a wide-ranging discussion on anti-Semitism today in which I took part.

8 *Response*, Simon Wiesenthal Center, Los Angeles, California, Fall 2001.

9 Quoted in L'Arche, October–November 2001, p. 66. "Cette guerre se poursuivra, de plus en plus violente, jusqu'à ce que nous ayons vaincu les juifs."

10 Raphael Israeli, "Anti-Semitism Revived: The Impact of the Intifada on Muslim Immigrant Groups in Western Democracies," in *Jerusalem Viewpoints*, no. 455, June 1, 2001, published by the Jerusalem Center for Public Affairs.

11 See *Actualité Juive*, no. 733, January 17, 2002, p. 6, 9–11, 22–24, 31–32, for different viewpoints — Israeli, French, and French Jewish — on the rising anti-Semitism in France.

12 Emmanuel Navon, "Pardon My French," *Jerusalem Post*, January 29, 2002.

13 David Landau, "Jewish Angst in Albion," *Ha'aretz*, January 23, 2002.

14 Op-ed article entitled "To Anthrax" in *Al-Risala*, November 7, 2001, by columnist Dr. Atallah Abu Al-Subh. The *Hamas* weekly in which this piece appeared is based in Gaza.

15 *Al-Maydan*, September 24, 2001. By editor Issam Al-Ghazi. This is an independent Egyptian weekly, Memri, no. 281.

16 Ibid.

17 Memri, September 21, 2001, no. 274. See the article by deputy editor Magdi Shandi and especially (on September 17) by columnist Muhammad Mustagab.

18 *Al-Arabi*, September 16, 2001. The article was by columnist Ahmad Murad.

19 Salim ʿAzzouz, *Al-Ahrar*, September 17, 2001.

20 Ammar Shammakh in Egyptian-based *Afaq Arabiya*, September 19, 2001, Memri, September 21, 2001, no. 274.

21 *Teheran Times*, Iranian newspaper, October 25, 2001. Islamic Republic News Agency, October 24, 2001.

22 *Al Thawra*, September 19, 2001.

23 *Al-Ahram Weekly Online*, September 27–October 3. Story by Omayma Abdel-Latif.

24 Ahmad Al-Muslih, in *Al-Dustour*, September 13, 2001, Memri, September 20, 2001, no. 270.

25 Ibid., Memri, article by Hayat Al-Hweiek `Atiya and Rakan Al-Majali, who added that Jews more than anyone "are capable of hiding a criminal act they perpetrate, and they can be certain that no one will ask them about what they do."

26 Interview for an official Al-Azhar University web site, <www.lilatalqadr.com>. Memri, October 17, 2001, no. 288.

27 Interview with Rod Nordland, *Newsweek*, September 14, 2001.

28 "Zionists Could Be Behind Attack on WTC and Pentagon," October 14, 2001, on website <www.islamweb.net/english>. The "facts" behind the article come from Pakistan though the site is registered to the State of Qatar Ministry of Endowments and Religious Affairs.

29 <ArabNews.Com>, Saudi English language daily; posted on November 5, 2001, by Hassan Tahsin.

30 *Iran Daily*, October 29, 2001.

31 IRNA (Islamic Republic News Agency), October 25, 2001.

32 Palestinian Daily Press Review, September 24, 2001.

33 See *Tishreen*, January 31, 2000, editorial.

34 *Al Thawra*, February 22, 2000, editorial. Daily commentary report on Syrian radio, February 24, 2000. See also *Al Baath*, February 10, 2000. "All those who saw Levy on television threatening Lebanon were reminded of the Nazi period."

35 Lebanese television footage from February 28, 2000, showing David Levy's speech to the Knesset threatening to "burn the soil of Lebanon" (in reprisal for Hizbullah attacks) alongside footage of Hitler's Nazi rallies.

36 *Al-Ittihad* (United Arab Emirates daily), February 25, 2000.

37 *Al-Watan* (semi-independent Qatari daily), February 21, 2000. Some of this material was compiled by the Anti-Defamation League. See its March 2000 background file on "Anti-Semitism and Demonization of Israel in the Arab Media," January–February 2000.

38 "Anti-Semitic Images in the Egyptian Media," Anti-Defamation League, New York, January 2000–February 2001. On the extraordinary prevalence of hostile anti-Jewish attitudes across the political spectrum in Egypt, see Rivka Yadlin, *An Arrogant, Oppressive Spirit. Anti-Zionism as Anti-Judaism in Egypt* (Oxford/New York: Pergamon Press, 1989).

39 Dr. Mahmoud Al-Said Al-Kurdi, *Al Akhbar*, March 25, 2001.

40 *Al-Musawwar*, no. 24, August 4, 1972, p. 13.

41 Ibid., Zbeir Sultan, "The Peace of Zion," January 1, 2000; Memri, January 6, 2000.

42 Ibid., see also *Al Ahram*, April 29, 2001, which recalled Mu`ammar al-Qadhafi's "revelations" that Libyan children had been injected with AIDS by foreign nurses. The government daily echoed the accusations of those who believed the CIA or Israeli Mossad were behind this crime.

43 Syrian News Agency, May 5, 2001.

44 *Jews, Israel and Peace in Palestinian School Textbooks 2000–2001 and 2001–2002*, Report, New York, Center for Monitoring the Impact of Peace, November 2001, p. 22–25.

45 Ibid., p. 17.

46 Ibid., p. 35.

47 Ibid., p. 28–29, 34–40.

48 Ibid., p. 42.

49 *Al Hayat Al-Jadeeda*, April 13, 2001. Hiri Manzour's article was published on Israel's Holocaust Remembrance Day. It was provocatively entitled "The Fable of the Holocaust" to cause maximum offense.

50 Al Hayat Al-Jadeeda, May 15, 1997.

51 *Yediot Aharonot*, June 25, 1997.

52 Fiamma Nirenstein, "How Suicide Bombers Are Made," *Commentary* (September 2001): p. 53–55.

53 Ibid., p. 54.

54 Ibid.

55 Ibid., p. 55.

56 Martin Kramer, "The Salience of Islamic Fundamentalism," *Institute of Jewish Affairs*, no. 2 (October 1995): p. 5–6.

57 Ibid., p. 6.

58 Ibid., p. 8.

59 See Fouad Ajami, *The Arab Predicament. Arab Political Thought and Practice Since 1967* (Cambridge, MA: Cambridge University Press, 1984), p. 50–76.

60 D.F. Green, editor, *Arab Theologians on Jews and Israel*, The Fourth Conference of the Academy of Islamic Research, 3rd edition, Geneva, 1976, p. 9.

61 Ibid., Kamal Ahmad Own, "The Jews Are the Enemies of Human Life," p. 19–24.

62 Ibid., p. 91.

63 Ibid., p. 95; Dr. Abdul Halim Mahmoud, *Al-Jihad wa al-Nasr* (Holy War and Victory), Cairo, 1974, p. 148–150.

64 Eliahu Salpeter, "Anti-Semitism Among the Arabs," *Ha'aretz*, February 9, 2000.

65 See *Holocaust Denial in the Middle East: The Latest Anti-Israel Propaganda Theme* (New York: Anti-Defamation League, 2001), p. 5–6. Abu Mazen never publicly retracted his Holocaust denial book despite a request to do so from the Simon Wiesenthal Center in Los Angeles. He told the Israeli newspaper *Ma'ariv* that he wrote the work at a time when the PLO was "at war with Israel." After Oslo, he claimed, he would not have made such remarks.

66 See Per Ahlmark, "Reflections on Combating Anti-Semitism," in Yaffa Zilbershats, editor, *The Rising Tide of Anti-Semitism* (Bar-Ilan University, 1993), p. 59–66. Mr. Ahlmark, who co-founded the Swedish Committee against Anti-Semitism, has called Rami's Holocaust denial statements "the most vicious anti-Jewish campaign in Europe since the Third Reich." Rami has been

prosecuted in Swedish courts on three occasions. He was again convicted and fined in October 2000.

67 See *Imam*, March and May issues of 1984, a publication of the Iranian Embassy in London. Also *The Imam Against Zionism*, Ministry of Islamic Guidance, the Islamic Republic of Iran, 1983, for the Ayatollah Khomeini's malevolent view of Israel. Also Emmanuel Sivan, "Islamic Fundamentalism, Antisemitism and Anti-Zionism," in Robert S. Wistrich, editor, *Anti-Zionism and Antisemitism in the Contemporary World* (New York: New York University Press, 1990), p. 74–84.

68 Olivier Carré, *L'Utopie Islamique dans l'Orient Arabe* (Paris, 1991), p. 195–201; Robert S. Wistrich, "The Antisemitic Ideology in the Contemporary Islamic World," in Zilbershats, *The Rising Tide of Anti-Semitism*, p. 67–74.

69 *Jerusalem Post*, April 25, 2001. A year earlier a conservative Iranian newspaper, the *Teheran Times*, had insisted in an editorial that the Holocaust was "one of the greatest frauds of the 20th century." This prompted a complaint by the British Member of Parliament Louise Ellman to the Iranian ambassador in London. Agence France-Presse, May 14, 2000.

70 *New York Times*, March 26, 2000. Sabri added: "It's certainly not our fault if Hitler hated the Jews. Weren't they hated pretty much everywhere?"

71 Quoted in *Holocaust Denial in the Middle East*, p. 12.

72 Muhammad Kheir al-Wadi, "The Plague of the Third Millennium," *Tishreen*, January 31, 2000.

73 Ibid.

74 *Al-Ahram*, March 14, 1998, defended Garaudy by arguing *inter alia* that there was "no trace of the gas chambers" which were supposed to have existed in Germany. In fact, there were no gas chambers erected in Germany itself — all the death camps were located in Poland.

75 *Holocaust Denial in the Middle East*, p. 8–9.

76 Roger Garaudy, *Les Mythes Fondateurs de la politique israélienne* (Paris, 1995). A former Catholic, then a Communist, Garaudy became a Muslim in 1982 and married a Jerusalem-born Palestinian woman. On the echoes in France, see Pierre-André Taguieff, "L'Abbé Pierre et Roger Garaudy. Négationisme, Antijudaisme, Antisionisme," *Esprit*, no. 8–9 (1996): p. 215. Also Valérie Igounet, *Histoire du Négationisme en France* (Paris, 2000), p. 472–483.

77 See the article by Mouna Naim in *Le Monde*, March 1, 1998.

78 *Memri Report*, February 20, 2001.

79 *Al-Istiqlal*, April 20, 2000.

80 Ibid.

81 This theme is particularly strong in Syrian, Iraqi, and Iranian government propaganda, but similar expressions can be found in more "moderate" Arab countries like Saudi Arabia, Jordan, and Egypt.

82 Y. Harkabi consistently argued that Arab anti-Semitism was "the outcome of political circumstances," not "a cause of the conflict but a product of it." See his "Contemporary Arab Anti-Semitism: Its Causes and Roots," in Helen Fein, editor, *The Persisting Question: Sociological Perspectives and*

Social Contexts of Modern Antisemitism (Berlin/New York: De Gruyter, 1987), p. 420.

83 See Sylvia Haim, "Arab Antisemitic Literature," *Jewish Social Studies*, no. 4, (1956): p. 307–309. Arabic translations of French anti-Semitic literature (made by Christian Arabs) were originally an important conveyor-belt for the transmission of anti-Jewish stereotypes originating in European Christian culture.

84 Yossef Bodansky, *Islamic Anti-Semitism as a Political Instrument* (Shaarei Tikva: The Ariel Center for Policy Research, 1999), p. 41–50.

85 Robert S. Wistrich, "The Antisemitic Ideology in the Contemporary Islamic World," in Zilbershats, *The Rising Tide of Anti-Semitism*, p. 70.

86 Dr. Lutfi abd-al-ʿAdhim, "Arabs and Jews: Who Will Annihilate Whom?" in *Al-Ahram al-Iqtisadi*, September 27, 1982. See the long extract cited by Raphael Israeli, in his pamphlet on *Arab and Islamic Anti-Semitism* (Shaarei Tikva: The Ariel Center for Policy Research, 2000), Policy Paper No. 104, p. 14–15.

87 Lewis, *Semites and Anti-Semites*, p. 286.

88 Ibid., p. 258. See also the pioneering study of Y. Harkabi, *Arab Attitudes to Israel* (London: Vallentine, Mitchell, 1972), p. 227.

89 Lewis, ibid., p. 259.

90 Robert S. Wistrich, *Antisemitism: The Longest Hatred* (New York: Pantheon, 1991), p. 265.

91 See my article "The New Islamic Fascism," *Partisan Review*, no. 1 (2002): p. 32–34 and my research paper for the American Jewish Committee entitled "Muslim Antisemitism — A Clear and Present Danger," published in May 2002. Much of the material in this essay has been drawn from that research and suitably recast.

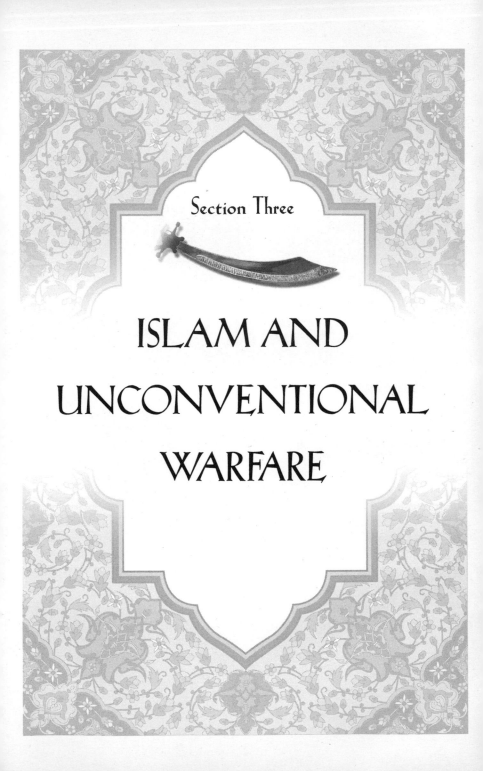

Section Three

ISLAM AND UNCONVENTIONAL WARFARE

Nuclear Programs of
Arab and Islamic States:
Capabilities, Strategies, and Implications

Gerald M. Steinberg and Aharon Etengoff

T he proliferation of nuclear weapons technology in the radical
states of the Middle East, Persian Gulf, and south Asia has been
steadily accelerating since the 1970s. Under Saddam Hussein,
Iraq spent billions of dollars on acquiring and developing ballistic
missiles and weapons of mass destruction. In 1991, at the time of
the U.S.-led counterattack following the invasion of Kuwait, the
totalitarian Iraqi dictator was only a few months away from being
able to fabricate a nuclear weapon. Iran has been working steadily
to follow this lead, as have Libya, Algeria, and other states. In May
1998, Pakistan followed India in officially entering the nuclear
weapons club.

The threats to security and stability posed by the spread of
nuclear weapons in the Islamic world go beyond the impacts of the
individual national programs and constitute a much wider regional
and global threat. These are highly unstable areas, in which terrorism, sponsored, used, and sheltered by states, is endemic, and the
concept of *jihad* (holy war) is central. In much of this region, the

degree of hostility toward perceived enemies ("Israel," "the West," the "Great Satan") is extremely high,[1] and the global strictures against the acquisition and use of weapons of mass destruction are ignored.

In addition, despite the many sectarian and nationalist conflicts among groups, the shared element of Islam is seen as providing a basis for cooperation in obtaining these weapons and technologies, and perhaps even the transfer of nuclear arms in times of crisis and conflict.[2] Pan-Islamic ideology is quite powerful, if often violated (as in the case of the Iran-Iraq war, Saddam Hussein's invasion of Kuwait, etc). In many cases, the development of an "Islamic bomb" is often understood "to be a nuclear weapon acquired for broad ideological reasons — a weapon that supposedly belongs collectively to the Muslim *ummah* or community and, as such, is the ultimate expression of Islamic solidarity."[3]

This concept has been stated explicitly by a number of Islamic leaders. Before he was executed, deposed President Zulfikar Ali Bhutto, the architect of Pakistan's nuclear program, wrote, "We know that Israel and South Africa have full nuclear capability. The Christian, Jewish, and Hindu civilizations have this capability. The Communist powers also possess it. Only the Islamic civilization was without it, but that position was about to change."[4] Similarly, in an address before an Islamic conference in Teheran in 1992, Iranian Vice President Sayed Ayatollah Mohajerani declared, "The Muslims must cooperate to produce an atomic bomb, regardless of UN efforts to prevent proliferation."[5]

Echoing similar sentiments, many Palestinians cheered the Pakistan nuclear tests as part of the extension of a wider Islamic military capability. The Palestinian newspaper *Al-Quds* printed an illustration of the nuclear mushroom cloud, with an Islamic crescent above it.[6] Pakistan's image and influence in the Islamic world rose significantly as a result of the nuclear tests. As Pervez Hoodbhoy noted in an article in the *Bulletin of Atomic Scientists* (1993):

> The bomb looms large in the popular Muslim consciousness as a symbol of Islamic unity, determination, and self-respect. It is seen by many as a guarantee against further humiliating defeats, as the sure sign of a reversal of fortunes, and as a panacea for the ills that have plagued

Muslims since the end of the Golden Age of Islam. Such sentiments are echoed by Muslims from Algeria to Syria, and from Iraq to Pakistan. A country that could turn this symbolism into reality would have the support of hundreds of millions of Muslims the world over. It is therefore natural that Pakistan, a Muslim country that is now a de facto nuclear state, should indeed enjoy considerable financial and political benefits from oil-rich Arab countries.[7]

While, for the most part, the nuclear weapons programs (and, in the case of Pakistan, capabilities) are primarily national, rather than "Islamic," in the sense of being made available to groups and causes that extend beyond national boundaries, this situation is likely to evolve. In the meantime, the threats to the United States, Israel, Europe, and other potential targets that will be posed by acquisition of nuclear weapons in Iraq, Iran, Libya, Algeria, Syria, and perhaps Egypt are very serious.

In this chapter, we will describe and analyze the 1) nuclear weapons capabilities and technologies, 2) development and acquisition plans and programs, and 3) statements on strategy and goals for Iran, Pakistan, Libya, Syria, Egypt, Saudi Arabia, and Algeria. For each country, we will present information based on a detailed study of the sources, including U.S. government and other official reports, the academic literature, and press reports. The country assessments will also include analysis of technological acquisitions (include dual-use systems, materials, and facilities), delivery systems such as ballistic missiles, and cooperation with third countries, including Russia, China, and North Korea, and well as between themselves. Because of the United States' destruction of Saddam Hussein's Baathist regime, our discussion of Iraqi nuclear capabilities will consist of historical background, with Iraq, at the present time, no longer considered a threat in the context of other regimes.

On this basis, the implications of the proliferation of nuclear weapons and technology in the Arab and Islamic world will be analyzed. In the case of Pakistan, this section will focus on the impact of the nuclear weapons capability on the balance of power in the region (including the Persian Gulf), on the nuclear ambitions and programs of the other states in the region, and the potential for transfer of technology and experienced personnel. Regarding the Iranian nuclear acquisition program, we will examine the security implications for the region (including Israel), and for future deployment of U.S. and NATO forces and interests in the region. We will also consider the implications of the accelerating nuclear proliferation process in this region for European security interests.

IRAQ

Iraq's efforts to acquire nuclear weapons began many years ago, and continued despite wars, attacks, and international sanctions imposed following the invasion of Kuwait in August 1990, and the war that followed.

In the early 1970s, Iraq attempted, unsuccessfully, to purchase a plutonium production reactor that was similar to the one France utilized in its nuclear weapons program.[8] In 1976, France and Iraq reached an agreement on the construction of the Osirak and Isis reactors — which were part of Iraq's sizeable nuclear research complex at Tuwaitha in Baghdad. This led to greater vigilance by outside powers, including Israel, leading to a series of setbacks in the Iraqi effort. However, Khidhir Hamza, a former physicist who worked on Iraqi nuclear weapons since 1970 (and defected in 1994), reports that in 1979 (when Saddam became president), the project was accelerated.[9] In June 1981, after efforts to gain international cooperation in stopping the flow of nuclear weapons technology to Iraq failed, Israel launched an air strike against the Osirak nuclear reactor, just before its first fuel was to be loaded.

Following the destruction of the reactor, the central effort was shifted to the production of highly enriched uranium, and Iraqi scientists investigated many different techniques for uranium enrichment. However, Iraq still maintained an interest in acquiring plutonium as fissile material for weapons, albeit on a lower level. Following the end of the war with Iran, more resources were made available for the acquisition of nuclear technology, and in 1988, Iraq attempted to obtain the components and technology for the URENCO gas-centrifuge process. During this period, Saddam Hussein increased the priority of acquiring a nuclear weapons capability, and accelerated the rate of development and acquisition of technology, materials, and expertise.[10] A wide acquisition network was formed, with branches in many countries around the world. In 1990, Iraq initiated a crash program to divert reactor fuel (highly enriched uranium) under IAEA safeguards, to the production of nuclear weapons.

At the time of the Gulf War (January 1991), Iraq maintained a sophisticated and wide-ranging nuclear weapons development program, which was supported by at least 16 primary and supporting facilities.[11] The program employed 10,000 people, and had a multi-year budget of approximately $10 billion.[12] According to Hamza, the project was close to completion at the time of the Gulf War.[13] (The prototype bomb was a "hulking, blimp-shaped, stainless steel device minus, of course, its uranium core," that would not fit on a missile.)

IRAN

Iran's nuclear program began in 1967, with the delivery of a U.S.-supplied 5 megawatt (MW) research reactor at Teheran University.[14] In 1974, Iran established the AEOI — the Atomic Energy Organization of Iran. Iran maintains two operational (5 MW and 30 kilowatt [KW]) research reactors, as well as a .01 KW critical assembly at Esfahan and Teheran.[15]

A third reactor, named Bushehr, is the core of the Iranian nuclear program. Construction was initiated by Germany (Siemans) in the 1970s, suspended in 1979 (due to the Islamic revolution[16]), and subsequently revived based on Russian assistance. The initial agreement (estimated to be worth $1 billion) was signed in 1995, but work on the 1,000 MW reactor did not begin until February 1998.[17] In March 1998, Iranian and Russian officials agreed in principle on construction of two more reactors for the Bushehr complex,[18] and in November 1998, Russia and Iran announced that they were studying the possibility of building three more nuclear reactors at Bushehr.[19]

Iran also turned to China for assistance, and in 1990, the two countries signed a ten-year nuclear cooperation agreement.[20] In 1994, a contract was signed with China's National Nuclear Corporation for the construction of two 300 MW power reactors,[21] but the contract was cancelled in 1997.

Although the U.S. administration initiated a series of high-level dialogues (the Gore-Chernomyrdin Commission) with the Russian government in the effort to slow the flow of Russian assistance, these efforts had little or no impact. In 1995, Iran attempted to purchase a uranium enrichment plant from Russia,[22] and in April 1998, Russia and Iran held talks regarding the construction of a research reactor utilizing 20 percent enriched uranium.[23] In May 1998, the head of the Iranian Atomic Energy Organization visited Russia, to discuss further cooperation and purchases.[24]

In October 1998, Western intelligence reported that Iran (led by the AEOI) was attempting to acquire equipment for laser enrichment of nuclear materials.[25] According to the American officials "there is no question that the turn-key facility was intended for" Iran's nuclear weapons program.[26] Laser enrichment is considered to be uneconomical for producing the low-enriched uranium used in civilian power reactors.[27] The official Russian response has been that Moscow did not know of the contract until early last year because the Science and Technology Center of Microtechnology (a unit of the government's D.V. Efremov Institute of St. Petersburg), had not sought an export permit, on the grounds that no sensitive technology was involved.[28] A senior U.S. official said that some Russian laser-related equipment theoretically could be cleared for export to Iran but that the U.S. government believed that, "taken as a whole package," the laser facility clearly "was intended and designed for weapons-grade enrichment."[29]

In April 1999, the Russian Izhorskiye Zavod (machine-building company in St. Petersburg) began producing equipment for the primary circuit at Bushehr.[30] This included the reactor vessel, steam generator casing, and internals.[31] In January 2000, Iran's President Muhammad Khatami sent a message to acting president of the Russian Federation Putin, stating the expectation that ties between the two states would be extended further. In mid-January, Russia's Foreign and Defense Ministers met with the Secretary of Iran's Supreme National Security Council, and declared that Moscow intended to fulfill its obligations under the relevant agreements. Atomic Affairs Minister Adamov denied reports that Russia had agreed to stop nuclear collaboration with Iran.[32]

In February 2000, the U.S. Senate approved legislation imposing sanctions on entities that assisted Iran's chemical, biological, and
nuclear weapons programs.[33] In June 2000, the U.S. government
reported that a nuclear research center in Teheran was importing
tritium from Russia. Tritium is a radioactive gas used primarily to
enhance the explosive power of nuclear warheads. One American
nuclear specialist noted that "This is an issue of concern and one
would expect Iran to be very forthcoming in providing assurances
about what it is being used for."[34]

Russian construction and engineering crews continued to work
on the Bushehr nuclear power reactor project. In May 2000, Iran's
ambassador to Russia, Mehdi Safari, declared that the nuclear power
station was 40 percent complete, and would become operational
in 2002.[35] However, work on the complex has been somewhat de-
layed due to American sanctions.[36] As such, the date of completion
remains highly speculative.[37]

Assessments of progress in the Iranian nuclear sphere vary
considerably. In 1993, the Central Intelligence Agency (CIA)
stated that Iran was eight to ten years away from acquiring nuclear
weapons; foreign assistance was said to be critical.[38] However, in
1999 the CIA warned that Iran might soon be able to produce a
nuclear weapon.[39]

Clearly, Russian and Chinese assistance has accelerated the rate
of Iranian nuclear development significantly. According to Marine
General Anthony Zinni, former head of U.S. Central Command,
"I would say they are on track, within five years, they would have
the capability [by then]."

Iranian officials formally deny that they are pursuing a military
nuclear path. Dr. Amrollahi (of the AEOI) declared, "We would like
to tell the world community that if our activities were not peaceful,
the IAEA would have said so."[40]

Yet, an earlier statement by President Ali Khamene`i, in a Feb-
ruary 1987 address to Iran's Atomic Energy Organization, sharply
contrasted Iran's policy of denying military nuclear intentions:

> Regarding atomic energy, we need it now. . . . Our na-
> tion has always been threatened from outside. The least we
> can do to face this danger is to let our enemies know that

we can defend ourselves. Therefore, every step you take here is in defense of your country and your evolution. With this in mind, you should work hard and at great speed.[41]

Missiles

- Approximately 150 Scud-Cs — 500 km range, 700 kg payload.[42]

- Up to 200 Scud-Bs — 300 km range, 985 kg payload.[43]

- Approximately 25 CSS-8s — 150 km range, 190 kg payload.[44]

- Unknown quantity of indigenous-manufactured *Mushak* missiles — range from 120 km to 200 km, payload from 150 kg to 500 kg.[45]

- Currently developing *Shihab*-3, over 1,000 km range, over 700 kg payload; the *Shihab*-4, 2,000 km range, 1,000 kg payload; and the *Shihab*-5, which will have a range of 10,000 km.[46] On July 15, Iran successfully conducted the second test of its *Shihab*-3 missile, reportedly using one of a dozen North Korean rocket motors supplied to Teheran in 1999.[47] (The first test was conducted in July 1998, but the missile did not complete a full trajectory.)[48]

In a report to the Subcommittee on Space and Aeronautics, Kenneth Timmerman stated that Iran is developing a new missile, named "*Kosar*." The *Kosar* is structured around the Soviet SS-5 missile, uses the same RD-216 liquid fuel rocket motor, and has a range of 4,250 km. There are reports that the *Kosar* is the basis for Iran's space launch vehicle.[49]

PAKISTAN

Although relatively removed from the conflicts in the Middle East, Pakistan clearly represents a major threat to India, as well as to other states in the region. The increasing political instability, as reflected in the military coup in October 12, 1999, that ousted the government of Muhammad Nawaz Sharif, and the role of radical Islam, are causes for growing concern, particularly given Pakistan's status as a de-facto nuclear weapons state.

On May 28, 1998 (a short while after five Indian nuclear tests), Pakistan announced that it had successfully completed five nuclear tests, which were reportedly carried out over a two-hour period in Balochistan.[50] According to the Pakistan Atomic Energy Commission, the nuclear tests measured up to 5.0 on the Richter scale, and had a (reported) yield of up to 40 kilotons (KT) (equivalent TNT).[51] One of the tested nuclear devices was said to be a boosted uranium device, while the other tests were (low yield) sub-KT devices.[52] On May 30, 1998, Pakistan tested an additional nuclear warhead (with a yield of 12 KT), bringing the total amount of Pakistani nuclear tests to six.[53]

Pakistan's nuclear program has reportedly progressed considerably following the successful nuclear tests in 1998.[54] Although the Pakistani government declared a moratorium on further nuclear weapons tests in June 1998,[55] two nuclear reactors, along with a plutonium processing facility, have since become operational. In addition, reports indicated that Pakistan may now be able to produce enough plutonium to manufacture one atomic bomb per year.[56]

In addition, concerns regarding Pakistani nuclear and missile cooperation with other states in the region are increasing. In 1999, the Saudi Arabian defense minister, Prince Sultan, visited Pakistan's secret nuclear facilities at Kahuta and a missile factory.[57]

History

The Pakistan Atomic Energy Commission (PAEC) was established in 1955, and in 1965, Pakistani Prime Minister Zulfikar Ali Bhutto declared: "If India builds the bomb, we will eat grass or leaves, even go hungry. But we will get one of our own."[58] In 1972, Bhutto assembled Pakistan's top scientists at Multan, and ordered them to build an atomic bomb.[59] In 1974, after India conducted a nuclear test, Bhutto declared that Pakistan must develop its own "Islamic bomb."[60]

Following Bhutto's statement, Pakistan's nuclear program accelerated considerably. In October 1974, Pakistan signed a contract with France for the design of a reprocessing facility for the fuel from its power plant at Karachi and others.[61] However, in response to pressure from the United States, the import of key components became more difficult.[62] China provided assistance in the development of gas centrifuges,[63] and the uranium enrichment facility began operation in the early 1980s.

In 1989, Pakistan tested a short-range missile, capable of carrying a nuclear payload. In 1990, the United States suspended military aid to Pakistan, after President Bush stated that he could not certify that Pakistan did not possess nuclear weapons.[64] In 1992, Pakistani Foreign Minister, Shahryar Khan, declared that Pakistan possessed the components and knowledge to manufacture at least one nuclear explosive "device."[65] In 1994, German officials announced the seizure of preforms for gas centrifuge scoops intended for use in Pakistan.[66]

However, by the mid-1990s, reports indicated that Pakistan's nuclear arsenal consisted of at least ten nuclear warheads based on a Chinese design.[67] In February of 1996, British custom officials seized a shipment of Swedish laser measuring equipment slated for a Pakistani company that was well known to be a "front" for Pakistan's nuclear weapon program.[68] In addition, the CIA revealed that China clandestinely sold 5,000 ring magnets to Pakistan's A.Q. Khan Research Laboratories.[69] In September 1996, reports indicated that China had sold (in 1996) an industrial furnace and high-tech diagnostic equipment, with military applications, to an unsafeguarded nuclear facility in Pakistan.[70]

The Pakistani nuclear program is based on enriched uranium weapons, using the fissile material produced at the Kahuta enrichment facility[71] and utilizing centrifuge technology based on *Urenco* G-1 and G-2 designs stolen by Dr. A.Q. Khan.[72] The plant[73] has an estimated 3,000 centrifuges in operation — generating a capacity of 9,000–15,000 SWU, and is capable of producing 55-95 kg of HEU per year.[74] Kahuta also houses the Dr. A.Q. Khan Research Laboratory, which began operating in 1984, and has the ability to produce centrifuge components.[75]

Pakistani officials also claim to be independent in the production of heavy water, enriched uranium, zirconium, and spare parts for its nuclear industry, and able to fabricate a nuclear weapon of any type or size, including a neutron bomb.[76] However, according to U.S. government sources, Pakistan acquired nuclear-related and dual-use equipment and materials from Western Europe and other sources.[77]

Among its goals, Pakistan is seeking to develop the capability to produce plutonium for potential weapons use.[78] A 50-70 MW heavy-water moderated plutonium reactor located at Kushab, and constructed with Chinese assistance, became operational in 1998.[79] A U.S. official was quoted as stating that Khushab is: "being operated as a dedicated weapons plutonium production reactor."[80] In March 2000, *Nucleonics Week* reported that Pakistan had successfully obtained (through smuggling) components, as well as equipment, for a heavy water production plant at Khushab.[81] Another non-safeguarded heavy water production facility supplied by Belgium in 1980 (with a yearly capacity of 13 MT) is located at Multan.[82]

The Pakistan Institute of Nuclear Science and Technology (PINSTECH) site with Pakistan's New Laboratories (also known as New Labs) includes an experimental-scale plutonium re-processing plant, capable of re-processing 10-20 kg of plutonium on a yearly basis.[83] Construction of New Labs (based on French design) began in 1976, and, according to reports, has been completed.[84] Apparently, both "cold"[85] and "hot"[86] tests have been conducted at the facility. PINSTECH also hosts a small-scale reprocessing laboratory that utilizes a solvent extraction method in addition to the Nuclear Track Detection Laboratory, an entity that carries out exploration for uranium.[87] The Center for Nuclear Studies, also based at PINSTECH, is Pakistan's primary nuclear training school.[88] (PINSTECH contains two small reactors, named Pakistan Atomic Research Reactor — also known as PARR.[89])

There is also a partially built plutonium reprocessing plant at Chashma. Construction of the plant was begun by the French, but was subsequently halted in 1978.[90] According to U.S. intelligent reports, either Pakistan or China may be re-building the plant.[91]

In 1987, Pakistan received a tritium purification and production facility (with a daily production capability of 5–10 grams of tritium) from West Germany.[92] PARR-1 is a 10 MW high flux, (upgrade from its original 5 MW capacity) pool type research reactor supplied by the United States in 1965.[93] PARR-1 is under IAEA safeguards, and originally utilized uranium enriched up to 90 percent, but has since been converted to use 20 percent enriched uranium.[94] According to reports, Lithium-6 targets were irritated on a test basis, for later use in tritium separation.[95]

Missiles

Pakistan's efforts to develop and manufacture long-range ballistic-missiles capable of carrying nuclear warheads is part of a strategy to counter India's military capabilities.[96]

Pakistan's missile arsenal includes:

- The *Ghauri* MRBM (Pakistani developed and manufactured) is a medium-range ballistic missile using liquid propellant, based on North Korea's *No Dong* MRBM, (range 1,500 km; payload 700 kg. However, it is more likely that its range is similar to the North Korean *No Dong* — 1,300 km.[97]

- The *Shaheen*-1 SRBM (Pakistani developed and manufactured) solid-fueled, 750 km range.[98]

- The *Hatf*-1 is a Pakistani developed and manufactured solid propellant missile with an 80 km range.[99]

- The M-11 SRBM is a (mobile) Chinese manufactured missile with a 290 km range, and is capable of carrying an 800 kg warhead.[100] According to reports, the M-11 is a single-stage, solid-propellant missile, with an inertial mid-course guidance system.[101] Reportedly, Pakistan's HATF III will be based on this model.[102]

According to Pakistani officials, Pakistan is currently developing two new missiles, the *Ghaznavi*, and the *Shaheen*-II. Both have a (intended) range of 2,000 km — a range sufficient to reach any location in India.[103]

LIBYA

Libya has attempted to obtain nuclear material and technology from Pakistan, China,[104] the Soviet Union (now Russia), Argentina,[105] India, and Belgium. Libya's December 2003 pledge to dismantle its weapons programs are encouraging, but we will still consider the country's weapons-development history.

Currently, Libya's basic nuclear program includes a small research reactor (which was provided by the Soviet Union in the mid-1970s at the Tajura nuclear research center[106]), and could be operating several minor nuclear research facilities. According to

Gordon C. Oehler, "Persistent efforts to deny Libya access to nuclear, BW, and delivery system technology have hobbled Qadhdhafi's programs and forced him to turn to less advanced technologies and less reliable sources available in the gray and black markets of the developing world."[107]

However, a CIA report notes that:

> Libya continues to develop its nascent and still rudimentary nuclear research and development program but still requires significant foreign assistance to advance to a nuclear weapons option. In the latter half of 1999, Tripoli and Moscow resumed discussions on cooperation at the Tajura Nuclear Research Center[108] and on a potential power reactor deal. Should this civil-sector work come to fruition, Libya could gain opportunities to conduct weapons related R&D.[109]

Libya ratified the NPT treaty in 1975, which had been signed earlier by the Idris regime in 1969, but has not signed the CTBT.[110] In 1980, Libya reached an agreement with the IAEA to place (all of) Libya's nuclear infrastructure under international inspection. However, despite the accord with the IAEA, Qadhdhafi has continually stated Libya's desire to acquire nuclear weapons.[111]

In 1977, Qadhdhafi embarked on a program of nuclear (and other) cooperation with Pakistan. For a while, it appeared as if this program had produced tangible results. Libya provided financial aid and delivered uranium "yellow cakes" (that originated in Niger), hoping that it would be compensated in the form of weapons from Pakistan.[112] However, Pakistan ended its nuclear relations with Libya before the success of Pakistan's atomic bomb — leaving Qadhdhafi without any nuclear gains.[113]

Nevertheless, despite reports of nuclear cooperation between Pakistan and Libya, Qadhdhafi (in 1986) stated that Libya would never help Pakistan acquire an atomic bomb. He said, "We consider nuclear weapons production a great mistake against humanity."[114]

In 1979, the Soviet Union supplied Libya with a 10 MW nuclear reactor, which was installed at a Libyan research center. The center was staffed with 750 Libyan specialists and technicians. Nevertheless, many students were sent abroad for additional training, and 200 Libyans studied nuclear science materials in the United States until 1983 — when nuclear training for Libyans was prohibited.[115]

In the early 1980s, Libya considered buying a power station from the Soviet Union, but displeased with Soviet technology, turned to the Belgian firm Belgonucleaire to take over the engineering contract and supply equipment. The United States objected to the deal, and Belgium decided (in 1984) to refuse the United States $1 billion contract. Subsequently, Libya re-confirmed their agreement with Moscow to construct an 880 MW power station to be located in the Surt region. The total cost of the power station was over $4 billion.[116]

In 1983, the Tajura nuclear research center became operational.[117] The research center includes a small research reactor, (provided by the Russians in the 1970s[118]) and, as noted above, in 1999, Libya and Moscow resumed discussions about resuming cooperation and discussed a potential power reactor deal.[119]

Missiles and Other Delivery Systems
- Scud-C variant — 550 km range, 500 kg payload.[120]
- 100+ Scud-B missiles — 300 km range, 985 kg payload.[121]
- SS-21 Scarab — 70 km range, 480 kg payload.[122]
- Current program to develop Al Fatah (Iltisslat) missile with 950 km. range — 500 kg payload. Has been under slow development for over 15 years.[123]

SYRIA

Syria does not have an active and advanced nuclear program, but following the pattern in a number of other states in the Middle East and elsewhere, the Syrians have been slowly building a foundation in both missile and nuclear technology. This foundation is largely based on civil research and dual-use applications, including a small 30 KW neutron research reactor in Damascus, which is operated under IAEA safeguards.[124] The fertilizer plant at Homs is owned and operated by the Atomic Commission of Syria, and this plant is being prepared for recovering uranium from phosphates.

According to the Federation of American Scientists, in 1979, Syria reportedly initiated a military nuclear program — and has not provided the IAEA with complete information regarding these activities.[125]

The Russian government has been seeking to expand its influence in the region through the export of sensitive and dual-use technologies (see the discussion of the Iranian case), and this process included the re-establishment of traditional ties between Moscow and Damascus. On February 23, 1998, the two countries signed an agreement regarding the "peaceful" use of nuclear energy, and in July 1998, a memorandum was signed regarding the construction of a 25 MW light water nuclear research center in Syria, which included the participation of Russia's Atomstroyeksport and Nikiet.[126] On May 19, Russia and Syria signed a cooperative agreement, in the fields of scientific, technical, and economic cooperation in the peaceful application of nuclear energy.[127]

In its 2000 report on WMD proliferation, the CIA stated: "As to Syria's embryonic nuclear research and development program, we will continue to monitor the potential for this program to expand. Moscow and Damascus agreed in 1999 to cooperate on peaceful uses of nuclear energy in a wide area of disciplines."[128]

Missiles and other delivery systems

- 60-120 Scud-C — 500 km range, 500 kg payload.[129]

- Up to 200 Scud-B missiles — 300 km range, 985 kg payload.[130]

- 200 SS-21 Scarab — 70 km range, 480 kg payload.[131]

- In the process of developing indigenous production capability for M-9 [CSS-6 or DF-15] missiles – 600 km range, 500 kg payload.[132]

EGYPT

Egypt continues to play a primary role in the Arab world, and has sought to maintain advanced military capabilities, including ballistic missiles, chemical, and, to a lesser degree, biological weapons as well. However, Egyptian policy in the area of nuclear weapons development is somewhat exceptional, and has been relatively dormant for some time. The major cause for concern is the possibility that following regional developments, and the India and Pakistani nuclear tests of 1998, the Egyptian pursuit of nuclear weapons may resume.

Egypt's nuclear program began in 1954, and significantly progressed in 1961, following the acquisition of a 2 MW research reactor from the Soviet Union.[133] Following the 1967 War, however, Egypt's nuclear program declined, after many of its nuclear experts emigrated abroad and economic difficulties increased.[134] Nevertheless, serious work in the nuclear sphere continued.

In the mid 1970s, as part of the realignment away from the Soviet Union and the beginning of peace negotiations with Israel, the United States agreed to provide Egypt with eight nuclear power plants. The U.S. proposal required accession to the NPT, and Egypt ratified the treaty in 1981. However, following the Israeli decision to forgo the American plan, the U.S. offer to Egypt lapsed. In September 1992, Egypt signed a contract with Invap, Argentina's nuclear organization, to build a 22 MW research reactor at Inshas.[135] Construction began in March 1993,[136] and became operational in 1998.[137] Egypt also continued to seek ways to expand its nuclear development capabilities, through a joint project with Canada.[138]

In addition to the two nuclear reactors, Egypt operates a hot cell complex[139] for plutonium extraction research, and a pilot nuclear fuel factory that is utilized to process natural uranium mined in Egypt.[140] Egypt is also striving to develop uranium fuel independently. Egypt has reportedly signed contracts with Australia, Canada, and Niger to buy mining technology — and aid in processing uranium ore.[141] Egypt also maintains scientific projects under the tutelage of the IAEA,[142] and has bilateral agreements regarding the peaceful use of atomic energy with Germany, the United States, Russia, India, China, and Argentina. The UK and India provide assistance to Egypt in scientific research training, and atomic projects as well.[143]

Although the evidence indicates that Egypt dropped its nuclear weapons efforts in the 1960s, some Egyptians have called for a renewed effort toward this goal. Officials and journalists often argue that Israel's nuclear capability is a justification for Arab nations to build atomic bombs.[144] Apparently, Egyptian rhetoric has given way to action — and Egypt is currently building ballistic missiles capable of carrying a nuclear payload.[145] Following the 1998 Indian and Pakistani tests, reports of Egyptian-Syrian and Saudi Arabian cooperation in this area increased.[146]

SAUDI ARABIA

Although Saudi Arabia is a signatory to the NPT and is not generally viewed as a country of concern in the area of nuclear proliferation,[147] a number of reports and allegations of Saudi efforts to acquire nuclear weapons have been published over the past years. In 1994, news reports indicated that Saudi Arabia had tried to acquire nuclear weapons from Iraq. These reports were based on the allegations of a former Saudi diplomat, Mohammed Khilewi, who later sought asylum in the United States. According to Khilewi, Saudi Arabia provided $5 billion for Iraq's nuclear program during the 1980s, in return for a nuclear weapon. Khilewi also alleged that Saudi Arabia possessed two (undeclared) nuclear research reactors. However, these claims were never corroborated — and U.S. officials have stated that they have no evidence of Saudi assistance to Iraqi nuclear development.[148]

In 1999, Saudi Defense Minister, Prince Sultan bin Abdul-Aziz, visited Pakistan's Kahuta uranium enrichment plant and missile factory.[149] Aziz denied the allegations, stating:

> Saudi Arabia is a signatory of the nuclear non-proliferation treaty and is committed to its international pledges. . . . [The visit did not] exceed the first entrances of the site and did not include secret facilities as was reported. . . . We are proud that our relations with Pakistan are always friendly and strong and they should not be interpreted as something else.[150]

The Saudi acquisition of long-range strategic missiles is also seen as an indication of intentions in this area. The missiles include 40 to 60 Chinese CSS-2[DF-3] missiles with 2,400 km range and 2,500 kg payload, deployed at al-Sulaiyil and al-Joffer, 500 km and 100 km south of Riyadh, respectively. Each site includes four-to-six concrete launch pads.[151]

ALGERIA

In 1984, Algeria purchased 150 tons of uranium concentrate from Niger, and there are numerous reports of cooperation with Iraq in this area dating from the 1980s.[152] Attention to Algeria's nuclear efforts was drawn in the early 1990s, when an unreported thermal heavy water moderated 15 MW nuclear reactor (with the potential for upgrading to 40 MW) was discovered via space imaging. The Es Salam reactor was supplied by China and apparently became operational in 1992 or 1993.[153] (In addition, Algeria operates a one MW Argentinian pool-type research reactor, which first went critical in 1989.[154]) Both nuclear reactors are now under IAEA safeguards.[155] The Es Salam nuclear is estimated to have the capability to produce three to five kilograms of plutonium per year.[156] In addition, reports claim that the nuclear facility includes a Chinese-supplied hot cell that can be used to separate plutonium, albeit on a small scale,[157] and a facility for the production of radioisotopes.[158]

The construction of this reactor in an isolated part of Algeria was kept secret for a number of years, until the construction activity and telltale security perimeter were discovered using satellite imaging.[159] A large, heavy-walled building nearby may have been intended as a full-scale plutonium plant, and a Soviet-made SA-5 surface-to-air missile battery was located at the site.[160] When it was first discovered, Algerian officials claimed that the reactor was designed for "peaceful purposes," such as electrical power generation and production of radioactive isotopes for medical research.[161] However, as analysts noted, "There are no electrical-power generation facilities at the reactor and no electric-power transmission lines are nearby. . . . This is clearly a military nuclear reactor for weapons production."[162]

China is also reported to have supplied Algeria with nuclear weapons technology, as well as expertise on matching nuclear weapons to various aerial and missile delivery systems.[163] Under pressure from the United States, Algeria accepted IAEA safeguards in 1992, joined the Nuclear Non-Proliferation Treaty (NPT) in 1995, and signed the CTBT on October 15, 1996.

As in the cases of Iraq, Iran, and other would-be proliferators, the capability for developing nuclear weapons continues, as does the concern regarding Algerian intentions. As Spanish government analysts noted in 1998:

> . . . the knowledge obtained by an impressive staff of experts and scientists, as well as the availability of the

installations which it will have at the end of the century, will place this country in an advantageous position to restart a military program if the corresponding political decision is taken.[164]

Similarly, David Albright concluded that Algeria "might have the facilities necessary to produce military plutonium, the key element in nuclear weapons" in two years.[165]

In addition, Algeria has been a transfer point for nuclear materials, and there is evidence that uranium dioxide purchased from Argentina was delivered to Iran.[166]

With regard to weapons delivery, the Algerian armed forces possess a variety of bombers, including the Su-24 Fencer, as well as short-range missiles and launchers, and (Soviet-manufactured) rockets.[167]

IMPLICATIONS

Despite the efforts of the United States government during the past decade, the proliferation of weapons of mass destruction and ballistic missile technology in the Middle East has accelerated. Most other countries and leaders around the world did not share these concerns, and even when they did, their actions were very limited.

The U.S.-led sanctions and export limitations may have slowed but did not prevent this process, particularly with respect to Iran. In the case of Iraq, the unprecedented degree of intrusion established in the UNSCOM inspection and verification regime, as well as ten years of sanctions, did not force Saddam Hussein to halt efforts to preserve and acquire new WMD and missile capabilities. Following the Iraqi lead, additional states will pursue such weapons without fear of censure or stigma.

For Israel, as well other countries in the region, and also for the United States and Western Europe, these developments require major adjustments in military strategy. The deterrence and defense against WMD threats has become the primary focus of Israeli security policy,[168] and in the United States, the need for greater attention to these threats was emphasized by the report of the Rumsfeld Commission and in other strategic planning frameworks. In NATO, the WMD and missile threats from the Middle East are also gaining increased attention,[169] as reflected in discussions of joint approaches and responses. Unless there is a radical change in the implementation of policies designed to slow or prevent proliferation, within the next decade, the number of states in the Middle East with a nuclear weapons capability, as well as biological weapons and long-range delivery systems, is likely to increase dramatically. In the Middle East, the emergence of a multipolar WMD environment in the next decade is increasingly likely.[170]

Endnotes

1. Samuel Huntington, *The Clash of Civilizations* (New York: Simon and Schuster, 1997).
2. Herbert Krosney and Steven Weismann, *The "Islamic Bomb"* (New York: Times Books, 1981), also the BBC documentary series of the same name; D.K. Palit and P.K.S. Namboodiri, *The Islamic Bomb* (Asia Book Corporation of America, 1979).
3. Pervez Hoodbhoy, "Myth-Building: The 'Islamic' Bomb," *Bulletin of the Atomic Scientists* (June 1993).
4. Ibid.
5. Ibid.
6. Danny Rubinstein, "The Islamic Bomb and the Palestinians," *Ha'aretz*, June 1, 1998, p. B1.
7. The combination of religious and ethnic hatreds, reactionary internal forces, and failed leadership in Muslim society grasping to achieve nuclear weapons capabilities are also major sources for criticism. One critic in the region has argued that it is difficult to recall a more demoralized and corrupt community in the annals of history. Each of the 30-odd "Islamic" governments are dominated by self-serving rulers. . . . All are addicted to armaments and to dependence on suppliers. All are littered with machines but command no technology. Not one is home to a university or research center of repute. They lack the will no less than the know-how to transform wealth into capital, importance into influence, resource into power.
    Hoodbhoy, "Myth-Building: The 'Islamic' Bomb."
8. Office of the Secretary of Defense, *Report of the Quadrennial Defense Review*, Washington, DC: U.S. Department of Defense, 1997, <http://www.defenselink.mil/pubs/prolif/me_na.html>.
9. Khidhir Hamza with Jeff Stein, *Saddam's Bombmaker: The Terrifying Inside Story of the Iraqi Nuclear and Biological Weapons Agenda* (New York: Simon and Schuster, 2000).
10. "Iraq-Early Western Assessments: What Did We Know and When Did We Know It?" *FAS*, <http://www.fas.org/nuke/guide/iraq/nuke/when.htm>.
11. The majority of the facilities were in Baghdad, and the periphery of the city, but others were located in Mosul in the north, and Al Qaim and Akashat, in

the west near the Syrian border, Office of the Secretary of Defense, *Report of the Quadrennial Defense Review.*

12 "Weapons of Mass Destruction in the Middle East," Monterey Institute Center for Nonproliferation Studies, <http://cns.miis.edu/research/wmdme/iraq.htm>.

13 A.H. Joffe, "Serious Talk About 'The Gang that Couldn't Bomb Straight,' " *Forward*, November 24, 2000.

14 "Iran Nuclear Milestones," *Risk Report*, vol. 6, no. 4, (July-August 2000), <http://www.wisconsinproject.org/countries/iran/nuke-miles.htm>.

15 "Weapons of Mass Destruction In The Middle East," Monterey Institute Center for Nonproliferation Studies, <http://cns.miis.edu/research/wmdme/iran.htm>.

16 *Risk Report*, vol. 6, no. 4, (July-August 2000), <http://www.wisconsinproject.org/countries/iran/nuke-miles.htm>.

17 *Risk Report*, vol. 6, no. 4, (July-August 2000): In January 1997, 200 Russian engineers laid the groundwork for the construction of a light-water VVER-1000 reactor in Bushehr.

18 "Nuclear and Missile Trade Developments," *NonProliferation Report*, vol. 6, no. 1 (Fall 1998): p. 167.

19 "Russia May Build Reactors in Iran," Associated Press, November 26, 1998. A detailed report on recruitment of Russian scientists and engineers for the Iranian missile program was published in the Russian newspaper *Novaya Gazeta* and summarized in the *Washington Post*, March 23, 1998, and in the *Washington Times*, April 8, 1998.

20 "Iran Nuclear Milestones," *Risk Report*, vol. 6, no. 4, (July-August 2000), <http://www.wisconsinproject.org/countries/iran/nuke-miles.htm>.

21 Ibid.

22 Ibid.

23 Ibid.

24 "Iran Nuclear Team To Visit Russia, China — Paper," Reuters, May 11, 1998.

25 "Iran Nuclear Milestones," *Risk Report*, vol. 6, no. 4, (July-August 2000), <http://www.wisconsinproject.org/countries/iran/nuke-miles.htm>.

26 Judith Miller, "Russia Sends Mixed Signals on Laser System to Iran," *New York Times*, September 20, 2000.

27 Walter Pincus, "Russia: Laser Deal With Iran Blocked," *Washington Post*, September 20, 2000, p. A25.

28 Miller, "Russia Sends Mixed Signals on Laser System to Iran."

29 Pincus, "Russia: Laser Deal With Iran Blocked," p. A25.

30 "Iran Nuclear Milestones," *Risk Report*, vol. 6, no. 4, (July-August 2000), <http://www.wisconsinproject.org/countries/iran/nuke-miles.htm>.

31 Ibid.

32 Programme for Promoting Nuclear Non-Proliferation (PPNN), Newsbrief No. 49, 1st Quarter 2000, p.4, <http://www.soton.ac.uk/~ppnn/newsbriefs/htm>.

33 "Iran Nuclear Milestones," *Risk Report*, vol. 6, no. 4, (July-August 2000), <http://www.wisconsinproject.org/countries/iran/nuke-miles.htm>.

34 Bill Gertz, "Russia Sells Missile Technology to North Korea," *Washington Times*, June 30, 2000.

35 According to Russian Atomic Power Minister Yevgeny Adamov, Teheran plans to place orders for three more reactors at Bushehr. Adamov also stated that the Russian leadership had to "occupy a more active position on the world arena." "Moscow To Supply 8 Atomic Reactors To India and Iran," *DPA*, April 2, 2000; "Iranian Nuclear Reactor 40 Percent Complete Says Ambassador," Agence France Presse, May 23, 2000.

36 Indeed, U.S. sanctions have played some part in slowing construction of Iran's nuclear reactor. Acceding to a U.S. request, the Czechoslovakian Parliament and government approved a law banning all Czech exports to the Bushehr nuclear power plant, including particularly the air conditioning ducts that were to be purchased from ZVVZ Milevsko company. In addition, Ukraine decided (as a result of American pressure) not to provide the turbines for the Bushehr reactors. Instead, Russia will provide Iran with the turbines — but this will delay the project and increase costs, "Czech Parliament Bans Exports for Nuclear Plant in Iran," Associated Press, April 5, 2000; NEB/AK/GE/RAE 08-Mar-2000 13:32 PM EDT (08-Mar-2000 1832 UTC) Source: Voice of America, <http://www.fas.org/news/iran/2000/000308-iran1.htm>; Michael R. Gordon, "Against US Wishes, Russia Will Sell Reactors to Iran," *New York Times*, March 7, 1998; "Iran Condemns Ukraine for Scrapping Nuclear Deal," Reuters, March 7, 1998; Gerald Steinberg, "Arms Control and Non-Proliferation Developments in the Middle East: 1998-1999," BESA Security and Policy Studies, No. 44, August 2000, <http://faculty.biu.ac.il/~steing/conflict/1999_Middle_East_Report.html>; Op. Cit., Programme for Promoting Nuclear Non-Proliferation (PPNN) Newsbrief No. 51, 3rd Quarter 2000, p. 4–5.

37 In October of 1999, Iran threatened to withhold further nuclear contracts from Russia for failing to complete the Bushehr plant in time. In February 2000, Russia's Ministry of Atomic Energy acknowledged that the project was running 18 months behind schedule, and in June 2000, Russia's deputy minister for atomic energy stated that the Bushehr plant would be completed in 2002. Although the date of completion remains highly speculative, press reports note that Bushehr is expected to be online by 2003, *Risk Report*, vol. 6, no. 4 (July-August 2000), <http://www.wisconsinproject.org/countries/iran/nuke-miles.html>; Modher Amin, "Iran Nuclear Power Plant to be Operational by 2003," UPI, January 31, 2001.

38 "Iran Nuclear Milestones," *Risk Report*, vol. 6, no. 4, (July-August 2000).

39 Programme for Promoting Nuclear Non-Proliferation (PPNN) Newsbrief No. 49, 1st Quarter, 2000, p. 16.

40 "Iran: Nuclear Suspicion Grows," *Risk Report*, vol. 1, no, 7 (September 1995): p. 3-4, <http://www.wisconsinproject.org/countries/iran/nuke.html>.

41 "Nuclear Weapons-Iran," *FAS*, <http://www.fas.org/nuke/guide/iran/nuke/index.html>.

42 "Weapons of Mass Destruction in the Middle East," Monterey Institute Center for Nonproliferation Studies, <http://cns.miis.edu/research/wmdme/iran.htm>.

43 Ibid.

44 Ibid.

45 Ibid.

46 Ibid.; W. Seth Carus, "Iran And Weapons Of Mass Destruction," *American Jewish Committee* (June 2000): p. 9–10, citing testimony of Kenneth R. Timmerman, President, Middle East Data Project, Inc., before the Subcommittee on Space and Aeronautics, Hearing on H.R. 1883, Iran Non-Proliferation Act of 1999, July 13, 1999, as found at <www.house.gov/science>; see also "Iran Preparing Bigger Missile Launch," Reuters, July 15, 1999.

47 The Shihab-3 is believed to be based on North Korea's *No Dong* ballistic missile. "Iran Tests Ballistic Missile," Reuters, July 15, 2000; W. Seth Carus, "Iran And Weapons Of Mass Destruction," *American Jewish Committee* (June 2000): p. 9.

48 Gerald Steinberg, "Arms Control and Non-Proliferation Developments in the Middle East: 1998-1999," *BESA Security and Policy Studies,* no. 44 (August 2000), <http://faculty.biu.ac.il/~steing/conflict/1999_Middle_East_Report.htm>.

49 W. Seth Carus, "Iran and Weapons of Mass Destruction," The American Jewish Committee, June 2000, p. 9–10, citing testimony of Kenneth R. Timmerman, President, Middle East Data Project, Inc., before the Subcommittee on Space and Aeronautics, Hearing on H.R. 1883, Iran Non-Proliferation Act of 1999, July 13, 1999, as found at <www.house.gov/science>; see also "Iran Preparing Bigger Missile Launch," Reuters, July 15, 1999.

50 The tests were carried out despite U.S. efforts (which included an offer of economic and military benefits) to convince Pakistan not to go ahead with the tests. Earlier U.S. efforts to curb Pakistan's nuclear program were apparently unsuccessful — limited sanctions were leveled at Pakistan in 1990, because of the uncertainty over whether or not Pakistan possessed a nuclear device. Following the Indian and Pakistani tests in 1998, the Clinton administration slapped economic sanctions on the two states — but did not sever ties. The Clinton sanctions halted economic aid, loans, and military sales, but significantly did not ban loans to non-government companies, or investment by U.S. companies. However, sales of dual-use items were stopped, and banks were prohibited from lending money to either government. It should be noted that the majority of other countries, i.e., Britain, France, and Russia, chose not to impose any sanctions. "Pakistan Nuclear Weapons," *FAS*, <http://www.fas.org/nuke/guide/pakistan/nuke/index.html>; "India-Pakistan: Nuclear Weapons Update 1998," *Risk Report*, vol. 4, no. 6, November–December 1998, <http://www.wisconsinproject.org/countries/pakistan/nuke98.html>.

51 It must be noted that Pakistani data regarding the nuclear tests cannot be confirmed seismically by outside sources. Indeed, Indian sources have suggested that only two nuclear weapons were detonated — and had lower yields than Pakistan claimed. Nonetheless, seismic information indicated at least two, and perhaps a third, test in the initial round of tests, and one on May 30th, "Pakistan Nuclear Weapons," *FAS*, <http://www.fas.org/nuke/guide/pakistan/nuke/index.html>.

52 Ibid.

53 Ibid. However, Pakistani sources have claimed that at least one nuclear device, (originally slated to be tested on May 30th) remains underground, and is ready for detonation.

54 Nonetheless, Pakistan has stated that it will not assemble or deploy its nuclear warheads, nor will it resume testing unless India does so first. . . . In addition, Pakistan has agreed to enter into negotiations to complete a fissile material cutoff agreement — but has not agreed to halt production of fissile material before signing the treaty. Office of the Secretary of Defense, *Proliferation: Threat and Response*, (Washington, DC: U.S. Department of Defense, January 2001), <http://www.defenselink.mil.

55 "Pakistan Nuclear Milestones," *Risk Report*, vol. 6, no. 5, September–October 2000, <http://www.wisconsinproject.org/countries/pakistan/nuke-miles.htm>.

56 Ibid.

57 Ibid.

58 Ibid.

59 Ibid.

60 "Pakistan Nuclear Weapons," *FAS*, <http://www.fas.org/nuke/guide/pakistan/nuke/index.html>.

61 Ibid.

62 Ibid.

63 In 1996, reports indicated that the A.Q. Khan Research Laboratory had received 5,000 ring magnets, which could be used in gas centrifuges, from a Chinese nuclear company, "Pakistan Nuclear Weapons," *FAS*, <http://www.fas.org/nuke/guide/pakistan/nuke/index.html>.

64 "Pakistan Nuclear Milestones," *Risk Report*, vol. 6, no. 5, September–October 2000, <http://www.wisconsinproject.org/countries/pakistan/nuke-miles.htm>.

65 Ibid.

66 Ibid.

67 It should be noted that China's nuclear aid to Pakistan began long before the 1986 Sino-Pakistani atomic cooperation agreement. Indeed, important Sino-Pakistan transfers occurred during the period of 1980–1985. Reportedly, China provided Pakistan with the design of one of its warheads, as well as enough HEU for a small amount of weapons, "Pakistan Nuclear Weapons," *FAS*, <http://www.fas.org/nuke/guide/pakistan/nuke/index.html>.

68 "Pakistan Nuclear Milestones," *Risk Report*, vol. 6, no. 5, September–October 2000, <http://www.wisconsinproject.org/countries/pakistan/nuke-miles.htm>.

69 Ibid.

70 Ibid.

71 Andrew Koch and Jennifer Topping, "Pakistan's Nuclear-Related Facilities, Center for Non-Proliferation Fact Sheet," *Non-Proliferation Review*, vol. 4, no. 3, 1997.

72 Ibid.

73 The Kahuta enrichment plant may be the location where highly enriched uranium is formed into weapons cores. Koch and Topping, "Pakistan's Nuclear-Related Facilities, Center for Non-Proliferation Fact Sheet," citing Col. S. Bakov, "Nuclear Ambitions," *Krasnaya zveda*, May 23, 1990, p. 3; in JPRS-TND-90-011 (June 28, 1990), p.21; Indranil Banerjee, "The Secrets Of Kahuta," *Sunday*, April 24, 1993, p. 34–38; in JPRS-TND-93-014 (May 18 1993), p. 12–15.

74 Koch and Topping, "Pakistan's Nuclear-Related Facilities, Center for Non-Proliferation Fact Sheet," citing David Albright, Frans Berkhout, and William Walker, *Plutonium And Highly Enriched Uranium 1996: World Inventories, Capabilities, And Policies* (Oxford: Oxford University Press, 1997), p. 275.

75 Koch and Topping, "Pakistan's Nuclear-Related Facilities, Center for Non-Proliferation Fact Sheet," citing David Albright and Mark Hibbs, "Pakistan's Bomb: Out of the Closet," *Bulletin of the Atomic Scientists* 48 (July/August 1992): p. 38–43; Koch and Topping, "Pakistan's Nuclear-Related Facilities, Center for Non-Proliferation Fact Sheet."

76 "Pakistan Nuclear Update," *Risk Report*, vol. 6, no. 5, September–October 2000, <http://www.wisconsinproject.org/countries/pakistan/nuke2000.htm>; "Pakistan Nuclear Milestones," *Risk Report*, Vol. 6, No. 5, September–October 2000, <http://www.wisconsinproject.org/countries/pakistan/nuke-miles.htm>; Office of the Secretary of Defense, *Proliferation: Threat and Response*, Washington, DC: US Department of Defense, January 2001, <http://www.defenselink.mil>.

77 In July 1999, British custom officials intercepted 20 tons of crucial components used in the manufacture of nuclear weapons, including high-grade aluminum — destined for Pakistan, "Pakistan Nuclear Milestones," *Risk Report*, vol. 6, no. 5, September–October 2000, <http://www.wisconsinproject.org/countries/pakistan/nuke-miles.htm>.

78 Office of the Secretary of Defense, *Proliferation: Threat and Response*, Washington, DC: US Department of Defense, January 2001, <http://www.defenselink.mil; Office of the Secretary of Defense, *Report of the Quadrennial Defense Review*.

79 Koch and Topping, "Pakistan's Nuclear-Related Facilities, Center for Non-Proliferation Fact Sheet," citing R. Jeffery Smith and Thomas W. Lippman, "Pakistan Building Reactor that May Yield Large Quantities of Plutonium,"

Washington Post, April 8, 1995, p. A20; "Pakistan Nuclear Update, 2000," *Risk Report,* vol. 6, no. 5, September–October, 2000, <http://www.wisconsinproject.org/countries/pakistan/nuke2000.htm>.

80 Ibid., *Risk Report,* "Pakistan Nuclear Update, 2000."

81 It should be noted that there is a disagreement between U.S. officials as to whether or not China supplied the heavy water plant. "Pakistan Nuclear Update, 2000," *Risk Report,* vol. 6, no. 5, September–October, 2000, <http://www.wisconsinproject.org/countries/pakistan/nuke2000.htm>.

82 Koch and Topping, "Pakistan's Nuclear-Related Facilities, Center for Non-Proliferation Fact Sheet," citing Aroosa Alam, *Muslim,* July 3, 1996, p. 1; FBIS-TAC-96-008, July 3, 1996; Indranil Banerjee, "The Secrets Of Kahuta," *Sunday,* April 24, 1993, p. 34–38; JPRS-TND-93-014, May 18, 1993, p. 12–15.

83 Koch and Topping, "Pakistan's Nuclear-Related Facilities, Center for Non-Proliferation Fact Sheet," citing Indranil Banerjee, "The Secrets Of Kahuta," *Sunday,* April 24, 1993, p. 34–38; JPRS-TND-93-014, May 18, 1993, p. 12-15; J.N Dixit, "India's Nuclear Options," *Indian Express,* August 30, 1994; "In the Aisles," *Der Spiegel,* June 26, 1989, p. 87–89; JPRS-TND-89-014, July 14, 1989, p. 39–40; "Hot Laboratories," *Der Spiegel,* February 27, 1989, p. 87–89, 113; JPRS-TND-89-006, March 28, 1989, p. 33–34; Koch and Topping, "Pakistan's Nuclear-Related Facilities, Center for Non-Proliferation Fact Sheet," citing U.S. State Department, The Pakistani Nuclear Program, Washington: GPO, June 23, 1983.

84 Koch and Topping, "Pakistan's Nuclear-Related Facilities, Center for Non-Proliferation Fact Sheet," citing David Albright and Mark Hibbs, "Pakistan's Bomb: Out of the Closet," *Bulletin of the Atomic Scientists,* vol. 48 (July/August 1992): p. 38–43.

85 Koch and Topping, "Pakistan's Nuclear-Related Facilities, Center for Non-Proliferation Fact Sheet," citing V.D. Chopra, *Patriot,* November 10, 1986, p. 4; *World Wide Report,* January 2, 1987, p. 63–64.

86 Koch and Topping, "Pakistan's Nuclear-Related Facilities, Center for Non-Proliferation Fact Sheet," citing "Hot Laboratories," *Der Spiegel,* February 27, 1989, p. 113; JPRS-TND-89-006, March 28, 1989, p. 33–34.

87 Koch and Topping, "Pakistan's Nuclear-Related Facilities, Center for Non-Proliferation Fact Sheet," citing "Pakistan: PINSTECH Fabricates Sensitive Track Detecting Material," *Nucleonics Week* (February 19, 1987), and U.S. State Department, "The Pakistani Nuclear Program," Washington: GPO, June 23, 1983; *Patriot,* August 23, 1989, p. 5; JPRS-TND-89-020, October 26, 1989, p. 30–31.

88 Koch and Topping, "Pakistan's Nuclear-Related Facilities, Center for Non-Proliferation Fact Sheet," citing *Dawn,* April 7 1985, p. 7; JPRS-TND-85-009, May 23, 1985, p. 78–79; "Twenty-Five Years of Research and Development at PINSTECH," *Muslim,* May 25, 1992, p. 10; JPRS-TND-92-020, June 25, 1992, p. 14–17.

89 Koch and Topping, "Pakistan's Nuclear-Related Facilities, Center for Non-Proliferation Fact Sheet."

90 Ibid.

91 Koch and Topping, "Pakistan's Nuclear-Related Facilities, Center for Non-Proliferation Fact Sheet," citing Bill Gertz, "China Aids Pakistan Plutonium Plant," *Washington Times*, April 3, 1996, p. A4.

92 Koch and Topping, "Pakistan's Nuclear-Related Facilities, Center for Non-Proliferation Fact Sheet," citing Michael Schneider, "Paris: Hub for Pakistani Nuclear Traffic," *Politis-Le Cityoen* (February 22–28, 1990): p. 50–55; JPRS-TND-90-021, July 18, 1990, p. 27–29; Mark Hibbs, "Illegal Export Charges May Spur Tighter German Export Controls," *Nucleonics Week* (January 5, 1989): p. 3–5; Heinz Vielan, "First Confessions — Pakistan's A-Bomb with German Help?" *Welt Am Sonntag*, December 25, 1988, p. 1–2; JPRS-TND-89-001, January 13, 1989, p. 25–26.

93 Koch and Topping, "Pakistan's Nuclear-Related Facilities, Center for Non-Proliferation Fact Sheet," citing "Research Reactors," *Nuclear Review* (April 1996): p. 18; "Pakistan," *Nuclear Europe Worldscan* (July/August 1991): p. 51; "PARR's New Lease Of Life," *Nuclear Engineering International*, vol. 36 (December 1991): p. 3.

94 Koch and Topping, "Pakistan's Nuclear-Related Facilities, Center for Non-Proliferation Fact Sheet," citing "Datafile: Pakistan," *Nuclear Enginnering Informational*, vol. 36 (May 1991): p. 52–54; Shahid-ur-Rehman Khan and Rauf Siddiqi, "PAEC Plans To Expand And Extend The Life Of Kanupp," *Nucleonics Week* (November 7, 1991): p.10.

95 Koch and Topping, "Pakistan's Nuclear-Related Facilities, Center for Non-Proliferation Fact Sheet."

96 After the successful 1999 tests of the *Ghauri* and *Sha-heen*-1 missiles, Pakistan announced the conclusion ("for now") of "the series of flight tests involving solid-and liquid-fuel rocket motor technologies." Pakistan also asked India to participate in a "strategic restraint regime" that would limit the development of missile and nuclear weapons technology, as well as deployment, Office of the Secretary of Defense, *Proliferation: Threat and Response*, Washington, DC: U.S. Department of Defense, January 2001, <http://www.defenselink.mil>.

97 Last tested in April 1999. "Unclassified Report to Congress on the Acquisition of Technology Relating to Weapons of Mass Destruction and Advanced Conventional Munitions, July 1 through December 31, 1999," <http://www.cia.gov/cia/publications/bian/bian_aug2000.htm#10>; Office of the Secretary of Defense, *Proliferation: Threat and Response*, Washington, DC: U.S. Department of Defense, January 2001, <http://www.defenselink.mil>.

98 Last tested in April 1999. "Unclassified Report to Congress on the Acquisition of Technology Relating to Weapons of Mass Destruction and Advanced Conventional Munitions, July 1, Through December 31, 1999," <http://www.cia.gov/cia/publications/bian/bian_aug2000.htm#10>.

99 Office of the Secretary of Defense, *Proliferation: Threat and Response*, Washington, DC: U.S. Department of Defense, January 2001, <http://www.defenselink.mil>.

100 Shirley A. Kan, Foreign Affairs and National Defense Division, "Chinese Missile and Nuclear Proliferation: Issues for Congress," CRS Report For Congress, October 20, 1993, <http://www.fas.org/spp/starwars/crs/93-10-20.htm.

101 Ibid., citing *Jane's Defence Weekly*, April 9, 1988.

102 Office of the Secretary of Defense, *Proliferation: Threat and Response*, Washington, DC: U.S. Department of Defense, January 2001, <http://www.defenselink.mil>.

103 Ibid.

104 In 1970, Qadhdhafi attempted to purchase an atomic bomb from China. "Libya Has Trouble Building the Most Deadly Weapons," *Risk Report*, vol. 1, no. 10 (December 1995): p. 1–4, <http://www.wisconsinproject.org/countries/libya/trouble.html>.

105 In 1974, Libya and Argentina finalized a deal, under which Argentina would provide Tripoli with equipment for uranium mining and processing. Apparently, Argentina had already extracted plutonium from spent reactor fuel, although it remains uncertain if the agreement with Libya provided any assistance in this area. However, in 1982, during the war over the Falkland Islands, Libya provided Argentina with $100 million in anti-aircraft and air-to-air missiles. It has been suggested that Argentina may have provided nuclear information or technology to Libya. Indeed, according to a May 1983 report, Argentina and Libya continued nuclear contacts after the war, during which discussions about reprocessing and enrichment technologies probably occurred. In 1985, reports indicate that Argentina planned on selling a hot cell facility to Libya — but pressure from the United States prevented the sale. Rodney W. Jones, Mark G. McDonough, Toby F. Dalton, and Gregory D. Koblentz, "Argentina," from *Tracking Nuclear Proliferation, Carnegie Endowment for International Peace, July 1998, <http://www.ceip.org/programs/npp/nppargn.htm>.

106 Office of the Secretary of Defense, *Report of the Quadrennial Defense Review.*

107 Gordon C. Oehler, National Intelligence Officer for Science, Technology, and Proliferation, Central Intelligence Agency, "The Proliferation of Weapons of Mass Destruction in the Middle East," *Washington Institute For Near East Policy,* Soref Symposium, April 27, 1992, <http://www.washingtoninstitute.org/pubs/oehler.htm>.

108 The research center is under IAEA safeguards. "Weapons of Mass Destruction in the Middle East," Monterey Institute Center for Nonproliferation Studies, <http://cns.miis.edu/research/wmdme/libya.htm>.

109 "Unclassified Report to Congress on the Acquisition of Technology Relating to Weapons of Mass Destruction and Advanced Conventional Munitions, July 1 through December 31, 1999," <http://www.cia.gov/cia/publications/bian/bian_aug2000.htm#6>.

110 "Weapons of Mass Destruction in the Middle East," Monterey Institute Center for Nonproliferation Studies, <http://cns.miis.edu/research/wmdme/libya.htm>, "Libya Special Weapons," *FAS*, <http://www.fas.org/nuke/guide/libya/index.html>.

111 "Libya Special Weapons," *FAS*, <http://www.fas.org/nuke/guide/libya/index.html>.

112 Ibid.

113 "Libya Has Trouble Building the Most Deadly Weapons," *Risk Report*, vol. 1, no. 10 (December 1995): p. 1, 3–4, <http://www.wisconsinproject.org/countries/libya/trouble.html>.

114 "Libya Special Weapons," *FAS*, <http://www.fas.org/nuke/guide/libya/index.html>.

115 Ibid.

116 Ibid.

117 "Libya's Nuclear Research Is Centered at Tajurae," *Risk Report*, vol. 1, no. 10 (December 1995): p. 10, <http://www.wisconsinproject.org/countries/libya/tajura.html#top>.

118 Office of the Secretary of Defense, *Report of the Quadrennial Defense Review.*

119 "Unclassified Report to Congress on the Acquisition of Technology Relating to Weapons of Mass Destruction and Advanced Conventional Munitions, July 1 through December 31, 1999," <http://www.cia.gov/cia/publications/bian/bian_aug2000.htm#6>.

120 "Weapons of Mass Destruction In The Middle East," Monterey Institute Center for Nonproliferation Studies, <http://cns.miis.edu/research/wmdme/libya.htm>.

121 Ibid.

122 Ibid.

123 Ibid.

124 30 KW nuclear research reactor, along with almost one kilogram of highly enriched uranium, was purchased from China in 1991. Both the reactor and enriched uranium are now under IAEA safeguards, "IAEA Annual Report for 1999 (annex), *IAEA*, October 31, 2000, <http://www.iaea.org/worldatom/Documents/Anrep/Anrep99/>; Michael Eisenstadt, *Jane's*, 1993, p. 169.

125 "Syria-Special Weapons," *FAS*, <http://www.fas.org/nuke/guide/syria/index.html>, "Weapons of Mass Destruction In The Middle East," Monterey Institute Center for Nonproliferation Studies, <http://cns.miis.edu/research/wmdme/syria.htm#2>.

126 "Syria-Special Weapons," *FAS*, <http://www.fas.org/nuke/guide/syria/index.html>.

127 "Russia, Syria Sign Nuclear Power Agreement," RFE/RL Newsline, May 20, 1999, <http://www.rferl.org/newsline/1999/05/200599.html>.

128 "Unclassified Report to Congress on the Acquisition of Technology Relating toWeapons of Mass Destruction and Advanced Conventional Munitions, July 1 through December 31, 1999," <http://www.cia.gov/cia/publications/bian/bian_aug2000.htm#7>.

Gerald M. Steinberg and Aharon Etengoff

129 "Weapons of Mass Destruction In The Middle East," Monterey Institute Center for Nonproliferation Studies, <http://cns.miis.edu/research/wmdme/syria.htm>.

130 Ibid.

131 Ibid.

132 Ibid.

133 The 2 MW research reactor was supplied by the Soviets, and began operating in 1961. It was shut down for renovation during the 1980s, but re-opened in 1990. The reactor runs on 10%-enriched uranium fuel. "Egypt's Budding Nuclear Program," *Risk Report*, vol. 2, no. 5 (September–October 1996), <http://www.wisconsinproject.org/countries/egypt/nuke.html>.

134 "Nuclear Weapons Program — Egypt," *FAS*, <http://www.fas.org/nuke/guide/egypt/nuke/index.html>.

135 "Egypt's Budding Nuclear Program," *Risk Report.*

136 Ibid.

137 Shawn Twing, "Egypt Opens Nuclear Power Plant," *Washington Report on Middle East Affairs* (April 1998): p. 38–42, <http://www.washington-report.org/backissues/0498/9804038.html>.

138 "Egypt's Budding Nuclear Program," *Risk Report.*

139 Ibid. Supplied by France.

140 Ibid.

141 Ibid.

142 In addition, both Egyptian nuclear reactors operate under IAEA safeguards, "Weapons of Mass Destruction in the Middle East," Monterey Institute Center for Nonproliferation Studies, <http://cns.miis.edu/research/wmdme/egypt.htm>.

143 "Nuclear Weapons Program — Egypt," *FAS*, <http://www.fas.org/nuke/guide/egypt/nuke/index.html>.

144 "Egypt's Budding Nuclear Program," *Risk Report.*

145 Egypt's missile capability and developments: 100+ SS-1 (Scud-B) with 300 km range and 985 kg payload; approximately 90 Project T missiles with 450 km range and 985 kg payload; developing Scud-C variant production capability with DPRK assistance; with 550 km range and 500 kg payload; developing Vector missile with 800 km to 1,200 km range and 450–1,000 kg payload. It has been alleged by U.S. and Israeli intelligence that Egyptian government companies are acquiring and exporting U.S. (and Western) technology to N. Korea for alterations — which is then returned to Egypt as advanced missile components. Egypt is also suspected of working with China and (N. Korea) to develop missiles and non-conventional weapons. "Egypt's Budding Nuclear Program," *Risk Report*, vol. 2, no. 5 (September–October 1996), <http://www.wisconsinproject.org/countries/egypt/nuke.html>; "Weapons of Mass Destruction In The Middle East," Monterey Institute Center for Nonproliferation Studies, <http://cns.miis.edu/research/wmdme/egypt.htm>.

146 "Nuclear Weapons Program — Egypt," *FAS*, <http://www.fas.org/nuke/guide/egypt/nuke/index.html>.

147 "Weapons of Mass Destruction in the Middle East," Monterey Institute Center for Nonproliferation Studies, <http://cns.miis.edu/research/wmdme/saudi.htm

148 Ibid.

149 "Saudi Arabia Denies Nuclear Link with Pakistan," Reuters, August 5, 1999.

150 Ibid.

151 "Weapons of Mass Destruction in the Middle East," Monterey Institute Center for Nonproliferation Studies, <http://cns.miis.edu/research/wmdme/saudi.htm>.

152 "Algeria Special Weapons," *FAS*, <http://www.fas.org/nuke/guide/algeria/index.html>, Bill Gertz, "China Helps Algeria Develop Nuclear Weapons," *Washington Times*, April 11, 1991.

153 "Weapons of Mass Destruction in the Middle East," Monterey Institute Center for Nonproliferation Studies, <http://cns.miis.edu/research/wmdme/algeria.htm>; *World Nuclear Industry Handbook, 1993* (Surrey, England: Nuclear Engineering International, 1993), p. 120; "Algeria Special Weapons," *FAS*, <http://www.fas.org/nuke/guide/algeria/index.html>; Bruce W. Nelan, "China: For Sale: Tools of Destruction," *Time* magazine (April 22, 1991).

154 Rodney W. Jones, Mark G. McDonough, Toby F. Dalton, and Gregory D. Koblentz, "Argentina," *Tracking Nuclear Proliferation, Carnegie Endowment for International Peace,* July 1998, <http://www.ceip.org/programs/npp/nppargn.htm>.

155 "Weapons of Mass Destruction in the Middle East," Monterey Institute Center for Nonproliferation Studies, <http://cns.miis.edu/research/wmdme/algeria.htm>.

156 "Algeria Special Weapons," *FAS*, <http://www.fas.org/nuke/guide/algeria/index.html>.

157 Ibid.

158 *Eurasian Politician's World Report*, no. 2, October 31, 2000, <http://www.the-politician.com/issue2/wr2.htm#mideast>, quoting "The Middle East," *ISIS* (June 2000).

159 Vipin Gupta, "Algeria's Nuclear Ambitions," *Nuclear Engineering International* (March 1992): p. 6; Vipin Gupta, "Algeria's Nuclear Ambitions," *International Defense Review*, no. 4 (1992): p. 329–330.

160 "Algeria Special Weapons," *FAS,* <http://www.fas.org/nuke/guide/algeria/index.html

161 Ibid.

162 Bill Gertz, "China Helps Algeria Develop Nuclear Weapons," *Washington Times,* April 11, 1991.

163 Ibid.

164 M. Gonzalez and J.M. Larraya, "Spanish Intelligence Warns of Algerian Nuclear Potential," *Madrid El Pais*, August 23, 1998, <http://www.fas. org/news/algeria/fbis-tac-98-235.htm>.

165 Albright's quote to *Jane's Terrorism & Security Monitor*, quoted by *Eurasian Politician's World Report*, no. 2, October 31, 2000, <http://www.the-politician. com/issue2/wr2.htm#mideast>.

166 Richard Kessler, "Panel to Guide Nuclear Technology Sales from Argentina to Algeria," *Nucleonics Week* (May 7, 1987): p. 6.

167 *Eurasian Politician's World Report*, no. 2, October 31, 2000, <http://www. the-politician.com/issue2/wr2.htm#mideast>, quoting "The Middle East," *ISIS*, June 2000.

168 Gerald M. Steinberg, "Parameters of Stable Deterrence in a Proliferated Middle East," *The NonProliferation Review*, vol. 7, no. 1 (Fall–Winter 2000).

169 "Biological Weapons: The Threat of the New Century?" North Atlantic Assembly, Science and Technology Committee, Sub-Committee on the Proliferation of Military Technology, Draft Interim Report October 1999; Ian O. Lesser and Ashley J. Tellis, *Strategic Exposure* (Santa Monica, CA: Rand, 1996); Thanos Dakos, Proliferation of Weapons of Mass Destruction and the Threat to NATO's Southern Flank: An Assessment of Options, NATO Research Fellowship Report, 1998.

170 Gerald M. Steinberg, "Parameters of Stable Deterrence in a Proliferated Middle East," *NonProliferation Review*, vol. 7, no. 1 (Fall–Winter 2000).

The Chemical and Biological Threat of Islam

Dany Shoham

BACKGROUND AND MAIN MILESTONES

On June 8, 1963, during a raid on native anti-Communist villagers in Yemen, the Egyptian Air Force employed aerial bombs containing chemical warfare agents. It was the first time chemical weapons have ever been used in the Middle East. That event marked the beginning of the Islamic non-conventional weapons era, an era bearing enormous strategic importance. During the 40 years since that time, Egypt and other Islamic states have armed themselves with dreadful chemical and biological weapons, forming a region of the world most intensely engaged in the acquisition of offensive chemical and biological capabilities. In conjunction with rapid ballistic proliferation in the Islamic countries of the Middle East, this development constitutes a strategic turn of paramount significance.

Egypt was the Islamic state that pioneered the procurement of chemical weapons. These were employed by her repeatedly from

1963 until 1967 against unprotected Muslim civilians in Yemen, far and away from the Egyptian borders. Later, chemical weapons were further employed again on various occasions, without hesitation and on a large scale, by Muslims against Muslims.

Iraq used chemical weapons many times against Iran throughout the lengthy war between the two countries (1982–88). The target population was often a civilian one. Thus far the climax of Iraq's brutality on this score was the massacre of some 4,300 Kurdish residents of the town of Halabja by chemical weapons. Also noteworthy are the numerous incidents where the Iraqi regime brought about the assassination of individual opponents by thallium poisoning. Biological weapons were used as well by the Iraqi regime against the Kurds.

In 1982, the Syrian regime killed some 18,000 "undesirable" Syrian *Sunni* residents of the city of Hama, primarily by means of cyanide. Three years before that horrifying event, in 1979, while conducting a vigorous effort to suppress religious dissidents occupying the holy *Ka`abba* of Mecca, the Saudi regime effectively employed on a massive scale a potent incapacitating CW agent, probably benzyl chloride, acquired for that purpose from France.

The cases mentioned here point to the distinct possibility that chemical or biological weapons of any sort might readily be used by Muslims against non-Muslims.

The disintegration of the USSR gave birth to new Islamic states throughout the last decade, which greatly facilitated the proliferation of chemical and biological weapons. Inevitably, these countries formed inter-nation connections for the transfer of the relevant technology. The relatively young Islamic state of Kazakhstan, for example, has mastered crucial technologies related to both chemical and biological weapons, hitherto possessed by the Soviet Union. Kazakhstan found itself in the position of being a potential key supplier, with the option for choosing one of the three alternatives:

a. responding positively to requests from her Islamic sisters

b. relating with indifference to such requests

c. actively hindering the migration of such technologies to other countries

On occasion it follows the second option, more frequently the first one. In effect, the intra-Islamic migration of this specific expertise began 1972. At that time, Egypt supplied Syria with chemical weapons produced in Egypt to provide Syria with an initial unconventional operational capability toward the October 1973 offensive against Israel. The Egyptian-Syrian connection, in preparation for the October 1973 War, constituted the most profound strategic-military-operational cooperation configured during the 20th century in the Islamic world, including, evidently, the element of offensive chemical capacity.

The Egyptian-Iraqi connection during the 1980s was aimed at the development and production of various ballistic missiles with warheads carrying all types of non-conventional armaments.

Politically, the Islamic states that so far avoided the biological and/or chemical conventions — namely Egypt, Syria, Libya, Iraq, Lebanon, Algeria, Morocco, Sudan, United Arab Emirates, Afganistan, Kazakhstan, Azerbaijan, and Kyrgystan — sustain a degree of coordination between them.

CONCEPTUAL FOUNDATIONS

The basic assumption of the Islamic system is that Israel possesses nuclear, biological, and chemical weapons. This constitutes a sufficient factor (though not a mandatory one) for an Islamic view supporting acquisition of chemical and biological weapons, alongside or instead of nuclear weapons. This view is shared mainly by the Arab world and Iran, and is approved by Pakistan and other peripheral Islamic countries. It constitutes the reason and/or excuse for continued efforts to acquire chemical and biological armament.

On a public and political level, this concept serves as a bargaining chip and as a stick with which to browbeat Israel into disarming itself in the realm of chemical, biological, and nuclear weapons. This concept is also fed by other factors, among them internal Arab affairs as well as Arab concern for protecting the balance of weaponry between Arab countries and Iran on both an actual and symbolic level. These concepts have been nurtured by the fact that Israel was victorious in all the wars; by the dramatic effect chemical weapons played in Iraq's war against Iran; by the relative ease in obtaining biological and chemical arms; and by the fearful image of such weapons. In practical terms, such weapons have great weight because their destructive ability allows them to serve as a tremendous threatening device, creating threat levels far higher than with conventional weapons both as deterrent, retaliatory, and as attack systems.

In addition to Iran, one has to recall that, among Islamic nations, Pakistan maintains profound relations with Iran and Arab countries, and it also believes in arming itself with nuclear, biological, and chemical weapons altogether. Furthermore, outside the Islamic orbit, North Korea holds a similar view, while maintaining close ties with Islamic countries such as Syria, Libya, Egypt, and Iran.

We shall examine the threat situation in each of the relevant countries.

SYRIA

Basic Characteristics

Syria has a consistent policy of biological and chemical arms acquisition that is systematic and determined, and has never been denied by Syria. More than any other country, Syria has a policy of seeking strategic parity with Israel, which, in military terms, means attaining biological and chemical weapons.

Syria apparently cooperates with Egypt in biological and chemical arms acquisition today; it certainly does with Iran and probably with Libya.

One must recall that Syria has switched from above ground to underground storage and production facilities, thus significantly limiting Israel's ability to detect and destroy such facilities.

Chemical Weapons

In 1972, Syria received aerial bombs and artillery shells from Egypt containing Sarin nerve gas and blistering mustard gas. Ten years later, it began production of Sarin for aerial bombs and later for Scud missiles. Syria also possesses reserves of cyanide gas which were used in part in the slaughter of 18,000 Syrian *Sunni* residents of the city of Hama in 1982.

In recent years, Syria has produced the deadlier and more stable VX nerve gas placed on bombs and in missile warheads.

This chemical agent surpasses Sarin in its toxicity, persistence, and virulence, thus complementing the operational flaws of Sarin. Syria was helped in these efforts by Russian scientists specializing in the Russian version of the gas, which is superior to the original American version. Recently Syria deployed chemical warheads on its Scud-C missiles. This is in addition to the aerial chemical bombs on its *Sukhoi*-22, *Sukhoi*-24, MIG-23 and some 200 chemical warheads adapted to Scud-B missiles. It is to be expected that Scud-D will follow.

The warning from the Syrian ambassador in Egypt that Syria would threaten the use of its chemical weapons against Israel to counter an Israeli chemical threat set a new level for this kind of statement. In January 1989, in a conversation with Senator McCain in Damascus, Assad confirmed that Syria had chemical weapons. In 1993, Assad hinted that Syria had a way to win the Golan back at any price, despite Israel's nuclear superiority. The Syrian Information Minister said in 1995 that Syria had "cards" it had not yet played, but which it would be willing to employ in a war with Israel. Assad has declared lately that Syria can cause great damage to Israel through the "special armament" it has, because the Syrian army has reached strategic balance with the IDF. The Syrian army did indeed perform a series of experimental launchings of different versions of Scud missiles tipped with chemical warheads. This activity points to an experimental program that American experts believe could lead to the use of chemical warheads if Syria intensifies its cooperation with Russia in the field of chemical weapons. Moreover, the exposure of the Syrian operational system of Scud-C missiles through satellite photographs, shows that it includes chemical weapons that provide Syria with the option of carrying out a surprise chemical attack. Parallel to this, the exposure of the nuclear operational system attributed to Israel by the well-reputed *Jane's* newspaper, as well as satellite photographs, allow Syria another major military option of directing a chemical attack at this system.

This cluster of developments makes clear Syria's intention to neutralize Israel's nuclear threat which might otherwise endanger Syrian military gains in the Golan Heights, if and when Syria decides to initiate action there using chemical weapons.

Dany Shoham

Biological Weapons

Syrian spokesmen have stressed that Syria is arming itself with a technical response surpassing Israel's nuclear arms, an allusion to biological weapons. These comments underscore a Syrian concept that even if chemical weapons are not sufficient to undermine Israel's nuclear deterrent, the addition of the even more powerful biological weapons will certainly complete the job.

Syria has been developing such weapons since 1985, producing botulinum toxin and ricin toxin, as well as anthrax and cholera germs. Russian experts recently hired by Syria are involved in the production of anthrax and its weaponization in missile warheads. The biological agents mentioned earlier are particularly deadly: botulinum is a poisonous protein made from a bacterium that surpasses the lethality of any other natural or synthetic substance; ricin is another deadly protein (made from castor beans, commonly grown in Syria) which has an optimal cost-effective ratio; and anthrax, an easily grown bacterium with long-term survivability for purposes of storage, eventual launching, and ability to last in the environment. Cholera bacteria are very suitable for contaminating water and food systems through guerrilla warfare.

EGYPT

Basic Characteristics

In addition to supplying Syria during joint plans for the Yom Kippur War, Egypt supplied chemical and biological weapons, and the means to manufacture them, to Iraq in the 1980s. It continues to maintain such arms, despite denials and despite consistent efforts to form the image of a country that wants to eliminate such weapons.

Since the 1993 Chemical Weapons Convention, there is a clear inter-Arab concept, led by Egypt, to refrain from joining the Convention, and to develop a chemical-attack option as well as a biological option, as Egypt has done, so long as there is no across-the-board regional ban on chemical, biological, and nuclear weapons in the Middle East. When the Chemical Convention was signed in January 1993, Mubarak was in Damascus with Assad, and both called on Arab states to refrain from joining the Convention.

During 1990, Egyptian-Iraqi cooperation in ballistic and bio-chemical armament reached its peak. Indeed, only a short while before Iraq's invasion of Kuwait, Egypt's defense and foreign ministers defended Iraqi acquisition of chemical and biological weapons, hopeful of reaping fruits from the Egyptian-Iraqi cooperation.

Against the background of Egypt's immense and unprecedented financial expenditures on its military power, and Egypt's non-participation in the chemical and biological weapons conventions, it is reasonable to assume that its military arsenal includes chemical-biological arms, contrary to public declarations by the top Egyptian leadership.

Chemical Weapons

Egypt's acquisition of chemical arms began in the 1960s with the principal installation in Abu-Za`abel (backed by local pesticide plants) and secondary installations in Abu Rawash (production of sprays) and Beni Sueif (an air force base). The main research and development area is in Dokki, and a support industrial installation is in the Egyptian Chemicals and Dyes Manufacturing Company.

At first, Egypt manufactured mustard gas (blistering) and phosgene (suffocating), using them in Yemen. Later, it developed Sarin nerve gas and VX nerve gas. These were all made on an industrial level and loaded in mines, artillery shells, aerial bombs, rockets (including cluster warheads), and finally missiles warheads. After the suspension of the Egyptian-Iraqi-Argentinean Condor Project, which the Egyptians and Iraqis wanted for chemical and biological weaponry purposes, the Egyptians turned to arming other missiles. Most probably this arming process has been completed. Concomitantly, many Egyptian experts have taken part in international forums where they attained knowledge and access in the field of chemical arms.

Biological Weapons

Anwar Sadat (in 1972) and Saddam Hussein (in 1990) were the only two Arab leaders until now who unequivocally declared, one 18 years before the other, that Egypt and Iraq had biological weapons on an operational level. Both were telling the truth.

Egypt began a combined chemical-biological weapons project in the 1960s code-named "*Izlis*." It took place (and probably continues to take place) at an Egyptian military-civilian consortium located at Abu-Za`abel that includes a military installation called

Industrial Plant Number 801. This is an industrial plant known as Abu-Za`abel Chemicals and Pesticides Company. A second site is a facility at the El-Nasser Chemical Pharmaceuticals and Antibiotics Company.

At the beginning of the 1970s, about ten years after the start of the project, and after stocking chemical weapons used operationally in Yemen, it seems that Egypt indeed also stockpiled appreciable quantities of biological weapons on an operational level, as well as the means to launch them. It also appears that Sadat's statement was not a chance utterance but timed to coincide with a decision to launch a surprise strike at Israel, and thereby strengthen Egypt's deterrent ability to preclude an Israeli non-conventional counter-strike of any sort.

"The Plagues of Egypt," which included "pestilence" and "mur-rain," have been preserved to this day, enabling Egyptian scientists to imitate the plague-producing agents as biological warfare agents. Indeed, Egypt's relatively advanced biotechnological abilities allowed it to deal with these two agents. The production and storage of the former agent, the plague (pest) bacterium, are not at all simple, while the latter one, the Rift Valley fever virus, is even more complicated to handle. To this, one must add Egypt's development of additional biological warfare agents, as, for instance, botulinum toxin and a virus that causes encephalitis, as further biological warfare agents.

LIBYA

Basic Characteristics

Libya has conducted a very wide biological-chemical weapons acquisition program, though seemingly only partially productive for the time being. In September 1983, the CIA already believed that Libya had chemical weapons. Since then, Libya has come a long way. Qadhdhafi has repeated several times that Libya has the right to acquire chemical and biological weapons no less than any other country, especially those already armed with weapons of mass destruction. And he transfers this right to the entire Arab world, although recently he has pledged to abandon Libya's weapons programs.

Indeed, immediately after the establishment of the Chemical Weapons Convention, Qadhdhafi met Mubarak to coordinate with him the steps to be taken by the entire Arab world. Only a few years earlier, Mubarak had said that, unlike the lies of Libya, Egypt had no chemical weapons and had no desire to acquire them. Syria was the only Arab country to defend Libya, which had tried in vain to conceal a massive chemical arms factory as a pharmaceutical plant. This comment also hinted at the cooperation between Syria and Libya along the Libya-Syria-Iran-North Korea axis of missile and biological/chemical weapons development.

Simultaneously, Libya is a partner in North Korea's development of long-range missiles (along with Iran and Syria) — the *Nodong* (1,000-1,300 km) — which are ultimately intended, evidently, for carrying chemical and biological warheads. This would boost Libya one step up as a potential threat *vis-à-vis* Israel and Europe. Other missiles in the Libyan ballistic program include the TD-1 and TD-2 (2,000-3,500 km) plus the OTRAG (2,000 km). Regretfully, the Libyan biological and chemical effort receives very significant support from South Africa.

Chemical Weapons

The Rabta complex can easily be switched to its original purpose of chemical weapons production at any time. The complex was inaugurated in the presence of the Egyptian Health Minister in September 1995. The plant is said to supply pharmaceuticals to the entire Arab world, inasmuch as it is supported by an Egyptian company, the El-Nasser Pharmaceutical Company, which provides support for Egypt's chemical-weapons factory. In December 1994, the CIA director said that Egypt and Libya were cooperating in the manufacture of chemical weapons. Libya is also cooperating with Iraq, Syria, and Iran in this field. Hence, the Libyan effort is unique in that it unites all five threatening countries.

Meanwhile, the Libyans found it wise to transfer activities to huge factories tens of meters beneath the ground, thereby creating two advantages: removal, or significant decrease, of the threat of satellite recognizance as well as the threat of being bombed. Indeed, the American director of Central Intelligence stressed these two difficulties when surveying Libya's extreme acquisition policies. He said joint international action could only delay the process but not prevent it.

Dany Shoham

Two new additional chemical installations are located at Sebha and Tarhuna in underground tunnels dug into mountains. These projects are camouflaged as civilian projects aided by contractors from around the world. The construction plans for the Tarhuna factory, described as the largest chemical arms plant in the world, were obtained by German intelligence from German and Austrian contractors, and there is great concern that they have reached Syria as well as Iran.

Biological Weapons

In addition to the three chief chemical weapons facilities mentioned above, which most probably contain hidden wings for biological weapons, Libya attempted to conceal her biological weapons program within two installations: the "Microbiological Research Center" and the "General Health Laboratories." In the field of biological weapons Libya developed two germs — anthrax and brucella — as well as botulinum toxin, as biological warfare agents, an effort assisted by foreign firms. It is fairly reasonable that Libya has already begun to produce and accumulate biological weapons.

IRAN

Basic Characteristic

Iran is the most advanced Islamic country in the Middle East, technologically and scientifically. Moreover, being a non-Arab Islamic state, it has a key role within the Islamic block in general, and in regard to the proliferation of chemical and biological weapons in particular. Further, it is possible that Iran constitutes the greatest biochemical threat for the following reasons:

- Its present biochemical armament procurement and its future nuclear armament procurement are the result of a long-term strategy, supported by significant capital and by careful supervision

- Its membership in the Chemical and Biological Conventions, despite the fact that it is arming itself with biological and chemical weapons (which it denies)

- Its emphasis on long-range missiles carrying biochemical warheads, and interest in an aircraft carrier

- Its fostering of terrorist capabilities, which include chemical and especially biological terrorism

- Its outstanding strategic interface with Syria

- Its Muslim fanaticism and enmity to Israel

- The remarkable profusion and physical decentralization of the installations included in the system, responsible for development, production and warehousing of chemical and biological warfare agents and of delivery means — located in Teheran, Isfahan, Kharge, Karai, Marv-Dasht, Shiraz, and Bandar-Khumeiny

- There was no substantial change in the policy and in the acquisition of strategic weapons following the change of regime.

Iran has succeeded in obtaining significant assistance from countries that have mastered key technologies. There is evidence of a recent increase in the aid Iran receives from China, Russia, North Korea, Pakistan, and South Africa, for its chemical-biological efforts. Concomitantly, there is extensive aid coming from German firms, largely the same firms that previously helped Iraq and as such, those firms have earlier been condemned, ironically, by Iran — a typical line of deceit by the Iranians — many of which compose the strategic Iranian concept.

Chemical Weapons

Iran learned more about chemical warfare than any other country in the world from the bitter experience of seven years of attacks by Iraq. Such cumulative experience has ramifications for Iran's chemical weapons acquisition program. During the war, Iran tried to manufacture its own chemical weapons, but it deployed them in a limited way only. Yet, by the end of the war, Iran had accumulated vast experience in the production of chemical weapons. Today it has such weapons on artillery shells, aerial bombs, rockets, and very likely on missile warheads as well. The chemical warfare agents it produces include: cyanide, mustard, luwisite, phosgene, tabun, and Sarin.

Biological Weapons

Iran is working relentlessly in the realm of biological weaponry. It has vast and sophisticated biotechnological infrastructures at its disposal along with skilled manpower. It therefore has only limited need for outside assistance, and its biological weapons program should bear fruit in the near future. Its biological weapons dovetail with those produced by Syria: botulinum, ricin, and anthrax. Still, its production capacity, especially of viruses, is far greater than that of Syria, and it undoubtedly aspires ultimately to achieve biological warheads for long-range missiles.

The Iranian effort to equip itself with biological weapons is accentuated by assistance from Russia. Russia contributes to the offensive biological capabilities of Iran at the operational level to the extent that, according to American intelligence sources, Iran's biological arsenal will have the power nearly equivalent to a nuclear effect. Nor has the importance of biological weapons in the context of terrorist actions escaped Iran's view, and it equipped itself with the means for guerrilla-warfare intended to employ biological agents by spraying and by the contamination of water systems.

PAKISTAN, KAZAKHSTAN, AND OTHER EMINENT ISLAMIC RESOURCES OF TECHNOLOGY TRANSFER

The Islamic system is blocked, chiefly by Israel and her only Islamic (NATO member) ally, Turkey, on its western wing, and by inferior African countries on its southern wing. Direct geographical interface allows for the effective transfer of technology and skills through the northern and eastern wings of the Islamic system of nations, and they do indeed function in this manner. Pakistan, the most advanced Islamic state, borders on the powerful nation of China, with which it maintains close and productive ties, and sensibly shapes the eastern connections of the Islamic nations. Being in such a paramount position, Pakistan constitutes an extremely important source of know-how and technology in itself, as well as a crucial bridge for the migration of essential expertise and components from the Far East, China, and North Korea in particular.

Moreover, the common border found in between Pakistan and Iran enables direct technology transfer. Movements of specialists, chemicals, components, know-how, or even weapon systems cannot be effectively monitored or detected thereupon. Also, Pakistan repays Libya and Saudi Arabia for the massive financial assistance they provided by advancing their nuclear and CB weapons development. All in all, the major contribution of Pakistan as an Islamic CB weapons proliferator cannot be measured as yet in realistic terms since it has been developed in secrecy. It is obviously significant, in any event.

The other Islamic peripheral country, Kazakhstan, though undergoing an opposite process, namely deproliferation, evidently still plays a similar role in regard to countries to the north. The disintegration of the USSR gave birth to several new Islamic states on the northern periphery of the Islamic system, including Uzbekistan, Tajikistan, Azerbaijan, Turkmenistan, Kyrgystan, and, the most northerly, significant, and largest one, Kazakhstan. The latter completely masters technologies related to all types of nonconventional weapons even though it proclaims that it is currently committed to total disarmament. The big sister, Russia, is situated to the north, whereas the Islamic little sisters shorten the distance to the Iranian, Pakistani, and Afghani borders. The paradoxical phenomenon emerging within this peculiar context is in that the more a particular nation declares that it is complying with the convention, the more resources of critical technologies and specialized manpower in that country become available to developers in other countries. That is precisely the case with Kazakhstan and some of her nearby Islamic sisters. One manner by which this worrisome situation is manifested is the knowledgeable "scientific mercenaries" that find their way to the Middle-Eastern Islamic developers.

Kazakhstan inherited large and advanced CB facilities from mother-USSR: two huge chemical weapons production facilities, one at Pavlodar and the other one at Zhambul — the former containing very sophisticated installations — and a chemical weapons storage facility on the Ili river. Furthermore, four major biological weapons facilities have been active in Kazakhstan: the so called Scientific Experimental and Production Base in Stepnogorsk (including a major Soviet anthrax brewing plant), the Vozrozhdenie Island open-air test site in the Aral Sea, the Scientific Research Agricultural Institute in Gvardeyskiy, and the Anti-Plague Scientific Research Institute in Alma-Ata.

Not expecting her own disintegration, the Soviet Union did not bother to concentrate her gigantic biological and chemical efforts within Russia itself, and various facilities situated in other parts of USSR were actively involved in the program. In Uzbekistan, for example, the Institute of Genetics, Tashkent, has for years been working on biological weapons to be used in agriculture, an advanced form of economical bio-warfare. A marginal country like Armenia, for instance, appears to possess chemical weapons originating in Russia. Also, it has been reported that Islamic segments still belonging to Russia, like Chechnya, have usable CB weapons.

Plausibly, one may assume that given the proper payment, the Islamic brotherhood overcomes obstacles that would otherwise hamper the migration of essential biochemical technologies, or even entire CB weapon systems or their components. Movement of these technologies, particularly through common borders, is taking place from peripheral Islamic countries into the Middle East. In practice, that is how it happens.

CHEMICAL AND BIOLOGICAL TERRORISM

The nature of many chemical and biological warfare agents allows them to be used by non-regular militants, namely saboteurs, in a very effective and horrifying manner. One of the greatest fears in the West, especially in the United States, concerns chemical and biological terrorism. This fear centers around terrorists who would function as human launchers, such as suicide bombers, in the extreme. They could be armed with such weapons by a terrorism-oriented Islamic country or by some Islamic organization acting on its own. Candidates include Iran, Libya, Syria, Sudan, and Algeria in terms of state-sponsored terrorism. *Al-Qaʻidah* (headed by Osama bin Laden), *Hizbullah*, *Hamas,* and *Tanzim* are the current candidate organizations prepared to conduct biochemical terrorism. The anthrax letters attack against the United States has been, unfortunately, a concrete illustration. Biochemical guerrilla warfare may be conducted without the possibility to trace the sponsor, be it a country or an independent organization. Not surprisingly, the threat of Islamic biochemical terrorism concerns even Russia, considering how Chechnya might act. Technically speaking, the feasibility of such a scenario is quite high, with the target being located in Israel, the United States, or elsewhere. Of particular concern in the United States is the problem of preparedness to face biological terrorism and whether it is being addressed by American authorities.

The leading Islamic organization to take practical steps to attain an operational biochemical capacity is *al-Qai`dah*. It has been implicated in what is called "multi-track biochemical microproliferation."

Al-Qa`idah is not the only Islamic organization that is a cause for worry in terms of biochemical terrorism. Former CIA director James Wolsey described the *Hizbullah* as a potential agent for biological terrorism. This is particularly realistic due to the fact that the *Hizbullah* is directly supported by Iran. Iran possesses various CB weapons, including specific means designed for guerilla operations.

One reason for the extreme position of the Syrians concerning their stipulated access to the Kinneret (Sea of Gallilee) could have been the feasibility of contaminating it.

Finally, the Palestinian terrorist organizations should be mentioned. Certainly, the *Hamas* and *Tanzim* are aware of various options that may be employed in biochemical terrorist acts against Israeli targets. Actually, during the past two decades Palestinian terrorists attempted sabotage by toxic materials in about a dozen cases, apparently on individual initiatives. Nevertheless, there is gradually increasing awareness within the *Hamas* regarding possible use of poisonous substances for purposes of sabotage. On several occasions the *Hamas* already attempted to carry out that mode. Also, one cannot rule out the possibility of "an ecological *intifada*" directed at poisoning the water sources in Judea and Samaria that serve Israel's Coastal Plain, inhabited primarily by Jewish citizens. The Kinneret might be regarded to be a preferable target for contamination by potent radioactive materials.

THE EVOLVING THREAT TOWARD EUROPE AND THE UNITED STATES

The biochemical threat posed by the Islamic block toward Israel is self-evident, and in time might take shape. This is but one dimension of the Islamic menace. As noted earlier, most Islamic countries that possess offensive biochemical capabilities seek to equip themselves with long-range ballistic missiles of up to thousands of kilometers, covering areas much wider than their immediate environment. The very long distance that missiles can traverse also goes far beyond their relevant strategic geopolitical arena, a fact that should arouse considerable amazement since it presents the obvious danger of a capacity to deliver chemical and biological agents to targets far away.

This biochemical-ballistic capacity even goes far beyond the needs resulting from the strengthening cooperation between Turkey, the Muslim country that separates Europe and the Middle East and belongs to NATO, and Israel. This cooperation serves as an excuse for the ostensible need for Islamic nations to cultivate multiple chemical-biological offensive strategies whose potential goals include Israel, Turkey, and a large part of Europe.

The 21st century will probably see enormous scientific bio-technological developments. Unfortunately, these developments will entail enormous unwanted military implications, and will significantly intensify the biochemical threat. Ballistic delivery systems for biochemical warfare agents will improve considerably. Also expected is the addition of biochemical warheads that contain cluster bombs armament that are carried by cruise missiles, thereby greatly increasing the threat. The leading Islamic countries are in all probability seeking to master those developments.

What the future threatens to produce is a "biochemical monster turning on its creators." For years the United States and various European countries, or, more precisely, many supply firms in Europe and the United States, have been contributing extensively and critically to this irreversible process. In practical terms, it means that in approximately five years or so, an ordnance of surface-to-surface ballistic missiles armed with warheads containing CB agents, might be deployed within the premises of Iran, Syria, and Libya, capable of reaching remote targets in Europe as well as in the United States. The chances of such a scenario taking place, in terms of both deterrence, retaliation, and threat of and first use, can be determined only in the future. At any rate, an impending shift in the balance of power is about to occur.

Further, the implementation of the chemical convention and the perfection of the biological convention should facilitate putting controls on the suppliers of prohibited biochemical technology, particularly in Europe and the United States, although past experience teaches that, in most cases, suppliers found ways to bypass the controls. The name of the game, in this connection, is early and much better intelligence as well as persistent determination.

THE OVERWHELMING MENACE OF BIOLOGICAL WEAPONS

During the recent decade, biological weapons re-emerged as ultimate practical weapons of mass destruction, in terms of both guerrilla warfare and large-scale warfare, whereas nuclear weapons constitute the ultimate weapon of deterrence. Mention should be made of the broad impact of biological weapons, which may be fully strategic and widely explosive, even when employed by means of guerrilla warfare. Also, biological weapons hold the ratio of cost to efficiency at its desirable limits that meets the needs of developing countries seeking non-conventional armaments which are not too complex to handle. Nuclear weapons are enormously more sophisticated and expensive, and they retain their status as the super deterrent weapon of mass destruction. Yet, the increasing attainability, diversity (toxins, non-epidemic pathogens, and epidemic pathogens), and versatility of biological weapons make them attractive to rogue regimes in search of a weapon with massive impact.

A lot has been said, and evidenced, with regard to the anticipated devastation resulting from the employment of the two supreme biological warfare agents, the anthrax bacterium and the smallpox virus. In practice, the former is an available, readily cultivated, highly infective, and yet non-contagious pathogen, marked by extreme environmental stability, remarkable virulence, and considerable sensitivity to certain antibiotics. The virus causing smallpox is an already globally eradicated pathogen, and, hence, difficult, but not impossible, to obtain. It is easily reproducible in fertilized chicken eggs, highly infective and contagious, less stable but fully resistant to antibiotics, and very virulent. Each of those pathogens is indeed a potent biological warfare agent that can be spread by guerrilla warfare or regular military operations. Regardless of the panic they can generate, which is extremely significant in itself, the affliction they cause directly is horrendous in terms of casualties and medical logistics.

Of interest here are two events during which rulers of Islamic nations threatened to use biological weapons. For quite some time, Iraq (until of course Saddam Hussein's fall) and Egypt have been the most powerful Arab nations, technologically and scientifically. Their presidents, Anwar Sadat (in 1972) and Saddam Hussein (in 1990), were the only leaders worldwide to voluntarily and purposefully announce that they possess usable stocks of biological weapons. Saddam's announcement was delivered a few years after the continuous Iraqi employment of chemical weapons against Iran, prior to the 1990 invasion of Kuwait. Both leaders lacked nuclear weapons, but in view of the fact that their possession of effective chemical weapons was public knowledge, they found it politically beneficial to add their possession of biological weapons.

CONCLUDING REMARKS

Driven by an exceptional conjunction of gradually intensifying pan-Islamic brotherhood and solidifying geostrategic motives, the leading Islamic countries have persistently paved the way of a virtually irreversible CB proliferation process, in contrast to the currently prevailing global deproliferation trends. This proliferation is fueled by two complementary processes: domestic increase and distribution of CB-related know-how, skill, and practical application within the Islamic world, and the simultaneous migration of the necessary technologies from non-Islamic countries. It seems as if the Islamic proliferators act as an absorbing apparatus of portions of the dismantled facilities and dismissed personnel affiliated with past military CB infrastructures located in non-Islamic countries. Intra-Islamic spreading, in parallel, of cardinal biochemical essentials is of no less importance.

The fact that most Muslim nations are full members of the CWC and BWC is misleading, because more than half of the Islamic states plainly do not have, and do not intend to have, CB weapons. Most possessors are not full members. Iran, though being a major possessor, is a full member, but the Iranian case is distinctly the case of well-orchestrated amazing deception. On the other hand, a non-possessor like Lebanon intentionally refrains from membership, so as to allow the deployment of CB weapons by Syrian forces in Lebanon.

Unfortunately, positive global developments such as the emergence of autonomous nations from the disintegration of USSR, and the worldwide tendency for disarmament and arms control especially in terms of non-conventional weapons, paradoxically played a role of paramount importance in arming Islamic nations with these weapons. This phenomenon is still taking place, and in all likelihood will continue in the future.

The anticipated outcome is the formation of a formidable Islamic menace toward Western countries where their former, and present, suppliers are located. Islamic terrorists, including CB-oriented ones, publicly declare that objective. Turkey, and certainly Israel, the only democracies in the Middle East, are severely threatened by the Islamic proliferators.

The existing geopolitical strategic formation of the Islamic system, together with its adjacent arenas, are plainly in her favor. The likely outcome of that entire conjuncture is indeed threatening. Ranging, potentially, from local small-scale CB terrorism up to the launching of CB-agents-carrying-ballistic missiles on an international scale, the Islamic CB weapons menace is emerging as an extremely serious issue. A future Islamic nuclear umbrella would certainly make matters worse. The fact that the leading Islamic countries are aware of the potential impact of their power propels their incentive for making more progress in this realm. All four modes of action are present: deterrence, retaliation, threat, and surprise attack. Globally, then, chemical and more biological weapons are considered to constitute an imminent menace from Islamic countries. Israel and the West are evidently the first priority targets. The prospects of effectively countering this threat are diminishing as time passes.

Integration of the Islamic world will most likely continue in the future. The reservoir of CB weapons' know-how presently scattered over different Islamic countries should be regarded as a potentially unitary resource of utmost importance, available for concrete armament needs of various Islamic nations.

Disregarding for a moment the Islamic nations that formerly formed part of the Soviet Union, no less than six Islamic countries — Egypt, Syria, Libya, Iran, Sudan, and Pakistan — currently possess chemical and biological weapons, while Algeria and Saudi Arabia are candidates to join the club. Moreover, in contrast to the ongoing global positive trend of chemical and biological deproliferation, the prominent and obvious path followed at this time by the leading Islamic countries leads to the augmentation of their chemical and biological capacities.

The described paradigm relates to the global perspective, as well. The formerly Central-European East-West frontline is seemingly being replaced, subtly, by a Middle Eastern one. Syria and Iran presently constitute the new frontline, as against Turkey, Israel, and Jordan — while Saudi Arabia is, in terms of a distinct strategically Eastern-supported Middle Eastern block, opposing a strategically Western-supported one.

COPING WITH THE THREAT

The Islamic countries can use their biochemical weapons the following ways:

- Practical scenarios: conquest, defense, neutralization, paralysis, forcing evacuation, causing massive losses, preventing immediate danger to the regime, damaging strategic targets

- Threat scenarios: spreading panic, deterring actions or re-actions of various opponents; undermining the deterrent capability of opponents

The two scenarios at the two ends of the spectrum — tactical operation for the purpose of military conquest of a given theater (the Golan Heights, for example) as opposed to a strategic operation against civilian population centers (such as the central coastal area of Israel) — serve totally different aims. There are several interim scenarios, as, for example, an aerial attack on military airfields, on reserve forces call-up stations, and on command and control centers. However, the common denominator and central guiding notion that would precipitate a decision to engage in action, would be the presumption that the use of chemical or biological weapons would have a high chance of devastating essential targets, and that the likelihood of success in any substitute fashion would be low or non-existent.

In the foreseeable future, if and when threatening states possess nuclear weapons, it is reasonable to assume that they will serve as a nuclear umbrella to an atomic threat against Arab states. Hence, there is no doubt that Iran and others will feel free to use chemical and biological weapons to the extent that they see fit, in the belief that they are protected from nuclear counterstrikes, and are even willing to absorb a chemical-biological attack. A situation such as this will bring about a drastic change in the equation of forces. Assuming for the moment that this development is still far off, one alteration in the equation of forces as perceived by the Arab countries must be taken into consideration: *The Arab and Iranian analysis of the current situation is that biological arms can nullify the threat of an Israeli nuclear counterstrike to a chemical attack launched by an Arab nation or by Iran.*

Unfortunately, in the face of the stockpiling of biological and chemical weapons by Arab countries and Iran, it is presently difficult to identify a way to critically limit the rate of that process, or to prevent new technologies from being available by non-Islamic countries. The North Korean and Chinese formal and semi-official aid extended to Syria, Iran, Libya, and Egypt, along with the informal transfer of invaluable technological knowledge (if not more) from Russia, may well create an incremental jump in the present rate of armament build-up. It is only a matter of time before the stockpiles of biochemical weapons in Islamic countries will include missile-carrying warheads. This will enable those countries to launch BCW from any site in their territory to any location within Israel. In terms of basic strategic time, there is no fundamental difference if this status will be achieved in three, six, or nine years.

Only with a sharp turnabout in the application of restrictions on international commerce, in the support provided by a radical nation such as North Korea, or in the powerful Arab-Iranian motivation to strengthen their strategic alliance in terms of unconventional armaments, can a real change be effected. Present international circumstances being what they are, none of these developments are imaginable now or in the foreseeable future.

The efficiency of physically striking at the source of the threat, such as an air strike on weapons stockpiles or their production plants, demonstrated clearly by the pinpoint surprise bombing of the Iraqi nuclear reactor but shown to be inefficient in the continuous bombings during the Kuwait campaign where the element of surprise did not exist, remains an option of considerable potential. However, two recent developments have made such an operation extremely difficult: a) underground production plants and storage sites make bombing problematic, and, b) doubts that an Arab country (or Iran) would react with restraint. Preventing the development of a situation which would encourage an Arab leader to utilize biological or chemical weaponry, or to assign the authority for their use to some lower echelon, is of the highest priority.

The following steps could also help target countries such as Israel a great deal:

- A defense capability that would greatly reduce the damage inflicted by a CB attack

- Preparation for an immediate and devastating Israeli reprisal that would include, at the same time, the neutralization of the remaining biochemical attack capability

- Identification of storage sites of CB weapons and production plants, and the creation of immediate and effective attack capability

- Early warning systems to identify such an attack and neutralize it by political or military means, including anti-missiles envelopes

- On the political-diplomatic-psychological warfare level — endeavor to identify an Arab line based on biochemical threatening, which is heightened by acute or continuous brinkmanship, and formulate an opposing operational line based on parallel yet more sophisticated brinkmanship

There appears to be a sharp increase in inter-Arab and Iranian cooperation. Can this cooperation reach the level of transferring chemical or biological weapons from one nation to another, or to operational strategic coordination in this connection? The enormous threat inherent in this matter requires close attention.

A different threat whose importance and many-faceted ramifications are well known, relates to inter-Arab and Iranian cooperation concerning the international conventions to eliminate chemical and biological weapons. The Arab countries that have not yet signed border on Israel or currently possess such a potential, including Syria, Egypt, Lebanon, and Libya. An Islamic country such as Iran that signed the convention could demand inspection of installations in another country that has signed, including Israel, the results of which would be passed on to other Arab allies that have not signed. It is difficult to see how this situation can be avoided, except by the adoption of a drastic amendment that would prohibit a country that initiated such an inspection from receiving all of the results even if they were positive. Moreover, Arab states and Iran could coordinate among themselves exactly which installations they would demand to be inspected.

Objectively speaking, the Arab demand for a Middle East without weapons of mass destruction is a positive step. Yet, the difficulty in accomplishing this state of affairs stems from severe, and in some instances, inherent constrains, and it is doubtful that it is basically feasible.

The main difficulty in the eradication of biological and chemical weapons is twofold:

- What is the probability of actually achieving complete (physical) eradication of such arms without the danger of countries hiding them?

- What are the chances of precluding the possibility that the weapons will be recreated within a short time period of time such as days or weeks, and of hiding this capacity?

Finally, what is the probability, in effect, that the Islamic-Arab lineup of forces could be weaned away from maintaining such weapons? Recent developments taking place with respect to the Libyan strategy of WMD may possibly reflect an affect-course of deterioration of the related Libyan CBW programs. The present analysis has been worked out, yet, regardless of such seeming course, it may turn inadequate during 2004.

BIBLIOGRAPHY

Bozheyeva, G. "The Pavlodar Chemical Weapons Plant in Kazakhstan: History and Legacy." *The Nonproliferation Review*, vol. 7, no. 4 (2000): p. 136–145.
Bozheyeva, G., et al. "Former Soviet Biological Weapons Facilities in Kazakhstan: Past, Present and Future." Occasional Paper No. 1, Center for Nonproliferation Studies, Monterey, US, June 1999.

Bruck, G.M., and C.C. Flowerree. *International Handbook on Chemical Weapons Proliferations.* New York: Greenwood Press, 1991.

Carus, W.S. "Chemical Weapons in the Middle East." Research Memorandum No. 9. The Washington Institute for Near East Policy (December 1988).

The CBW Convention Bulletin – Quarterly Journal of the Harvard-Sussex Program on CBW Armament and Arms Limitation, 1990–2002; in: <www.fas.harvard.edu/`hsp> and <www.sussex.ac.uk/spru/hsp/>.

Collins, J.M. "Weapons of Mass Destruction: The Impact of Proliferation on U.S. Military Posture." Congessional Research Service Report for Congress (1995).

Cordesman, A.H. *Weapons of Mass Destruction in the Middle East.* United Kingdom: Brassey's Ltd., 1991.

Douglass, J.D., and N.C. Livingstone. *America the Vulnerable: The Threat of Chemical and Biological Warfare.* New York: New York Free Press, 1987.

Eitzen, E. "Potential Biological Threat Scenarios." Testimony before the U.S. Senate Permanent Subcommittee on Investigation. Washington DC (October 31, 1995).

Cameron, G. "Multi-Track Microproliferation: Lessons from Al-Qa`idah and Aum Shinrikyo." *Studies in Conflict and Terrorism,* vol. 22 (1999): p. 277–309.

Godsen, C. Presentation at the meeting on "Saddam Hussein War Crimes and Crimes against the Iraqi People." The Middle East Institute, Washington DC (September 18, 2000).

Haikal, M.H. *Illusions of Triumph.* London: Harper Collins, 1992.

Holger, K., and E. Kock. *Bomb Matters — Lethal Weapons in the Third World.* Berlin, Verdens Gang Verlag (January 1990).

Howe, H. "Syria Preparing Option of Sudden Chemical Attack on Israel Cities." *Yediot Aharonot,* Tel Aviv (September 12, 1997): p. 5–7.

The Journal of the American Medical Association. Special issue on biological warfare. Vol. 278, No. 5 (1997).

Levran, A. *The Military Balance in the Middle East — 1986.* The Jaffe Center for Strategic Studies, Tel Aviv University, 1987.

London Times. "The Non-Parties to the CW Convention." Editorial, September 20, 1993, p. 4.

Politics and the Life Sciences. Special issue on chemical and biological terrorism. Vol. 15, no. 2, (1998).

Pugwash International Forum Periodical Reports on Chemical and Biological Warfare. In: <http://www.pugwash.org>, and <http://pugwash.org/reports/cbw/cbw1.htm>.

Purver, R. "Chemical and Biological Terrorism: The Threat According to the Open Literature." The Canadian Security Intelligence Service, Ottawa, 1995.

Russian Foreign Intelligence Service Report – "The Proliferation of Weapons of Mass Destruction," 1993.

Sayigh, Y. *Arab Military Industry.* United Kingdom: Brassey's Ltd., 1992.

Schumeyer, G. *Chemical Weapons Proliferation in the Middle East.* U.S. Army War College, Pensylvania, April 1, 1990.

Shoham, D. "Chemical Weapons in Egypt and Syria: Evolution, Capabilities, Control." BESA Center for Strategic Studies, Security and Policy Studies No. 21, Bar-Ilan University, June 1995.

Shoham. D. "Libya, Egypt and Weapons of Mass Destruction." *Nativ*, vol. 9, no. 3, p. 15–16 (1996).

SIPRI (Stockholm International Peace Research Institute). *The Problem of Chemical and Biological Weapons*. New York: Humanities Press Inc., 1971.

SIPRI periodical reports and publications on chemical and biological warfare, in: <www.sipri.se> and <www.databases.sipri.se/index/html>.

Task Force on Terrorism and Unconventional Warfare. "The Iraqi Weapons of Mass Destruction Challenge: Myths and Reality." U.S. House of Representatives, Washington, DC, 1997.

United Nations Conference on Disarmament. Periodical reports and publications, in: <http://www.unorg.ch/disarm.htm>.

UNSCOM periodical reports and publications; in: <www.unorg/Depts/unscom> and <cns.miis.edu.research/iraqucreport/index.htm>.

U.S. Arms Control and Disarmament Agency. "Status of BW Programs of Key Countries." Report submitted to Congress, July 1996.

U.S. Department of Defense, Office of the Under Secretary of Defense for Acquisition. The Military Critical Technologies List. October 1992, p. 13.

Facing Insurgent Islam: A Grand Strategy for the West

Yehezkel Dror

PART ONE: ESTIMATE OF DYNAMICS

I. Approach

One of the more significant global processes very likely to characterize the 21st century is the continuing and escalating rise of Islam. In terms of self-consciousness, energy, demography, economic power, and military capacities, Islam is "standing up," as the usual phrase in Arabic puts it. As a civilization and belief system and as a cluster of states and non-state actors, Islam is sure to become increasingly potent and to exert increasing influence on geo-political processes and structures.[1] This potency can, from a Western and global perspective, be very benevolent or/and very malignant. Under optimistic assumptions, Islam can again become a very creative civilization making significant contributions to a peaceful global order, to humankind, and to global culture as a whole, while advancing the people of Islam to high individual and collective pluralistic qualities of life. However, under pessimistic assumptions, rising Islam can take very aggressive forms, combining religious fanaticism with mass killing weapons,[2] bringing about neo-barbarism in significant parts of the world, and moving toward a post-modern form of religious and cultural wars. In particular, resurgent Islam is likely to be aggressive toward the West, causing it much damage, while also causing much harm to the adherents to Islam themselves and possibly endangering the future of humanity as a whole.

Given this evolutionary potential of Islam, a main challenge facing the West and its partners is to influence the actual developments of Islamic states and societies so as to increase the probability of positive trajectories and reduce the probability of negative ones while containing the damage potential of the latter.

The basic position of this chapter is that, therefore, the West needs a well-considered grand strategy[3] which serves as grounding both for long-term policies and for crisis improvisation in the face of the many unpredictable and also in part inconceivable[4] situations sure to come about. This chapter is devoted to an effort to develop such a grand strategy.[5]

The concept of "grand strategy" poses serious dangers if taken in an unsophisticated way. Statecraft has to deal with unique concrete situations that resist simple categorization. Still, a well-considered grand strategy can provide principles helping policymakers to take a deeper, more comprehensive, and longer-term view of "hot" issues and to cope with specific situations in ways taking into account broader contexts and fundamental goals. Thus, improved grand strategic thinking would have led to quite different European Union policies toward Turkey and Western policies in Bosnia, avoiding grave error that cannot but strengthen the malignant potential of Islam.

II. Islam in Transformation

Different Islamic states moved through various phases of evolution according to unique timetables. Thus, Turkey followed after the First World War a very different path from Saudi Arabia and Malaysia; changes in ways having little in common with the Islamic parts of India which later became Pakistan and Bangladesh. Still, there is a historic unity to Islam and its states as belonging to a shared, though pluralistic, civilization. This unity justified discourse on a "grand strategy" dealing with Islam as a whole. However, to try to understand the present situation and the evolutionary potential[6] of Islam and develop an appropriate grand strategy, thinking in terms of long-term history[7] is essential. But long-term perspectives must be combined with detailed analysis of contemporary processes within a view of history as nonlinear,[8] systemic,[9] and partly open-ended.[10]

Reducing such "thinking-in-history"[11] to bare essentials, four phases characterize much of the path of Islam from the past into the present and toward uncertain and contingent issues in the future.

In the first phase, Islam was an extremely successful religion and civilization, with tremendous achievements in expanding, building societies and states, and reaching peak cultural creativity. The domain of Islam extended over large parts of the then-known world, succeeded for generations to hold on to large segments of Europe, and constituted what would today be called a "super block."

In the second phase, with the emergence of pre-modern and modern Europe, the crystallization of the Western state system, and the scientific and technological revolution, the White Christian West conquered the domain of Islam and subordinated it.[12] From the perspective of Islam, this was a period of colonization, foreign occupation, enforced subjugation, and cultural humiliation.[13] However, the elimination of Islamic sovereignty in no way eroded adherence to Islam.

In the third phase, Islamic states regained independence and most of them tried to modernize on lines of the West. The nation-state pattern was taken over in many Islamic countries, together with Western ideas and ideologies. However, this "Westernization" was in most societies superficial and did not touch grass root adherence to Islam and its political potentials, with the partial exception of Turkey, thanks to the unique Ataturk reforms.

Following failures of modernization, weakening of the West, and discrediting of some of its main ideologies, all Islamic countries are now to some extent in a fourth phase; some more so and some less. Bewilderment and search for selfhood and individual and collective self-identity characterize this phase.[14] Following the failures of Western-type nationalism and various versions of state socialism, it is increasingly characterized by re-Islamization.

Yehezkel Dror

Individually and collectively, Moslems and Islamic societies search for self-identity and an appropriate place in the modern world. Quasi-westernization continues to be an attractive option for some elites, but is losing ground, with growing portions of the educated and of professionals too becoming more Islamic. There is a return to "roots" with much turning to "fundamentalism,"[15] with search for ways to combine Islamic traditions with modern technologies and economies, and with a very strong desire to make Islam again into a major global power. All this goes hand in hand with much resentment toward the West and a continuing feeling of humiliation,[16] combined with a contradictory mixture between envy and unwillingness to accept Western *Zeitgeist* and "post-modernity."

The present phase is loaded with contradictions, such as desire for economic prosperity and technological modernization together with clinging to traditions; a sense of power together with strong feelings of inadequacy; resentment of the West combined, as noted, with not a little envy; and more.

A number of additional "drivers" of the future[17] add to instability while strengthening the likelihood of developments harmful to the West. Let me start with demography. Populations in most Islamic countries increase rapidly and become urbanized, producing explosive situations. However, some countries have a rather stable and relatively small indigenous population, including some of the oil-richest states. In some countries, demographic changes, including immigration, entry of refugees, and import of labor, disturb ethnic-political balances, as in Lebanon, Kuwait, and Jordan. All in all, demographic factors aggravate instability, by overloading governments, retarding economic and social welfare, and creating urban masses prone to fundamentalism and also fanaticism. This applies both to domestic situations and to relations between states, with large and growing populations on one hand and very rich countries with small populations on the other, such as in the Persian Gulf, producing very unstable disparities. Similarly, the growing populations of North Africa facing southern Europe, of Turkey facing east Europe and of Malaysia and Indonesia facing Australia, may well produce radical geo-strategic shifts including violent eruptions changing global cultural and power relations.

To move on to socioeconomic trends as a second main driver of the future closely related to the demographic one, widespread poverty and unemployment are unavoidable in the foreseeable future in most Islamic countries. No economic policy and no achievable international support can rapidly increase per capita real income, produce employment opportunities, and provide social services and amenities of life, satisfying growing aspirations and expectations. Therefore, extreme social frustrations and tensions are assured, with much potential for instability and Islamic fundamentalism at least in part hostile to the West.

Demographic and socioeconomic processes add up to deep social traumatization, producing search for "anchors" in life[18] and also for "enemies" to blame,[19] including anti-Western intentions. At the same time, the action capacities of Islamic countries and non-state actors are rapidly increasing, including ability to cause grievous harm to the West. Economic and professional elites are developing, with significant investments in education, including technical training. Most governments follow a selective technological modernization policy including modernization of military capacities.

Another factor characterizing the present phase is the growth of Islamic Diasporas and their radicalization. Large-scale migration from Islamic countries to the West, as caused mainly by economic motifs, is sure to increase despite all countermeasures. Intensifying radicalization of many of these migrants, because of clinging to roots and harsh barriers to their cultural absorption in their new countries of residence, is also to be expected. In combination, these two provide a strong basis for counter-Western Islamic actors residing in the West itself.

Significance of individual rulers in determining national policies, characterizing most Islamic countries, adds much uncertainty, with personal choices having significant consequences for better and worse. But this does not change the overall estimate of the dynamics of Islam for the next 50 years or so: Unless the West strongly intervenes with ongoing future-making processes, Islamic countries are sure to be quite unstable with much fundamentalism. Some state and non-state actors are very likely to be extremely fanatic, up to readiness to endanger their survival in order to cause grievous harm to the West by using all the means at their disposal.

Yehezkel Dror

All in all, Islam is "standing up." This is sure to be a super-turbulent process,[20] with discontinuities and eruptions, internal conflicts and external tensions dominating the scenery during at least the next 50 years. It is this current and foreseeable phase of the evolution of Islam and its evolutionary potential that poses a fateful challenge to Western grand strategies.

III. Alternative Pathways into the Future

The domain of Islam is surprise-prone, permeated with uncertainty, and sure to be in turmoil with a high probability of low-probability contingencies occurring. But the future is only in part chaotic, with main possibilities being constrained in central features by ongoing processes as discussed above. Therefore, main alternative pathways of Islam into the future can in part be depicted from the perspective of the West in a number of scenarios and structured futures. I will first present some scenarios, beginning with what appear to be dangerous ones for the West, moving on to some *prima facie* positive ones. But it should be noted that "bad" scenarios often also constitute an "occasion," in the sense of "opportunity" in Machiavelli's terminology, which can be utilized to influence the future for the better. And "good" ones may prove in the longer run to be Pandora boxes, especially if mishandled.

But, first, a comment on the impacts of global contexts. It makes a lot of difference to the future of Islam if the world as a whole moves rapidly toward an "end of history," with free markets and liberal democracy irresistibly permeating all societies.[21] Or, instead, if the world continues in the main on a trajectory of an uneasy mix between globalization and "tribalism," with some advancement of global regimes but a lot of "chaos."[22] My assumption is that at least till the middle of the 21st century, the first image of the future is beyond the limits of the possible, and in the second half of the 21st century it probably will not be relevant any more. Rather, the second image, with many possible variations, is the most likely future on which discussion of the evolution of Islam should be predicated. Jumps may occur and, indeed, I will present a contingent grand strategic recommendation to break the continuity of global history by instituting a "global leviathan," as a last resort against the self-destruction of humanity if lesser measures fail. If and when such or another mutation occurs or is brought about, this chapter will be obsolete. But until such an historic leap into a different geo-strategic and geo-cultural cosmos takes place, the proposed working assumption is that global impacts will not be radical and forceful enough to shift Islam beyond the alternative futures inherent in its present evolutionary potential.

However, external influences can shape parts of the future of Islam within its alternative futures as, in part, discussed in the following. This, indeed, is the purpose of the proposed grand strategies for the West — which, in essence, constitute deliberative interventions with historic processes designed to influence the actual pathway into the future taken by Islam and its actors.

Moving on to the substance of alternative futures of Islam, let me start with a number of scenarios that are, initially at least, dangerous from a Western perspective:

- Sudden destabilization of some countries because of internal coup d'etat or upheavals, such as in Jordan, Iraq, Saudi Arabia, and Egypt

- Outbreak of war between Iran and a combination of Arab states, between Egypt and Sudan, and more

- Violent conflict between some Arab states and Israel endangering important Western interests, whether starting in a limited way, such as on the Golan Heights, escalating from some local destabilization, such as in Jordan or Lebanon, or initiated as a major war

- Dramatic terrorism against Western high-value targets with chemical materials, massive hostage taking, etc.

- Escalating inter-cultural conflicts, such as between Pakistan and India, between Turkey and Greece, and between Moslem and non-Moslem actors in the Balkans or the former USSR

- New types of conflict with the West, such as large scale "boat people" migration from North Africa into Spain and from there into West Europe

- Acquisition of nuclear and other mass-killing weapons by some Islamic countries and also by non-country actors, including by unstable states and jihad groups, coupled with rumors on possible surprise-use of such weapons against Western countries and their allies

- Increasing likelihood of a nuclear conflict between some Islamic and some non-Islamic countries, which, however "local," may cause much damage to large areas and is likely to mutate global geo-politics as a whole

- A steep decline in oil prices, resulting from break-throughs in energy technology, producing severe economic crises and regime destabilization with propensities to engage in external aggression (llustrating the negative side of what may in many respects be a very positive development for the West and the world as a whole)

- Alternatively, increasing dependence of the West, Russia, and Japan on Middle Eastern oil, with its availability being endangered by a mixture between internal instability in main oil-producing countries and withholding of oil as a way to blackmail the West to make very costly and, in part, impossible concessions

- Development of an Islamic bloc with "super-power" capacities, confronting the West on global values and issues and demanding from main Western ex-colonial countries compensations for "generations of enslavement and robbery"

What are initially positive scenarios include, for instance:

- Rapid economic and social development in most Islamic countries, together with democratization including some unique features, accompanied by cultural creativity of global significance and peaceful cooperation with the West

- Increasing differentiation between Islamic countries, with many of them becoming more "Western" in main features

- Solution of main points of conflict between Islamic and Western countries, such as the Palestinian issue, integration of Turkey in the European Union, and the Kashmir conflict

- Large oil discoveries bringing about economic and social stabilization, including in Egypt and North Africa

- Strong reversals of fundamentalism, with new ideas combining basic Islamic values with democracy, human rights, and cooperation with the West gaining the upper hand

Many additional scenarios, negative and positive, can be designed. However, the ranges of the likely and of the possible, even if unlikely, are constrained by some basic historic structures and processes shaping the future of the domains of Islam. Therefore, despite the already mentioned likelihood of surprise possibilities including inconceivable ones, coherent main alternative futures of large parts of the Islamic areas, bringing out main features of evolutionary potentials and main alternative lines of evolution into the future, can be constructed. These include four main structures of the future:

Future One: Cooperation and Development

This is the most optimistic alternative future, with a majority of Islamic states cooperating peacefully among themselves and with the West. Successfully economic and social development takes place with much domestic stability. Regimes combine Western democracy and Islamic traditions and values. Islamic religious thinking downgrades hostility toward other civilizations and abandons the idea of Holy War. And cultural creativity leads toward an Islamic renaissance with important contributions to global cultures.

Future Two: Cohesion with Fanaticism

The second future is the most pessimistic one. Pan-Arab and Pan-Islamic forces dominate large parts of the area of Islam, including the Middle East, West Asia, and East Asia. Turkey and Egypt become increasingly fundamentalist. An Islamic block is formed, overcoming schisms and demonstrating increasing hostility toward the West. Fanaticism-prone countries engage in economic and technological advancement, building up strong action capabilities, while keeping society mobilized. Pushing back Western-Christian global dominance, aggressively advancing Islam in Africa and Asia, confronting Hindu India, and eliminating Israel are among the main goals, consistently pursued.

Future Three: Mixed Conflict and Cooperation, with Limited Upheavals

This future continues more or less present processes, *raison d'etat* being the main motive of Islamic state behavior, inter-state relations moving between cooperation and conflict, and domestic upheavals being limited. In this future, fundamentalism does not grow significantly and Iran becomes less extreme. Relations with the West continue as now, with ups and downs and limited conflicts combined with selective cooperation, without Islam forming a coherent cultural geo-political block.

Future Four: Mixed Conflict and Cooperation, with Many Upheavals

This future illustrates situations in between the second and third structures presented above, with a potential for further development into either direction. Such a future can last for quite some time, but is basically unstable because of non-sustainability of a structure including antinomies actively conflicting one with another.

Various combinations are likely and additional variations are possible. But these four alternative future structures, together with the scenarios outlined earlier, do add up to a sketch of the evolutionary potentials of Islam. Thus, they pose the main challenge posed by insurgent Islam to the West.

Before taking up the daunting task of indicating some principles for a Western grand strategy for coping with insurgent Islam, three widespread delusions must be deconstructed, namely clinging to the status quo, relying on westernization and trust in separation.

IV. Hollowness of Status Quo, Doubtfulness of Westernization, Impossibility of Separation

Three policy orthodoxies preventing development and application of an effective grand strategy of the West in respect to Islam include 1) clinging to the status quo and hoping it is sustainable, with some improvements such as settling the Arab-Israeli, Indian-Pakistan, and Turkey-Greece conflicts and prevention of escalation of

Islamic terrorism, 2) westernization of the main countries of Islam, and 3) separation of the world into zones of peace and zones of turbulence that can be kept apart, with the latter including turbulent and anti-Western Islamic states and non-state actors.

These are serious misperceptions caused by lack of understanding of ongoing socio-cultural dynamics, of the uniqueness of Islam, and of the processes shaping regional and global futures. They are based on and aggravated by "motivated irrationalities," "end of history" phantasmagoria, Western parochialism, a-historical thinking, and many additional causes of distorted images of reality and its trends as prevalent in governments, elites, societies, and civilizations.

True, maintaining the status quo in large parts of the Moslem world, with some obviously needed improvements and subject to socioeconomic progress and movement toward Western political values, is desirable from a Western perspective, especially when compared with some of the alternatives. But this is a vain hope, with efforts to realize it likely to be more counter-productive than helpful.

In view of the strength of change drivers, such as globalization, science, and technology, no status quo is maintainable, certainly not in the domain of Islam as shaped also by internal very turbulent processes, as already discussed. Therefore, instead of striving for the impossible, efforts should concentrate on trying to channelize cascading transformations in desired directions and, at least, avoiding the worst. However, this can be done only if inherent instability of the status quo is recognized, main change factors are diagnosed, and robust policies focus on efforts to influence main trajectories of change, including revolutionary ones, without any ambitions of "fine tuning." Alternatively, if maintaining of some main features of the status quo is regarded as essential, large-scale interventions are necessary to dampen change forces, and such efforts too are sure to fail after some time unless alternative channels for radical change fitting Islam and its potentials are provided.

To clarify this crucial point, let me mention two examples, however much they may contradict status quo-oriented policy dreams:

- The kingdom of Jordan is basically unstable and becoming hyper-unstable with the establishment of a Palestinian state. Therefore, Western policies based on an assumption of long-range stability of Jordan as a Hashemite kingdom are mistaken and should be changed. Thus, if after careful consideration priority is given to maintaining Jordan and its regime, this has far-going implications. These include, for instance, not letting the Palestinian state acquire action capabilities that can endanger Jordan and deterring it from action against Jordan; encouraging Israel to keep most of the Jordan valley so as to minimize borders between Jordan and the Palestinian state; supporting effective law-and-order policies in Jordan; providing massive help to Jordan to significantly improve its socioeconomic situation; and gearing for effectively helping Jordan, directly and indirectly, if its stability is endangered. An alternative policy is to assist in a smooth transformation of Jordan into a part of a Palestinian state. Waiting for events to happen in the hope that the status quo is likely to prevail is the worst posture of all, sure to fail, with bad consequences that are avoidable.

- Turkey poses a pivotal problem with a status quo that cannot continue for long and with a critical crossroad likely to lead either to westernization or to Islamization. The case of Turkey illustrated strikingly the lack of grand strategic thinking in the West, as demonstrated by the absurd policies of the European Union on Turkish membership and by actions of some Western states on the Armenian issue and its history. Instead, needed is a determined effort by the West to strengthen the westernization of Turkey while preserving and developing its unique culture. This may be possible, thanks to the radical cultural engineering of Attaturk and may help to pose a model for some other Islamic states that can help to prevent and also to reverse Islamization. But this requires a determined high-quality policy by the West. Lack of such a policy is very likely to be evaluated by future historians as a very grave error, contributing significantly to the decline of the West by its own fault.

These examples serve to introduce the second delusion of much of present Western thinking and feelings on Islamic states, namely trust in westernization as a main grand policy. Efforts to protect human rights and prevent atrocities are a moral imperative not to be judged too much in terms of realpolitik interests. But the situation is different in respect to efforts to export to Islamic countries Western forms of liberal democracy and free markets. Even much more dangerous as bases for policies are images of Islamic countries becoming rapidly similar in main features to the West, such as the Middle East somehow leaping into a quasi-European-Union pattern of cooperation.[23]

Doing so may well be unjustified morally in terms of global ethics of pluralism. Worse, it is not only in vain but positively dangerous, speaking in terms of realpolitik.

The economic policies proposed by the West are sure to increase unemployment and thus to accelerate destabilization and encourage anti-Western fundamentalism. The argument that in the long run Western types of free markets and globalization are sure to bring about economic prosperity to the countries of Islam is doubtful, unrealistic, and irrelevant. It is doubtful because main aspects of Western economic structures do not fit the social conditions and values of most of the Islamic countries. It is unrealistic because many Islamic rulers do not want to accept crucial aspects of Western economic systems because of their power implications and political consequences. And it is irrelevant, because if in the shorter run transition crises produce Islamic fundamentalist states, then the longer-run benefits of Western-type economies will not be reached.

Even more of a delusion is involved in efforts to push Islamic countries toward Western-type democracy. It is quite clear that democratic elections, given the present socioeconomic and political situation in most of the countries of Islam, will bring to power parties and rulers supporting deeper Islamization of their countries, often coupled with fanaticism and hostility toward the West. Also, in the view of many Western experts, there are serious contradictions between Islamic cultures and political theology on one side and democracy on the other,[24] making the latter into a wrong model for good regimes in Islamic states. In this respect, it is interesting to note that Iran has the most democratic elections

---

of any Islamic country, while seeming to move in the direction of a unique mixed democratic-religious regime. The nature of such a regime, if it achieves a long-term balance, is hard to comprehend to Western minds and its future is unknown — but most likely is very different from Western liberal democracy.

The emerging recommendation is to be very careful and selective about urging Islamic countries to adopt Western-type liberal democracy. Less ambitious attempts to upgrade the consent-basis and welfare-orientation of regimes, together with respect for basic human rights, have a much higher probability of beneficial results, both for the people of the area and for the West.

This recommendation in no way implies any moral or political "judgment" on those countries as "unripe" for the "higher" values of the West. Rather, the recommended posture recognizes the right of other cultures to live by their values, as long as those are not aggressive.

The third delusion of the possibility of "separation" is less expressed explicitly, but tacitly underlies some Western security thinking[25] with sure-to-follow bad results. It is most pronounced in respect to Africa, with major upheavals, warfare, and all genocide there being assumed to have no costs for the West and, consequently, being left to burn out with very little efforts at effective intervention. This is a mistake not only in humanitarian but also in terms of realpolitik because of growing probability that earlier or somewhat later some of the protagonists will take action against the West, up to direct threats with mass killing weapons.

This is all the more true with Islamic states and non-state actors, where conflicts which at first are local in scope being often likely to broaden and involve Western interests and states. True, the West is more prone to intervene, as illustrated by the Gulf War, because of very visible dangers posed by local conflicts to its interests. But hopes to "isolate" local warfare in less obviously sensitive areas than the Middle East linger in the background, as illustrated by "do nothing" strategies in conflicts involving Islamic former parts of the Soviet Union and diminishing interest in such conflicts in the Balkan.

This is much more of an error than neglect of conflicts in Africa, with broad Islamization sure to undermine any efforts to separate local conflicts involving Islamic actors from the West.

The deconstruction of mainstream Western policy orthodoxies regarding Islam does not imply that all Western policies toward Islamic countries are wrong. Many Western strategies and actions are well taken. These include, for instance, maintaining close contact with leaders of non-aggressive Islamic countries and sharing with them some decision making; economic assistance; efforts to slow proliferation of mass killing weapons; trying to calm local conflicts; confronting Iraqi aggression; and more. But, driven by often wrong assumptions and lacking a well-considered grand-strategic base, policies are inadequate and also counterproductive. Hence, the need for a reconceptualized grand strategy for the West that fits the realities and prospects of insurgent Islam.

PART TWO: GRAND STRATEGY RECOMMENDATION

V. Intermezzo: On Building the Grand Strategy

Building a grand strategy requires outstanding cognitive and moral capacities and is a task for high-quality interdisciplinary policy research, development, and creativity organizations ("think tanks").[26] Obviously, I cannot do so on my own. However, to indicate some directions and illustrate a few of the principles, I will present and explain eight main suggested dimensions for building a grand strategy for the West toward Islam: (1) relating respectfully to Islam, (2) selective accommodation, with red lines, (3) helping socioeconomic development, (4) curbing aggressive actors, (5) reducing aggressive capacities, (6) holding states and rulers strictly accountable, (7) damage limitation, and (8) if all fails, moving toward a global leviathan.

But first, the main hyper-goals of such a grand strategy must be explored.

VI. Hyper-Goals: Avoiding the Worst and Advancing the Good

Grand strategies of the West should serve two partly overlapping hyper-goals:[27] namely "bad-reducing" and "good-advancing." The first aims at containing dangers and threats, including prevention of their development and realization and decreasing their damage if they do occur. The second aims at advancing a "good world" as positively defined by Western values as changing with time.

Preventing fanatic states from having nuclear weapons and reducing Western sensitivity to a breakdown of oil supplies from the Middle East, illustrate the containment of bad possibilities. And helping the Arab Middle East to prosper through peaceful cooperation illustrates the achievement of desirable futures. These examples also indicate the overlap between the two hyper-goals as well as their distinct nature.

The means to be used for reducing bad situations and their consequences and/or for advancing good ones are multifarious and not dictated by the "negative" or "positive" nature of the goal. Thus, threats of sanctions can be used to advance desirable situations, such as respect for human rights; and economic assistance is sometimes effective for preventing bad situations, such as societies becoming more fanatic. The preferable mix of measures to be used in order to contain the bad or/and advance the good depends on the particularities of sub-goals and situations and on availability of policy instruments. Still, the distinction between danger-containment and "good"-advancement is very significant and serves as a main compass for the recommended grand strategies.

Given Western values, classifying situations as "bad" is often not difficult, but there are many exceptions with processes being ambiguous and containing both bad and good aspects. The distinction also serves to bring out a main problem, namely different conceptions of what constitutes a "good" future. Cultural differences can here easily result in shallow judgments. Thus, Western *Zeitgeist* embraces human rights, individualism, and liberal democracy, while most of Islam has quite different values based on religious norms — but this does not justify evaluating the latter as "bad" and to be counter-acted. Instead, I propose to base the Western grand strategy primarily on a distinction between Islamic values and processes which are inner-directed and those that are aggressive toward the West and its associates. Thus, when Islamic countries reject the equality of women, this is anathema to Western values, but poses no danger to the West. But when Islamic countries and groups engage in terrorism against the West, this poses a clear threat.

From the perspective of the West, a grand strategy toward Islam should first of all aim at reducing the dangers built into fanatic and aggressive Islam, especially when equipped with effective damage-causing instruments of both "low intensity" and mass killing potential. This includes, for instance, reducing the probability and limiting the damage of negative developments, such as:

- New types of quasi-religious wars, with large confrontations having an ideological or cultural basis, such as between an emerging Islamic block of "true believer" nations and Western countries

- Regional conflicts that endanger the West, by jeopardizing the flow of essential materials such as oil; or by inaugurating a new epoch of atrocities with increasingly lethal weapons

- Action which is dangerous from a global perspective, even though non-violent and within what has traditionally been regarded as "domestic matters," such as destruction of natural resources on a scale endangering important global ecological assets

- Non-violent action which can destabilize Western societies, such as illegal mass movement of population from Islamic countries; or drug production and diffusion on a scale having serious social consequences

- Neo-barbaric behavior that, though initially not directly endangering Western security transgresses against basic values which must morally be protected to preserve the viability and integrity of the West

Containment of such dangers is a first grand strategic imperative, leading to a number of specific policies, some well known and some in need of much innovation. Thus, prevention of proliferation of mass killing weapons and their delivery instruments and of diffusion of dangerous knowledge belong to the expanding family of arms control, though requiring much more determined measures. However, prevention of fanaticism armed with mass killing weapons and reducing its damage potentials requires radically novel approaches. As further discussed within the proposed grand strategic dimensions, these range from suitably targeted intelligence collection up to neutralization of dangerous "prophets of holy wars" and surgical operations against their centers and facilities, coupled with painful action against countries providing them with safe havens.

Despite some overlaps, quite different in nature are policies aiming at advancement of positively desired situations, such as respect of human rights, democracy, socioeconomic development, regional economic cooperation, peaceful settlement of disputes, promotion of global equity in a meaningful sense, and so on. However, as already discussed, priority should be given to the advancement of inner-directed instead of aggressive Islam. This may or may not involve advancement of some of the enumerated Western values. But this is secondary to the main aim of reducing dangers to the West, all the more so as "pushing" of the Western values may often be counter-productive and is also in part doubtful in terms of a pluralistic global morality.

Opinions may differ on this point, with a counter-argument claiming that only by adopting some main Western values can the benign future of Islam be assured. Available empiric data and reliable theories are inadequate for supporting or disproving this conjecture. But this very uncertainty accentuates the importance of danger-containment as the primary foundation of a Western grand strategy on Islam, in combination with advancement of desired positive situations as far as possible and not carrying serious risks of boomerang effects.

When the proposed hyper-goals are contrasted with the dynamics of Islam, as discussed earlier, the net assessment is one of a large and increasing security deficit likely to pose serious direct and indirect dangers to the West. Reducing the growing security deficit and turning it into a security surplus — this is the challenge facing construction of grand strategy for the West, to the eight main dimensions of which I now turn.

VII. Main Dimensions of Proposed Grand Strategy

(1) Relating Respectfully to Islam

The first recommended dimension is to respect the integrity of Islam and help it to "stand up" and develop in light of its own values and traditions as a main civilization and global factor. Any and all anti-Islamic elements and impressions should be strictly avoided.

It is essential to differentiate between "fundamentalism" and "fanaticism." Fundamentalism, as noted, is a phenomenon belonging to modernity while reacting against it, can be inner-directed, and strives to transform society. As put by Anthony Giddens:

> Fundamentalism is not the same as either fanaticism or authoritarianism. Fundamentalists call for a return to basic scriptures or texts, supposed to be read in a literal manner, and they propose that the doctrines derived from such a reading be applied to social, economic, or political life.[28]

In Islam, fundamentalism often leads to fanaticism, but this is not always or necessarily the case. Also to be taken into account in rejecting any automatic correlating of fundamentalism with aggression is the fact that non-fundamentalist Islamic regimes can be very aggressive, as illustrated throughout the modern history of the Middle East. Therefore, respect of fundamentalism as long as not accompanied by aggressive intentions, coupled with efforts to encourage and support its non-aggressive forms, though not meeting Western values in other respects, is a main requirement of the proposed grand strategy.

The essence of the proposed posture is respect toward Islam, sincerely felt and convincingly demonstrated, together with support for unique styles of life which Islamic societies prefer. Thus, the West disparages Islamic legal norms, such as punishments regarded as "inhuman" and differential gender roles, and to regard them as regressive and contradicting human progress. However natural, such reactions are counter-productive in terms of realpolitik.

Many such expressions of Western disapproval of Moslem values are a matter of public opinion, mass media, and other channels which cannot and should not serve in the West as strategic policy instruments. Western leaders should demonstrate respect for Islamic norms and for the right of Islamic countries to live according to whatever values they prefer, within the limits of a minimum set of compelling global norms and as long as aggression toward others is avoided. But care must be exercised not to camouflage feelings. What is needed is bona fide respect for Islam and for the right of other cultures to live according to their values, as long as some basic norms regarded as obligatory for all societies are complied with.

Yehezkel Dror

Concomitantly, space should be provided for Islamic states to play an increasing role in global affairs, such as giving Islam a permanent seat on the UN Security Council, without veto rights, to be rotated between core states. Strict care should be taken to avoid actions or omissions which may be interpreted as reflecting negative attitudes toward Islam and Moslems, or lack of concern for them. Absence of rapid and effective help to Moslems in Bosnia and failure to adequately punish those who are responsible for barbarities committed against them, including senior politicians, is therefore, as already stated, a very serious blunder contradicting the required posture of the West toward Islam.

(2) Selective Accommodation, with Red Lines

To reduce friction and agitation, as well as for moral reasons, ambitions and desires of Islam should be accommodated as long as they are non-aggressive and do not impair important values and interests of the West. At the same time, red lines should be maintained and, at appropriate opportunities, explicated and explained, beyond which Islamic demands and actions will be rejected and counter-acted.

Obviously, there is a large gray area between those two policy principles. Also, often the positive or negative implications for the West of various actions of Islamic countries and non-state actors are uncertain. A guide for such situations is provided by the first grand strategic dimension discussed above, which leads to the recommendations to give to Islamic actors the benefit of doubt. However, governments tend to ignore dangers and over-accommodate aggression so as to avoid taking controversial and risky actions. Therefore, a Western "red line" in respect to Islam should be strictly enforced, including select demonstration actions so as to maintain deterrence and aggression while providing support for non-aggressive Islamic interests and values.

Thus, conflicts between Islamic and non-Islamic actors, such as in the Balkan and the Middle East, should be settled in a fair way, meeting legitimate interests of all parties, while avoiding giving in to extortion, threats, and violence, and making sure that agreements are fully kept. Also, as indicated, specific issues should be handled in ways taking into account their impact on the future relations between the West and Islam as a whole, such as in reducing tensions while maintaining credible images of strength and determination.

Three examples may help to clarify the importance of credible and enforced red lines:

a. Iraq's action against Kuwait was clearly an act of "state aggression," justifying and requiring counter-action.

b. Oil boycotts endangering supplies essential to the West are, according to the proposed yardsticks, a clear instance of grave aggression. Therefore, forceful counter-action to stop them is recommended.

c. The offering of a prize by an Iranian body enjoying governmental support for the assassination of Salman Rushdie. Expressions of understanding for Islamic reactions to writings regarded as defaming the faith, with explanation as to why such writings cannot be repressed in the West, were in order as part of the proposed posture of respect toward Islam. However, sympathetic understanding should have gone together with a clear declaration that any support for hurting the author is not only abhorrent to Western values regarded as having global significance, but that encouragement of action to hurt a person residing in the West is a gross act of aggression which will be met with serious sanctions. If this, together with helping Iran to find a way to "climb down from the tree," had not worked, then escalating counter-measures against Iran should have been taken till they withdrew from this act of aggression.

(3) Helping Socio-Economic Development

Attractive are policies helping peaceful progress of Islam and its societies. However, as noted, care should be taken to avoid defining "progress" in terms of Western value. As long as Islamic states are peaceful and meet some minimum of universal values, the West should help with socioeconomic development.

Special attention should be given to measures that strengthen non-aggressive social development and counteract fanaticism. But to be avoided is wishful thinking, such as assuming that democratization will for sure produce "nice" governments after a relatively short learning period, and that free market economies will produce employment and raise standards of living for most of the populations. Also misleading is the widespread belief that economic progress necessarily reduces fundamentalism, ethnic tensions, fanaticism, and aggression.

Despite such problems and risks, helping socioeconomic and political development can be of much help, in addition to being ethically mandatory and serving as a step toward a global grand strategy. But to seriously implement this grand strategic dimension, much more is needed than giving some money, providing advise based on Western experiences (and often serving Western economic interests), and helping with conflict resolution.

A relevant issue is more equitable distribution of windfall profits among Islamic countries. Thus, the oil incomes of very rich countries with small populations should be used to help development of oil-poor and population-rich countries. This implies that Saudi Arabia, Libya, and the Persian Gulf countries should be persuaded and obliged to share a lot of their wealth with other Islamic countries. But convincing them to do so may require quite some arm twisting, will hurt relations with the oil rich countries, and may also bring about their destabilization. However, such steps are in the interest of Islamic countries and civilization as a whole and may be of much help in assuring benign development.

(4) Curbing Aggressive Actors

However difficult it may be to classify a concrete actor as belonging to one of the categories, crucial to the proposed grand strategy is the distinction between non-aggressive actors on one hand and aggressive and fanatic actors on the other.

"Fanatic" or "crazy states" or non-state actors[29] present an extreme case of both immorality and danger. Such Islamic states[30] or non-state actors are committed to an ideology favoring and urging aggressive action, are willing to take high risks and pay high prices for engaging in such action up to risking destruction, and are building up action capacities devoted to realizing their "holy war" beliefs.

Global values converge with imperatives of realpolitik and require either eradication of such actors or making them completely ineffective. This is becoming more and more essential because of the increasing ease with which such states and, in the foreseeable future, also non-state actors, can acquire mass killing weapons with which they will be able to blackmail and harm the West. Doomsday-weapons for holding the world at ransom are also likely to become a possibility in the not far-off future. Therefore, radical countermeasures become necessary when milder treatments do not work.

A first line of counter-action is persuasion, economic incentives and disincentives, international pressures, isolation, prevention of acquisition of dangerous weapons, "coercive diplomacy," etc. But, if such steps fail, direct intervention before a fanatic state acquires significant action capacity may constitute the most humane and cheapest strategy, as well as often the only effective one. Such intervention should change the regime and, if essential, impose an "educational interim government" (as done in Germany and Japan after World War II).

As discussed in the next dimensions, a minimum disarmament of countries with fanatic-aggressive tendencies is essential. However, fanatic states and actors can cause a lot of damage also with easily available means, are always suspect of acquiring mass killing weapons in clandestine ways, and serve as an encouragement to fanatization of additional states and non-state actors. Therefore, making them non-fanatic is often the only reliable countermeasure, to be achieved by changing their leadership into a more benign one. If this cannot be done by conventional means (support of internal opposition, etc.), then direct action against the fanatic leaders is morally justified, in terms of realpolitik, as long as there is a high probability that less fanatic ones will take their place.

These examples raise issues of cost-benefit thinking and of maintaining reasonable proportions between the threats against the West and counteraction. No automatic program-solving equations can be provided; each case needs discretion fitting specific circumstances. But as a recommended guideline, the proposed grand strategy allocates much weight to long-range impacts, proposing a readiness to pay now a higher price in order to improve trajectories into the future.

(5) Reducing Aggressive Capacities

Limiting the action capacities of aggressive or potentially aggressive Islamic actors is in many respects a more attractive option than taking action to change their nature to become non-aggressive. Arms control regimes are an increasingly important feature of emerging global governance and are on high moral grounds. However, they suffer from major weaknesses.

It is desirable to apply arms control regimes with discrimination, supporting armament of inherently non-aggressive countries, especially Western democracies threatened by aggressive Islamic states. This applies, in special cases, also to letting them maintain mass killing weapon systems. However, global arms control regimes cannot sanction such differentiation, even if morally justified in realpolitik. Indeed, the opposite is true: It is easier to cause non-aggressive and especially Western democratic countries to join disarmament agreements and they are more trustworthy to comply with such agreements than aggressive countries. Thus, the net effect may be to let aggressive countries gain a net advantage. The ease with which countries, and in some respects even more so non-state actors, can acquire and hide weapons, including mass killing ones, further makes reduction of aggressive capacities less reliable than transforming aggressors into non-aggressors in intention.

Another difficulty is being able to identify in advance the transformation of non-aggressive into aggressive countries. Denying weapons to all is quite impossible, all the more so because defense cooperation is an integral part of maintaining friendly relations and also reducing motives to become hostile. But benign countries acquiring advanced weapons can rapidly become aggressive ones, as illustrated by the mutation of Iran.

Given all these difficulties, reducing the attack capacities of aggressive and potentially aggressive countries is a main grand strategic dimension.

The proposed robust principle is to prevent any and all potentially aggressive, and especially fanatic states and non-state actors, from possessing mass killing weapons. This requires determined action to prevent flow of such weapons, and of the materials and knowledge to make them, to such countries, enforced inspection of suspect sites in such countries, and destruction of dangerous tools and weapons — if necessary, by surgical strikes. But these are very difficult endeavors, because of "dual uses" of many types of materials and knowledge, multiplication of potential suppliers with diverse interests, domestic political and economic considerations in the West, and accepted norms of "sovereignty." Therefore, given present realities, proliferation of mass killing weapons to aggressive Islamic states and non-state actors cannot be prevented.

This is the justification for active defense measures, such as anti-missile systems. However, these cannot be relied upon because of the variety of ways to deliver mass killing weapons, in addition to the errors inherent in technologically very complex systems. Also to be taken into account are the high costs of anti-missile systems and their global geo-strategic problem. Therefore, annihilation of attack capacities should have priority, if feasible.

Any success, however partial, in limiting aggressive action capacities is well worth the effort. But such policies cannot be relied upon. Therefore, it is necessary to combine efforts to reduce the capacities of dangerous actors with changing their motivation, parallel with preparing for failures of both lines of action. Ultimately, moving toward a global leviathan may be essential for preserving the West and humanity as a whole. But let me leave this dimension of last resort to the end, after considering additional less radical and costly grand strategic possibilities.

(6) Holding States and Rulers Strictly Accountable

An especially troublesome case is posed by fanatic non-state actors who in fact are supported or at least granted safe havens by states, as illustrated by a number of Islamic terrorist and guerilla organizations. Coping with the increasingly serious threats posed by such actors requires holding states and rulers strictly accountable for terrorist and guerilla activities supported by them, never mind disclaimers of responsibility.

In terms of international law, all states are duty-bound to take all feasible measures to prevent their territory being used as a basis for aggression against other countries. All the more so, direct or indirect support of aggressive groups is itself an act of "state aggression" which, if serious in scale and consequences, is an act of war. Therefore, an effective grand strategy against Islamic (and other) fanaticism requires states and their rulers to be held strictly accountable for supporting aggressive non-state actors in whatever way. Active sanctions against such states and rulers, including military operations if lesser measures prove inadequate, are therefore in principle recommended — again, subject to adjustment to specific situations.

(7) Damage Limitation

Whatever is done, failures are unavoidable and serious threats and attacks by fanatic Islamic states and non-state actors are likely, including mass killing weapons. Instability in Islamic countries and state failures increase the probability of partial failure and also counterproductive effects of even the best grand strategy, with dangerous situations likely to come about. Therefore, preparing for failure is an essential dimension of the proposed grand strategy.

Coping with failure involves two lines of action: reducing the sensitivity of the West to bad developments, and preparing capacities to intervene and reverse negative events and trends. Reducing dependency on oil from the Middle East and hardening essential facilities sensitive to fanatic attack illustrates the first approach. Preparing planning-wise and operationally to engage in surgical operations against revealed mass killing capacities in the hand of fanatic countries illustrates the second.

(8) If All Fails, Moving Toward a Global Leviathan

It is quite likely that only some parts of the proposed grand strategy will be adopted and implemented. Furthermore, even if an optimal Western grand strategy against Islamic fanaticism armed with mass killing weapons is effectively applied, adequate success cannot be assured. This is all the more likely because even if only a small number of fanatic states and non-state actors possessing new types of mass killing weapons, such as biological ones, successfully evade countermeasures, this is enough to pose an intolerable threat to the West, and to humanity as a whole.

In other words, when fanaticism armed with mass killing weapons is at stake, then 90 percent success in neutralizing this threat is not enough. And to achieve 100 percent success is impossible within given global regimes. Therefore, if and when the threat of use of mass killing weapons by fanatic actors passes a certain threshold, radical changes in global regimes become a necessity. What may become essential for the survival of civilization as a whole in the face of the specter of a new barbarism is a global leviathan, that is a global authoritarian security regime led by the West which effectively controls all mass killing weapons and stops fanaticism in the making.

This is the ultimate grand strategic option, the time for which, regretfully, may come. If so, it is preferable to gear for such a possible need in advance in order to be ready if and when the hour strikes, such as after a "minor" nuclear attack by a fanatic actor.

VIII. Democratic Morality Versus "Evil"

The contingent recommendation to establish a global leviathan poses in full measure tragic moral dilemmas raised by the proposed grand strategy, which recommends harsh measures such as surgical operations against fanaticism-suspect states and their rulers. Thus, the grand strategy would have clearly supported an assassination in 1938 of Hitler organized by France, Poland, Czechoslovakia, a Jewish underground, or the Zionist movement — but this surely would have been harshly condemned by Amnesty International,[31] had it existed at that time.

If the main assumption on the future of humanity is that it is sure to thrive despite some minor interim "accidents,"[32] then indeed the proposed grand strategy should be rejected as "immoral" and as "undermining the values of the West." However, if fanaticism armed with mass killing weapons is regarded as being a dangerous form of "evil" having the potent to bring about a new form of barbarism, then we are in a situation of "bad moral luck"[33] where the tragic necessity is to pay with very important values for even more important ones.[34]

This is the moral justification for the proposed grand strategy and for the changes required by it in some of the thinking and practices of Western states and their legal systems. True, the required moral balance between preserving the integrity of the Western moral canon and meeting the requirements of protecting the security of the West and of humanity as a whole is a difficult and delicate one and requires much care. But such difficulties must not be permitted to avoid the issue till grave harm is done, with likely overreaction to follow.

IX.   Epilogue: Counting on Statesmanship — or on Catastrophe?

Throughout this chapter I have used the term "the West." Implied is the need for much cooperation between Western countries and their allies, together with other countries, civilizations, and global institutions, with maximum participation of non-fanatic Islamic states and non-state actors. The USA has to take the lead, together with the European Union, in facing the dangers of Islamic aggression and fanaticism, as integral to its role of leader of the West and the only global hyper-power.

Implementation of the proposed grand strategy requires new types of intelligence capable of estimating reliable fanaticism potential. Also needed is development and readying of novel action instruments, doctrines, and units, such as lethal but temporarily very disabling weapons for surgical operations against fanatic rulers. Even more difficult is integration of the various dimensions into a coherent grand strategy and its measured application to shifting situations. Most difficult of all to achieve are the moral and cognitive capacities to govern and the crystallization of political will essential for facing the evil of fanaticism equipped with mass killing weapons.

This is the task of statesmanship and stateswomanship, supported by high quality policy professionalism. The realities of contemporary politics, with single exceptions, provide little ground for hope that the West will be equal to the task. If so, the much worse second best is rapid learning from limited crises before real disasters strike. However, whether Western statecraft on insurgent Islam will improve before much damage is caused or not, strategic thinkers and planners should follow a "supply side" approach and prepare grand strategies to be ready when "demand" realizes, out of understanding or pain.

To prepare some elements of such a grand strategy and, hopefully, stimulate more and better grand strategic thinking and planning on crucial issues, including grand strategies for the West on insurgent Islam — these are the ambitions, intentions, and hopes underlying this chapter.

Endnotes

Work on this chapter was initially supported by a Senior Fellowship at the Washington Institute for Middle East Policy in autumn 1990 and by the Leonard Davis Institute for International Relations at The Hebrew University of Jerusalem. Its present form is very different from what I first wrote more than ten years ago. But I would like to express my appreciation to the two policy research institutes that stimulated me to think in terms of a grand strategy for the West on Islam.

1 The single most important book putting forth this proposition is Samuel P. Huntington, *The Clash of Civilizations and the Remaking of World Order* (New York: Simon and Schuster, 1996). But readers should be careful not to be overwhelmed by this outstanding analysis, which suffers from trying to understand and predict very complex and heterogeneous processes within one paradigm. Also relevant is John L. Esposito, *Islamic Threat: Myth or Reality?* (New York: Oxford University Press, 1992).

2 The commonly used term "weapons of mass destruction" (WMD) is inadequate. What really is at stake are "mass killing weapons."

3 On the concept of "grand strategy," see Paul Kennedy, editor, *Grand Strategies in War and Peace* (New Haven: Yale University Press, 1991), and Williamson Murray, MacGregor Knox, and Alvin Bernstein, editors, *The Making of Strategy: Rulers, States, and War* (Cambridge, UK: Cambridge University Press, 1994), But the best book I know which clarifies the idea of grand strategy by applying it to a historic case is Edward N. Luttwak, *The Grand Strategy of the Roman Empire: From the First Century A.D. to the Third* (Baltimore, MD: Johns Hopkins University Press, 1976) (to be followed by a study of the grand strategy of the Ottoman Empire).

4 On the distinction between uncertainty and inconceivability, see Yehezkel Dror, "Beyond Uncertainty: Facing the Inconceivable." *Technological Forecasting and Social Change,* vol. 62, no. 1 & 2 (August/September 1999): p. 151–153.

5 Literature abounds with suggestions on how to deal with particular pressing issues, such as Iran. But efforts to develop grand strategies for the West for dealing with Islam as a whole are sorely lacking. Huntington (see endnote 1) takes some steps in this direction, but much more is needed. This is but one expression of the overall scarcity of grand strategic thinking after the end of the Cold War.

6 The concept of "evolutionary potential" as fundamental to the frames of thinking of this chapter, is developed in C.R. Hallpike, *The Principles of Social Evolution* (Oxford: Oxford University Press, 1988).

7 Very relevant is the approach of Fernand Braudel. A convenient collection of relevant writings of his is *On History* (Chicago, IL: University of Chicago Press, 1980). Especially salient for our subject is his work on the Mediterranean, as conveniently abridged in Fernand Braudel, *The Mediterranean and the Mediterranean World in the Age of Philip II* (New York: HarperCollins, 1972).

8 For interesting treatment see Courtney Brown, *Serpents in the Sand: Essays on the Nonlinear Nature of Politics and Human Destiny* (Ann Arbor, MI: University of Michigan Press, 1995).

9 As discussed in Robert Jervis, *System Effects: Complexity in Political and Social Life* (Princeton, NJ: Princeton University Press, 1997).

10 My analysis and recommendations are based on a view of the future as shaped by a dynamic mix between "necessity, contingency, mutations, chance, and choice," that is partly open and partly constrained by the past. Very relevant is Geoffrey Hawthorn, *Plausible Worlds: Possibility and Understanding in History and the Social Sciences* (Cambridge, UK: Cambridge University Press, 1991). For an underlying model of reality as a whole as partly open and partly determined by the past, see McCall Storrs, *A Model of the Universe: Space-Time, Probability, and Decision* (Oxford: Clarendon Press, 1994).

11 Two studies that well present the sweep of evolution of Islam are Ira Lapidus, *A History of Islamic Societies* (Cambridge, UK: Cambridge University Press, 1988), and Bernard Lewis, *The Middle East: 2000 Years of History from the Rise of Christianity to the Present Day* (London: Weidenfeld & Nicolson, 1995). To be added is at least an introductory text to Islam as a religion, such as David Waines, *An Introduction to Islam* (Cambridge, UK: Cambridge University Press, 1995).

12 This is concisely discussed in William H. McNeill, *Rise of the West: A History of the Human Community* (Chicago, IL: University of Chicago Press, 1963).

13 Illumination are Amin Maalouf, *The Crusades Through Arab Eyes* (New York: Schoken, 1987), and, differently, Karen Armstrong, *Holy War: The Crusades and Their Impact on Today's World* (London: Macmillan, 1988).

14 Revealing are literary expressions, as discussed in M. M. Badawi, *A Short History of Modern Arab Literature* (Oxford: Clarendon Press, 1993). Also relevant, though focusing on intellectuals who do not necessarily reflect most of reality, are two books by Fouad Ajami, *The Arab Predicament: Arab Political Thought and Practice Since 1967* (Cambridge, UK: Cambridge University Press, 1981), and *The Dream Palace of the Arabs: A Generation's Odyssey* (New York: Pantheon, 1998). Providing a different impressionistic view is Robert D. Kaplan, *Eastward to Tartary: Travels in the Balkans, the Middle East, and the Caucasus* (New York: Random House, 2000).

15 Many insightful chapters on fundamentalism in the domain of Islam are included in the publications of the Fundamentalism Project at the University of Chicago, such as the volumes edited by Martin E. Marty and R. Scott Appleby published by the University of Chicago Press: *Fundamentalism Observed*, 1991; *Fundamentalisms and Society: Reclaiming the Sciences, the Family, and Education*, 1993; and *Fundamentalisms and the State: Remaking Politics, Economies, and Militance*, 1993.

A broad perspective is supplied in Gillis Kepel, *The Revenge of God: The Resurgence of Islam, Christianity and Judaism in the Modern World* (Cambridge, UK: Polity Press, 1994). The theological bases of Islamic fundamentalism are examined in Emmanuel Sivan, *Radical Islam: Medieval Theology and Modern*

Politics (New Haven, CT: Yale University Press, 1985). On fundamentalism as paradoxically an expression of modernity however opposed to some parts of it, see Shmuel. N. Eisenstadt, *Fundamentalism, Sectarianism, and Revolution: The Jacobin Dimension of Modernity* (Cambridge, UK: Cambridge University Press, 1999).

16 It is interesting to consider in this context the impacts on the world of Islam of the establishment of Israel and its victories over Arab countries. Arab reactions to the Gulf War and continuing sanctions against Iraq are also significant in this context.

17 High-quality uses of this concept to map alternative futures are illustrated by CIA, "Global Trends 2015: A Dialogue About the Future with Nongovernment Experts" (IC 2000-02, December 2000, <www.cia.gov>).

18 More enlightening on ongoing processes in Islam than most of the modern literature is Karl Jaspers, *Psychologie der Weltanschauungen,* second edition (Berlin: Springer, 1960), first published in 1922. Only parts of this book have been translated into English.

19 Some of the ideas and concepts of Carl Schmitt are very useful for analyzing the politics of contemporary Islam. Especially salient are Carl Schmitt, *Der Begriff des Politischen* (Berlin: Duncker & Humblot, 1963), shorter version first published 1927; as well as his writings on political theology and political romantics: *Politische Theologie II: Die Legende von der Erledigung jeder Politischen Theologie* (Berlin: Duncker & Humblot, 1970), and *Politische Romantik* (Berlin: Duncker & Humblot, 1982), reprint of second edition, 1925. Studies of Carl Schmitt's works showing the way for an exploration of their relevance to an understanding of the politics of Islamic states (which is quite ignored in writings in English on Islam), include Friedrich Balke, *Der Staat nach seinem Ende: Die Versuchung Carl Schmitts* (München: Wilhelm Fink, 1996), and John P. McCormick, *Cart Schmitt's Critique of Liberalism: Against Politics as Technology* (Cambridge, UK: Cambridge University Press, 1997).

20 As discussed in James N. Rosenau, *Turbulence in World Politics: A Theory of Change and Continuity* (Princeton, NJ: Princeton University Press, 1990).

21 As forcefully, but wrongly, argued by Francis Fukuyama, *The End of History and the Last Man* (New York: The Free Press, 1992).

22 Important, but too short-term in part are CIA, "Global Trends 2015: A Dialogue About the Future With Nongovernment Experts" (see endnote 17), and Zalmay Khalilzad and Ian O. Lesser, editors, *Sources of Conflict in the 21st Century: Regional Futures and U.S. Strategy* (Santa Monica, CA: The RAND Corporation, 1988). Pertinent is Robert D. Kaplan, *The Coming Anarchy: Shattering the Dreams of the Post Cold War* (New York: Random House, 2000).

23 A striking illustration is provided by a well-known and widely discussed book by one of the most outstanding Israeli statesmen, namely Shimon Peres, *The New Middle East* (New York: Henry Holt, 1993). This book is very important as a utopia — which may well exert positive influence on long-term thinking and

also have impacts on reality beyond the time horizons of this chapter. However, I am sorry to say, if main Israeli policies were to be based in the foreseeable future on its images, before a mutation occurs in the Arab Middle East, the results would be dismal.

24 The difficulties and perhaps impossibility within the foreseeable future of combining democracy with Islam are considered in Bernard Lewis, *The Political Language of Islam* (Chicago, IL: University of Chicago Press, 1988); Elie Kedourie, *Politics in the Middle East* (Oxford: Oxford University Press, 1992); and Daniel Pipes, *In the Path of God: Islam and Political Power* (New York: Basic Books, 1983).

25 As illustrated, in a well-hedged and sophisticated way, by Max Singer and Aaron Wildavsky, *The Real World Order: Zones of Peace / Zones of Turmoil*, revised edition (Chatham, NJ: Chatham House, 1996).

An interesting small-scale case of the problems of separation as a strategy is posed by proposals in Israel to "disconnect" from the Palestinians, as discussed, for instance, in Dan Schueftan, *Disengagement: Israeli and the Palestinian Entity* (Tel Aviv: Zmora-Bitan, 1999), in Hebrew.

26 For some of the requirements of grand strategic thinking see Yehezkel Dror, *Grand-Strategic Thinking for Israel* (Shaarei Tikva: Ariel Center for Policy Research, Policy Paper 23, 1998).

27 Following Charles Taylor's definition of "hypergoods," I use the term "hyper-goals" in a somewhat weaker sense of goals that provide the standpoint from which other goals must, in part, be weighted, judged, decided about. See Charles Taylor, *Sources of the Self: The Making of the Modern Identity* (Cambridge, MA: Harvard University Press, 1989), p. 63.

28 Anthony Giddens, *Runaway World: How Globalization Is Reshaping our Lives* (New York: Routledge, 2000), p. 66.

29 The widely used concept of "rogue" states is inadequate for presenting the true nature of the problem, which is better reflected in the terms "fanatic" or "crazy" actors. See Yehezkel Dror, *Crazy States: A Counterconventional Strategic Problem* (Millwood, NY: Kraus Reprints, 1980), updated edition. On "rogue states," see Robert S. Litwak, *Rogue States and US Foreign Policy: Containment After the Cold War* (Washington, DC: Woodrow Wilson Center Press, 2000), and Raymond Tanter, *Rogue Regimes: Terrorism and Proliferation* (London: Macmillan Press, 1999), updated edition.

30 It should be emphasized that Islam has no monopoly on fanatic states, though in its present phase it is more prone to produce such entities than other civilizations. The most dangerous fanatic state in modern history has been Nazi Germany.

31 If Hitler had been assassinated in 1938, most of the history books, too, would have condemned this act as "murder," not knowing what would have happened had he not been killed, with genocide for instance never being considered as a conceivable act of his. Therefore, historic evaluation of events and acts is often, though not always, very doubtful, lacking knowledge of what would have happened if. . . . Thus, we cannot even be sure what would

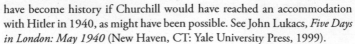

have become history if Churchill would have reached an accommodation with Hitler in 1940, as might have been possible. See John Lukacs, *Five Days in London: May 1940* (New Haven, CT: Yale University Press, 1999).

32 For such a recent philosophy, or biology, of human evolution regarded as reliably bringing about a "good" future, see Robert Wright, *Non Zero: The Logic of Human Destiny* (New York: Pantheon, 2000).

33 For this concept in modern moral philosophy, see Daniel Statman, editor, *Moral Luck* (Albany, NY: State University of New York Press, 1993). I use the term somewhat differently as referring to situations where we have no choice but to make a "tragic choice," as conceptualized in Guido Calabresi and Philip Bobbit, *Tragic Choice* (New York: Norton, 1979).

34 There is nothing new about the need for "dirty hands" in statecraft, but post-modern liberal-democratic discourse tends to repress this unpleasant necessity and thus gets out of tune with global realities in the foreseeable future.

SUMMARY

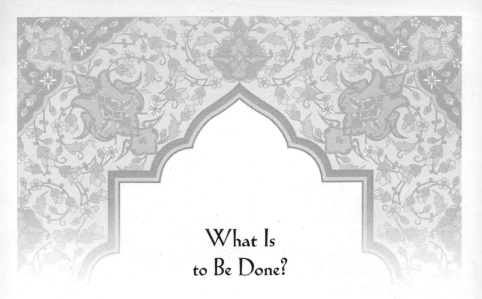

What Is
to Be Done?

David Bukay

The amazing phenomenon is that fundamentalist Islamic terrorism has been with us for many years, and it is only the irresponsible complacency of leaders, who repeatedly deny the reality and rationalize their inactivity,[1] that causes them to act only when catastrophe is at their doorstep.

The Afghan example is instructive. The United States acted to aid the Afghan rebel forces with funding and military equipment on an enormous scale. It viewed bin Laden as a man of vision, and the *mujahidin al-Afghan* as freedom fighters. After the loss of Iran in February 1979, the United States feared that the conquest of Afghanistan by the Soviet Union constituted a substantial threat to its influence in the oil states, as well as possible Soviet control over strategically sensitive central Asia.

The size of American aid to the Afghans began at $100 million in 1980, and by 1986 reached a half a billion dollars. Altogether, the United States poured three billion dollars into Afghanistan and bin Laden's organization. Although the United States acted in co-ordination with Saudi Arabia as a means of protecting its interests,

Saudi Arabia's agenda was to disseminate its religious influence. It played a central role in the activity of the "Arab Afghans," and in the aggressive spread of fundamentalist Islam. It funded and supported the Taliban's activity, and bin Laden retained close ties with the Saudi royal house. Its aim was to disseminate the Wahabi school of Islamic thought and practice, while encouraging radical religious movements such as *al-Ittihad al-Islami* and funding *jam'iat al-mujahidin al-Islamiyah* or "graduates of Afghanistan," which fought alongside the Muslims in Bosnia, or funding the Islamic Palestinian organizations, including the *shuhada* families. The United States knows well that the Saudi regime is not much different from the regime the Taliban set up in Afghanistan. Saudi Arabia occupies a high place in the list of fundamentalist Islamic terrorist nations.

It is important to refute two notions that have gained currency in the West, which are interrelated and fundamentally erroneous. One concerns economic welfare, the other education. The cultural assumption in the West is that economic welfare means pliancy, and education means moderation, and both of these lead to "sane" and rational politics. This view is a "mirror image" of the West and bears no relation to reality. Poverty leads to crime but not to terrorism. The major leaders and activists of the terrorist organizations are from the middle class or sometimes from the upper class, and the preponderant majority of them have higher education. Rarely does a formal leadership develop among the poor and socioeconomically oppressed. Terrorism does not grow from hunger, rather from radical ideologies and especially fanatic religion. Bin-Laden and Muslim terrorist leaders never declared that the reasons for their activity are poverty, ignorance, and hunger. They have mentioned the Western Crusades, the belligerency of the Jewish state, and the authoritarian Arab regimes.

In the mid-1990s, fundamentalist Islam became one of the hottest topics in academic, media, and government circles in the United States. In the era of "politically correct," Perlmutter rightly and notably compared Islamic radicalism with Nazism and fascism, stating that its goal was to create a totalitarian Islamic state. He recommended that the West kill the phenomenon in the cradle,[2] and asserted that any conciliatory policy would be a terrible mistake. The only way to deal with fundamentalist Islam, Charles Krauthammer argued, is the "pure stick approach."[3]

The attack on the World Trade Center on February 26, 1993, brought home to the policymakers and citizens of the United States the essential threat embodied in fundamentalist Islam. Not since the international activity of the PLO led by the arch-terrorist and serial liar Arafat, has there been such a menacing and imminent threat to the basic interests of the United States. Meanwhile, several large terrorist attacks had to occur to induce a zero-hour realization that what is at hand is an all-out cultural assault.

Strategic experts and political advisers disagree about the operative means and methods of struggle. One model, for instance, is that of Egypt and Jordan's fight against the Islamic terrorist organizations, as Indyk proposes.[4] This entails a determined military struggle and uncompromising enforcement, with the aim of restricting the groups to the socioeconomic domain only. A second model of action is that proposed by Murphy and Gause — namely, to adopt the approach the Turks used against Erbekan, the leader of Islamic party, and fit Islamic activity into an agreed framework so as to avoid political polarization.[5] Still another model is the assessment that if radical Islam gains power, it need not necessarily harm Western interests, because it is an authentic representative of the Islamic public.[6]

As for academic research, two main approaches crystallized regarding the Islamic fundamentalist danger to Western civilization: the first, the *clash of civilizations* approach, maintains that fundamentalist Islam is on a direct collision course with the West.

Huntington was the first to characterize the problem in terms of a clash of civilizations and a reformulation of the world order. He counted the conflicts that occurred during the 1990s, and found that most of them were located on the fault line between Islamic civilization and other civilizations.[7] The West refuses to acknowledge what it itself clearly sees: the struggle is between democracy, pluralism, modernity, tolerance, openness, civic freedoms, individualism, and a critical attitude on the one hand, and mental absolutism and cultural closure, tribal traditionalism and social anarchy, religious fanaticism, intolerance, and an unbridled violence directed against all infidels on the other.[8]

David Bukay

This is also the position of Lewis, who was the first to point out the Islamic threat to the West.[9] Islam is an aggressive and expansionist religious ideology, a reaction to the Judeo-Christian cultural heritage.[10] Pipes regards Islamic fundamentalism as a threat similar to communism. This ideology, the "green threat," jeopardizes human society,[11] which is Kramer's view as well.[12]

Second is the *integrated approach*, which views fundamentalist Islam as a phenomenon that is natural to Arab-Islamic society, and sees no essential contrast and antagonism with the West. Islamic fundamentalism is not a threat, but rather a deeply rooted response to the Arab governments' failure to address socioeconomic problems. The main scholars espousing the integrated approach are Voll and Esposito. In their view, most of the Islamic movements constitute a positive, dynamic force rather than militant extremism. Islam is a religion of peace, tolerance, and fraternity, and does not threaten the West.[13]

Even though the debate has been clearly decided, and even the greatest skeptics no longer have any pretext after the terrorist attack of September 11, 2001, unfortunately the issue has not yet been internalized in Israel. Once a nation that served as a model for all the world of effectively fighting terror, Israel became defeatist and flawed in its approach.

The greatest threat posed by fundamentalist Islam remains the non-conventional threat. As former CIA director James Woolsey pointed out, the United States does not have to wait for another Pearl Harbor to understand that there is no greater threat to its security than terrorism involving weapons of mass destruction.[14] Fundamentalist Islam in the form of *al-Qaʿidah* and the World Islamic Front for Holy War against Jews and Christians is a clear and immediate danger, and these forces have enough motivation to go all the way and thereby hasten apocalyptic processes of redemption.

Yet the most deadly and dangerous terrorism, in our view, is computer terror, or cyber-terrorism. The destruction it could wreak on human society stands in inverse proportion to the threat it is perceived as embodying. Because it is very effective and low cost, it is impossible not to regard it as the preferred battlefield. A planned computer terrorist attack would likely cause a total disruption of modern society: information, electricity, banking, and industrial systems, as well as a total disruption of the political and military systems. Deutsch, another former CIA director, rightly remarked that the electron is the ultimate precision-guided weapon. When Islamic fundamentalist terrorism gets over its yen for open, demonstrative terrorism, it is likely to turn to computer terrorism, even if this does not involve manipulative use of the media.

There are two approaches to the war on terrorism. 1. Different means of defense such as protection of important individuals and technical-physical security of different kinds (checkpoints, means of exposure and detection, wiretapping and electronic surveillance, and preventive intelligence). Yet if the war on terrorism is restricted to the preventive dimension alone, there is no doubt that terrorism will triumph. 2. Proactive measures such as preemptive as well as retaliatory and punitive actions. The principle is to hit terrorism first, before it organizes and takes action. Harming or weakening the intelligence on terrorism is like making a country blind. Instead, intelligence must provide all the necessary means for functioning.

Proactive measures include clear strategic policymaking, and well-defined objectives in a determined war on terrorism. If only short-term steps are taken, failure is certain. Simply to rest on one's laurels is not permissible. Action against the foci of terrorism must be aggressive and consistent. Terrorism succeeds when for military and/or political reasons its adversary refrains from applying its full resources to the war. The key precept is that terrorism, like guerrilla warfare, must be fought by its own tactics. That, in a nutshell, is the strategy and formula for success.

There should be extensive activity in the realm of disseminating, including the establishment of a national information authority whose task is to gather information for use on that key battlefield of the modern era, the field of the media and world public opinion where terrorism also concentrates most of its efforts.

In Israel, there is some question whether terrorism can be defeated and its dangers overcome. World experience shows that terrorism cannot be terminated. It remains part of the society for generations despite its profound threat to the survival of given societies. Nevertheless, terrorist groups can and must be defeated. Examples include the Baader-Meinhof gang in Germany, the Red Brigades in Italy, the Japanese Red Army, the *aum shinrikio* (Pure

Truth) in Japan, the Tupamaros and the Monteneros in South America. As for nationalist organizations, it is worth learning from Turkey's experience with Ocalan and the PKK; Spain's struggle with ETA, the Basque underground; the situation of the Islamic *jihad* for five years after the assassination of its leader Fathi Shkaki (until it recovered under the auspices of the arch-terrorist Arafat); or the situation of *Hamas* for more than a year after the `Awdallah brothers were killed until, once again, it was resuscitated with Arafat's assistance.

The question on the international agenda is what to do for the future of humanity? Should the Islamic approach be adopted that calls for the restoration of the traditional-anarchic past, should the West continue with its policy of human progress and social welfare? The two are basically incompatible. Any attempt to avoid coping with this question will only exacerbate the problems, and intensify the dangers to the point that they threaten our sheer existence. On September 11, 2001, a world war broke out. The attack on the American targets was a challenge to Western society. Until it is understood that the struggle against fundamentalist Islam is a war of the Sons of Light against the Sons of Darkness, until the means are made available for an all-out war on the terrorists and the nations that support them, the world will continue to face an existential threat. Bin-Ladenism is the new Hunnism, bent on the destruction of modern civilization and on installing the reign of total anarchy. The new Huns threaten everything that goes against their fanatical values. Unless they are denied the chance to do so, they will succeed in turning the past into the future.

Endnotes

1 N.F. Dixon, *Our Own Worst Enemy* (London: J. Cape, 1987).
2 A. Perlmutter, "Wishful Thinking about Islamic Fundamentalism," *Washington Post,* February 6, 1992.
3 C. Krauthammer, "America's Great Success Story," *Middle East Quarterly,* vol. 1, no. 4 (December 1994): p. 71–79. See also A. Stav, "The Muslim Threat to the Western World," *Midstream,* vol. 39, no. 1 (1993): p. 2–6.
4 M. Indyk, "The Implications for US Policy," in Y. Mirsky and E. Rice, editors, *Islam and the US: Challenges for the Nineties* (Washington, DC: Institute for Near East Policy, 1992).
5 R.W. Murphy and G.F. Gause, "Democracy in the Middle East," *Middle East Policy,* vol. 5, no. 1 (January 1977).

6   R.H. Pelletreau, "Not Every Fundamentalist Is a Terrorist," *Middle East Quarterly*, vol. 2, no. 3 (September 1995): p. 69–76; see also, "Symposium: Resurgent Islam in the Middle-East," *Middle East Policy*, vol. 3, no.2 (April 1996).

7   S.P. Huntington, "The Clash of Civilizations?" *Foreign Affairs*, vol. 72, no. 3 (Summer 1993): p. 21–49.

8   S.P. Huntington, "If Not Civilizations, What? Paradigms of the Post-Cold War World," *Foreign Affairs*, vol. 72, no. 5 (November–December 1993).

9   B. Lewis, "The Return of Islam," *Commentary*, vol. 61 (January 1976): p. 39–49.

10 B. Lewis, *Islam and the West* (Oxford: Oxford University Press, 1993), p. 133–135.

11 D. Pipes, "There Are No Moderates: Dealing with Fundamentalist Islam," *The National Interest*, vol. 41 (Fall, 1995); D. Pipes, "The Western Mind of Radical Islam," in M. Kramer, editor, *The Islamism Debate* (Tel Aviv: Tel Aviv University, 1997).

12 M. Kramer, "The Mismeasures of Political Islam," in Kramer, *The Islamism Debate,* see endnote 11.

13 J. Esposito, "Clash of Civilization? Contemporary Images of Islam in the West," in G.M. Munoz, editor, *Islam, Modernism and the West* (London: Tauris, 1999); J. Esposito, *The Islamic Threat* (Oxford: Oxford University Press, 1992); J.O. Voll and J.L. Esposito, "Islam's Democratic Essence," *Middle-East Quarterly* (September 1994; December 1994).

14 J. Woolsey, *Time*, June 1, 1997, p. 4.

Glossary of Islamic Terms

A

`adah	custom
`ahd	covenant
`alim (pl. `ulama`)	religious scholar
`aql	reason
`asabiyah	Arab tribal solidarity
`ashurah	day of mourning in *Shi`i* tradition; in *Suni* tradition, the "tenth" day, after the Jewish Yom Kippur
`asriyun	modernists
Ahl al-dhimma	people of the covenant, protected status
Ahl al-kitab	people of the book: Jews and Christians
Ahmadiya	a Muslim sect, located in the far periphery of Islamic religion
Al-Islam huwa al-hal	Islam is the solution
Al-`uruba	the Arab *qawmi* ideology, as inter-Arab relations
Alawites	a sect located in northern Syria, the political elite there (not considered Muslims)
Allahoo akbar	Allah is the greatest
Amir al-mu`minin	commander of the faithful
Ansar	the followers of the prophet in Medina
Arkan al-islam	the five pillars of Islam

B

Baiy`ah/ mubaya`ah	oath of allegiance to the ruler
Bid`ah	apostasy, heresy; innovation practice

D

Da`wah	religious propaganda, propagation of the Islamic faith
Dar al-harb	abode of war, the world outside Islam
Dar al-Islam	abode of Islam, Muslim land
Dar al-sulh	regions considered at temporally peace with Islam (by contract)
Dawlah	state
Din	faith, religion
Duniah	world

F

Faqih (pl. fuqaha)	legal expert, jurisprudent
Fard `ayn	obligatory duty
Fard kifaya	voluntary duty
Fatwah (pl. Fatawat)	authoritative religious ruling
Fidayeen	Infiltrators, fighters, guerrilla warrior
Fiqh	jurisprudence
Fitna	rebellion, especially during classical Islam, in connection with the power question

G

Ghulat	exaggerators

H

Hadith (pl. Ahadith)	narration, traditions of the prophet

Hajj	pilgrimage to Mecca
Hakmiyah	sovereignty
Halal	permitted, lawful activities
Haq (pl. Huquq)	right
Haram	unlawful activities, sacred territory, sanctuary
Hijab	veil, covering for Muslim women in public
Hijrah	the prophet's migration on July 16, 622 C.E. from Mecca to Medina
Hizbullah	party of Allah
Hukm	authority, rule
Hukumah	government
Hurriyah	freedom

I

`ibadah	worship
`id	festival
`id al-adh`a	the feast of sacrifice
`id al-fitr	the feast of breaking the *Ramadan* fast
`ilm	knowledge, science
`ilmaniyah	secularism
`ird	woman honor
Ijma`	consensus of Muslim community
Ijtihad	innovative thinking, interpretation of Islamic law
Ikhwan -	brotherhood

Imam	religious and prayer leader
Iian	faith
Islah	reform

J

Jahiliyah	the times of pre-Islamic Arabia, sinful society
Jama`ah	association or society
Jihad	holy war (in *Qur`an*: strive, effort for the sake of Allah)
Jihad al-akbar	striving for the path of Allah when the whole world is Muslim
Jihad al-saghir	the holy war against the enemies of Islam
Jizyah	an exemption tax
Juhhal	common people, those without religious knowledge

K

Kafir (pl. Kuffar)	disbeliever, infidel
Khali`	one who deported from his tribe
Khawarij	Islamic radical sect
Khutbah (pl. Khutab)	sermon, preaching

M

Madhhab (pl. madhahib)	school of legal thought or jurisprudence
Madrasah	school, school of thought, religious college
Majlis al-shura	consultative assembly

Mawla (pl. Mawali)	non-Arab Muslim convert in early Islamic history
Mu`min (pl. Mu`minun)	believer or faithful
Mufty	Muslim religious scholar
Mujahid	soldier of God
Mullah	local religious leader
Murtad	he who rejects Islam, an apostate
Muruwah	tribal manhood
Mushrik (pl. Mushrikun)	polytheist, idolater

N

Nahdah	resistance
Niyah	intention
Nizam islami	Islamic system

Q

Qadi	Islamic judge
Qawm	nation, race
Qias	reasoning by analogy
Qiblah	direction of pray
Qur`an	the holy book of Islam
Quraysh	the prophet's tribe

R

Rak`ah	bowing during prayer
Ray	opinion, personal speculation
Ridda	civil war, the first war fought between Muslims

S

Sabr	endurance and steadfastness
Sadaqah	charitable donation
Sahabah	companions of the prophet
Salafiyah	movement of Islamic revival
Salat	prayer
Shahada	the confession of faith: there is no God but Allah and Muhammad is the messenger of Allah
Shahid (pl. Shuhada)	martyr, witness to faith
Shari`ah	the path, the Islamic law according to the *Qur`an* and *hadith*
Shaykh	tribal leader, religious teacher
Shi`ah	party, faction, the adherents of `ali
Shura	consultation
Sufi	follower of Islamic mysticism
Sufism	Islamic mysticism and asceticism
Sunnah	the practices of the prophet
Sura	chapter in *Qur`an*

T

Ta`awun	solidarity, cooperation
Ta`ifiyah	sectarianism
Tajdid	renewal of Islam
Tali`ah	vanguard
Tanzimat	the reform policy in the Ottoman empire, during the 18th and 19th centuries

Taqiyah	dissimulation about one's religious identity
Taqlid	imitation
Tariqah	religious order
Tashmis	deportation, banishment
Tawhid	unity of Allah

U

Ummah	the Islamic community
Uqqal	those who are acquainted with the religious secrets; opposite of *juhhal*
Urf	local custom
Usuliyah	roots, fundamentalism

W

Wahabiyah	the Islamic movement in Saudi-Arabia in the 19th century
Waqf	endowment of property for religious purposes
Watan	homeland, fatherland

Z

Zakat	voluntary charity

About the Authors

Dr. **David Bukay** teaches in the political science department at the University of Haifa. Among his fields of specialization are: the Arab-Israeli conflict; inter-Arab relations and the Palestinian question; international terrorism and fundamental Islam; theoretical issues and political applications in the Middle-East; Asad's foreign policy toward Israel and Lebanon; the culture approach to understanding the Middle-East. Dr. Bukay has written a number of articles on Middle East issues and for *Nativ*. He is the author of *Total Terrorism in the Name of Allah: The Emergence of the New Islamic Fundamentalists* (Shaarei-Tikva: ACPR Publications, 2003); *Arab-Islamic Political Culture: A Key to Understanding Arab Politics and the Arab-Israeli Conflict* (Shaarei-Tikva: ACPR Publications, 2003); and *Arafat, the Palestinians and Israel: The Politics of Masks and Paradox* (Brighton: Sussex University Press, 2004).

Anthony J. Dennis is a lawyer, human rights activist, and independent scholar living in the United States. An acknowledged expert on Islamic affairs, he has appeared as a guest on over one hundred syndicated talk radio and television programs in the United States. Most recently, he served as editor and contributor of a historic and unique collection of essays entitled *Letters to Khatami: A Reply to the Iranian President's Call for a Dialogue Among Civilizations* (Bristol, IN: Wyndham Hall Press, 2001). He is also the author of an earlier book concerning the political aspirations of the Muslim fundamentalist movement entitled *The Rise of the Islamic Empire and the Threat to the West* (Bristol, IN: Wyndham Hall Press, 1996).

Yehezkel Dror is professor of political science at the Hebrew University of Jerusalem and a member, Club of Rome. He has engaged in research and served as an international adviser on statecraft, global issues, security affairs, and policy planning. His experience includes two years as a senior staff member of the RAND Corporation in the USA; two years as senior planning and policy analysis adviser in the office of the Israeli Minister of Defense; high-level advisory positions in the offices of Israeli prime ministers; two years at the European Institute of Public Administration in Maastricht working on European Union issues; and more. Dror has published 15 books in nine languages, including *Crazy States: A Counterconventional Security Problem, A Grand-Strategy for Israel, Refounding Zionism,* and *The Capacity to Govern: A Report to the Club of Rome.*

Aharon Etengoff is a student at Bar Ilan University, and is senior researcher in the Arms Control Program. He has contributed to many of the research projects published by Prof. Gerald Steinberg and other members of the Bar Ilan faculty, including: "Israeli Landmine Policy and Related Regional Activity," in the *Journal of Mine Action* (Fall, 2001); and "2000–2001 Middle East Arms Control and Proliferation Report," BESA, 2002.

Joseph Farah, an Arab-American, is founder, editor, and chief executive officer of WorldNetDaily.com, the leading independent English-language Internet news site. He is also a weekly columnist for the international edition of the *Jerusalem Post.* The former editor-in-chief of the *Sacramento Union* has written for the *Los Angeles Times, Chicago Sun-Times, Wall Street Journal,* and dozens of other publications. He co-authored with Rep. Richard Pombo, *This Land Is Our Land* (New York: St. Martin's Press, 1996).

K.P.S. Gill is the publisher and editor of *Faultlines*, the founding president of the Institute for Conflict Management, and a former member of the National Security Advisory Board (NSAB). An officer of the Assam cadre of the Indian Police Service, he served in a number of theaters of civil strife and low intensity warfare, and, as director general of the Punjab Police, led the successful campaign against terrorism in that state. Among other activities after his retirement from the police, he writes on internal security, political, and developmental issues for a number of newspapers and magazines. He has also published a book, *The Knights of Falsehood* (New Delhi:

Har-Anand Publications, 1997), exploring the abuse of religious institutions and ideas by the politics of terrorism in Punjab.

Raphael Israeli is a professor of Islamic, Middle Eastern, and Chinese history at Hebrew University, Jerusalem. Professor Israeli is the author of 15 books and some 80 scholarly articles in those domains. A member of the Steering Committee of the ACPR, his work in Hebrew, French, and English frequently appears in leading international publications, including *Nativ.*

Dr. **Mordechai Nisan** lectures on Middle East studies at the Hebrew University of Jerusalem. Among his books are *Minorities in the Middle East: A History of Struggle and Self-Expression* (London and Jefferson, North Carolina: McFarland, 1991), *Toward A New Israel: The Jewish State and the Arab Question* (New York: AMS, 1992), and *Identity and Civilization: Essays on Judaism, Christianity, and Islam* (Lanham, MD: University Press of America, 1999). Dr. Nisan has researched and written of late on Lebanon as part of his ongoing investigation of foreign involvement in that country and the fate of Christians in the Middle East.

David Pryce-Jones was educated at Eton College, and then read history at Magdalen College, Oxford. He has published nine novels and nine books of non-fiction, including *The Closed Circle* (Chicago, IL: I. Dee, 2002) and *The War that Never Was* (London: Weidenfeld & Nicolson, 1995), about the end of the Soviet empire. He is a senior editor of *National Review* in New York.

Dr. **Ajai Sahni** is executive director of the Institute for Conflict Management and the South Asia Terrorism Portal and executive editor of *Faultlines: Writings on Conflict & Resolution.* He has researched extensively on terrorism and low intensity warfare in the Indian subcontinent, and is the co-editor (with K.P.S. Gill) of *Terror & Containment: Perspectives on India's Internal Security* (New Delhi: Gyan Pub. House, 2001).

Dr. **Charles Selengut** is professor of sociology and of religious studies at Drew University in Madison, New Jersey. He is the author of many scholarly studies on the rise of fundamentalism and new religious movements in the Middle East, that foresaw, early on, the advent and intensity of the current strife in Israel and around the globe. Among his latest works are a monograph on the religious roots of the Muslim/Israeli conflict, and his books, *Jewish Identity in the Post Modern Age* (St. Paul, MN: Paragon House, 1999), and *Jewish-Muslim Encounters: History, Philosophy, and Culture* (St. Paul, MN: Paragon House, 2001), based on an international conference he organized in Europe, which brought scholars from divergent branches of these faiths, face to face. Dr. Selengut was the recipient of an NEH Fellowship at Harvard University and is currently conducting research for a study on apocalyptic Messianism in Israel and the United States.

Dr. **Shaul Shay** served as a senior career officer in the military intelligence of the Israeli Defense Forces (IDF) and holds the rank of Col. (Res.). He is a graduate of the Israeli National Defense College and completed both M.A. and Ph.D. at Bar Ilan University in Political Science — International Affairs. Dr. Shay is a lecturer at Bar Ilan University, senior research fellow of the International Policy Institute for Counter Terrorism (ICT) at the Interdisciplinary Center, Herzilya, and heads the Department of Military History of the IDF.

Dany Shoham is a researcher at the Begin-Sadat (BESA) Center for Strategic Studies, Bar-Ilan University, Israel. He investigates chemical and biological warfare in Arab countries and around the world. Formerly, he was a senior analyst and lieutenant colonel in military intelligence. Dr. Shoham received a Ph.D. in medical microbiology from Tel Aviv University. He has published numerous articles on virology and a monograph on chemical weapons in Syria and Egypt, and is a frequent contributor to the ACPR policy paper series as well as *Nativ* on these topics.

Canon Dr. Patrick Sookhdeo was born in Guyana, South America, of Pakistani-Indian heritage. He is director of the Barnabas Fund, which assists Christians suffering for their faith in Muslim contexts, through prayer and fund-raising. He lectures internationally on Islam, multiculturalism, and race, and is the author/editor of eight books, the most recent being *A Christian's Pocket Guide to Islam* (Christian Focus Publications, Ross-shire, U.K., November 2001). He holds a Ph.D. from London University's School of Oriental and African Studies and a D.D. from Western Baptist Seminary, Portland, Oregon, for work on pluralism. He is the canon-theologian of the Anglican Diocese of Kaduna, Nigeria and non-residentiary canon of Peshawar, Church of Pakistan. He was awarded the 2001 Coventry Cathedral Prize for Peace and Reconciliation and the Spring 1990 Templeton UK Project Award.

Prof. **Gerald Steinberg** directs research in proliferation and regional security at the BESA Center for Strategic Studies and heads the program on conflict management at Bar Ilan University. He received his doctorate from Cornell (1981) in international relations, and publications include "Parameters of Stable Deterrence in a Proliferated Middle East: Lessons from the 1991 Gulf War," *The NonProliferation Review*, 7:3 (Fall–Winter 2000); "Arms Control and Non-Proliferation Developments in the Middle East: 1998/99," Security and Policy Series Paper #44, BESA Center for Strategic Studies, Bar Ilan University, 2000; "Dual Use Aspects of Commercial High-Resolution Imaging Satellites," Security and Policy Series Paper No. 17, BESA Center for Strategic Studies, Bar Ilan University, 1998; "Chinese Policies on Arms Control and Proliferation in the Middle East," "China Report," special issue on *China and the Middle East: The Quest for Influence* (New Delhi; Thousand Oaks, CA: Sage Publications, 1999), edited by R. Kumaraswamy, no. 3–4.

Robert S. Wistrich is Neuberger Professor of Modern European and Jewish History at the Hebrew University in Jerusalem. Among his books are *Hitler's Apocalypse* (New York: St. Martin's Press, 1986), *Antisemitism: The Longest Hatred* (New York: Pantheon Books, 1991), and *Hitler and the Holocaust* (New York: Modern Library, 2001).